The
Resilience
Factor

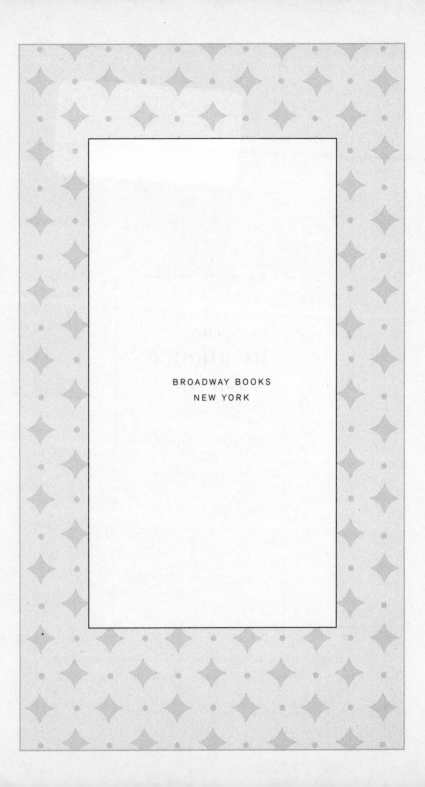

BROADWAY BOOKS
NEW YORK

The
Resilience
Factor

7 Keys to Finding
Your Inner Strength and
Overcoming Life's Hurdles

Karen Reivich, Ph.D.,
and Andrew Shatté, Ph.D.

BROADWAY

A hardcover edition of this book was published in 2002
by Broadway Books.

PRINTED IN THE UNITED STATES OF AMERICA

BROADWAY BOOKS and its logo, a letter B bisected on the diagonal,
are trademarks of Broadway Books, a division of Random House, Inc.

Visit our website at www.broadwaybooks.com

First trade paperback edition published 2003

Book design by Lisa Sloane

The Library of Congress has cataloged the hardcover edition as follows:

Reivich, Karen.
The resilience factor: 7 essential skills for overcoming life's inevitable
obstacles / Karen Reivich and Andrew Shatté.—1st ed.
p.   cm.
Includes index.
1. Resilience (Personality trait)   I. Shatté, Andrew.   II. Title.

BF698.35.R47 2002
155.2'4—dc21   2002074396

ISBN 0-7679-1191-1

20 19 18 17 16 15

For Veronica and for my parents,

Betty and Lloyd

— AJS

✦ ✦ ✦

For my

husband, Guy, and our three sons,

Aaron, Jacob, and Jonathan

— KJR

Contents

How many times in the last week have you said to yourself, "I can't take this stress anymore," or "Why do I keep overreacting to such little things," or even "Is this all there is to life?" Or maybe things are going "just fine," but you keep thinking that something's missing. If you're like most Americans, burning the candle at both ends or just feeling worn out from juggling too many obligations, you've probably had thoughts along these lines recently. What you need is more resilience—the ability to persevere and adapt when things go awry.

Everyone needs resilience, because one thing is certain, life includes adversities. There are the inevitable daily hassles—work dumped on your desk at 4:45 P.M., children who need to be in different places at the same time, disagreements with your significant other. There are probably major setbacks too—a lost job, a failed relationship. And recent events have shown that our lives may also be touched by great trauma. But if you increase your resilience, you can overcome most of what life puts in your way.

It's such an important concept that it bears repeating: Everyone needs resilience. More than fifty years of scientific research have powerfully demonstrated that resilience is the key to success at work and satisfaction in life. Where you fall on the resilience curve—your natural reserves of resilience—affects your performance in school and at work, your physical health, your mental health, and the quality of your relationships. It is the basic ingredient to happiness and success.

How resilient are you? Our research shows that most people consider themselves to be fairly resilient. But the reality is that most of us aren't emotionally or psychologically prepared to handle adversity, which means that instead of facing our problems bravely and confidently, we risk giving up and feeling helpless. And even though you may be resilient in certain ways and in specific areas of your life, you may need help in others. Our studies indicate that resilience is made up of seven distinct abilities, and almost no one is good at them all.

Can you boost your resilience? Absolutely. It's all about changing the way you *think* about adversity. For more than three decades psychologists have investigated how our thinking processes affect our resilience, and the role of resilience in achieving success and satisfaction. As therapists and scientists, we have focused on how to change people's thinking so they can build greater resilience, and we've had enormous success—enhancing the resilience of parents, of couples, of workers in the corporate world, and helping children at risk for depression and college freshmen who were underachieving.

In this book you will get to measure your own resilience, and we'll show you your resilience strengths and those areas on which you could improve. Our goal is to teach you the seven skills of resilience that we have developed over the last fifteen years. These seven skills will lead you to a thorough understanding of how and why you think the way you do. Armed with the self-awareness they provide, thousands of children, adolescents, parents, and corporate employees have used the skills to become happier, more productive, more successful, and more balanced in their lives.

A Thought Experiment

Would you indulge us for a minute or two? We ask that you vividly cast yourself as the lead actor in the following scene. Imagine, if you will, that you have been working longer hours than usual lately. While your job does have periodic project crunches that last a few days or even a week, this latest stint has been a marathon—weeks of ridiculously long days that have left you sapped and spent.

Today's been particularly trying. The tribulations began as soon as you arrived at the office at 8:00 this morning. Awaiting you were three voice-mail messages. The first was from a customer complaining that they still had not received a deliverable from your department that they had expected days earlier. A second was from your assistant, who glumly announced that the figures he gave you yesterday, and which you spent most of your day folding into your major project, had a "minor inaccuracy." The third came from your director, demanding to know when the work would be completed and reminding you, as if you needed reminding, that the project was already overdue and over budget. All this before 9:00 A.M.

The rest of the day is more of the same. When you finally call it quits at 6:30 that evening and point the car toward home, you're lost in a fantasy about being with your loved ones and sinking into that big, comfy sofa. Your youngest child will already be asleep—this makes the second time this week you've missed her bedtime. Still, you'll read to your son for a while, have a bite to eat, and catch up with your spouse. But it's not to be.

As you walk through your front door, you can already feel the tension. You've barely had time to decompress when your spouse angrily says to you, "I know we both agreed that you should take this job, that it would be good for your career. But this is getting pretty frustrating. I'm stuck doing most of the chores around here and the kids really miss you."

What is going through your mind as you experience this scene? What emotions are you feeling? What would you do?

Likewise, what goes through your mind when you hear those persistent rumors of downsizing in your organization? How do you feel? What do you do? How do you react when you're making that lengthy commute and someone cuts you off on the freeway? What do you think, feel, and do when you catch your teenage daughter smoking? Or when the team you manage fails to meet its project deadline? When you lose your job or when your significant relationship falters? Or when you notice that the health of your aging parents is beginning to fade?

Are you quick to anger? Do you often feel guilty? Do you stifle your feelings and worry silently? Perhaps you often feel defeated. This book will teach you to identify your own *thinking style*. More than twenty years of research conducted around the world shows conclusively that how we analyze the events that befall us has a profound effect on our resilience. How you respond to situations like those just described reflects something called thinking style. Thinking style is like a lens through which we view the world. Everyone has such a lens, and it colors the way we interpret the events in our lives. Your thinking style is what causes you to respond emotionally to events, so it's your thinking style that determines your level of resilience—your ability to overcome, steer through, and bounce back when adversity strikes.

Building Resilience

We all know resilient people. They inspire us. They seem to soar in spite of the hardship and trauma they face. In fact, the most resilient people seek out new and challenging experiences because they've learned that it's only through struggle, through pushing themselves to their limits, that they will expand their horizons. They are not danger seekers, yet they don't wither when confronted with risky or dangerous situations. Resilient people understand that failures are not an end point. They do not feel shame when they don't succeed. Instead, resilient people are able to derive meaning from failure, and they use this knowledge to climb higher than they otherwise would. Resilient people have found a system—and it is a system—for galvanizing themselves and tackling problems thoughtfully, thoroughly, and energetically. Resilient people, like all of us, feel anxious and have doubts, but they have learned how to stop their anxiety and doubts from overwhelming them. We watch them handle threat with integrity and grace and we wonder: Could I do that?

The answer is yes. Your capacity for resilience is not a genetically fixed trait like how tall you are, nor are there genetic limits on how resilient you can become. While you may be able to improve your time in a 5k run, if your body is not built for speed, practice will not transform you into an Olympic track star. But with practice, anyone can master resilience.

Resilience is under your control. You *can* teach yourself to be resilient. You can profoundly change how well you handle setbacks, how enthusiastically you approach challenges. In fact, you probably *need* to learn how to be resilient. Although some of us are born into circumstances that forge resilience early, most of us have to learn how to face adversity without shrinking. We have to learn how to think keenly when embroiled in conflict, how to derive knowledge and meaning from our setbacks and failures. And we have to learn how listening to our thoughts, our inner voice, can guide us through the havoc that life sometimes brings.

Resilience enables you to achieve at the highest levels at work, to have fulfilling, loving relationships, and to raise healthy, happy, successful children. It allows you to meet the needs of your job and still have time and energy to be there for your family. It is what enables you to bounce back quickly after a crisis at work or home. Resilience helps you handle the stressful moments with your adolescent, your ex, or your new partner.

Resilience is of vital importance when making quick and tough decisions in moments of chaos. What's more, it grants you the ability to do so with grace, humor, and optimism. Resilience transforms. It transforms hardship into challenge, failure into success, helplessness into power. Resilience turns victims into survivors and allows survivors to thrive. Resilient people are loath to allow even major setbacks to push them from their life course.

Who needs resilience? Is it important only for people who are struggling or had a tough childhood? No. Regardless of the amount of money you have, or the degree to which your parents were neglectful or caring, or how well you are doing at work or with relationships, you will benefit by increasing your resilience. Resilience is not an either/or trait. It's a continuum, and no matter where you fall on that continuum today, you can increase your ability to rise to tomorrow's challenges with doggedness and spirit.

What makes one person resilient and another not is often determined during childhood. How we analyze events depends on thinking styles that we have learned over our lifetime and that operate reflexively, in knee-jerk fashion, when things don't go our way. Nonresilient thinking styles can lead us to cling to inaccurate beliefs about the world and to inappropriate problem-solving strategies that burn through emotional energy and valuable resilience resources.

So, how can we make you more resilient? We have spent the last fifteen years applying what was learned in the lab and in therapy rooms toward developing seven skills that anyone can use to think more accurately about themselves and their world. Mastering these skills will lead you to more fulfilling relationships, to a more productive career, and to feeling excited and energized in life. We have worked with corporate executives, parents, children, teachers, and athletes—and we have proof that the skills we teach work. This book will show you how to increase what is right in your life as well as fix what is wrong.

Scan the titles in the self-help section of any bookstore and you will find books that offer advice on how to overcome depression, forgive your alcoholic parents, or manage your child's attention deficit disorder or ADHD. Although these books are important, they are remedial. They are geared toward fixing what is broken. And while it's important to minimize the damage that depression, alcoholism, or ADHD cause, if you are stuck in a damage-control approach to life, you will never flourish. In this book we do not get stuck in fix-it mode. You'll learn foundational skills that you can use to overcome areas of weakness and, just as important, enhance areas of strength. You will learn how to develop your resilience and use it to live with vitality, curiosity, and inspiration.

Your Commitment to the Journey

Let there be no mistake: The skills imparted in this book can change your life, but they are not a quick fix. If we could offer a pill, or a catchy phrase, or a simple rule that would enable you to leap over the inevitable obstacles of life in a single bound, believe us, we would. But let's face it, in the real world it takes real work to change your life for the better. You won't put down this book and suddenly, magically, have a tenfold increase in resilience. This is not a pump-up seminar in book form, where you leave feeling ready to conquer the world and then, three days later, can't quite remember how it was that you were supposed to do that. We may live in a quick-fix world, but quick fixes rarely last. Our research shows that everyone can increase their resilience—permanently—by learning the seven skills that we have developed and by putting them to use.

Increasing resilience will require work on your part. And it will require you to be honest about how you see yourself and others. It is going to take energy and commitment. Fortunately, learning the skills of resilience is not like dieting. Most dieters generally go through weeks of deprivation and frustration before seeing results that make them look and feel better.

Building your resilience is the opposite. As soon as you learn to fight off your negative thinking style, such as harsh, unfounded self-criticisms ("I'm so selfish," "I'm screwing up my kids," "I'm never going to make it in this job"), you can stop yourself from spiraling into a major funk, and that feels good—immediately. You like yourself better. You have more energy and you are ready to deal with your problems. Likewise, if your thinking style leads you to blame others or outside circumstances for your problems ("Hey, it's not my fault I'm not selling—the market's impossible" or "We're not getting along because she doesn't make *me* a priority"), once you use the skills to stop ducking responsibility, you put yourself in the driver's seat to solve the problem.

In this book you will learn to "hear" the nonresilient thoughts that run through your mind automatically when you are faced with a problem or under stress and to identify how this nonresilient thinking generates counterproductive feelings and behaviors. You will see that these thoughts and beliefs are like a ticker tape that threads through your mind, over and over again, reinforcing inaccurate interpretations of the adversity you face. You will learn how to override this tape so you can see problems more clearly and solve problems more effectively. You will learn how to recognize unproductive "rules for living"—such as "I must succeed in all things, at all times, or else I am a failure," or "If *he* doesn't love me then I must not be lovable"—that are unwittingly sapping your motivation and hindering your success. You will learn how to fight back against your nonresilient beliefs the moment they occur, so your time is not wasted and your energy is not drained. You will learn how to minimize negative emotions and increase your experience of positive emotions. Put simply, you will learn to build your resilience so you can reach your personal and professional goals. We guarantee that after reading this book and mastering these skills, you will have a better understanding of who you are and why you behave in the way you do than ever before.

PART ONE

The

Commitment

to

Change

CHAPTER ONE

Resilience Matters

To the casual observer, Robert was living the American dream. Through hard work and a measure of serendipity, he had moved through the ranks of a Fortune 1000 company. He and his wife, Jeannie, had just celebrated twenty good years together. They lived in a modest but tasteful home in a leafy suburb of Philadelphia, and in a few short years of mortgage payments the house would be theirs, free and clear. Robert and Jeannie's three children, ages seventeen, fifteen, and nine, had always been a source of great joy.

But lately for Robert, the dream had faded. His nine-year-old son had struggled in school since the first grade, and six months ago his academic difficulties were given a label—attention deficit disorder. His vivacious and expressive fifteen-year-old daughter had been replaced by a brooding, rebellious stranger. Once her greatest confidant, Robert found himself relegated to moody yes or no responses, on the increasingly rare occasions when she was home. Robert's job and his marriage had been the two linchpins in his life, but neither provided the spark it once did. He had devoted fifteen years to his company, but his career had plateaued in the last few years, and the promotional path was no longer clear. With the recent rumors of downsizing, Robert became increasingly anxious about his family's financial future. Three college tuition bills lay ahead, and little money had been invested for retirement. And then there was his marriage. Robert and Jeannie had always been close, but between the demands of work and the kids they rarely got any time alone.

At age forty-seven, Robert was ill-prepared to manage the adversities in his life, as routine or commonplace as they may seem. Somehow, somewhere, Robert had lost his way. The parts of his life that had once given him such fulfillment now left him feeling empty.[1]

What Is Your "Bottom Line"?

Which aspects of Robert's situation resonate most strongly with you? What in your life do you most wish to change? Do you want to increase your productivity at work? Is it that your relationships with family or friends are not as rich and fulfilling as you would like? Do you need help balancing work and home? What is it that led you to pick up this book? Whatever you are seeking, you are almost certainly not alone. A majority of people worry about their future prosperity and happiness.[2] As a culture we are searching for ways not only to improve our lives but to "supersize" them. We are searching zealously and we are searching en masse.

Most of us can identify with one aspect or another of Robert's disappointments. You might be failing to actualize your career potential and are struggling to understand why. It's unlikely that the problem is lack of commitment; Americans already work the longest week in the world, and the United States is the only industrialized country in which work hours are increasing.

Perhaps you want to increase your intimacy at home. As we work harder and longer, we spend less time nurturing the relationships that matter to us most. It's not that we're avoiding intimacy with our partners and our children. In fact, we're seeking it frantically. John Gray's relationship guide *Men Are from Mars, Women Are from Venus* sold over 7 million copies in the United States alone.[3] His newspaper column attracted 30 million readers weekly. And still we search for an answer.

For many of you the impetus is more personal. You may be looking to end that nagging anxiety that keeps you awake at 3:00 A.M., or you're wrestling with an addiction. Perhaps recent world events, like terrorism and war, have shaken your sense of security and control. You may have experienced bouts of depression that left you unmotivated and disconnected. You are not alone. At any one time, more than 20 million Americans attend self-help support groups, for everything from drug and alcohol addiction, bereavement, cancer survival, emotional problems, and cross-dressing.[4] Or perhaps you have a child with low self-esteem and who feels down a lot of the time, and you want to infuse her childhood with confidence and accomplishments, fun and adventure. How can this book help you?

For almost fifteen years, at the University of Pennsylvania, we have been conducting research on the role resilience plays in people's lives, and we've found that it's essential to success and happiness. To that end, we've developed a set of skills to help people from all walks of life achieve their goals by enhancing their capacity for resilience.[5] We have equipped patients with the skills to enable them to bounce back from the adversities—recovering from addiction, coping with bereavement, dealing with job loss or divorce—that so often lead to clinical depression and anxiety. We created a prevention program for children at risk for depression, helping them to overcome the high levels of family conflict and low levels of family cohesion they experienced on a daily basis. As long as two years after they learned the skills, children from the program showed half the rates of depression of their control peers. We designed a parallel program for new college students at risk of underachieving, helping them to steer through the obstacles to success that all freshmen encounter. And we have worked with others who, while generally satisfied, wanted to optimize their lives and reach their full potential. In this vein, the skills we've identified as crucial to building resilience have helped athletes perform to their peak, parents to enhance their parenting, teachers to better address the complex needs of their students, and corporate employees to improve their productivity and job satisfaction and to better balance work and home.

The skills are a means to achieve diverse ends—overcome childhood obstacles, steer through new adversities, bounce back from major setbacks, and reach out to broaden your worlds. In other words, they promote resilience, leading people to solve their own problems, take appropriate risks, and accurately forecast the implications of an adversity. The skills also provide a remarkable opportunity for people to look inward, to get to know themselves—really know themselves—and connect more deeply with others.

Our research has demonstrated that the number-one roadblock to resilience is not genetics, not childhood experiences, not a lack of opportunity or wealth. The principal obstacle to tapping into our inner strength lies with our cognitive style, which we'll refer to in this book as thinking style—ways of looking at the world and interpreting events that every one of us develops from childhood. Humans are not passive recipients of sensory data from the world around them. We actively process information, simplifying and organizing it in idiosyncratic ways. When adversity strikes, we use mental shortcuts to figure out its causes and implications so that we can quickly make sense of the abundance of information that barrages us. At times these shortcuts help us manage the information overload; at other times they lead us astray. As we navigate our way through the world, we assume that we are responding to a direct readout of that world, one that is comprehensive and accurate. But we are not. Our thinking styles bias and color our viewpoint, leading us to develop patterns of behaviors that are often self-defeating. For example, some people have a thinking style that leads them to see problems as insurmountable, so they give up even in situations in which they do have control.

How can you increase your resilience? By learning to understand your thinking styles and developing skills to circumvent them so that you can see the true causes of adversity and its effect on your life. And it is re-silience that will help you achieve your goals—whatever it is you hoped to achieve when you picked up this book.

Our Journey, Our Process

We want to accompany you on a voyage of self-discovery. We want to share with you the process that has helped the thousands with whom we've worked—and helped us too, as you'll see from the examples we of-fer from our own lives. We will guide you to understand your thinking styles and provide insight into what those styles are buying and costing you in your life. We will equip you with seven skills of resilience that you can use to maximize your performance at work, improve your significant relationships, boost your health, and find the courage to embrace new ex-periences.

The first leg of our journey, Part One of the book, defines resilience. What is this potent quality that underlies all our problem-solving efforts? We share with you research that has revealed seven major factors that contribute to the development and strengthening of resilience. In Chap-ter 2 we give you the opportunity to measure your level of resilience with our RQ Test and to determine your relative strengths and weaknesses. Overcome your resilience weaknesses, build on your strengths, and you will be amazed at how much easier it will be for you to approach life—and all of its inevitable obstacles and conflicts—with flexibility, adaptabil-ity, and confidence. In Chapter 3 we describe the philosophy of our program and the foundations upon which it was based.

We'll give you a brief overview of the skills now, and in Part Two we will take you through each one, showing you why it's necessary and teaching you how to use it effectively.

1. **LEARNING YOUR ABCs.** When confronted with a problem or challenge, are you ever surprised by how you react or wish you could respond differently? Do you ever assume that you know the facts of a situation, only to find out later that you misinterpreted them? If the thoughts running through your head when you're faced with adversity are inaccurate, your ability to respond effectively to that adversity will be severely compromised. We'll teach you to "listen" to your thoughts, to identify what you say to yourself when faced with a challenge, and to understand how your thoughts affect your feelings and behavior.

2. **AVOIDING THINKING TRAPS.** When things go wrong, do you automatically blame yourself? Do you blame others? Do you jump to conclusions? Do you assume that you know what another person is thinking? When faced with adversity, people regularly make eight mistakes that undermine resilience. We'll teach you to identify the ones you habitually make and how to correct them.

3. **DETECTING ICEBERGS.** Everyone has deeply held beliefs about how people and the world should operate and who they are and want to be. We call these iceberg beliefs because they often "float" beneath the surface of our consciousness so we're not even aware of them. Often these beliefs guide us to behave in ways that are true to our values. Sometimes, however, these deep beliefs interfere with our ability to live the kind of life we want, and they explain why we overreact to seemingly minor issues or have a hard time making what seem like simple decisions. We'll teach you how to identify your deep beliefs and determine when they are working for you and when they are working against you.

4. **CHALLENGING BELIEFS.** A key component of resilience is problem solving. How effective are you at solving the problems that you encounter day to day? Do you waste time pursuing solutions that don't work? Do you feel helpless to change situations? Do you persist on one problem-solving path even when you see that it's not getting you where you want to be? It's your thinking style that often leads you to misinterpret the causes of a problem, which then leads you to pursue the wrong solutions. We'll teach you how to test the accuracy of your beliefs about problems and how to find solutions that work.

5. **PUTTING IT IN PERSPECTIVE.** Do you get caught in what-if thinking in which you turn every failure or problem into a catastrophe? Do you waste valuable time and energy worrying yourself into a state of paralyzing anxiety about events that have not even occurred? We'll teach you how to stop the what-ifs so that you're better prepared to deal with problems that really do exist or are most likely to occur.

6. **CALMING AND FOCUSING.** Do you feel overwhelmed by stress? Do your emotions sometimes come on so quickly and fiercely that you can't seem to think straight? Do "off-task" thoughts make it hard for you to concentrate? We'll show you how to stay calm and focused when you're overwhelmed by emotion or stress so you can concentrate on the task at hand. This "fast skill" is often used with Skill 7.

7. **REAL-TIME RESILIENCE.** Are there times when counterproductive thoughts make it hard for you to stay engaged and in the moment? Do certain negative thoughts tend to recur over and over again? We'll teach you a powerful skill so that you can quickly change your counterproductive thoughts into more resilient ones—with immediate results.

You don't need to use every skill every day to see improvement in your resilience. In fact, many people find dramatic changes in their resilience after mastering and using just two or three of these skills. We will explain what your scores on the RQ Test say about your personality and point out which resilience factors each of the skills is designed to enhance so you can concentrate your energy on learning the skills that will most benefit you.

In Part Three we apply the resilience skills to the primary domains in life—relationships, parenting, work, and reaching out. You'll be able to develop more satisfying relationships with friends and family or with your intimate other. You'll benefit from the same training we've provided to thousands of employees, from senior executives to front-line salespeople and customer service representatives, so that you can maximize your productivity and have greater balance between work and home. You'll learn techniques to help you become a more effective and nurturing parent. We'll show you how you can use the skills of resilience to improve your physical and mental health. And together we'll explore how the skills can help us deal with the large existential issues that all humans must face—grief and bereavement, our own mortality, and creating meaning in our lives.

The Nature of Resilience

The mantle of research into resilience has been taken up by a small core of mental health professionals made up of psychologists, psychiatrists, and sociologists. Though their work has focused almost exclusively on children, their findings reveal to us the characteristics that forge resilient adults. The modern era of inquiry into the nature of resilience dates back almost fifty years, to a landmark study that tracked the trajectory of high-risk children across their first thirty-five years of life, a study we will visit in Chapter 3. Since then, armed with an array of research designs and statistical methodologies, researchers have comprehensively mapped the resilience terrain, delineating the variables that erode resilience and those that function to protect it.

Their work indicates that the process that determines our resilience as adults is a dynamic one—a complex interaction between elements of a child's external and internal worlds. Many of the early external pressures on resilience—low birthweight due to poor maternal nutrition, childhood poverty, divorce, or physical abuse—can themselves never be reversed.[6] They are in the past. But some of the internal causes of low resilience, such as thinking styles, can be modified, even counteracted. And, more important, once your thinking style has changed, you can use it to undo the ongoing negative consequences that stemmed from events in your childhood that were outside your control.

Research has also revealed that humans have four fundamental uses for resilience. Some of us must apply our reserves of resilience to *overcome* the obstacles of childhood—a broken home, poverty, or even emotional neglect or physical abuse. We need resilience to put behind us the damage that may have occurred in our youth and to take responsibility for creating the adulthood we want.

All of us need resilience to *steer through* the everyday adversities that befall us—arguments with friends and family, disagreements with the boss, or an unexpected expense. Life is rich in stress and hassles, but if you're resilient you will not let the daily tribulations of life interfere with your productivity and well-being.

Most of us at some point in our adult lives come up against a major setback, a life-altering event that blows us off course. For some it's a job loss or a divorce. For others, the death of a parent or child. These are monumental crises that tax our resilience. And depending on our supplies of resilience, we will either become helpless and resigned, or we will *bounce back* and find a way to move forward.

These three uses of resilience are reactive in nature, determining our response to adversity. We also explore a fourth use of resilience that transcends our desire to protect and defend ourselves. Those of you whose goal is to find renewed meaning and purpose in life and to be open to new experiences and challenges can apply resilience to *reach out* so that you can achieve all you are capable of.[7]

Overcoming

We met Deb in the summer of 2000 when she enrolled her front-line staff in our resilience workshop in anticipation of the high burnout rates common in social service organizations like hers. We admired her from the very first. In spite of the odds, this courageous woman had performed her way to executive status in a Fortune 500 company. Then, having achieved her goals in the corporate world, she resigned her position to fulfill a dream—to found an organization devoted to helping new immigrants find work. She had built her dream from the ground up.

Deb's clients take classes in computer skills, assertiveness skills, and presentation skills. They learn what to wear to interviews, how to describe their talents, what questions to ask regarding benefits and compensation. Deb developed skill-development programs to guide her clients toward success. She wanted her graduates to get and keep jobs but, as important, she wanted them to experience dignity and pride. We had enormous respect for Deb and all she had achieved. And gradually, over several months, her life story emerged, and our respect and admiration turned to awe as we came to see what Deb had overcome to be where she is today.

Deb grew up in Miami, the child of drug-addicted parents. She and her siblings were placed in a series of foster families, but somehow Deb overcame all the disadvantages she faced. In spite of a childhood mired in chaos and unstable family relationships, she flourished academically, socially, and spiritually, ultimately achieving substantial professional success. Rather than rest on those laurels, she chose to reach out a hand to help others prevail. Deb is a paragon of how resilience can be used to overcome. But how did a child who suffered most of the classic setbacks that foster low resilience become such a resilient adult?

When we hear such stories of deprivation in the early years, we know intuitively that these children are disadvantaged—they are at high risk of failing to achieve later in life. Research has isolated many of the childhood circumstances that present the greatest threat to resilience: Low birthweight, low socioeconomic status, low maternal education, unstable family structure, and maltreatment put any child at risk for underachievement. But how is it that these characteristics of the world outside the child come to exert their influence on the internal life of the child, on her motivation, achievement, and on her resilience?[8]

With some variables, the impact is direct. Low birthweight often correlates with a compromised brain structure, which limits the child's intellectual functioning, which then interferes with the development of competent coping strategies. Other variables contribute indirectly. Poverty may have a direct impact on resilience if it is severe enough to lead to malnutrition in the child, but it also has a more subtle indirect path. Parents who are struggling with poverty often become depressed. Depression, in turn, disturbs the relationship between parent and child, usually resulting in low parental involvement. This means the child often is left to fend for himself and is not provided the protection and care that he needs to ensure his healthy development.

The same is true for marital discord. In the wake of separation and divorce, parents often become absent physically and emotionally. Parents who are themselves struggling often lack the emotional stamina to provide their children with the attention, caring, and supervision that they need. Following a divorce, many children become more emotional, often angry at the parent who moved out, and sad and more difficult to comfort at home. For a parent who already feels emotionally depleted, the child's emotional needs may be too much to bear. Indeed, research shows that the aspect of divorce that is most important in predicting how children will fare is the quality of the relationship with the parent with whom they subsequently live. Although the residential parent (typically mothers) often works hard to maintain close relationships with her children, disruptions in child rearing—poor communication and supervision, not enough outward expressions of love and affection—are so common and so intense that the first few years after a divorce have been dubbed by researchers as a time of "diminished parenting."[9]

What leads to these parenting problems? In most cases, a number of interacting factors make it difficult for the parent to remain as engaged and attentive as she once was. Following a divorce, it is not uncommon for one or both parents to experience symptoms of depression that interfere with good parenting. It's nearly impossible to be genuinely interested in your child and to respond with love and patience when you're fighting the demons of depression. Real-world changes also contribute to changes in parenting practices. Routines of the family typically change following divorce. A full-time mother might need to go back to work. Those already employed might need to work longer hours. The parent's change in schedule usually means periods of less supervision for the child or more time in the company of babysitters or child care providers, which brings less consistency in styles of play, discipline, and overall quality of interaction. Put simply, it is difficult to remain in tune with your child and responsive to his needs when every ounce of your resilience is being used to get yourself through a painful divorce and the cascade of life changes it brings. Yet just as Deb was able to overcome the negative aspects of her childhood, research shows that some children cope with the stress of divorce better than others.[10]

Clearly the world in which we are raised matters, and as children, there's little we can do to alter that world. But, as proven by people like Deb, not everyone in difficult circumstances succumbs to the risk. Some children do fine, others even flourish, despite their impoverished backgrounds. What then are the specific characteristics that determine how well a child will fare? What does the child herself bring to the table? Resilience researchers have searched for the factors that enable people like Deb to thrive while many others succumb to similar adversities. One such factor is IQ. It has emerged as an important ingredient in overcoming unavoidable disadvantages, even in the most impoverished of circumstances. In general, those with higher IQs end up being more successful than those with lower IQs. Does that mean that Deb succeeded only because she was smart? Not necessarily. As important as IQ is, other factors play even more significant roles in predicting a child's successful transition to adulthood and subsequent success. As Harvard psychologist Howard Gardner argues, intelligence measured by standardized tests (verbal and quantitative aptitude) contributes no more than 20 percent to the entirety of possible factors that determine one's success in life. Indeed, it was discoveries of that sort that led psychologists Peter Salovey and John Mayer to study what they called emotional intelligence—the ability to monitor one's own and others' emotions, to regulate them, and to use emotion-based thinking to guide actions.[11]

The research on emotional intelligence shows that although traditional intelligence matters, the way in which it exerts its effect is not as straightforward as it may seem. In one study that tracked children into adulthood over a twenty-two-year period, researchers found that those with higher IQs used more effective, more mature social and cognitive coping strategies, such as the ability to understand another person's perspective, and had good problem-solving skills that enabled them to succeed. That is, the children with higher IQ scores were more successful as adults because they had more sophisticated social and cognitive skills, best described as emotional intelligence. While not much can be done to improve your IQ, a lot can be done to improve your resilience, a key component of emotional intelligence. That's where we come in.

We cannot take away the poverty into which you were born, nor can we reverse your parents' divorce or improve your score on standardized intelligence tests. We cannot change your childhood. How then can we help you overcome the circumstances of your life when you were young? By teaching you how to analyze and change the nonresilient beliefs you developed about yourself and your ability to control your life during those early years. We can teach you a process that you can use to stay motivated, productive, engaged, and happy even when facing stress at work or home.

As the Debs of the world well know, breaking free from a difficult childhood takes hard work and determination. It requires the ability to stay focused and to make accurate distinctions between where you have control and where you do not. The seven skills of resilience that we describe in this book will give you the tools to do just that.

Steering Through

Perhaps you had a happy and contented childhood—enough money, enough love, good values, and the support and supervision of caring adults. Not everyone has a history that needs overcoming. But does that mean that resilience is less important for you? No. Everyone needs resilience because everyone is confronted with problems, stress, and hassles—they are a daily part of life. Resilient people use their inner resources to deal with the normal grind of life—running late for meetings, squabbling with coworkers, managing a child's hectic schedule, staying on top of an ever-growing to-do list—without becoming overwhelmed and negative. The resilient "coper" can steer through the whitewater of life and remain on course. Research shows that the essential ingredient in *steering through* chronic stress is self-efficacy—the belief that you can master your environment and effectively solve problems as they arise.

People high in self-efficacy stay committed to solving their problems and don't give up when they find that their original solution doesn't work. They are more likely than people who doubt their ability to cope to try new ways to solve a problem, persisting until they find a workable answer. And, by solving problems, their confidence is enhanced, which in turn increases the likelihood that they will persevere even longer the next time they are faced with a challenge. In contrast, people who don't believe they have the ability to bring about good things in their lives are more passive when faced with a problem or when placed in a new situation. They shy away from new experiences—taking on a new hobby, applying for a new job, joining a social group—because they assume that they are unequipped to meet the challenges that the new situation will bring. When a problem arises at work or in the family, such as a negotiating with a tough client or connecting with a noncommunicative adolescent, they hang back and rely on others to search for solutions. If they are forced to solve a problem themselves, their lack of confidence causes them to give up at the first sign of difficulty. This too becomes a self-fulfilling prophecy. Each time they give up or fail to solve a problem, the belief that they cannot handle the pressures of life is reinforced and their self-doubt increases.

We opened this chapter with a brief profile of Robert and Jeannie and their three children. When Robert came to us, he felt "off his game." His life wasn't going horribly wrong—he loved his family and felt committed to his work—but he saw that it was veering off course and he didn't know how to get it back on track. He told us that he had always been the kind of man who took charge when things went wrong, but lately he no longer felt like he was "the captain of the ship." His self-efficacy had bottomed out.

Let's examine a day in Robert's life and notice how he describes his ability to handle the stress he is feeling. When the alarm goes off at 5:45, Robert reflexively hits the snooze button, knowing that his New Year's resolution to run every day will once again go unfulfilled. Breakfast is chaotic. His fifteen-year-old daughter, Dianne, is still refusing to speak to him over some perceived slight, and his son, Jeff, is loudly chanting some TV theme as he splashes his cereal across the table. Robert feels a twinge of guilt as he finds himself thinking that he can't wait to get to work. "I sit there and look at my family and I don't know how to begin to make things better. I want to understand why Dianne is mad, I want to connect with Jeff, but I just don't know how to anymore. So, instead, I eat as quickly as I can and make a hasty retreat to work." Robert is keenly aware that his ability to connect to his family has been compromised, and his knowledge of his ineffectiveness leads him to want to escape.

Robert's desire to be at the office fades as soon as he arrives. There, awaiting him, are several urgent e-mails that signal another morning spent dousing office spot fires. On the way to the cafeteria he runs into Brenda and Jim, two colleagues who used to work in his division. They're bemoaning the waning fortunes of their 401ks, the company's stock price, and the recent rumors of downsizing. Brenda and Jim are speculating on which division, theirs or Robert's, is likely to be slashed the most and wonder who will have jumped in the right direction when the smoke clears. "That kind of negativity and panic never used to bother me. I knew that I was good at my job and that as long as I continued to produce and continued to lead, I would be safe. But now that kind of talk shakes me. Instead of going back to my office and going about business as usual, I get distracted by self-doubt. What if my division is cut? What if I can't afford college for my kids? I what-if myself into a panic and end up squandering the day. By the time I get myself focused, there is no time left to tackle the project work that I'm forced to shelve each day in favor of the demands that are triaged to top priority." Rather than leaving work satisfied that he has accomplished his goals for the day, Robert leaves worried and further doubting his ability to get his career back on track.

Robert arrives home to find Jeff's report card, documenting even further academic decline. Ironic how the cost of Jeff's ADD medication continues to go up while his grades go down. When Robert sees the phone bill, he knows he has to speak to Dianne about the calls she's been making—a conversation he dreads. His seventeen-year-old daughter, Cathy, just asked for the keys to the car and he agreed, meaning another evening spent in worry until he hears the garage door close around midnight.

Robert's not a whiner, nor does he overlook the successes and blessings that are present in his life. His work securing a client was publicly acknowledged at one of the morning meetings. After dinner, he and Jeff bonded as they surfed the Internet together to track down some information on Benjamin Franklin for a class project. Later that evening Robert and Jeannie sat on the porch with a glass of wine and talked like they used to before they had kids. But the everyday adversities, minor as each one may seem, are draining Robert's reserve of resilience, and there seem to be a dearth of positive experiences in his life to replenish the supply.

Robert is an insightful man. When he came to us he already understood that all that had changed for him was his belief in himself; life was no more difficult, the challenges were no more severe than they had been before. As he put it, he was used to "the permanent whitewater" of life. But what had changed was his belief in his ability to negotiate the rapids. "Somewhere along the way, I lost confidence in myself. My faith in my ability to handle the daily hassles of life eroded away and left me feeling at the whim of whatever life put in my path."

Robert was experiencing a crisis of self-efficacy that stripped him of his ability to steer through chronic stress. He could not pinpoint a specific moment in which he lost faith in his abilities, and, frankly, we did not believe knowing why it changed was necessary for helping him regain it. Instead, our focus was on helping Robert to regain his faith in himself, by working with him to tackle the current problems of his life, one problem at a time. The worst possible way to build someone's self-efficacy is to pump them up with you-can-do-it platitudes. At best, putative self-esteem–enhancing slogans and motivational talks do nothing. At worst, they actually further undermine resilience and effective coping. Why? Because self-esteem is the by-product of doing well in life—meeting challenges, solving problems, struggling and not giving up. You will feel good about yourself when you do well in the world. That is healthy self-esteem. Many people and many programs, however, try to bolster self-esteem directly by encouraging us to chant cheery phrases, to praise ourselves strongly and often, and to believe that we can do anything we set our mind to. The fatal flaw with this approach is that it is simply not true. We cannot do anything we want to in life, regardless of the number of times we tell ourselves how special and wonderful we are and regardless of how determined we are to make it so. Karen could spend the rest of her days dreaming about becoming a Nobel physicist, and Andrew of that Olympic gold in the 100-meter sprint. But even if we devoted the rest of our lives to achieving these goals we'd fail—our talents lie elsewhere.

We know that as people start to build a track record of small successes by solving problems, self-efficacy follows naturally. Building self-efficacy is more difficult and time-consuming than pumping up your self-esteem. Our resilience training works because the skills we teach equip you with tools to solve the problems in your life and to meet the challenges that confront you. Although we didn't know why Robert's self-efficacy had faded, we knew what skills he needed to learn and practice to get it back. So, that's where we started with Robert; over the next two months we met with him regularly and taught him the seven skills of resilience. Some of the skills were familiar to Robert; he had been "unconsciously competent" in them. Our goal was to improve his resilience by making him aware of what skills he already had so that he could use them more effectively and more deliberately. The skills that were new to him became additional tools to add to his "resilience" tool kit. When we last spoke to Robert, he told us, "I feel like I'm back. My life is still rich in hassles and stress, the number of problems is as steady as ever. But I'm handling them each as they come. I know where I want to be five years from now professionally, I've got a plan to get there, and day by day I am finding ways to get closer with my kids and with Jeannie." Once again Robert is captain of the ship, able to steer through daily adversities thanks to his inner strength and resilience.

Bouncing Back

Some adversities are particularly traumatic and seem to require higher levels of resiliency than the ones we rely on to steer through. The setback is so extreme, so emotionally devastating, that it takes every ounce of resilience to recover.

In 1979 Cindi Lamb was driving with her infant daughter, Laura, in their home state of Maryland when, without warning, they were struck head on by a car traveling at 120 miles per hour. As a result of the crash, Laura, five-and-a-half months old at the time, became a quadriplegic. The other car was driven by a habitual drunken driver.

Less than a year later, across the country in Sacramento, California, a drunken driver with two prior convictions and a still-valid driver's license climbed behind the wheel and struck and killed thirteen-year-old Cari Lightner as she walked from her softball game to a school carnival. A highway patrol officer told Cari's mother, Candace, that the driver of the vehicle would probably not spend any time in jail. It was just the way the system worked, he said.

Most of us can only imagine how devastating events like these would be. It wouldn't be unusual for these two mothers to withdraw from the world—into a lifetime of ruminations, recriminations, and depression. But Lamb and Lightner did no such thing. Instead, they got MADD.

In 1981 Lamb and Lightner formed Mothers Against Drunk Driving (MADD). Beginning with little more than a national highway safety grant, they began to spread their message. By the fall of 1982, MADD consisted of 70 chapters. By March of 1983, 192 chapters were operating in 35 states. By its tenth year, MADD had mushroomed to 492 offices with affiliates in Canada, England, New Zealand, and Australia. And now, on the verge of its twentieth anniversary, Lightner and Lamb's organization rounds out at more than 600 chapters in all 50 states and affiliates around the globe.[12] These two mothers, though devastated, found the inner strength to bounce back, to channel their grief into a campaign against the very cause of their terrible loss.

What does it take to recover from trauma like that suffered by Lightner and Lamb or those unfortunate people touched by school shootings or a national disaster like the September 11 attack on America? Immediately after a traumatic event, it is normal to experience debilitating symptoms of depression and anxiety and for coping resources to become overwhelmed, even if we are not personally touched by trauma. Disasters of the sort that we witnessed on September 11 can cause both children and adults to experience extreme anxiety, problems sleeping, loss of appetite, and feelings of depression. It is very likely that after the terror attacks you suffered one or all of these symptoms. For people who were particularly close to the trauma, the reaction may have been far more severe. Post-traumatic Stress Disorder, or PTSD, is a serious psychological disorder that affects many people following exposure to severe trauma. Those who develop PTSD continue to relive the trauma through recurrent images, thoughts, or dreams. They attempt to avoid thoughts, feelings, or conversations associated with the traumatic experience. PTSD sufferers have heightened levels of physiological arousal—their bodies are on high alert—which causes them to startle easily, makes sleep and concentration difficult, and leads to irritability and anger. In the days following a trauma, many people experience an acute anxiety reaction, which includes the symptoms just described, but these people start feeling better within a few weeks. In PTSD, the symptoms can last for months and, if untreated, even years. Research shows that the best predictors of who will develop PTSD following a trauma are characteristics of the event: the severity, duration, and proximity of the person's exposure to it. People living in New York City or Washington, D.C., those who lost a friend or family member on September 11, and those working in the recovery effort are more likely to have developed PTSD than those experiencing the events through television and radio.

This is not to say that resilience plays no role in recovery from trauma or in minimizing risk of PTSD. Renowned trauma expert Dr. Judith Herman, author of *Trauma and Recovery*, describes how resilience actually increases a person's resistance to stress and lowers their chances of developing PTSD.[13] People who are most resilient in the face of trauma display three primary characteristics that work in concert to protect them from PTSD and hasten their recovery. They exhibit a task-oriented coping style—they take incremental, purposeful actions to deal with the adversity; as their actions show, they have a deeply held belief in their ability to control the outcomes of their lives; people who bounce back more quickly from trauma know how to use their connections to others as a way to cope with their experience.

We can see this triad of resilience at work in a young mother's reaction to September 11. Stacey, a mother of three, lives in Greenwich, Connecticut, and works in New York City. Although her family and close friends were not injured in the attack, she knew of people who died when the towers collapsed. Like most of us, Stacey was profoundly affected by what occurred and found herself shaken to the core. Her first concern was to protect her young children from images and conversations about the devastation. She kept the television and radio off whenever her children were present and even kept her four-year-old son from playing at a friend's house where the television was kept on and discussion of the horrors continued uncensored. When Stacey was alone, however, she was glued to the news reports and alternated between overwhelming sadness and rage as she learned of the individual stories of loss and suffering. She often cried uncontrollably at night and spent many evenings rehashing the details of the tragedy with her husband and friends. Stacey slept little, felt irritable and jumpy, and was distracted and forgetful. She muddled through.

Eventually, though, Stacey was able to marshal her strength to get herself and her family through the trauma of the terror attacks. As Herman would describe it, a key ingredient in her recovery was her ability to stick to a routine and exert control where she could. Doing this helped restore her belief in predictability and safety. Stacey explained, "Like a lot of people, I felt scared and kept thinking about how unsafe and unpredictable our world had become. And I didn't know how to argue myself out of that. But then I made myself get back to my routine—going to the gym like always, taking my kids to the park like always, even having Thursday nights out with my husband. And I found that the predictability of my routine was enough to make me feel safer. I didn't have to convince myself of a safe world, just that my little piece of it was safe."

Along with faith in the ability to control one's own destiny, Stacey relied on her connections to others to get herself through the first few weeks. She was willing to talk openly with her husband and friends about her feelings, and the more she talked, the better she felt. It's well known that social support reduces the psychological distress following trauma and helps people to bounce back from events that threaten to stop them in their tracks. Less resilient people have a harder time sharing their experiences with others, sometimes because they lack the intimate connections such openness requires, sometimes because they are less comfortable with their emotions and feel embarrassed to discuss their reactions. A lack of connection to others hinders recovery; resilience keeps you connected, and connection helps you heal.

But connection, reaching out to others for help or comfort, goes beyond sharing your thoughts and feelings about a trauma. According to Herman, highly resilient people are able to connect with others through purposeful action, whereas less resilient people find themselves easily paralyzed and isolated by the terror. For Stacey, connecting to others through purposeful action took the form of organizing a neighborhood relief fund and sending the money to the Red Cross. She also worked with teachers at her child's preschool to sponsor two evening "support groups" for anyone who wanted to come and share their experiences. Although Stacey felt upset for several weeks, her resilience enabled her to find a way to help herself and others heal.

Resilience Is Not Just Reactive

When we talk with parents, managers, and CEOs about resilience, most understand the need for resilience in dealing with adversity. They know that resilience is the capacity to respond in healthy and productive ways when faced with adversity or trauma, that it is essential for managing the daily stress of life. But we have come to realize that the same skills of resilience are as important to broadening and enriching one's life as they are to recovering from setbacks. How do we know this? We know it because the people we've taught these skills to have told us. When we talk to the students, parents, and corporate clients we have worked with about the changes they have seen in their lives, they start off by telling us that they are less fazed by problems—their "skin" feels thicker, they feel stronger and more confident. But they don't stop there. They also tell us that they feel more connected to people, eager to seek out new experiences, and more willing to take risks. As one woman told us, "My life just seems bigger now."

We want to convince you that the importance of resilience does not stop with recovering from setbacks; you can apply the same seven skills to creating a more enriching life for yourself. Resilience is a mind-set that enables you to seek out new experiences and to view your life as a work in progress. Resilience creates and maintains the positive attitude of the explorer. It confers the confidence to take on new responsibilities at work, to risk embarrassment by approaching a person you'd like to know, to seek experiences that will challenge you to learn more about yourself and connect more deeply with others. We call this application of resilience *reaching out*. By reaching out, your life becomes richer, your connections to others become deeper, and your world becomes broader.

Reaching Out

Some people live narrow lives. They have a routine that works—get up at seven, ride the exercise bike, work by nine, lunch at one (sandwich and a salad), home by six, dinner, an hour of television, return a few phone calls, twenty minutes of reading, then bed—and they stick to it. They feel comfortable, even happy, when the routine runs smoothly. Life for these people is best when it's predictable and known. For the most part, they don't complain and don't feel like they are missing out. You probably know someone like this. Perhaps it is you.

And then there are people who approach life as if it were an all-you-can-eat buffet. Plate in hand, they go back for more, trying a little of this and a little of that. Sometimes they happen upon caviar, while other times it's tuna casserole that's been sitting too long under the hot lights. But they don't let the tuna stop them from coming back. They find joy in reaching out to others and seeking new experiences. What's their secret? Just as resilience is necessary to overcome negative life experiences, cope with stress, or recover from trauma, it is equally necessary for a life that is rich in meaning, deep in connections, and committed to the pursuit of learning and new experiences.

Joan is in her mid-sixties and proudly displays photographs of her fourteen grandchildren around her home. She enjoys new experiences, even though sometimes they don't work out. She's realized that scuba diving, skiing, and salsa dancing aren't for her. But she has been delighted with her progress on her new computer, she has loved her class in meditation, and the trip she took through Alaska a few years ago was a great adventure.

Joan wasn't raised to be a risk taker. In fact, she had a more insular childhood than most. Her parents, frightened by what had happened to European Jews during the war and fearing the anti-Semitism that was still around, restricted her friendships to a small group of fellow Jews in town. Joan lived at home until she graduated from college and got married one month later.

"Fortunately, my husband won a fellowship to study abroad and we moved to London," Joan says today. "The move changed my life." Joan grew up in a difficult time for many American Jews. Her parents tried to protect her by keeping her world narrow. But as an adult, Joan was fortunate to be given the opportunity to broaden her world—and she took it. She found that through traveling she could make connections with people across the globe, and as these connections grew, so did her belief in herself. Her life became enriched. She says, "As an adult I learned how to push back the boundaries of my life and to feel safe and trusting when tackling new experiences and meeting new people. It didn't come easily for me. In the beginning I was anxious, but through trying new things I developed confidence in myself."

Travel deepened Joan's connection to the world, and activism gave her the opportunity to help shape the world she felt so connected to. She has devoted her life to creating a world that is safe for all people. She has worked as a human rights activist; she has organized demonstrations against nuclear weapons. Currently she is coordinating a local campaign to raise public awareness of land mines and to ban their use.

Many people believe that individuals like Joan just got lucky, that she was somehow blessed with the ability to find purpose in life, a capacity for intimacy, and a love of learning. How many times have you heard someone described as "not equipped for relationships" or "a real homebody," implying that it is something in the person's character that is impervious to change? There certainly exist basic temperamental differences among people that might be nudged a little, but dramatic change is unlikely. It makes no sense, for example, to try to make an introvert gregarious. But Joan's willingness to try new things did not come naturally. She has worked hard at living an enriched and meaningful life. Our work has shown that the core components of reaching out are based on a combination of desire and skill. We can't instill in you a desire for intimacy or a passion for new experiences. But if you want them, we can help you develop the resilience you'll need to get them. And you may even find that once you're more resilient, an interest in reaching out will emerge in you.

People who reach out, like Joan, do three separate things quite well: They are good at assessing risks; they know themselves well; they find meaning and purpose in their life.

First, individuals who assess risk well have sound judgment and they use it to distinguish reasonable risk from unreasonable risk. They are realistically optimistic—they can forecast with accuracy the potential problems that may arise, and they develop strategies to prevent them from occurring and to handle them when they do occur. Their confidence in their ability to assess risk and deal with problems provides them with an internal safety net that makes it easier for them to pursue new experiences and forge new relationships. When you have faith in your ability to respond to uncertainty, reaching out becomes less daunting.

Second, people who have a keen sense of themselves are comfortable expressing their thoughts and feelings. This authenticity is coupled with a sophisticated awareness of other people and a genuine desire to learn what life is like for them. Like Joan, they are socially comfortable and at ease when meeting new people. This is not to say that they are social butterflies, dropping into one relationship after another, openly sharing the most intimate of life stories over the first cup of coffee. Don't confuse purging with intimacy. People who reach out do not impose themselves on others, nor do they probe and prod for inappropriate self-disclosure. Rather, they use their emotional awareness to track subtle signs in the receptiveness of others. Their honed interpersonal skills enable budding relationships to bloom.

People who reach out need to know when to continue and when to desist. They must be able to assess if there is a "true fit" between who they are and what they're experiencing. As Joan explained, not all of the activities she tried were a good fit. "I tried snow skiing, water skiing, scuba diving, and ice skating. As much as I would like to see myself as an athlete, I realized that my favorite sports were walking and miniature golf at the Jersey shore. I guess I could have forced myself to get better at those things, but I know that athletics is not an area in which I have any natural skill, so it made more sense to try other activities that were a better fit with who I am." Because Joan knows herself and is comfortable with who she is, she feels no shame or sense of failure when her pursuits don't work out. The ability to pull back is just as important to reaching out as is the ability to forge ahead. The resilience skills help you figure out when to do which.

Third, people who live broad lives have found meaning and purpose in their endeavors, and are appreciative of what they have and experience. Finding meaning in life requires a focus on the here and now, a mindfulness that many of us lack, coupled with the ability to see the big picture. Joan describes how she sticks to her mission despite slow progress. "I know that my activities will not bring about 'world peace,' and sometimes I feel hopeless. But I've learned two ways to remind myself of the meaningfulness of the work. First is to stay present-focused, to be in the moment as much as possible, and to find something of immediate value in what I am doing. So, when I am giving a talk on the dangers of land mines, I say to myself, 'I am doing a good job giving this talk and that's valuable.' The second way I find meaning is to shift my focus to the big picture. I think about the millions of other people around the world who also care about the same things I do. I feel connected to others who share my values about justice and personal responsibility for making a better world, and I feel like my life has purpose."

Reaching out is risky. Meeting new people, trying new things, being willing to pursue activities that provide meaning takes a tremendous amount of courage and inner strength. Each time you open your heart to someone, each time you undertake to learn something new, you risk rejection and failure; you risk embarrassment and sadness. Every time you reach out, you put yourself in harm's way. But resilience fortifies you. The skills of resilience improve your ability to assess risk and plan for potential problems. They deepen your emotional awareness and your interpersonal skills. And they can be used to increase your ability to stay present-focused and find meaning in your life. With the seven skills of resilience under your belt, you can reach out if you desire to.

What enabled Deb to overcome her impoverished childhood? What reserve of strength enabled Cindi Lamb and Candace Lightner to turn their tremendous losses into humanitarian wins? And why does Joan search for opportunities to master something new and stay committed to her ideals? Each of them has natural resilience, and thanks to decades of scientific research, we can now teach you how to find that resilience within yourself.

CHAPTER TWO

How Resilient Are You?

Michael and Mary were born in the same place in the same year: Kauai, 1955. Kauai is a tropical island of mountains, rain forest, and pristine beaches located at the northwest end of the Hawaiian chain. The name itself conjures up images of idyllic childhoods spent fishing, hiking, and swimming. And so it probably was for many of the children born there in the mid-1950s, but not for Michael and Mary.

Michael, a premature baby, spent his first three weeks of life in a hospital ward, separated from his teenage mother. His father was absent with the military until Michael was two. By his eighth birthday Michael had three younger siblings, his parents were divorced, and his mother had left Kauai, breaking all ties with her family. Mary was born into poverty, the daughter of an unskilled farm laborer and a mentally ill mother. Mary's life between the ages of five and ten was one of repeated physical and emotional abuse, punctuated by her mother's several hospitalizations for mental illness.

Two children with the odds against them. And yet by their eighteenth birthdays, Michael and Mary were popular and successful at school, possessed solid moral values, and were very optimistic about their futures. How did these two children emerge from the turmoil of their early lives to be so resilient?

Michael and Mary were part of an ambitious, landmark study conducted by two eminent developmental psychologists, Emmy Werner and Ruth Smith.[1] This study, to which we alluded in Chapter 1, marked the beginning of the modern era of research into the early childhood factors that shape resilience. In 1955, 833 children were born on Kauai, and Werner and Smith tracked some 698 of them from their prenatal months to beyond their thirtieth birthdays. Their goal was to determine why some children thrive and others suffer severe deficits despite similar experiences. The data they gathered help us to understand the ingredients that comprise resilience.

Most of the children Werner and Smith followed were descendents of Southeast Asians who came to Kauai to work on the sugar and pineapple plantations. They found that one in every three children was born with the odds against them; they were "vulnerable" for many of the reasons we noted in Chapter 1—socioeconomic and family factors that were beyond their control. Their parents had not graduated high school and worked in low-paying laboring jobs. The families of these vulnerable children were particularly poor, and home life was marked by fighting and divorce. Many of the parents were alcoholic and had high rates of mental illness. For two out of three vulnerable children, their resilience was clipped, and the negative implications of this manifested themselves early on. They suffered significant learning deficits and displayed behavior problems such as hyperactivity and acting out by the time they were ten. By the time this group had turned eighteen, arrests, pregnancies, and serious mental health problems were common. The circumstances of their early childhoods had robbed them of their resilience, and they were now set on a downward trajectory that would affect their levels of achievement well into adulthood.

But there was one child in every three who developed into a confident, accomplished, connected adult like Michael and Mary. The resilience of those children was somehow preserved and enabled them to overcome the circumstances of their childhoods. In fact, most studies have shown that even among children exposed to several risk factors—like poverty, poor parenting, and genetic loading for mental illness—only half succumb. The other half thrive.

Werner and Smith found that a significant proportion of the vulnerable children went on to excel. When we examine the interviews with these children through the lens of our notion of resilience, we see that the children applied their resilience in all four ways we listed in Chapter 1. They overcame the early obstacles of poverty, ill health, and abuse, steered through the ongoing adversity of absentee parents, bounced back from the trauma of their parents' divorces, and had enough resilience to reach out for life's adventures and new experiences. As one of the study participants reported in a final interview, "I thank God that he gave me the power and strength to be where I am. I just think I am thirty years young—I have so much more to do in life. . . . I can't possibly do all I want to do in sixty to seventy years."[2]

How Can We Impact Resilience?

The work of Werner, Smith, and others demonstrates clearly that early childhood circumstances affect a person's resilience well into adulthood. Why are these effects so longlasting? Because they shape children's belief systems and abilities, and these remain stable even as they grow into adults. In Chapter 1 we noted some of these personal characteristics, these beliefs and abilities, that lead people to be resilient. We found that resilient people are able to monitor and regulate their own emotions and monitor the emotional states of others. Like Deb, they stay focused and intent on solving problems. They can accurately distinguish between those aspects of an adversity over which they have control and those they do not. Like Robert, they rate high on self-efficacy—they believe they can master their environment and they have the confidence to take action. Resilient people, like Stacey, have strong connections to others, and they rely on those connections to help them through the tough times. And those who reach out, like Joan, see challenges as opportunities and they are willing to take risks if it means broadening their lives. Nonresilient people lack these abilities and beliefs.

And again, this is where we, as psychologists and researchers, come in. Childhood environmental factors—poverty, divorce, mentally ill parents, to name a few—are history. They are beyond our ability to change. But beliefs can be changed and abilities can be boosted. Resilience is a nebulous concept—difficult for us to get our arms around—so how can we go about the task of making someone more resilient? Our work on the nature of resilience shows that it is comprised of seven abilities: emotion regulation, impulse control, empathy, optimism, causal analysis, self-efficacy, and reaching out. These seven concrete factors can be measured, taught, and improved.

We have developed a resilience test that measures a person's current standing on the seven abilities as well as their overall Resilience Quotient, or RQ.[3] It has been completed by thousands of people in diverse job types and from all walks of life, and has proven to be highly predictive of success in the real world. For example, in our work with a large telecommunications company, we compared the RQs of front-line employees with those of the managers who had been promoted from their ranks. The scores of the managers were significantly higher. With another client, a financial investment company, we measured the RQs of their newly hired financial consultants and tracked their performance on the number of clients and the dollar assets under their management. Those with higher RQs at the time of hiring did better on both.

The seven skills we have developed are designed to boost the seven abilities, and our research indicates that they work. We trained representatives in a customer service and sales division of a Fortune 100 company in the seven skills of resilience that we present in Part II of this book. Three months after the training they had outstripped their control group peers on each of the four most important performance ratings of their jobs. In another study we taught the seven skills to salespeople and office managers who had lower RQs than their peers. A month after they learned the skills they were outperforming those same peers by 50 percent on one performance measure and 100 percent on another. Resilience matters and it can be learned.

Remember that we promised to take you on a journey. Well, you've come to the beginning. The first step is to measure your own RQ. Once you know how strong you are on the seven factors of resilience, you'll have a better idea of which of the seven skills you need most.

Take the RQ Test

Please complete the following fifty-six-item RQ Test.* Do not spend too much time on any one item; it should take you only about ten minutes.

Please rate each item for how true it is of you, using the following scale.

> 1 = not at all true
> 2 = sometimes or somewhat true
> 3 = moderately true
> 4 = usually true
> 5 = very true of me

_____ 1. When trying to solve a problem, I trust my instincts and go with the first solution that occurs to me.

_____ 2. Even if I plan ahead for a discussion with my boss, a coworker, my spouse, or my child, I still find myself acting emotionally.

_____ 3. I worry about my future health.

_____ 4. I am good at shutting out anything that distracts me from the task at hand.

_____ 5. If my first solution doesn't work, I am able to go back and continue trying different solutions until I find one that does work.

_____ 6. I am curious.

_____ 7. I am unable to harness positive emotions to help me focus on a task.

_____ 8. I'm the kind of person who likes to try new things.

_____ 9. I would rather do something at which I feel confident and relaxed than something that is quite challenging and difficult.

_____ 10. By looking at their facial expressions, I recognize the emotions people are experiencing.

_____ 11. I give in to the urge to give up when things go wrong.

_____ 12. When a problem arises, I come up with a lot of possible solutions before trying to solve it.

_____ 13. I can control the way I feel when adversity strikes.

_____ 14. What other people think about me does not influence my behavior.

_____ 15. When a problem occurs, I am aware of the first thoughts that pop into my head about it.

_____ 16. I feel most comfortable in situations in which I am not the only one responsible.

_____ 17. I prefer situations where I can depend on someone else's ability rather than my own.

_____ 18. I believe that it is better to believe problems are controllable, even if that is not always true.

_____ 19. When a problem arises, I think carefully about what caused it before attempting to solve it.

_____ 20. I have doubts about my ability to solve problems at work or at home.

_____ 21. I don't spend time thinking about factors that are out of my control.

_____ 22. I enjoy doing simple routine tasks that do not change.

_____ 23. I get carried away by my feelings.

_____ 24. It is difficult for me to understand why people feel the way they do.

_____ 25. I am good at identifying what I am thinking and how it affects my mood.

_____ 26. If someone does something that upsets me, I am able to wait until an appropriate time when I have calmed down to discuss it.

_____ 27. When someone overreacts to a problem, I think it is usually because they are just in a bad mood that day.

_____ 28. I expect that I will do well on most things.

_____ 29. People often seek me out to help them figure out problems.

_____ 30. I feel at a loss to understand why people react the way they do.

_____ 31. My emotions affect my ability to focus on what I need to get done at home, school, or work.

_____ 32. Hard work always pays off.

_____ 33. After completing a task, I worry that it will be negatively evaluated.

_____ 34. If someone is sad, angry, or embarrassed, I have a good idea what he or she may be thinking.

_____ 35. I don't like new challenges.

_____ 36. I don't plan ahead in my job, schoolwork, or finances.

_____ 37. If a colleague is upset, I have a pretty good idea why.

_____ 38. I prefer doing things spontaneously rather than planning ahead, even if it means it doesn't turn out as well.

_____ 39. I believe most problems are caused by circumstances beyond my control.

_____ 40. I look at challenges as a way to learn and improve myself.

_____ 41. I've been told I misinterpret events and situations.

_____ 42. If someone is upset with me, I listen to what they have to say before reacting.

_____ 43. When asked to think about my future, I find it hard to imagine myself as a success.

_____ 44. I've been told that I jump to conclusions when problems arise.

_____ 45. I am uncomfortable when meeting new people.

_____ 46. It is easy for me to get "lost" in a book or a movie.

_____ 47. I believe the old adage, "an ounce of prevention is worth a pound of cure."

_____ 48. In most situations, I believe I'm good at identifying the true causes of problems.

_____ 49. I believe I have good coping skills and that I respond well to most challenges.

_____ 50. My significant other and/or close friends tell me that I don't understand them.

_____ 51. I am most comfortable in my established routines.

_____ 52. I think it's important to solve problems as quickly as possible, even if that means sacrificing a full understanding of the problem.

_____ 53. When faced with a difficult situation, I am confident that it will go well.

_____ 54. My colleagues and friends tell me I don't listen to what they say.

_____ 55. If I decide I want something, I go out and buy it right away.

_____ 56. When I discuss a "hot" topic with a colleague or family member, I am able to keep my emotions in check.

Emotion Regulation and Resilience

Emotion Regulation is the ability to stay calm under pressure. Resilient people use a well-developed set of skills that help them to control their emotions, attention, and behavior. Self-regulation is important for forming intimate relationships, succeeding at work, and maintaining physical health. People who have difficulty regulating their emotions often emotionally exhaust their partners at home and are difficult to work with. Re-

Emotion Regulation

Add your scores on the following items:		Add your scores on the following items:	
Item 13	_____	Item 2	_____
Item 25	_____	Item 7	_____
Item 26	_____	Item 23	_____
Item 56	_____	Item 31	_____
Positive Total	_____	Negative Total	_____

Positive Total minus Negative Total = _____ This is your Emotional Regulation score.

Above Average:	A score higher than 13
Average:	A score between 6 and 13, inclusive
Below Average:	A score lower than 6

search shows that people who lack the ability to regulate their emotions have a hard time building and maintaining friendships. There are probably many reasons why this is so, the most basic of which is that negativity is a turnoff. People don't like to spend time with people who are angry, sullen, or anxious. Not only is it a drain, but emotions are contagious. The more you associate with the angry, sullen, and anxious, the more angry, sullen, and anxious you become.

Of course, not every emotion needs to be repaired or controlled. We don't believe that all anger, sadness, anxiety, and guilt should be minimized, managed, or stifled. To the contrary, the expression of emotions, negative and positive, is healthy and constructive; indeed, proper emotional expression is a part of being resilient. But just as life's luster is dulled if we keep our emotions under total wraps, so does being a slave to your emotions interfere with your resilience and drain it from those around you.

Some people are prone to experience greater amounts of anxiety, sadness, and anger than others and have a harder time regaining control once they are upset. They are more likely to get stuck in their anger, sadness, or anxiety and are less effective at coping with adversity and solving problems. And they find it nearly impossible to reach out to others and new experiences when they are being held captive by their emotions.

Consider Beth, a manager in a telecommunications company. As a child, Beth was emotionally volatile and remembers feeling powerless to shift her mood once it took hold. Her mercurial style didn't soften as she grew to adulthood. As Beth candidly describes, the emotional roller coaster she rides undermines her effectiveness as a parent. "I have two teenage daughters, and I know they are reluctant to talk with me about their problems. I know they worry that I won't be able to handle my own emotional reactions and that instead of helping them to sort through what they are feeling, I'll get lost in what I am feeling. I try to show them that I can stay calm and listen to them, but the truth is, I really struggle with it. My emotionality has gotten in the way of being a good mother."

If Beth's story sounds familiar, emotion regulation is probably an ability you need to develop. But how do you go about regulating your emotions? There are a variety of effective techniques for calming yourself down when angry, for lifting your mood when sad, and for quieting anxiety, many of which we further discuss in Chapter 9. Of the many techniques for regulating emotions, we have found most effective those strategies that work to alter your beliefs about adversity—the actual thoughts you have when problems arise and that are the source of your emotions.

If you feel that you need to work on your emotion regulation, you'll find Skills 1 and 6 particularly useful. Learning your ABCs will enable you to detect the belief that produces your counterproductive emotion, while Calming and Focusing will provide you with the means to invoke the relaxation response you need to begin reining in those emotions.

Impulse Control

Add your scores on the following items:		Add your scores on the following items:	
Item 4	_____	Item 11	_____
Item 15	_____	Item 36	_____
Item 42	_____	Item 38	_____
Item 47	_____	Item 55	_____
Positive Total	_____	Negative Total	_____

Positive Total minus Negative Total = _____ This is your Impulse Control score.

Above Average:	A score higher than 0
Average:	A score between -6 and 0, inclusive
Below Average:	A score lower than -6

Impulse Control and Resilience

Dan Goleman, author of *Emotional Intelligence*, performed a fascinating study in the 1970s.[4] Young children, around seven years old, were brought one by one into a small room where another researcher was waiting. The researcher explained to each child that he had to leave for a few minutes, but before he did, he wanted to offer the child a marshmallow. The child could eat the marshmallow now, the researcher explained. But if the child held off on eating it and waited until the researcher returned, he'd give the child a second one. Ten years later Goleman tracked the children who had participated in the experiment; who were by now high school seniors. Those children who could control their impulses, who could delay the gratification of one marshmallow to get two, were doing significantly better socially and academically.

It's lack of impulse control that's getting Louis, a thirty-five-year-old college professor, into trouble. He is liked by most of his colleagues—they see him as fun and lively—but he is also the punch line of a great many jokes. He blurts out inappropriate comments in faculty meetings, giving voice to each thought as he thinks them. He's quick to apologize but equally quick to re-offend. He drinks too much socially, he overeats, and some colleagues have wondered about some of his relationships with students. Louis is too much id, not enough superego, which means that time and time again his hedonistic desires win out over his rational mind. His typical pattern is to get excited about a new project, throw himself into it full steam ahead, but then suddenly lose interest and drop the project altogether. As Louis puts it, "I'm like a twelve-year-old boy. I'm impulsive in my personal life and I'm impulsive professionally. I have a hard time controlling my emotions and a harder time telling myself no. I get all hyped up about something and go after it full throttle but I can't sustain my interest."

It makes intuitive sense that emotion regulation and impulse control are closely related, and our analyses bear this out—people who are strong on the RQ factor of impulse control also tend to be high on emotion regulation. We believe the connection in these areas exists because they tap into similar belief systems in us. So if your impulse control is low, you will accept your first impulsive belief about the situation as true and act accordingly. Often this produces negative consequences that can hamper your resilience. As with emotion regulation, the first key skill for impulse control is Learning Your ABCs, which we introduce in the next section. ABC tracks how our thoughts determine our emotions and behavior. Having mastered ABC, you can move to Avoiding Thinking Traps, which will

Optimism

Add your scores on the following items:		Add your scores on the following items:	
Item 18	_____	Item 3	_____
Item 27	_____	Item 33	_____
Item 32	_____	Item 39	_____
Item 53	_____	Item 43	_____
Positive Total	_____	Negative Total	_____

Positive Total minus Negative Total = _____ This is your Optimism score.

Above Average:	A score higher than 6
Average:	A score between -2 and 6, inclusive
Below Average:	A score lower than -2

guide you to detect the impulsive beliefs you commonly entertain and how they work to derail your resiliency. And once you get to Challenging Beliefs, you'll be able to boost your impulse control and generate more accurate thoughts that will lead to better emotion regulation and result in more resilient behavior.

Optimism and Resilience

"Oh, yes, the game was to just find something about everything to be glad about—not matter what 'twas," rejoined Pollyanna earnestly. "And we began right then—on the crutches."

"I can't see anythin' ter be glad about—gettin' a pair of crutches when you wanted a doll!" . . .

"Goosey! Why, just be glad because you don't need 'em!"

—ELEANOR H. PORTER, *POLLYANNA*[5]

Resilient people are optimistic. They believe that things can change for the better. They have hope for the future and believe that they control the direction of their lives. Compared to pessimists, optimists are physically healthier, are less likely to suffer depression, do better in school, are more productive at work, and win more in sports. These are facts borne out by hundreds of well-controlled studies.

Optimism, of course, means that we see our futures as relatively bright. Optimism implies that we believe we have the ability to handle the adversities that will inevitably arise in the future. And, of course, this reflects our sense of self-efficacy, our faith in our ability to solve our own problems and master our world, which is another important ability in resilience.

Our research shows that optimism and self-efficacy often go hand in hand. Optimism is a boon if it is linked with true self-efficacy because optimism motivates you to search for solutions and to keep working hard to improve your situation. It's worth noting that people who harbor unbridled optimism, of the Pollyanna variety, may not derive any advantage at all. In fact, unrealistic optimism may lead people to ignore real threats for which they need to prepare. A Pollyanna optimist, if diagnosed with a serious illness, might say to herself, "Oh, this is no big deal. My condition isn't serious. I'll be fine," which will make it unlikely that she will do the things she needs to do to improve her chances of recovery. The key to resilience and success, then, is to have realistic optimism coupled with self-efficacy. And as we shall see, self-efficacy is a result of successful problem solving, which in turn can be significantly enhanced using Challenging Beliefs and Putting It in Perspective—two skills that enable us to gain mastery over those elements of our world that are in our control.

Causal Analysis

Add your scores on the following items:		Add your scores on the following items:	
Item 12	_____	Item 1	_____
Item 19	_____	Item 41	_____
Item 21	_____	Item 44	_____
Item 48	_____	Item 52	_____
Positive Total	_____	Negative Total	_____

Positive Total minus Negative Total = _____ This is your Causal Analysis score.

Above Average:	A score higher than 8
Average:	A score between 0 and 8, inclusive
Below Average:	A score lower than 0

Causal Analysis and Resilience

Causal analysis is a term we use to refer to people's ability to accurately identify the causes of their problems. If we're unable to assess the causes of our problems accurately, then we are doomed to make the same mistakes over and over again.

Our mentor, Martin Seligman, and his colleagues identified a thinking style that's particularly important to causal analysis: explanatory style.[6] It's the habitual way you explain the good and bad things that happen to you. Everyone's explanatory style can be coded on three dimensions: personal ("me–not me"), permanent ("always–not always"), and pervasive ("every-thing–not everything") ways of thinking. A "Me, Always, Everything" person automatically, reflexively believes that she caused the problem (me), that it is lasting and unchangeable (always), and that it will undermine all aspects of her life (everything). Here are two "Me, Always, Everything" beliefs:

1. "My son is doing poorly at school *because I don't spend enough time making sure he does his homework. I'm a bad mother.*"

2. "I didn't get the promotion *because I am too timid and just don't have good people skills.*"

When problems arise, a "Not Me, Not Always, Not Everything" person believes that other people or circumstances caused the problem (not me), that it is fleeting and changeable (not always), and that it will not af-fect much of her life (not everything). Such a person interprets the same situations very differently from the "Me, Always, Everything" person:

1. "My son is doing poorly at school *because he has not been studying lately.*"

2. "I didn't get the promotion *because they don't understand how much I have to offer.*"

Explanatory style plays such an important role in resilience that we will take the issue up again in the next chapter. In Chapter 7, "Challeng-ing Beliefs," we'll give you a chance to map your own explanatory style and guide you through a process to get outside the thinking-style rut that your explanatory style represents.

We've witnessed firsthand how explanatory style can profoundly af-fect performance. Kathy and Len are a middle-aged married couple we met when they were students in an evening class we cotaught on abnor-mal psychology. We were impressed by Len and Kathy's insightful ques-tions and the tough but respectful way in which they challenged some of the theories we presented. Prior to the first exam, we predicted that they would both score among the highest in the class. To our surprise, Kathy got a B and Len scored in the C range. When they came to talk to us about the exam, it became apparent that they had different agendas.

Kathy was clearly more upset than Len although she got the better grade, and this made sense given their explanations. For Kathy, she got a

B because, as she put it, "I'm not smart enough for psychology." Len, in contrast, said, "I think I got a C because I'm having a hard time figuring out the best way to prepare for the exams." Kathy's "Me, Always, Everything" style led her to become discouraged, whereas Len's style drove him to look for solutions.

It's easy to see how explanatory style affects our causal analysis. Those people who ruminate about the "always–everything" causes of their problems cannot see a way to change their situation. They become helpless and hopeless. People who focus on the "not always–not everything" causes are galvanized and capable of generating solutions that they can put into action. But the most resilient people are those who have cognitive flexibility and can identify all the significant causes of the adversities they face, without being trapped in any specific explanatory style. They are realists in that they do not ignore the factors that are permanent and pervasive. They also don't reflexively blame others for their mistakes in order to preserve their self-esteem or absolve themselves of guilt. Nor do they waste their valuable reserves of resilience ruminating about events or circumstances outside their control. They channel their problem-solving resources into the factors they can control, and, through incremental change, they begin to overcome, steer through, bounce back, and reach out. Like someone who feels the need to improve his impulse control and optimism, if you need to improve your causal analysis, then Challenging Beliefs probably will be the skill that helps you the most.

Empathy

Add your scores on the following items:		Add your scores on the following items:	
Item 10	_____	Item 24	_____
Item 34	_____	Item 30	_____
Item 37	_____	Item 50	_____
Item 46	_____	Item 54	_____
Positive Total	_____	Negative Total	_____

Positive Total minus Negative Total = _____ This is your Empathy score.

Above Average:	A score higher than 12
Average:	A score between 3 and 12, inclusive
Below Average:	A score lower than 3

Empathy and Resilience

Your empathy score represents how well you're able to read other people's cues to their psychological and emotional states. Some of us are adept at interpreting what psychologists call the nonverbals of others—their facial expressions, their tone of voice, their body language—and determining what people are thinking and feeling. Others have not developed these skills and therefore are unable to place themselves in the other person's shoes, estimating what the person must feel and predicting what he or she is likely to do. This inability to read nonverbal cues can be costly in business, where progression through the ranks often requires networking skills, and for managers, whose job it is to understand how best to motivate their employees. It also can be costly in personal relationships, where people need to feel understood and valued. People low in empathy, even well-intentioned ones, tend to repeat the same old nonresilient patterns of behavior, and they're known to "bulldoze" others' emotions and desires. But your empathy score can be improved.

In Part Two of this book you will learn to use Learning Your ABCs and Detecting Icebergs to understand what motivates you as you navigate your way through the world. These same skills can be applied to how you deal with others—to better understand why the person you manage procrastinates on important projects, why your teenage son has become withdrawn and somber, and to better connect with the people you love.

Self-efficacy

Add your scores on the following items:		Add your scores on the following items:	
Item 5	_____	Item 9	_____
Item 28	_____	Item 17	_____
Item 29	_____	Item 20	_____
Item 49	_____	Item 22	_____
Positive Total	_____	Negative Total	_____

Positive Total minus Negative Total = _____ This is your Self-efficacy score.

Above Average:	A score higher than 10
Average:	A score between 6 and 10, inclusive
Below Average:	A score lower than 6

Self-efficacy and Resilience

Self-efficacy is our sense that we are effective in the world. It represents our beliefs that we can solve the problems we are likely to experience and our faith in our ability to succeed. We've already devoted a lot of time to the discussion of self-efficacy, so let's show you how it is used in a real-life situation. At work, people who have faith in their ability to solve problems emerge as leaders, while those who aren't confident about their efficacy find themselves lost in the crowd. They unintentionally broadcast their self-doubt, and their colleagues listen—and learn to seek the counsel of others.

Lynn and Greg work in the same department of a Fortune 500 telecommunications company. They are both new to the company and have had similar education and similar training. After being in their positions for six months, two different career trajectories have emerged. Greg has had small successes, but none of them convinced him that he was equal to the job. He still doesn't believe he can complete the project work expected of him. On the other hand, Lynn's small successes have added to her confidence. With each victory, she grows in her knowledge that she has genuine talents and skills that she can use to control her work environment. The difference lies in how Lynn and Greg respond to normal work challenges. Lynn's self-confidence and belief that she could solve problems enabled her to negotiate the inevitable complications that arise at work. Greg, in contrast, was passive in response to similar challenges. He felt incapable of generating solutions and ill-equipped to carry out solutions offered by others. As a consequence of her resilience, Lynn has

Reaching Out

Add your scores on the following items:		Add your scores on the following items:	
Item 6	_____	Item 16	_____
Item 8	_____	Item 35	_____
Item 14	_____	Item 45	_____
Item 40	_____	Item 51	_____
Positive Total	_____	Negative Total	_____

Positive Total minus Negative Total = _____ This is your Reaching Out score.

Above Average:	A score higher than 9
Average:	A score between 4 and 9, inclusive
Below Average:	A score lower than 4

caught management's eye. She has been asked to take on more responsibility and has been offered the opportunity to participate in an advanced training seminar, which, although not billed as such, is known as a special training for those being put on the fast track.

Lynn's resilience places her on a positive career trajectory, whereas Greg's self-doubt and ineffectiveness actually serve to increase the difficulties he will encounter. In Part II we will teach you skills for building your confidence and improving your efficacy—Avoiding Thinking Traps, to head off your assumptions about the causes of your problems, and Challenging Beliefs, to become more accurate in your problem solving. When you use these skills, you'll do better at work and in your relationships, and with those improvements in your life will come a newfound confidence and sense of self-efficacy.

Reaching Out and Resilience

We've shared with you six abilities that enable a person to be resilient in the face of adversity. But as we've seen, resilience is not just about overcoming, steering through, and bouncing back from adversity. Resilience also enables us to enhance the positive aspects of life. Resilience is the source of our ability to reach out, and a surprising number of people can't do it. Why are some people afraid of reaching out? For some people, it's because they learned early in life that embarrassment was to be avoided at all costs. Better to remain in one's shell, even if it means a life of mediocrity, than to expose oneself to public failure and ridicule. For others, as we shall see in Chapter 8, this reflects the tendency to overestimate the likelihood of future adversity. And as we shall see in Chapter 5, people often overvalue sins of commission and underplay sins of omission. That is, failure due to an action is falsely considered more detrimental to success than the failure to act.

The reaching out of other people is compromised by their fear of plumbing the true limits of their ability. People with this thinking style, known as self-handicapping, subconsciously place limits on themselves: "If I don't try and then don't succeed I can always tell myself that I failed because I didn't really try, rather than having to face the fact that I just might not be good enough." Such people tend to overestimate the probability that failed attempts will lead to catastrophic outcomes. If you want to improve your ability to reach out, then our skills will surely help. We'll show you how to use Detecting Icebergs to uncover the deep beliefs that may be holding you back from intimacy and from taking on new challenges. We'll show you how to use Challenging Beliefs to test out your assumptions, and we'll guide you to use Putting It in Perspective to curb your fears about reaching out. We'll introduce you to Real-time Resilience so that you can fight back against your nonresilient beliefs as they occur.

Remember: You Can Increase Your Resilience

Some people are surprised that they didn't score higher on the RQ Test. Don't be disheartened—by using the skills we describe in this book, you can significantly improve in each of these seven abilities. As you'll see in the next chapter, meaningful change is possible.

CHAPTER THREE

Laying the Groundwork

In buying this book, you have made an important statement. You've declared your belief that your destiny can be changed and molded—that you can take control of your behavior and pilot your own life. We share in that belief. But before you begin to use the seven skills to bring about those changes in your resilience and your life, it's helpful, as with all new skills, to consider the history behind them. To this end, in this chapter we present the platform on which our work is built.

Our work is founded on decades of research devoted to the study of resilience, the variables that erode it, the factors that buffer it, and the effects of compromised resilience on later achievement.[1] However, in many ways we have navigated by a different star and charted a different course from the scientists before us. Here we'll share with you four principles on which our work is based—the four research-driven pillars that provide the foundation for the skills of resilience. We have learned in our years of presenting to audiences that some people want to review the underpinning theory before they commit to the skills. This chapter gives you the chance to "kick the tires" of our philosophy. Others will be less concerned with the theoretical platform and may instead be keen to jump in and use the skills. Feel free to skim this chapter and move to Part II of the book.

As we look back on the last fifteen years of our research, we have a sense that the route we traveled was, somehow, inevitable. As scientists, we believe that our philosophy should be shaped by the data, and the research findings in our field propelled us toward the four principles we hold. And once we arrived at those principles, our mission was set—to develop and validate real-world programs that boost resilience through more accurate thinking.

Pillar 1: Life Change Is Possible

As noted, we share in the belief that people can change their lives. This is a powerful concept, but it is a modern one. The notion that humans are not bound and gagged by the fallout of their early childhoods, that they can change their behavior at any time in their lives, seems such a truism to some people today. But, historically, people have believed that lasting change was not possible. And even now many people still cling to the notion that the first few years of life determine everything about a person and her future. In the early 1900s, Sigmund Freud, whom you probably know as the "father" of modern psychology, claimed that our personalities are largely fixed by about age five and was pessimistic about our ability to change. Freud had borrowed heavily from the rationalistic philosophy of Thomas Hobbes, who had a dim view of humankind, condemning our nature as nasty and selfish and our lives as brutish and short. Could we transcend this selfishness and redeem ourselves? According to Hobbes, no, we could not. Our personalities were innate and fixed, and nothing could change them. Freud was willing to concede that after years of expensive and time-consuming therapy, some positive outcomes could be wrought. But certainly, in Freud's view, no one could be trusted to fix him- or herself, and no self-help book could put a dent in the pathology in us all.

The last eight decades in psychology represent a battle over human nature. Freud was part of the debate that raged around a crucial question: What are the forces that shape our behavior, and can they be controlled? The answers that are offered define the very core of what it means to be human.

By the 1920s there were gathering murmurs of discontent with Freudian ideas among psychologists. The dissenters embraced a very different philosophy from Freud, one grounded in the empiricism of John Locke and Jean-Jacques Rousseau, which proposed that we are born *tabula rasa*, "clean slates," not with innate selfishness and greed but as fresh pages awaiting the formative imprints of our experiences. They concluded that just as learning shapes who we are and what we do, so we can direct new learning to overcome the past. What is learned can be unlearned.

According to this approach, people are not fatalistic victims of their ancestries or of their pasts. We are free to change our lives at any point—

Freud's Pessimism

Why was Freud so pessimistic about our ability to radically change ourselves and our lives? Two facets of his theory led him to this pessimism. First, he believed it was the mysterious forces of the unconscious mind that led us to behave as we do, that we can snatch only occasional glimpses into that unconscious realm, so it is almost impossible to bring the mind's activity under any kind of manual control. Second, he believed that the core of our personality development happened in the first five years of life. All subsequent development merely wrapped itself around the core like a second skin, but it couldn't affect the essence of who we were. That essence lay deep within our psyches—largely out of the reach of any positive effects brought by new experiences or short-term therapy.

It is an accident of history that Freud centered his theory on the unconscious. As a new graduate of the University of Vienna's medical school, Freud made his way to Paris to take up an internship with Jean-Martin Charcot. Charcot, a renowned hypnotist, specialized in the treatment of hysteria. Hysterical patients typically were functionally blind or paralyzed, but no doctor could find any obvious physical cause. Under Charcot's hypnosis, the blind were able to see and the lame, to walk—at least until the hypnotic spell was lifted. Once out of hypnosis, their maladies returned.

His experience with Charcot left a profound and lasting impression on the twenty-nine-year-old Freud. He suspected that the blindness and paralysis were due to conflicts being fought in the patients' unconscious minds. These unconscious conflicts generated enormous guilt, anxiety, and aggression as well as impulses to act that, if expressed, could overwhelm them. The ego worked to protect them from these dark secrets, to keep the conflicts from the patients' awareness. The blindness or paralysis was part of the ego's strategy. But with the ego weakened under hypnosis, the repressed behavior could not be contained, and the patients were able to see or walk. After his experiences with Charcot, Freud resolved that the unconscious mind, with all its conflicts and fixated energy, was the major engine of human behavior. And because the unconscious was, by definition, outside people's awareness, it was largely impossible for them to change themselves and impossible for a therapist to facilitate change for them without a very lengthy therapy process. Hence Freud's pessimism.

if we have the motive and the drive, and if we are equipped with the appropriate skills. That we are the masters of our own destinies is a liberating theory in line with modern thinking. And the research data support it—people *can* change positively and permanently. We have adopted this principle as the first pillar in our platform.

What unfolded during those pivotal forty years, roughly between the 1920s and the 1960s? The optimistic followers of Locke and Rousseau, who emphasized our ability to change through learning, disagreed with Freud on another fundamental issue. Freud was a great thinker, even a philosopher, but he was not a scientist. He developed much of his theory before the scientific method became the vogue. The new breed of psychologists wanted to inject scientific practice into their discipline.

Scientists perform experiments. Against the dogma of the time, Galileo believed that objects fell through the air at the same rate, regardless of their weight. To test this he climbed to the top of the Tower of Pisa (a straight climb in those days, since it hadn't started to lean), dropped several balls of different weights, and timed their falls. In systematic fashion, he changed one aspect of the environment and observed the result. This is true scientific method. So for psychology to be a science, it was argued, psychologists must be able to systematically change, or "manipulate," to use scientific lingo, one observable variable at a time.

Freud's theories could not be tested in this way. Unresolved conflicts cannot be experimentally manipulated; unconscious ego defenses cannot literally be observed. The new psychology insisted there was only one true grist for the psychology mill—not emotions or mental states, which cannot be seen, but the only thing that can be observed: behavior. And so it was that the new wave was dubbed *behaviorism*.

But as the emphasis on behavior as the only proper level of study became more radical, psychologists became disenchanted with the behavioral school, a situation that was almost certainly fueled by its leaders. John B. Watson, the first great American behaviorist, wanted all reference to mental and emotional states banished from psychology. The other great proponent of behaviorism, B. F. Skinner, presented an equally nonhumanitarian face. In fact, he developed and advocated an infant's crib that would tend to all the child's needs without the caregiver needing to be present, since he saw the hour-to-hour tending of the baby as an onerous chore. In his very first television interview, Skinner was asked, "Would you, if you had to choose, burn your children or your books?" Without pause he replied that he would burn his children, since his contribution to the future of society through his work was much greater than that through his genes.[2]

How foreign this all seems to us from our twenty-first-century perspective. But in the 1920s, '30s, and '40s psychology plunged headlong after behaviorism, building laboratories across the country on the assumption that the study of reinforcement and punishment in rats, dogs, and pigeons would reveal all we wanted to know of human behavior. All mention of emotions, mental states, and the mind was purged from the psychological landscape. Morton Hunt, a masterful historian of psychology, cites a clever commentator of the time: "Psychology, having first lost its soul to Darwin, now lost its mind to Watson."[3]

It may be easier to apply science to the study of behavior than to the study of thoughts and emotions. But if thoughts and emotions power behavior, then, even if the scientific method is more difficult to apply, thoughts and emotions must be studied if we are to understand people—including their resilience. There is an old joke among psychologists about behaviorism. A behaviorist loses his car keys and frantically begins looking for them in the parking lot. A colleague discovers him looking for his keys in the dirt under a bright overhead light and offers his help. After about thirty minutes of searching, the helper asks if his friend is sure he lost the keys here. "No," replied the behaviorist. "In fact, I'm pretty sure I lost them over there in that dark alley. But the light is much better here." It may be easier to shine the light of science on behavior, but if the key to boosting resilience is thinking, that's what we need to study.

Pillar 2: Thinking Is the Key to Boosting Resilience

By the 1960s the time was ripe for a resurgence of interest in the study of emotions and thoughts. This quiet revolution was led by an unassuming psychiatrist from Providence, Rhode Island: Dr. Aaron Beck. Beck presents a grandfatherly figure. There is nothing about his appearance and demeanor to suggest that he was a revolutionary, effectively overturning the practice of psychology. Only the shock of white hair and his brightly colored bow ties give any indication of the iconoclast. But revolutionize psychology he most certainly did.

When Beck was born in July 1921, Freud was at the zenith of his career. Aaron Beck stepped into this tradition when he entered Yale's psychiatry program in 1942. As a psychiatrist in training, Beck found himself in the therapy room attempting to follow the psychoanalytic model in which he'd been trained, peeling back his patients' layers of defenses to release, from unconsciousness, the fixated energy that supposedly caused their depression and anxiety. But when he plied the psychoanalytic techniques, his patients gave "strange" responses. For most of them, it didn't come naturally to talk about their dreams or their mothers. They wanted to talk about what was going on in their lives *now*, about what had driven them into therapy. And they shared their thoughts about themselves, about their world, and about their futures. "I can't do anything right." "My life is out of control." "No one could love me."

Beck noticed that these thoughts, or *cognitions*, shared about equal session airtime with the patient's emotions. Over the years he came to recognize what an enormous body of research now confirms—cognitions cause emotions, and emotions matter in determining who remains resilient and who succumbs. Beck developed a system of therapy, called cognitive therapy, in which patients learn to change their thinking to overcome depression and anxiety. Cognitive therapy gained world renown, and Beck established his Center for Cognitive Therapy at the University of Pennsylvania. We were training as therapists there when Joe entered our care.

Joe came to the center after eight unsuccessful years of Freudian psychoanalysis. He had become skeptical, jaded, and disillusioned, and was very pessimistic about his ability to change anything in his life. His first words to Andrew were unforgettably inauspicious: "I don't really expect this cognitive therapy to work. But since it's costing me money, I'm just happy that you'll fail in less time than my last doctor." Joe's was a difficult case. He felt helpless and hopeless and often vented his frustration. The first few weeks of therapy with him were like weathering a storm. It was not unusual for him to hurl pens and other missiles across the therapy room, and on one occasion he used his hefty frame to tear a bookshelf from Andrew's office wall. But once armed with the skills necessary to bolster his resilience, in surprisingly little time, he was able to get his life back on track and become a functioning human being again.

Joe made it very clear exactly how he wanted this therapy to differ from the psychoanalytic therapy he'd just left. "I felt like an accident victim in that therapy," he said. "I felt like anxiety and depression had hit me like a truck and I was lying injured in a ditch by the side of the road. My old doctor spent eight years examining me—right there while I was in the ditch. She gave me details about every broken bone and ruptured organ, every bump and bruise. But she didn't change anything. She didn't mend the bones or ease the pain. She didn't even get me out of that ditch. I don't want to know any more about how damaged I am. I'm looking for someone who's going to help fix me."

Joe's memories of feeling anxious and depressed went back as far as preschool. He could not recall more than a few snatches of time throughout his life when he had felt truly happy. By his early thirties, things had begun to escalate. He showed all the signs of full-blown panic disorder—distressing anxiety attacks that come out of the blue and bring intense fear, sweating, shaking, heart palpitations, choking sensations, and a persistent thought that one is dying or going crazy. Joe had begun to choke at work, and this was interfering profoundly with his performance as a marketing rep. He was also diagnosed with generalized anxiety disorder, characterized by chronic, unfounded life worries. He was depressed a lot of the time, felt hopeless and helpless, and often collapsed into crying jags for no apparent reason.

Joe turned to cognitive therapy on the recommendation of a friend. Cognitive therapy takes the form of a dialogue between the therapist and client. Together they tackle the client's inaccurate belief systems and thoughts—cognitions. It is technique based and time limited, with the emphasis on quickly and efficiently equipping patients with skills to get them back to normal as soon as possible. It is focused on the here and now, with little or no time devoted to exploring childhood relationships with parents or the vagaries of toilet training. It is optimistic about people's ability to radically alter their lives for the better. It holds that real, lasting change can be effected in a matter of weeks or months.

Andrew and Joe set to work on tackling Joe's complicated symptom profile, employing all of the state-of-the-art cognitive-behavioral techniques. Within months Joe was symptom free, back at work, and feeling better than he could remember. After a couple of booster sessions, it was clear that Joe had mastered the skills, and he and Andrew bid each other farewell.

Cognitive therapy works for most people, just as it did for Joe. An enormous body of evidence demonstrates that cognitive therapy is a highly effective treatment for anxiety and depression. The post-Freudian optimism was warranted—people can bring about real change in their lives if they find the right tools. These tools had worked for Joe because he had focused on what really mattered: his beliefs, thoughts, and emotions. The success of cognitive therapy highlights what many of us already suspect—that our thoughts and emotions are the very core of who we are; that they represent our essential humanity. And the skills of cognitive therapy form the basis of the seven skills in this book.

Pillar 3: Accurate Thinking Is the Key

For a very long time, a basic assumption in psychology has been that mental health is predicated on a firm grasp of reality. The paragon of mental health, according to this view, is the person who can accurately assess his or her strengths and weaknesses, accurately identify risks and consequences, accurately determine the true causes of problems, and accurately evaluate self and others. The notion that realistic thinking is important was reinforced by early theorists in cognition, who claimed that people generally interacted with the world just as a scientist would. In other words, people gather data in an unbiased way, aggregate the data in a logical manner, and then draw a conclusion that is accurate and empirically supported. Of course, real-life human cognition is much less tidy. When it comes to appraising ourselves, others, and situations, we are downright shoddy scientists. We collect incomplete data, we use shortcuts to process it that lead to biased appraisals, and we make errors in interpretation that often support our favored hypothesis. As two psychologists described it, "instead of a naïve scientist entering the environment in search of the truth, we find the rather unflattering picture of a charlatan trying to make the data come out in a manner most advantageous to his or her already-held beliefs."[4]

Certainly everyone acknowledges that drastic distortions of reality, such as delusions and hallucinations, are hallmarks of severe mental illness, like schizophrenia and bipolar disorder. Similarly, most would agree that a man who cannot make a simple layup, misses most of his free throws, and cannot dribble without tripping over himself or the ball yet steadfastly maintains that he is a star athlete is deceiving himself and others. We would find fault in his version of reality and would question his mental health. But some psychologists have started to take a second look at the importance of accuracy and realism and have begun to question how firm the grasp actually needs to be.

Two psychologists, Shelley Taylor and Jonathan Brown, are responsible for psychology's renewed interest in the importance of accuracy in mental health. They argue that people process the world in a way that often leads to positive illusions—general, enduring patterns of error and bias that lead to unrealistically positive self-evaluations, exaggerated perceptions of control, and unrealistic optimism. Taylor and Brown report that far from being balanced in their evaluation of positive and negative, most people have perceptions of themselves that are heavily weighted toward the positive side of the scale. What's more, Taylor and Brown suggest that these illusions actually may improve mental health. They argue that healthier people tend to overestimate the degree of control they have on the environment, tend to see themselves in an overly positive light, and tend to be unrealistically optimistic about the future.[5]

But we're willing to debate this claim. We believe that the preponderance of data suggest that there are clear dangers to optimistic illusions and clear advantages to what we call "realistic optimism." For example, research shows that people who are unrealistically optimistic tend to underestimate their risk of health problems and that, far from being helpful, their can't-happen-to-me attitude leads them to forgo preventive actions.

Cigarette smokers who don't believe in their personal susceptibility to cancer are less likely to quit smoking, and they often use self-deceptions so that they can continue to enjoy the experience of smoking. After all, it would be quite hard to savor the taste of a cigarette if, as you inhaled, you were focused on the belief that your lungs were blackening and your risk of dying from lung or throat cancer was real. Likewise, adolescents who believe that they will not contract a sexually transmitted disease or become pregnant are less likely to use condoms, and when symptoms arise they are less likely to go for treatment. Unrealistic optimism also has been found to decrease resistance to stress. In one study researchers found that people who were unrealistically optimistic about the state of their health were actually less resistant to stress as measured by physiological symptoms such as accelerated heart rate and elevated diastolic blood pressure than either people who were truly healthy or, more important, people who were openly distressed about their health problems. Similarly, people who repress their negative emotions and try to focus only on their positive feelings have stronger physiological reactions to stress than people who are more realistic and accepting of their negative emotions.[6]

Realistic optimism is the ability to maintain a positive outlook without denying reality, actively appreciating the positive aspects of a situation without ignoring the negative aspects. It means aspiring and hoping for positive outcomes, and working toward those outcomes, without assuming that those outcomes are a foregone conclusion. Realistic optimism does not assume that good things will happen automatically. It is the belief that good things may happen and are worth pursuing but that effort, problem solving, and planning are necessary to bring them about.

Pillar 4: Refocus on the Human Strengths

We do not live our life out and full; we do not fill all our pores with our blood; we do not inspire and expire fully and entirely enough. . . .

Might not a bellows assist us to breathe? That our breathing should create a wind in a calm day! We live but a fraction of our life. Why do we not let on the flood, raise the gates, and set all our wheels in motion? He that hath ears to hear, let him hear.

—HENRY DAVID THOREAU, *JOURNAL*, JUNE 13, 1851

Remember Andrew's patient Joe? About a year after Joe left therapy, free of depression and anxiety, Andrew picked up the phone to hear Joe's baritone voice. "Doc," he said, "do you remember my story of the ditch?"

How could Andrew forget? "Well, you helped me walk again. But can you help me to run?"

Joe had rid himself of the symptoms of anxiety and depression that had dogged him most of his life. He was no longer crying unexpectedly, choking at work, or feeling afraid when separated from those he loved. But it wasn't enough. He was no longer "ill," but he wasn't flourishing. In the final moments of the phone call, as Joe and Andrew set up an appointment for the following week, Andrew scanned the titles in his book shelf. *Walden* by Henry David Thoreau. The noise of anxiety and depression had abated in Joe's life; now his desperation was of the quiet sort. Now he wanted to fill all his pores with blood, to set all his wheels in motion. But even with all the clinical tools at Andrew's disposal, he had no techniques to guide Joe to "the good life." But he soon would.

Cognitive therapy gave Joe the "overcoming" resilience that enabled him to dispel the fears that had haunted him from childhood. Therapy gave him the "steering through" resilience that enabled him to deal with the day-to-day worries at work and at home. Cognitive therapy even gave him the "bouncing back" resilience that enabled him to handle a cancer scare with his sister. But resilience is more than that—Joe wasn't "reaching out."

Psychology's New Mission: Reaching Out

Ours was not always a discipline of illness and remediation. Certainly, diagnosing and curing mental illness has been a core part of psychology since the age of Hippocrates in the fifth century B.C. But prior to World War II, psychology held two additional focal missions: to nurture above-average talent and to promote life satisfaction and fulfillment in all people. However, with the advent of the Veteran's Administration in 1946, practitioners found that they could make their livings treating "the sick." In 1947 came the establishment of the National Institute of Mental Health, which provided large grants to research psychologists, provided that their area of inquiry was mental disorders. Thus, due to narrowly defined funding areas, psychology shifted its focus profoundly from the positive aspects of life to the negative.[7]

The postwar years saw a sea change in psychology from which it is only now beginning to recover. Psychologists became dedicated chroniclers of mental illness, exploring the many varieties and developing convoluted categories and subcategories of disorders with increasing zeal. The American Psychiatric Association first published its *Diagnostic and Statistical Manual of Mental Disorders* in 1952, a symptom checklist that has become the diagnostician's bible. That edition was 100 pages long. *DSM-IV*, the most recent edition published in 1994, exceeds 900 pages. Each successive generation of psychologists has been steeped in this illness model, meaning that our student clinicians are being trained in the methodologies of diagnosis and the lore of treatment.

In 1998, then president of the American Psychological Association, Martin Seligman, recognized that a window of opportunity lay open to restore the twin forgotten missions to prominence within psychology. Societies under conditions of threat or deficit, as was the case in the immediate postwar years, trend naturally toward a focus on the negative aspects of life. But America at the tail end of the twentieth century was experiencing unprecedented prosperity. With the cold war all but thawed and economic indicators at all-time highs, it was time to move "beyond the remedial." Technological innovations had enabled the measurement and categorization of the mental disorders and investigation of their neurological underpinnings, and had led to the creation of effective treatments. These same methodologies, Seligman argued, could be brought to bear on the human strengths and civic virtues—courage, interpersonal skill, rationality and realism, insight, optimism, honesty, perseverance, capacity for pleasure, putting troubles into perspective, future mindedness, and finding purpose, for example. Seligman called for the construction of a new science and practice—a discipline devoted to the neglected twin missions.[8]

Dubbed positive psychology, this new social science aims to create an empirical body of knowledge of optimal human functioning. The positive psychology movement has two basic goals: To increase understanding of the human strengths through the development of classification systems and methods to measure those strengths; To infuse this knowledge into effective programs and interventions designed to build participants' strengths rather than remediate their weaknesses

How well we are functioning in the world can be thought of as a dial, with numbers in the negatives and the positives. When Joe first arrived for therapy, he was clearly in the negatives, struggling with severe symptoms that were hampering his ability to hold a job and to find a caring relationship. As a young man, all but convinced that therapy could not help him, he felt terribly hopeless as he looked down the barrel of many years of emotional turmoil and pain. He had often thought of ending his own life.

Cognitive therapy had dialed Joe from the negatives to zero, but he wasn't making the most of life and pursuing opportunities with courage and determination. It takes "reaching out" resilience to dial us well into the positives. When Joe and Andrew met again, they mapped out a plan to foster the strengths in him. What did he hope to achieve? Certainly they considered what beliefs were holding Joe back—keeping him in the low positives on the dial. But more important, they looked at those domains of his life where he was already unconsciously using "reaching out" resilience and, adapting those lessons, expanded his reach to those areas where he was shrinking back. They once again parted ways, with Joe determined to implement his new plan.

A couple of years later Andrew received a letter from Joe, updating him on his life. Since they had last seen each other, Joe and his girlfriend had married and they'd bought a house. He'd accepted a promotion at work that had long been offered, but which he had avoided out of fear of failure. He had reestablished his relationships with family and extended his circle of friends. He and his wife were trying out a number of different hobbies, spending their weekends renovating the house and buying antiques to furnish it. Joe was flourishing.

Resilience, then, is the basic strength, underpinning all the positive characteristics in a person's emotional and psychological makeup. A lack of resilience is the major cause of negative functioning. Without resilience there is no courage, no rationality, no insight. It is the bedrock on which all else is built. Some of us need more resilience just to get us out of the negatives. Others, like Joe, want more resilience so they can flourish. The skills you learn in this book can help you do both.

Our Road to Resilience

We have both always been interested in doing research that made a difference for real people, not just to provide filler for the hundreds of psychology journals. Throughout our collaboration, we've adhered to a principle: If you develop a theory about the world, don't test it in a lab, test it in the world. Our research convinced us that thinking styles determine people's resilience and that resilience determines how well they do in life. We knew that if we could develop interventions that corrected thinking styles, we could increase people's resilience and improve their performance in the world. We recognized the enormous potential to enhance people's lives. And so we constructed programs and tested them in real-world settings—in schools, in colleges, and in the workplace.

PREVENTING DEPRESSION IN SCHOOLCHILDREN AND COLLEGE STUDENTS

The rates of depression are accelerating in epidemic proportions. In Western countries, we have witnessed a tenfold increase in the incidence of depression across two generations in the twentieth century. And the disorder is striking at younger and younger ages. When we were undergraduate students, our professors taught us that 10 percent of Americans experience clinical depression at least once in their lives and that the first bout usually strikes in the late twenties or early thirties. And now we stand at the podium and regrettably report to our undergraduates that 20 percent of Americans will fall to clinical depression and that the epidemic is striking school-age children.[9]

It was clear to the mental health profession that something had to be done. And to us it seemed that finding a way to prevent depression was better than attempting to cure depression after it has already taken hold. So, in the early 1990s, Dr. Martin Seligman and some of his graduate students (Karen among them) began to develop a depression prevention program, known as the Penn Resilience Program (PRP), for schoolchildren at high risk for depression. Andrew, who had been working on prevention programs in Australia, joined the PRP team in 1992, at which time the team was eagerly awaiting the results of a two-year follow-up study with the children.

The program was remarkably successful. Not only were the children who received the resilience training showing significantly fewer symptoms of depression than the control group at every testing phase, but the size of that effect grew over time. After two years, without any booster sessions, children who learned the skills taught in the program had half the rate of depression of those who didn't participate.[10]

For the next eight years, funded by the National Institute of Mental Health, we worked with teachers, guidance counselors, social workers, and nurses in several school districts to include resilience training along with the basic skills of reading, writing, and math.[11] And just like our first study, the students who learned the skills of resilience showed less depression compared to controls. We have since trained hundreds of teachers and counselors as PRP facilitators, and they have implemented the PRP in more than twenty sites nationally and internationally, including inner-city and suburban America, rural Australia, and Beijing.

As we were working with schoolchildren, our colleagues and we also developed a similar program to prevent depression and anxiety in college students with at-risk thinking styles.[12] Three years after the program was implemented, participants showed significantly less anxiety and depression and were physically healthier than their peers who were also at risk but who did not learn the resilience skills.[13]

Equipping Parents with Resilience

"It's great that you have a program for the kids. And I like that you train our teachers in these skills so that they can teach them to our students. But what about the parents?" The school superintendent, a parent himself, went on to describe the struggle schools have building bridges to parents and working with them as a team. He talked about other programs, such as peer mediation and refusal skills, that are offered in the schools to reduce drug use but that lack, in his words, "staying power" because they do not incorporate parents. As he spoke, other heads in the audience nodded. We agreed, and in the fall of 2000, we piloted a parent program in the Cherry Hill School District in New Jersey. Parents attended a six-week parenting program, and their kids participated in PRP. When we looked at how they were doing six months later, we found that 33 percent of the children who were in the control condition reported moderate to severe levels of depressive symptoms, but only 10 percent of the children who participated in the resilience workshop with their parents reported symptoms in this range.[14]

Corporate America Needs Resilience Too

In the summer of 1994 we got a telephone call from the director of training of a Fortune 100 company in the healthcare industry. The company's employees were facing critical adversities at work. Perhaps most stressful was the omnipresent personal accountability for bottom-line results, with the persistent threat of downsizing. Employees felt compelled to spend longer hours in the workplace in a vain attempt to keep pace, with consequent difficulty balancing responsibilities at work and home. The traditional training the director had in place was failing to meet the needs and demands of the contemporary workplace. The employees needed more resilience.

In response to the need, we created a company, Adaptiv Learning

Systems, through which we deliver resilience training in the corporate arena.[15] Adaptiv has worked with thousands of participants in a diverse realm of organizations and industries, including front-line customer service representatives in the telecommunications industry; sales reps in insurance, retail, and money management; managers in commerce, government, education, and research; and vice presidents in Fortune 1000 companies. We have successfully boosted their resilience, quantified in bottom-line results.

All of our research, all of our consulting represents a response to a genuine need. Initially our goal was to prevent depression in children at risk. We soon learned that the best way to do that was to boost their resilience. This led to the discovery that resilience had much broader implications than depression, and as we responded to these diverse needs, we realized that the unifying theme is resilience. Whether the goal is to overcome depression, sell more insurance, or strengthen relationships—resilience is the key.

PART TWO

Mastering

the

Seven Skills

CHAPTER FOUR

Learning Your ABCs

Know Thyself, Then Change

We have grouped the seven skills of resilience into two categories: know thyself skills and change skills. The three know thyself skills are designed to guide you toward a better understanding of how your mind works. They help build your self-awareness. The know thyself skills—Learning Your ABCs, Avoiding Thinking Traps, and Detecting Icebergs—give you a map of your beliefs, feelings, and behaviors and how they are interconnected. After you've mastered these three skills, you will have greater insight into how you see yourself and the world and why you react to events as you do.

Insight is the first step of change, but it is not sufficient. Remember Joe? He spent eight years in insight-oriented therapy and had reached the apex of self-awareness, yet he remained unable to become the author of his life—to write a new chapter. Change remained elusive because, for most people, insight alone is not enough. That's why after you have learned the know thyself skills, we will teach you the four change skills. You'll learn to identify the true causes of a problem and accurately assess where you have control to fix or recover from it. You'll learn how to keep the implications of problems in perspective and how to fight back against your nonresilient beliefs in real time.

You Are What You Think

The foundation of the seven skills of resilience is built on the simple realization that our emotions and behaviors are triggered not by events themselves but by how we interpret those events. The first skill is Learning Your ABCs. Specifically, it guides you to a greater understanding of the recurrent situations in which you are least resilient. ABC equips you with the skill to detect your thoughts when you are in the midst of an adversity and to understand the emotional impact of those beliefs. How often has this happened to you: You come home after a long day at work to discover that, once again, even though your spouse is home before you, dinner hasn't been started? How do you respond? Do you get angry? Do you feel let down? And if someone were to ask you that very minute what was making you feel that way, you'd probably point to the empty dining room table and state the obvious: "That's why I'm upset. No dinner. Again." But even though the reason for your anger seems obvious, this obvious answer is not correct. You're not angry because your spouse failed to make dinner, you're angry because you interpreted this failure to make dinner as a violation of your rights. Your *interpretation* of his actions, not his actions themselves, caused your anger.

We all experience adversity, the "A" in the ABC model. In this case, the adversity would be that your spouse didn't make dinner. Adversities are events that precipitate a reaction from us. They can be big—like losing a job, ending a relationship, or the death of a loved one. Or they can be relatively small—like missing a deadline, arguing with a friend, being late for a meeting. Most of us believe that adversities lead directly to emotional and behavioral consequences (the "C" in the model)—what we feel and do in response to the event. Your C in this scenario is anger or sadness. On the surface, it seems accurate to say that the world operates A–C. When something good happens, we experience a positive emotion. Promotions, dates accepted, sunny days should make all of us feel happy, proud, or joyous. When something bad happens, we experience a negative emotion. Flat tires, flat soufflés, clingy preschoolers should make all of us feel annoyed, cranky, or dejected.

But as logical as this seems, it's simply not accurate. In fact, it is not the events that happen to us that cause our feelings and behaviors—it is our thoughts or, as we'll call them, Beliefs ("Bs") about the events that drive how we feel and what we do. The world does not operate A–C, but A–B–C. A flat soufflé will lead to dejection in the person who thinks "Of course it's flat. I'm lucky if I can manage a grilled cheese sandwich." But a flat soufflé will lead to anger in the person who thinks "This cooking magazine is ridiculous. I followed the recipe perfectly and the thing is ruined. I bet those editors don't even bother to try out their own recipes." And it may even lead to delight in the person who thinks "Wow! A fancy pancake! The kids will love it. We'll all have a good laugh about it at dinner." Very simply, in most situations, our beliefs cause our feelings and behaviors.[1]

A. Adversity—What Pushes Your Buttons?

In most cases, we respond appropriately and productively to the events in our lives. We rise to the occasion and successfully react to setbacks and achievements, sometimes even with grace. Certain events, however, rob us of grace. These events are our button-push adversities. The first step in the ABC skill is to identify the adversities that challenge your resilience. Adversities vary in the degree of negative emotions and behavior that followed. They vary in how much they rob us of resilience. One person's adversity may be a positive event for another. For most of us, finding time to be alone is a relished event that happens too rarely. For most of us, being promoted at work is a great boon. But there are people for whom time alone is a great stressor, bringing self-doubts and sadness. And we have had a surprising number of clients who, when promoted, experienced no joy and instead spiraled into anxiety.

Here is a partial list of possible adversities:

+ Maintaining balance between work and family
+ Juggling several tasks at once
+ Recovering from a bad breakup
+ Dealing with other people's anger
+ Negotiating household responsibilities with your partner
+ Losing your job
+ Hosting dinner parties
+ Being diagnosed with a serious illness

We easily glide through days in which adversities don't crop up. But watch Andrew's anger explode when he's cut off in traffic. And catch Karen on a morning when her four-and-a-half-year-old twins are whining in cacophonous concert with their two-and-a-half-year-old brother. (Yes, even psychologists struggle with adversities that push their buttons.)

When we're confronted with our button-push adversities, we are more likely to derail because our thinking tends to muddy and our problem solving becomes lackluster. We may feel the urge to close the door and huddle in an armchair. Everyone has adversities that push their buttons. Resilience fortifies us against them.

Read the following list and rate on a scale of 1 to 5 your difficulty in dealing with the various situations and emotions written there. A 1 means that the situation or emotion is not at all difficult for you and a 5

Which Adversities Push Your Buttons?

1= not at all difficult; 2 = somewhat difficult; 3 = moderately difficult; 4 = very difficult; 5 = extremely difficult

Conflicts at work with colleagues	1	2	3	4	5
Conflicts at work with authority	1	2	3	4	5
Conflicts with family members	1	2	3	4	5
Conflicts with friends	1	2	3	4	5
Receiving positive feedback	1	2	3	4	5
Receiving negative feedback	1	2	3	4	5
Success	1	2	3	4	5
Failure	1	2	3	4	5
Spending time alone	1	2	3	4	5
Not having enough time for yourself	1	2	3	4	5
Taking on new responsibilities at work	1	2	3	4	5
Managing a hectic schedule	1	2	3	4	5
Juggling many tasks at once	1	2	3	4	5
Adapting to change	1	2	3	4	5
Attending social functions	1	2	3	4	5
Balancing your professional and personal life	1	2	3	4	5
Responding to negative emotions in others	1	2	3	4	5
Responding to positive emotions in others	1	2	3	4	5
Dealing with your own:					
anger	1	2	3	4	5
sadness	1	2	3	4	5
anxiety	1	2	3	4	5
embarrassment	1	2	3	4	5
guilt	1	2	3	4	5
boredom	1	2	3	4	5
frustration	1	2	3	4	5
shame	1	2	3	4	5
Savoring happiness or contentment	1	2	3	4	5

means it's extremely difficult for you. For any situation rated a 4 or 5, try to remember a specific example of a time when you felt unhappy with your attempt to respond to the situation.

Each situation that you scored as a 4 or 5 is an adversity for you. Take a moment to look for any patterns in your adversities. Do you have more adversities in one domain of your life, personal or professional? Are there certain themes, such as conflict, time management, or dealing with authority, that are particularly troublesome for you? Do you feel stuck in certain emotions, whether they are positive or negative? When you take a look at your list of adversities, do they share common features?

Rachel works in the human resources department at an Ivy League university where we offered our resilience training. She is a single mother who, like many of us, struggles to maintain a gratifying career while raising her family. As Rachel thought more about her adversities, she discovered a thread that connected many of them: Most were related to conflict and anger. Conflicts at work were the most difficult for her to deal with, especially conflicts around dividing work equitably among people in her office, but clashes with her children left her feeling off-balance as well. At home conflicts that occurred around transitions, like dinnertime, bath time, and bedtime, were the most upsetting for Rachel. She wondered if her tendency to become overwhelmed by conflicts with her children at mealtime and bedtime might be related to the anger she sometimes felt because she didn't have a partner to help her take care of the children. As you begin to notice which adversities cause you the greatest problems, pay attention to what they have in common. This will give you insight into why these adversities—but not others—get under your skin.

B. Your In-the-Moment Ticker-Tape Beliefs

Once we've identified our As—our adversities—we can start to concentrate on our Bs—our beliefs. We asked Rachel and the rest of her department who were participating in this training session to imagine that they were sitting in their office with the door closed. Suddenly there is a loud knock on the door and a colleague comes in flushed with anger. The colleague shakes a stack of papers and says, "I can't believe you turned this in without checking with me. You know I've been working on this project from the very beginning. Didn't it even occur to you that I might want to take a look at the report before you sent it off? I'm trying my best to believe that it was just a careless mistake, but I've got to say, I'm finding it very difficult. I'd really like an explanation." Then we asked Rachel and the others to write down three things: how they would feel, what they would do, and what they would be thinking right as they heard this.

If the world operated A–C, we would see uniformity in how these people responded to the adversity. The colleague's tirade should elicit a certain pattern of bodily sensations, perhaps anger or fear, and the awareness of these sensations ought to produce the same emotion in each individual. But that is not what we found. When we asked Rachel and her colleagues what they would feel in this situation, a few people said angry, a few said guilty, one said embarrassed, and one said sad. When we asked them what they would do in this situation, we also heard a variety of responses. A few people said they would start yelling back. A few others said they would apologize repeatedly, and one person said he would try to get out of the office as quickly as possible. Rachel said she would "lose it." She imagined that she would blow up at her colleague and storm out of her office.

We asked Rachel to tell us what she was thinking during the imaginary conflict with her colleague. She told us she'd be thinking "Wow. He's angry. He really shouldn't talk like that to me. It's not polite." We granted that while this was probably a censored version of what she was thinking, it didn't sound real. We wanted to know her *in the moment* beliefs, just as if we were able to read them off a ticker tape right as she was thinking them. A bit nervously, Rachel told us the unadulterated version: "Who the hell does he think he is? This ass thinks he can just storm into my office and bawl me out and that I'm going to sit here and take it?! And who's he kidding anyway? I worked my butt off on that report and he coasted like he always does. Now he's just trying to cash in on the glory. Well, he can forget it!" Now we are privy to Rachel's raw, uncensored ticker-tape beliefs, what she said to herself in the moment. Rachel predicted that she would scream at her colleague and storm out of her office, and this seems likely, given her ticker-tape beliefs. Ticker-tape beliefs are the thoughts that run through your mind— sometimes outside your awareness—that determine how you feel and what you decide to do in the midst of an adversity, challenge, or new experience. Most often, these are the beliefs you will focus on when using the skills of resilience. (We discuss more deeply held beliefs—iceberg beliefs—in Chapter 6.) Your ticker-tape beliefs place you squarely on an emotional and behavioral trajectory that will either facilitate your ability to handle the situation or cause you to stumble and falter. In other words, they directly affect the emotions you feel and the actions you take in response to adversity.

How aware are you of your ticker-tape beliefs? What are your ticker-tape beliefs right now while you read this? For those of you who are already keen listeners to your stream of ticker-tape beliefs, the next step is to develop your ability to identify the specific feelings and behaviors that flow from those beliefs. Those of you who don't spend much time listening to that stream need to learn how to tune in more often. You don't need to tune in every minute of every day—that would be a waste of your mental resources. But if you want to improve your ability to respond to adversity, you must listen to what you are saying to yourself when it occurs.

THE BEEPER ACTIVITY

The beeper activity is a useful way to develop your awareness of your ticker-tape beliefs. It's quite simple. Program your watch or computer to beep at random intervals (or every hour if you cannot make it beep randomly). Whenever you hear the beep, shift your attention to your beliefs and record whatever it is going through your head at that moment. Initially you may be surprised at the monotony of your ticker tape. As one college student who used the beeper activity told us: "Wow. There's not much happening in there. It's just one repetitive string of 'I'm hungry. I'm bored. I'm hungry. I'm bored.' " But as you develop your ability to listen to yourself, you will find that there is much more going on than you noticed at first. It may, however, take some time. Plan on doing the beeper activity two or three times a week, until you are able to hear your ticker tape without much effort. As you get better at this, stop doing the beeper activity and instead train yourself to listen for your ticker tape whenever you're confronted by an adversity. If conflicts at work are an adversity for you, each time a conflict occurs, ask yourself: "What am I thinking right now?" The more you become attuned to your beliefs, the easier it will be for you to master the other six skills of resilience.

WHY BELIEFS AND WHAT-NEXT BELIEFS
"Why Did This Happen?"

Two categories of ticker-tape beliefs are particularly important to understand when building resilience: causal beliefs—which we call "why beliefs"—and implication beliefs—"what-next beliefs."

As program developers in a computer software company, Jennifer and William worked collaboratively on many projects. Unfortunately, their usually fruitful collaboration had deteriorated. Much of their time was spent in bullheaded disagreements, arguing over semantics and interminably debating of the costs and benefits of every decision that they had to make. By the time they met with us, their collaboration had become a detriment to their careers.

For both Jennifer and William, the work conflict was an adversity. We asked them to tell us about their ticker-tape beliefs, what they were thinking to themselves as they battled each other. Jennifer's ticker tape involved why beliefs: "William is being disagreeable on purpose. He's mad that our boss shot down his last idea and he's taking it out on me. He's trying to make me feel as bad as he does." Her beliefs were oriented on the past. In essence, her ticker tape answered the questions: Why did this happen? What caused the problem? In her mind, Jennifer believed that they were having a hard time working together because William was taking out his frustration on her. And this belief made her angry.

As a species, we are probably evolutionarily prepared to search for the causes of the adversities that befall us: The accurate identification of causes is essential to locating workable solutions—and acting on solutions provides an evolutionary edge. Research shows that we do spontaneously ask ourselves "why" questions when problems arise, particularly when an outcome is unexpected, such as failure when we expected to succeed or when a desire has not been fulfilled.[2] It makes good sense for us to attempt to understand the causes of problems and surprise outcomes because doing so helps us redress the situation and increases the likelihood that we can reach our goals. If Jennifer didn't ask herself "why" questions, she would be at a loss to know what to do to improve her collaboration with William.

The leading "causal attribution" researchers, Martin Seligman among them, have found that every answer to the question "why" can be described along three dimensions. You'll remember that Seligman called these dimensions personal (me versus not me), permanent (always versus not always), and pervasive (everything versus not everything) and that people tend to answer the question "why" the same way, over and over again. As you begin to listen to your why beliefs, start to look for patterns. When adversity strikes, do you tend to blame yourself or others? Do you see the cause of the problem as permanent or fleeting? Do you believe the cause will undermine everything else in your life, or is it specific to the one adversity? The better you are at identifying and labeling your why beliefs, the easier it will be for you to change them when they interfere with your ability to respond to adversity.

"What's Going to Happen Next?"

William's ticker-tape beliefs didn't focus on why he and Jennifer were struggling but on what that meant for them in the future, which we call "what-next beliefs": "We're just not getting along these days. If we can't work it out, the project is never going to get off the ground and then our careers will be shot. These projects require teamwork, and if Jennifer and I can't work together, then I don't see how I'll be able to work with anyone else either." His ticker tape is oriented toward the future and expresses what he believes will happen next given the situation at hand. In this instance, the future looks bleak, so of course anxiety results. Like why beliefs, what-next beliefs provide evolutionary advantage. Those human predecessors who failed to look for threats were dramatically unprepared when a genuine threat emerged—perhaps they roamed too far from the clan campfire because they didn't anticipate the predators in the shadows. But many of us experience what-next beliefs that are catastrophic and highly improbable. Far from preparing us for real threat, the anxiety that these beliefs cause hampers our problem-solving efforts—and undermines our resilience.

WHAT IS YOUR PATTERN?

Sometimes ticker tapes are neither why beliefs nor what-next beliefs. For example: "Mike and I are fighting again. This is our fifth argument today. We just seem to fight and fight and fight." This explanation doesn't address the cause of the problem, nor does it make claims about the future. This string of beliefs is simply a narration of the events as they unfold. Other times our ticker tapes are evaluations: "I'm so tired of fighting with Julie about these things. I can't do this anymore. I can't stand it when we argue like this."

Some people's ticker tapes are a hodgepodge of beliefs: some evaluation, some narration, a few ideas about why, a couple of predictions. But for the most part, people have a dominant style. Their ticker tape focuses almost exclusively on the causes of problems, or on the implications of the event, or is mainly a play-by-play account of what has transpired. If your ticker-tape beliefs are mostly a play-by-play account or simply evaluate how you feel about the situation, you need to train yourself to think about the causes and implications of adversity because resilience requires a balance between thinking about the past and planning for the future. In Chapters 7 and 8 we will teach you how to make sure your why and what-next beliefs enhance your resilience, not thwart it. For now it is important for you to listen to your ticker tape and notice if there is a pattern. Do you tend to be why focused or what-next focused? Do you spend most of your internal life narrating or evaluating? The challenge for you today is to start refining your understanding of how you think. The tinkering process comes later.

C. Consequences Are Feelings and Behaviors

By now you've started thinking about As—the adversities that push your buttons—and Bs—the beliefs that run through your head when you are confronted with adversities. Beliefs matter because they shape the quality and intensity of your feelings and influence your behaviors—your Consequences (Cs)—the way you feel and what you do *in the moment* of an adversity or challenge. But why all the concern about feelings and behaviors? We care about feelings and behaviors for a very simple reason: Your success at work and in relationships, your mental health, and even to a large extent your physical health is nothing more than a composite of your mood and behaviors. Resilient people are able to regulate their emotions and control their reactions so that they respond appropriately in any given situation. The goal is not to be in a good mood at all times or to never give up. Rather, the goal is to have your emotions and behaviors be productive, appropriate responses to the facts of the situation, not knee-jerk reactions to your ticker-tape beliefs.

Take a moment to think about your in-the-moment emotions and reactions to setbacks, challenges, and new experiences. Do you seem to get stuck in an emotional rut: When you feel angry, guilty or embarrassed, is it hard to stop feeling that way? Is your emotional life narrow? If you tallied up the emotions you feel across a week, would you have a preponderance of one emotion, perhaps anger, or sadness, or anxiety? Or maybe you don't get stuck in one negative emotion, but, on reflection, you realize you don't experience too many positive emotions. On the behavioral side, do you find yourself repeating mistakes over and over again, such as procrastinating, or coming on too strong, or giving in too easily, despite the fact that the strategies aren't working? Alternatively, do you handle problems effectively but find yourself hesitating to step outside your comfort zone? You "forget" to sign up for the wine-tasting class you've been meaning to take. You can't find the time to invite a mother from your son's preschool class over for coffee. The fall foliage is at its peak yet you appreciate the color only as you race between errands. Once you're more resilient, you'll be able to overcome life's inevitable obstacles and still make time to learn new things and enjoy your life.

Belief-Consequence Couplets

So far we've talked about the important role beliefs play in determining our emotions and behaviors. Everyone's internal dialogue has its own meter and language, yet despite these differences, beliefs can be categorized. For each type of belief we label, we can predict which emotion and behavior will follow. We refer to these as B–C connections, and they always hold. These belief–consequence couplets are universal and, as we will discuss, make good sense from an evolutionary perspective. Let's take a closer look at the various types of beliefs and the emotions and responses they cause.

B-C Connections	
BELIEF	**CONSEQUENCE**
Violation of your rights	Anger
Real-world loss or loss of self-worth	Sadness, depression
Violation of another's rights	Guilt
Future threat	Anxiety, fear
Negative comparison to others	Embarrassment
© Copyright Adaptiv Learning Systems	

You may have noticed that all five Cs in our B–C list are negative. Where are the positive emotions like happiness, pride, and serenity? Of course, the positive emotions are an important part of our lives. But they're less important to our resilience than the negative ones. What matters in resilience is how we deal with adversity—and adversity normally leads to negative emotions.

Violation of Your Rights Leads to Anger

The anger family of emotions, including annoyance, irritability, acrimony, outrage, fury, and wrath to name just some, is brought on by the belief that someone has intentionally violated your rights, that someone has set out to harm you. Psychologist Dolf Zillmann has studied the triggers of anger and has found that, most often, insults to our self-esteem cause us to feel harmed or that our rights have been violated.[3] Anger comes when we believe we have been treated unfairly, thwarted in the pursuit of a goal, even when we believe, however irrationally, that it is an inanimate object doing the transgressing:—"Damn this car. It simply refuses to start up"—or circumstance—"It's raining just for spite."

Usually, however, we see another person as the agent of harm and we believe that that person's behavior was under her control. Imagine that someone darts in front of you in the parking lot, taking the spot you had your eye on. What do you think? "He saw I was waiting for that spot and took it anyway" is what we call a violation-of-rights belief. Or imagine that your child ignores you when you ask him to help set the table. If you think, "He thinks I'm his personal servant," that's a violation-of-rights belief, as is "My wife always leaves it to me to discipline the kids. It's not fair." In each of these examples, two beliefs are being expressed:

✦ Another person is to blame for the harm that comes to us.
✦ That person could have done otherwise.

Notice that in each example, the ticker-tape beliefs that precede anger are why beliefs—they answer the question "Why did this happen to me?" Are you a "why" person? If you are, and if you tend to see external causes for the problems you encounter, particularly involving other people, then you will likely experience a lot of anger in your life.

From an evolutionary perspective, the primitive form of the violation-of-rights belief is a belief that centers on the perception that an enemy is present. Our ancestors who were quick to perceive and react to enemies, and the potential harm they represented, had a greater chance of survival than those who failed to interpret danger when it was present. This is not to say that all anger is beneficial. As we will see, people who misperceive harm and believe their rights have been violated when they have not lack resilience and suffer a great deal. People who anger easily and have poor impulse control wreak havoc in their own lives and in the lives of those around them. To paraphrase Aristotle, becoming angry is easy. Becoming angry with the right person, at the right time, in the right way is hard.[4] Resilient people have mastered Aristotle's challenge.

Real-world Loss or Loss of Self-worth Leads to Sadness and Depression

Perhaps you don't get angry very often but instead find yourself feeling sad, down, dejected, or depressed more than you'd like. Sadness and depression result when you believe that you have lost something real—like a relationship, job, or loved one—or intangible—like self-worth. For example, imagine that you pride yourself on being a good writer. You send off an essay you wrote to a number of magazines, only to have it rejected by each. If you think, "I guess I'm not talented after all," sadness will result. Or imagine that you have become friends with a colleague at work. You find out that she has invited other people from the office to her house but not you. If you think, "She mustn't like me as much as I thought," you'll feel hurt or sad.

What is the survival value of sadness? On the surface, sadness and certainly depression seem to be disadvantageous. Sadness brings crying, loss of energy, and bodily complaints. It results in passivity, difficulty concentrating, and thoughts of death and dying. Why would evolution smile on these behaviors? Evolutionary psychologists argue that the function of sadness is to facilitate our adjustment to abandonment, such as the death of a loved one. The introspection and withdrawal is supposed to provide us with the opportunity to search for meaning in the loss and think about plans for the future. Sadness is an uncomfortable emotion, and it goads us to change what's wrong in our life and reduce the sadness in the process. The loss of energy may have kept the sad and cognitively impaired—hence more vulnerable—individual close to home where she was safe from dangers. Weeping and passivity may have elicited caretaking behaviors from other kin, which might have ultimately strengthened family connections. Thus, the evolutionary benefit of sadness, perhaps even depression, is to produce a supportive and protective reaction from other members of one's group following an experience of loss or abandonment.

The questions for you to answer now are: What is the nature of my ticker-tape beliefs? Am I someone whose emotions cluster around a sense of loss? Do I tend to blame myself for my problems, even when it probably isn't wholly my fault? People who are "why" oriented and who focus on internal causes of problems are more likely to feel sadness and depression when things go wrong. Nothing erodes resilience more quickly than depression. Nothing.

The Violation of Another's Rights Leads to Guilt

We asked college students to monitor their emotional lives for a day. Happiness, perhaps not surprisingly, was the most common positive emotion reported; guilt was the most common negative emotion. Students felt guilty for using up their roommates' shampoo, for not calling their parents, for flirting with people other than their boy- or girlfriends. They also felt guilty for not exercising, for eating and drinking too much, and for wasting their parents' money. In another study of guilt, researchers had adults in their twenties wear preprogrammed digital watches for one week. Each time the watch beeped, the person recorded feelings, thoughts, and activities at that moment. Guilt was pervasive. When the researchers extrapolated from their findings and allowed for eight hours of sleep per night, the data suggested that, on average, adults feel moderate guilt for thirty-nine minutes per day. That's a lot of guilt.[5] And just like what we heard from the college students, the situations that elicited guilt in these young adults can be neatly grouped into two categories:

✦ Breaches in self-regulation, including procrastinating, binge eating and drinking, failing to exercise, and overspending
✦ Breaches in commitments, including sexual infidelities, not spending enough time with family, and ignoring the needs of friends

How many minutes are you spending each day feeling guilty? And what are you feeling guilty about?

If your emotional life is governed by guilt, you are wasting too much energy on that emotion. That's not to say that all guilt is bad—some guilt is a good thing. Guilt may have evolved because it helps us to change our course of action and make amends. When our guilt stems from situations like overeating, procrastinating, or wasting money, it signals us that there has been a breakdown in self-control. Guilt acts as an internal brake of sorts, forcing us to notice what we are doing that makes us feel this way. It forces us to pause and provides us the opportunity to regain control of ourselves. We've all experienced the "internal brake" function of guilt. Remember the last time that you skipped going to the gym, or had too many drinks, or perhaps splurged a tad too grandly? Guilt, and the accompanying remorse and regret, is the emotion that gets us to haul our heavy bodies onto the treadmill, to pay the bartender and leave, to sheepishly plunk the $400, six-piece, cast-iron, artisan-crafted cookware set onto the counter at Williams-Sonoma and ask for a refund. Guilt is a powerfully motivating emotion.

One useful function of guilt is to get us to stop doing whatever it is that we are doing that is generating the guilt. Another is to motivate us to make amends. When we feel guilty about having harmed others, we can apologize and try to repair the damaged relationship, which, for a species that is dependent on others for survival, is an evolutionarily sound strategy. Ideally, of course, we would experience guilt *before* we did or said something stupid so that we would not need to regain control of ourselves or repair broken relationships. (After all, apologies are not always accepted.) Well, we do. All of us know the feeling of a spreading, growing, creeping wave of guilt even though we haven't actually done anything wrong. Perhaps you are on your way home after work and fantasize about driving right past your house, leaving your cranky toddlers, messy kitchen, and annoying bedtime routine for your spouse to deal with. Or maybe as you watch late-night television you get lost in reverie about how much fun it would be to return the not-so-innocent looks from that attractive person in your office. Or even though you have been sticking to your diet and exercise routine so well for so long, wouldn't it be great to stop off for a Krispy Kreme doughnut, maybe even two? In these cases, merely *considering* a transgression is enough to trigger what psychologists refer to as anticipatory guilt. Before our car passes the driveway, or we return a flirtatious look, or we consume a dozen chocolate glazed doughnuts, we feel guilty. Often, but not always, the anticipatory guilt is sufficiently unpleasant that we stop ourselves before we misstep.

Just as blue and green are basic colors, anger and sadness are considered basic emotions; even very young children experience them. The development of guilt, however, takes time. As we have seen, guilt involves a concern with a specific behavior or transgression. When we feel guilty, we are consumed with the notion that we have done a "bad thing" or have failed to do a good thing. As adults, we feel guilty when we believe that we have willfully harmed another person (or ourselves) or have done a bad thing when we could have done otherwise. Unlike anger, which is sparked because of a perceived external cause (the "why"), guilt is brought on by internal beliefs about cause. For example, imagine that you don't make it to your child's school play because your boss asks for a report by the end of the day. If you think, "I should have said no to my boss and told him that I'd get the report to him first thing in the morning. My daughter is going to be so upset," you'll feel guilt—you've emotionally harmed your daughter, and you could have done otherwise by standing up to your boss. Notice that you will also feel some sadness because you have lost the image of yourself as a good parent. Guilt and sadness overlap on the internal dimension. If, instead, your ticker tape is "I'm so sick of this job. They talk a good game about respecting the balance between work and family, but it's all just talk," then you will be angry because you are attributing the problem to external, volitional reasons. Your boss could decide to stick to his word, but he chooses not to.

Guilt has a close cousin that bears mentioning. When we've asked people to tell us their quintessential experience of guilt, we hear a lot about shame. The guilt and shame stories were both about things people wished they could undo: cheating on an exam, divulging the confidence of a friend, betraying a lover. Differences emerged, however, at the level of why beliefs. The ticker-tape beliefs that preceded guilt were focused on having done a bad thing, having behaved in a way that was wrong. Shame, in contrast, was related to beliefs about being a bad person; that is, the preceding beliefs focused on character rather than behavior.

Researchers point out that, although some of us experience guilt and shame, many people appear to be prone to one more than the other.[6] Shame-prone people believe that weaknesses in their character and flaws in the self are the cause of most of the transgressions they commit. Guilt-prone people tend not to look past the level of behavior; they believe, as it were, "I did a bad thing, but I am not a bad person."

Are you more guilt-prone or shame-prone? It is important to know this about yourself because shame is toxic. As we have already suggested, guilt functions to facilitate reparations. Indeed, guilt-proneness appears to be adaptive, particularly in the realm of relationships. People who scored high on "shame-free" guilt (they tend to experience guilt but not shame) were more empathic in their relationships and used more constructive anger management strategies compared to those who experienced more shame. The shame-prone people, in contrast, had a much more difficult time being empathic; they were more angry and hostile and weren't as effective at controlling their anger; and, in general, they were more likely to be depressed. The lethal nature of shame perhaps can best be understood by the powerlessness it engenders. We know how to change behaviors, but we feel helpless to change our character. The helplessness and powerlessness of shame propel us not toward better self-control and apologies but to flee and make ourselves disappear.

Future Threat Leads to Anxiety and Fear

How often do you feel anxious? Does that anxiety interfere with your ability to handle the situation, or does it propel you to practice and prepare? Everyone experiences anxiety. For some of us, it's a mild wave every now and then—just enough to get us to stay up extra late to prepare for work or to practice making the crème brûlée for the dinner party on Saturday night. For others, anxiety is crippling. One of Karen's patients,

Cara, was an accomplished singer. She came to therapy because in the past year she had been experiencing panic attacks, and lately when she performed solos she became gripped by anxiety. "I used to love to sing but something has changed. Now, when I have a solo, I become overwhelmed by anxiety. When I stand on the stage and look out at the audience, I start to worry that my voice will shake and that I won't be able to hit the full range of notes. Then my heart starts to pound and I can feel my hands shake. My chest starts to feel so tight and I can't even remember the first words of the song. I can barely look at the audience because when I do, it seems like they are sneering and laughing at me. I know I should just get started, but I feel frozen, absolutely frozen. Sometimes when I do get myself to sing, my voice really does sound constricted and flat and that, of course, just makes the whole thing so much worse."

Anxiety and fear affect almost every system of our bodies. Our physiology changes. Anxiety leads to disturbances in our cardiovascular system—we have heart palpitations, our blood pressure increases (or decreases), and our hearts race. Our respiratory system is affected. Our breathing becomes shallow and rapid, and we may feel as if we are choking. In fact, it is this latter symptom that is the root of the word "anxiety"—the Latin word *angere* means "to choke" or "to strangle." Our gastrointestinal system shows the effects of anxiety. We lose our appetite. We have abdominal pain, and when we do eat, we get heartburn. There are changes to our neuromusculature: Our startle response is heightened, our eyelids twitch, our extremities wobble and shake, our muscles spasm, we pace. Even our urinary system is affected. We feel a pressure to urinate and may need to run to the bathroom every few minutes.

As if that weren't bad enough, our behavior and thinking changes as well. Our speech lacks fluency, our coordination becomes impaired, our posture collapses. Our minds become hazy, the world seems unreal, we become increasingly self-conscious, our memory fails, we become distracted, our reasoning slips, our fears and worries increase. As anyone who has ever suffered from severe anxiety will tell you, it can be hell.

It was not until cognitivists like Aaron Beck gained prominence that beliefs were seen not only as a symptom of anxiety, but, more important, as its cause. Beck and other cognitive therapists argued that, even though the body goes haywire, the central feature of anxiety is actually a person's thoughts, specifically thoughts about threat and danger. Anxiety-prone people tend toward what-next beliefs. "Why" people look back and consider causes; what-next people look forward and, in the case of anxiety, see danger on the horizon. If you are a what-next person, pay close attention to your beliefs. Do you imagine the future as pleasant and safe or threatening and overwhelming? Naturally, anxiety will follow from the latter.

Even if the level of anxiety you experience is mild, you can still learn to identify the what-next beliefs that brought on the emotion. When you're feeling anxious as you walk into a staff meeting, what is it that you are saying to yourself? Perhaps something like "This is not going to go well" or "I bet he's going to dump another project on us. There's just no way I can take any more on." When you're feeling anxious as you get ready for a date, try to capture your thoughts. Are you thinking "He's going to think I'm boring" or "I bet she's going to give me the 'it's not you, it's me' speech." The point is that, with practice, you can capture the thoughts that trigger anxiety. Once you do, you'll find that they are all about some imminent future threat.

If anxiety is often debilitating, what evolutionary advantage could it possibly confer? Beck describes how anxiety and fear may have served as a check on overly careless behaviors.[7] For example, although aggressive behavior is a necessary part of exploration and competitiveness, both of which serve the survival of the species, if these behaviors are left unchecked, they can lead to injury and death. Imagine two of our early human predecessors, cave dwellers that we'll call Throgg and Dregg. Throgg has a passion for exploration. One day, as he is traveling across uncharted territory, something about the conditions leads him to think "There might be saber-toothed tigers out there." For Throgg, this belief leads to the physical signs of anxiety, and the anxiety response is uncomfortable and aversive—he wants it to end. Throgg is able to end the anxiety by heeding its warning and turning around to safer, known territory. But what if the connection between the belief and the physical response did not exist? Imagine that Dregg suspects that tigers are about but has none of the physical symptoms in response. He experiences no discomfort. He has no internal signal of potential danger, so he continues on into harm's way. In arguably the earliest episode of *Survivor*, Throgg will outlast Dregg because he has a strong connection between his cognitive appraisal of threat and his bodily experience of anxiety. Dregg likely will perish because when he considered the possibility of threat, his body continued to, as it were, whistle a happy tune.

Some anxiety, then, has survival value, but, as we will discuss in Chapter 8, too much anxiety interferes with successful living. If you're stuck on future threat, if you habitually catastrophize—seeing imminent danger when there is none—you not only waste time and energy worrying about bad things that will never happen, but you experience levels of anxiety that can disrupt resilience and wreak havoc on your performance and mental health.

Comparing Yourself Negatively to Others Leads to Embarrassment

Remember the flat soufflé? Imagine that you have invited friends over for dinner. You are sipping drinks and sharing stories in the kitchen as you put the finishing touches on the meal. Everything complete, you open the oven to remove the pièce de résistance and you discover, as do your friends, that the soufflé is flat and burned. Upon the moment of discovery, how would you feel? Now imagine that you discover the same flat, burned soufflé, but this time no one is present. What do you feel in that moment of discovery?

André Modigliani, a leading emotions researcher, argues that embarrassment is an acute loss of self-esteem, caused not by any behavior (such as failing to produce a fluffy soufflé) but, rather, by our knowledge that the behavior has been observed and negatively evaluated by others.[8] Embarrassment requires an audience. But other researchers have shown that embarrassment sometimes occurs when we have acted in a way that is inconsistent with our personal standards.[9] Promptness, athleticism, liberalism, creativity—all are examples of personal standards. Although breaching a personal value in the presence of others—the athlete who strikes out in front of his peers at the company softball game—intensifies the embarrassment, the social aspect is not a *necessary* condition. If the personal account of embarrassment is correct, we could feel embarrassed regardless of whether others were present when we opened the oven door.

The notion of personal standards helps explain why there is great variability in the situations that trigger embarrassment; what generates embarrassment in some people does not disturb the equanimity of others because we do not all have the same personal standards. Peter, a self-professed epicure, would feel embarrassed by the soufflé because his ticker tape would be "And I call myself a cook! I am clearly not a cook." Meanwhile, Lynn, a contented frozen food junkie, would not feel embarrassed because she has no such "competent cook" standard.

The debate regarding the role of an audience in embarrassment continues. It's probably true that some people feel embarrassed even when alone. But it may be that even when we are alone and misstep, we imagine how others would react if they had witnessed our actions. (Take the literal case of misstepping. What do you do immediately after you trip? You look around to see if anyone noticed.) Clearly, however, embarrassment is rooted in social comparison. We feel the greatest embarrassment in the presence of others.

What matters most in the context of resilience is how you respond in moments of social interaction—when your idea is nixed by your work team, when you are chastised in front of your friends, when your boss tells you that she is underwhelmed by your performance. When we listen to people's ticker-tape beliefs in the moment of their embarrassment, they almost always include references to others. They center around the fear that they have lost standing in front of people whose opinions matter.

How to Use the B–C Connections

The knowledge of these B–C connections is the foundation of self-awareness. By listening to your ticker tape, you can make sense of, even predict, what emotions and behaviors will follow. And, as you will see, each of the next six skills of resilience build on ABC.

There are two important uses of the B–C connections. You can use them to disentangle the mixture of emotions you experience when faced with a button-push adversity; or to identify the beliefs that are causing you to get "stuck" in a particular emotion, gain understanding of why you reacted as you did, and learn to keep your bearings in even the most stressful of circumstances.

DISENTANGLING YOUR EMOTIONS

Our emotions are not always singular but seem, at times, to come in a dizzying jumble. A hodgepodge of emotions is particularly common in the wake of a major stress. As Paul found, the B–C connections can help tease apart a tangle of emotions.

Paul joined a prestigious law firm in Manhattan and moved with his wife and baby to the city. He selected this firm because he had heard from a number of the lawyers that the firm recognized the importance of family and made it possible for the employees to find a workable balance. Six months into the position, Paul believed that he was doing well at work and felt a close camaraderie with the other lawyers. Around this time, Paul's daughter, Mary, now thirteen months old, began experiencing one respiratory infection after another. Jody, his wife, missed a lot of work to take their daughter to doctor's appointments or because she was too ill to go to day care. One morning Jody called Paul at his office and asked if he could take Mary to a doctor's appointment, because she was worried that her boss was becoming annoyed by the number of times she left early or came in late. When Paul mentioned to one of the partners that he needed to leave early to take his daughter to the doctor, the partner said snidely, "Don't make it a habit." Paul reacted with a flood of emotions. He felt a mixture of anger, guilt, embarrassment, even shame, and was bewildered by the complexity of his reaction. "I pride myself on being a pretty straightforward, what-you-see-is-what-you-get kind of guy. I usually have a good sense of why I'm feeling the way I do and I think I'm pretty resilient. This just threw me. I couldn't understand why one sarcastic comment would trigger so many emotions, and it kind of leveled me. I did leave to take Mary, but I was upset about it for much longer than was warranted."

Paul was overwhelmed by the sheer number of his emotions. He had a hard time concentrating for the rest of the day; he felt distracted and on edge. Paul decided that he wanted to confront the partner about the remark and understood that if he wanted to handle himself with composure, he first needed to disentangle his emotions. Paul's knowledge of the B–C connections helped him gain clarity on the situation. By articulating his thought process, he could identify, and thus control, the emotions that were overwhelming him. "I was angry because I believed that the partner's comment betrayed an institution-wide hypocrisy. One of the reasons I joined this firm is because they talked up their commitment to family. I never left early before, and I felt disrespected when he reacted so smugly." Paul interpreted the comment as a violation of his rights—he believed the company had mislead him during the courting period.

"I didn't think I was doing anything wrong by leaving early so I couldn't figure out at first why I was feeling guilty. I certainly didn't want to apologize if I hadn't actually done anything wrong. Then I realized that I wasn't feeling guilty about leaving early, the guilt was related to my role as a father. As I was leaving the office I remembered thinking that I wanted to be able to help out more with our daughter's illness and that my decision to work for this company may actually mean that I won't be able to help out much at all. I kept imagining that if my first request to leave early was met by such hostility, then it would be unlikely that future requests would be accepted. I guess I felt I was letting my wife and daughter down, and that's why I was feeling guilty." Paul's beliefs about causing harm to his family led to his feeling of guilt.

Paul was also able to pinpoint the ticker-tape beliefs that brought on his embarrassment: "As I was leaving the office, I looked up at the clock and saw it was two-fourteen. I immediately scanned the room to check to see if any of my colleagues noticed that I was leaving. Of course, even if they did see me leave, they probably wouldn't have any idea why and wouldn't have cared, but my thought was 'If they see me leaving early, they'll think I'm not as committed to the firm as they are and they'll look down on me for it.' " Paul experienced embarrassment in response to his imagined public scrutiny.

By systematically identifying the beliefs that brought on each of his emotions, Paul was able to clarify the many issues that were brought to the surface by a single offhand comment. This process helped him separate the issues he should discuss with his employers—their hypocrisy—from those that were personal. The ten minutes it took Paul to work through the B–C connections saved him from hours of ruminating and possibly even reacting inappropriately with his boss and colleagues. He was able to steer through the conflict more effectively by using the self-awareness fostered by the B–C connections to inform his problem solving.

IDENTIFY THE BELIEFS THAT HAVE TRAPPED YOU

Although the B–C connections have evolved to help humans make sense of their world and respond appropriately, sometimes people develop biases and gravitate to one or two types of beliefs. They apply these interpretations like cookie cutters, stamping every ambiguous situation into the same shape. Another way to think of the B–C connections is as a radar. Some people, perhaps because of their early experiences, scan their world for what could hurt them next. They have a future-threat radar and so feel anxious a lot of the time. Mark, who has a violation-of-rights radar, spends most of his life seeing himself as a victim. He was late for work because the city planners were thoughtless and scheduled road work during his commute. He and his mother quarreled because she didn't respect his privacy. He and his colleague clashed over priorities because she refused to acknowledge his seniority. Mark's tendency was to believe that people set out to annoy, undermine, and betray him—a violation of his rights—so he spent most of his time feeling angry.

Joy, however, is always looking for danger. Her anxiety moves between a low hum and a deafening crescendo. If a friend doesn't return her call, Joy begins to worry that she has somehow offended. If a second call goes unreturned, Joy convinces herself that the friend is angry and is certain that the friend wants nothing more to do with her. When the friend calls a few days later—explaining she was out of town on business—Joy feels annoyed at herself for wasting so much energy worrying about the demise of the friendship. After the birth of her first child, Joy's anxiety worsened—the health and safety of her son opened a whole new world of worries. Joy's tendency to see threat and danger around every corner caused stress in her marriage and, as her son got older, made his struggle for autonomy more difficult.

Individuals don't become trapped by beliefs that cause only negative emotions. Beverly is confident, happy, and accomplished, but she gets stuck in pride. At first blush, it seems a little odd to describe someone as "stuck" in a positive emotion. But just as problems arise when you feel constantly angry or anxious, problems also crop up when you feel certain positive emotions when they are unwarranted. Whenever things go well—contracts are negotiated successfully, meetings run efficiently and smoothly, the softball team wins—Beverly takes credit for the success. Her bias is to believe she brought about the good events and to miss the contributions of others. Initially, people gravitated to Beverly because her upbeat, confident style was pleasant to be around. But it didn't take long for them to become disenchanted with her. Her colleagues saw her as arrogant and boastful, and she developed the reputation of a glory hound. Beverly's bias, although it made her feel good, created professional and personal problems.

Perhaps you are not angry or overwhelmed by anxiety, or inappropriately proud like Beverly, but you may have a bias in how you interpret the good and bad events in your life. If you do, you are undermining your resilience because your bias is preventing you from seeing the facts of the situation. Sometimes Mark is correct—at times people intend to do harm. And Joy is certain to notice any real dangers that crop up. But biased thinking styles lead you to misinterpret the meaning of events much more often than they help you to get it right. Mark spends too much time responding to imagined hostility and Joy to imagined danger. Beverly's relationships are suffering because her friends find her tiresome. Each person is less effective in what he or she does, and less happy, because of biased thinking styles.

KEEP AN EMOTIONS LOG AND FIND OUT IF YOU ARE STUCK

Use your knowledge of the B–C connections to identify the pattern of beliefs that are limiting your emotional life. For the next week, keep a log of your emotions. Whenever you feel a strong emotion or experience a sudden shift in emotion, jot down what you are feeling and how intense the emotion is. At the end of the week, group the emotions you experienced into "families" of anger, sadness, guilt, anxiety, and embarrassment.

There is no rigid formula, but notice whether your emotions span the spectrum of feelings or if they tend to clump into one family. If they clump together, you may be biased in your thinking style and overly focused on one of the five varieties of beliefs, such as violation of rights or negative comparison to others. Pay particular attention to the emotions that follow from your button-push adversities; these are the situations in which your resilience may need the most bolstering. Sometimes people find that when they encounter relatively few of their button-push adversities, their emotional life is broad and varied, but when faced with stressful situations, their emotional lives become dominated by one feeling. As you learn the "change" skills of resilience, you will want to focus those skills on the beliefs that are dominating your emotional life.

How to Use ABC in Your Own Life

Use the ABC skill whenever you are confused by your reaction to an adversity or whenever your reactions are counterproductive. The goal of ABC is to parse your experience into A, B, and C. Until you separate your beliefs about the event from the facts of the event, and then separate these facts from your reactions to the event, you cannot do the work of changing your counterproductive beliefs. To scrutinize your beliefs, you first must isolate them.

Think of a recent adversity that you didn't handle very well. The first step is to describe the adversity (A). You can do this as a mental exercise, but it's better to get it down on paper. Use the Learning Your ABCs Worksheet on page 90 as a template. Make sure you describe the adversity objectively; do not let your interpretations of the event bias your description of the facts. Focus on providing just the who, what, when, and where of the situation. For example: "My boss and I had a disagreement about how I should approach a client whom we suspect may be disseminating our materials in violation of copyright. I wanted to call him directly, but she thinks I ought to send a letter first." This is a clear and objective description of the adversity. The following is not: "My boss and I had a disagreement about how I should approach a client who we suspect may be disseminating our materials in violation of copyright. I wanted to call him directly, but she thinks that I'll be too aggressive on the phone and will make the problem worse. She never trusts that I'll handle myself professionally and is constantly undermining my authority." The problem with the latter description is that it is injected with your beliefs—which are important, but the goal here is to separate the facts of the situation from your beliefs about those facts. Your beliefs are how you understand an event; we'll get to those in a moment.

The second step is to identify your Cs. What did you feel and how did you react as the event unfolded? Try to identify both your emotions and your behaviors, and note the intensity of the emotion. Was your emotion mild, moderate, or intense? The reason we jump from A to C and skip the Bs for now is that this is how we most often experience the flow in the real world. An event happens; we notice our feelings and responses to the event next, before we notice what we have said to ourselves (our Bs). Our Bs usually are not as salient as our reactions. Continuing with our example, then, here is a good description of the Cs: "I felt both irritated and anxious. Very irritated. Mildly anxious. My first reaction was to make a provocative remark, which, of course, did not go over so well. Then I started procrastinating. I did just about every other task I could think of but couldn't bring myself to work on the letter."

The third step is a mental version of connect-the-dots. After you've noted the adversity and the consequences, the task is to figure out the beliefs that connect the A to the C. Ask yourself: What was I thinking that brought on these feelings and actions? The goal, remember, is to identify the beliefs as you actually thought them, not to convert them to what you may view as a more acceptable version. The content of your ticker tape, the very words that it is constructed from, is important because those words capture the meaning with which you imbue the event. Thus, if your actual ticker tape is "She's a ball breaker" and you translate it to "She is tough," you lose important information regarding how you understand her motivations and the dynamics of your relationship. In our example, two emotions and behaviors flow from the situation: moderate to extreme irritation, which results in you making a provocative remark, and mild anxiety coupled with procrastination.

Use your knowledge of the B–C connections to make a mental check of your logic. We know that anger will follow a belief about violation of rights and anxiety will follow a belief about impending danger. If the beliefs you have generated do not fall into these categories, then you haven't clearly identified your beliefs. Remember that the B–C connections on page 75 always hold. If you didn't get your assessment right the first time, try it again now. Here's how our example would look on a worksheet.

As you practice applying ABC across a number of situations in your

---

Learning Your ABCs Worksheet

1. Describe the Adversity objectively (the who, what, when, and where) and record here: "My boss and I had a disagreement about how I should approach a client whom we suspect may be disseminating our materials in violation of copyright. I wanted to call him directly, but she thinks I ought to send a letter first."
2. Identify the Consequences (your emotions and behaviors during the Adversity) and record in the C column.
3. Identify your Ticker-tape Beliefs during the Adversity and record in the B column. (Remember, don't censor!)
4. Cross-check: Make sure you've identified a Belief for each Consequence and that there is a Consequence for each Belief.

B: Ticker-tape Beliefs	C: Consequences (Emotions and Behaviors)
She thinks that I'll be too aggressive on the phone and will make the problem worse. She never trusts that I'll handle myself professionally and is constantly undermining my authority.	I'm very irritated. I made a provocative remark.
What if we're wrong? The client is going to be very upset and may even try to make trouble for us.	I'm mildly anxious. I procrastinated.

© Copyright Adaptiv Learning Systems

---

life, begin to look for patterns. Do your ticker tapes have a certain theme? Do you tend to have more why beliefs than what-next beliefs? Do you notice a predominance of a particular kind of belief—violation of rights, loss, comparison to others? The more you are able to detect patterns the better, because pattern detection enables you to anticipate, and later prevent, nonresilient reactions. As you practice applying ABC, you may find that your list of Cs grows or you may realize that your ticker tape is more complex than it first appeared. That's a good sign. It shows growing self-awareness.

The final step of ABC is to cross-check. Each belief you have identified ought to connect with a feeling and behavior, and each feeling and behavior ought to connect with a belief—your Bs and Cs should be coupled. If you have a solitary B or C, take a moment to check for lingering emotions you did not immediately notice or beliefs that may have been playing with the volume too low. As with most skills, there is a learning curve. Don't be surprised if the first few times you practice ABC, you have fewer B–C couples than at a singles' night at your local community center.

How will you know that you've used the skill effectively? You will have what we call an aha! experience—you will say to yourself "Oh, no wonder I was feeling that way. I get it now." You will understand what you are feeling and why you are feeling that way. Once you've had the aha! experience, you are ready to more closely study the beliefs that are driving your reactions to make sure that you are not falling into thinking traps, a process we'll explore in the next chapter.

ABC Exceptions

Sometimes your beliefs don't matter quite so much.

Here we must contradict ourselves: In some cases, events are so severe that your reactions *are* driven by the event itself, not your beliefs about the event. When a loved one dies, the emotions that follow largely stem from the tragedy itself, not from one's interpretations of the tragedy. In the hours or days after a disaster—such as September 11—the magnitude of the event dictates your beliefs, and questioning their accuracy or usefulness is not particularly useful.

This fact does not mean that one's beliefs play no role in healing from tragedies and that the ABC skill serves no purpose. To the contrary, your beliefs and resilience determine how quickly and how easily you will regain control of your emotions and behaviors following colossal experiences.

There's another instance in which the ABC model doesn't hold true. Have you heard the phrase "amygdala hijack"?[10] Consider this story. Barb and Jim had been dating for two years. On Barb's birthday, Jim proposed, and they planned an elaborate wedding for the following summer. Three months before the wedding, Barb found out that Jim had slept with a woman from his office, and she broke off the engagement. Barb didn't return his phone calls and wouldn't answer the door when he came by. She hadn't seen him or spoken to him for three weeks. One night her friends convinced her to meet them for a drink after work. She's standing at the bar, scanning the room, when she sees Jim sitting with his back to her at a table with an attractive woman. Barb, drink in hand, storms the table. She calls his name, he turns in surprise, and she throws her drink in his face. That's an amygdala hijack.

The amygdala is an almond-shaped neural structure located above the brainstem, one half on each side of the brain. They are part of the limbic system, and their primary role is the service of emotions: generating emotions, storing emotional memories, providing emotional meaning to our lives. Without an amygdala, you would experience no joy, no sorrow, no fear or rage; life would be absent emotions and passion. The hippocampus (another structure in the limbic system) is responsible for storing the facts of the event. For Barb, the hippocampus encodes what she was drinking, where she was standing, what the boyfriend was wearing when she encountered him at the bar. The amygdala, in contrast, stores the emotional aspects—the rage she felt when she saw Jim with another woman, the humiliation she felt when she learned of his affair.

In some situations, the amygdala can override the neocortex, which serves motor, sensory, and cognitive functions, causing our emotions to prevail over our thinking. In most situations, the neural pathway goes from the thalamus to the neocortex, where the signals are processed and information regarding the object (what it is, what it means, what its value is) becomes known. The rest of the brain receives signals from the neocortex, and the body ultimately responds. But in some situations, the signal received by the amygdala acts as an alarm and the rest of the brain is mobilized before the neocortex completes its processing. For Barb, the sight of Jim triggered the amygdala alarm. Without complex processing of the stimuli, Barb saw Jim and reacted with rage. Her amygdala, in essence, shouted out "Danger! Danger!" and her body reacted.

The speed with which the amygdala reacts has clear survival value. Signals traveling directly from the thalamus to the amygdala go milliseconds faster than those traveling the long route from thalamus, to neocortex, to amygdala. The good news is that these milliseconds matter in emergency situations. The bad news is that important, detailed information is lost when the neocortex is left out of the loop. This trade-off between speed and thoroughness works to our advantage in some situations but to our disadvantage in others. Certainly speed is more important than thoroughness in true moments of crisis—the make and model of the oncoming car are of little importance. But in many situations when our emotions override our thinking, the richer information provided by the neocortex would have been to our advantage. Barb would have spared herself deep embarrassment had she noticed that the man in the navy shirt had blue eyes and a pierced ear, unlike Jim, who has brown eyes and would rather be seen naked than with an earring. The amygdala can save us but it can also cost us dearly.

Often when people first learn about the amygdala hijack, they wrongly conclude that we are slaves to our emotions and that any kind of intervention at the "thinking" level is useless. This is simply not true. It is important to remember that these amygdala moments are the exception, not the rule. Most of the emotions we experience follow more extensive processing from the neocortex, including our interpretations of the stimulus before us. Although, like Barb, occasionally we fly off the handle with very little thinking going on, it happens infrequently for some people, rarely at all for others. More common are the moments when we ruminate ourselves into a state of anxiety or anger or when we feel a growing sense of sadness as we engage in a detailed play-by-play of our last fight with a significant other, or when we get angry, or embarrassed, or feel guilty following a biased but belief-laden assessment of the current situation.

The very fact that in some situations our emotions cloud our thinking indicates a greater, not lesser, need for rationality. Granted, it is more difficult to assess a situation accurately when your emotions are at full throttle, but it is possible, even necessary. A crucial intervening step makes it possible to shift out of amygdala mode and into more rational thinking mode. When your emotions are coming on too fast and too strong, the most effective strategy is to calm your body. Then your mind can take over. In Chapter 9 we teach you the skills of Calming and Focusing so that you can reclaim your resilience even when your brain is working against you.

One Down, Six to Go

You have just learned your first resilience skill—the foundation of all the others. With your knowledge of ABC, now you can identify the adversities that are most challenging for you, you can recognize your in-the-moment beliefs—what you say to yourself when confronted with adversity—and you can identify how your beliefs make you feel and behave. You can use your understanding of ABC to make sense of a response that surprised you: "Oh, no wonder I felt so guilty. It's because I believed it was all my fault." And you can apply the same B–C information to increase your empathy for others: "She must be comparing herself negatively to me if she is feeling that embarrassed. Maybe I better check it out with her and make sure she's okay."

Practice Learning Your ABCs everyday. When you detect a sudden change in your mood, ask yourself: What did I just say to myself that made me feel this way? When you know an adversity is about to happen—say a meeting with a difficult colleague or a chaotic day at home—make sure to listen to your ticker-tape beliefs and notice the effect they have on you. The better you are at identifying what you say to yourself the moment adversity strikes, the easier it will be for you to change your nonresilient beliefs so they don't throw you off course. And, better yet, you can use your understanding of the B–C connections to anticipate how you will respond in the future: "I know I'm going to start to feel really anxious if I keep looking for the threat in every situation. Maybe I better try to think about this differently."

You are now ready to move on to the second skill of resilience—Avoiding Thinking Traps.

CHAPTER FIVE

Avoiding Thinking Traps

What a piece of work is a man! How noble in reason!
How infinite in faculty! In apprehension how like a god!
—WILLIAM SHAKESPEARE, *HAMLET*

Hamlet was supremely confident in the power of human intelligence and in our ability to think and act rationally. In fact, when it comes to intellect and logic, Hamlet believed that we were godlike—that our abilities were far above those of other animals. We think it's important to note here that comedian Jerry Seinfeld disagrees. Seinfeld poses it this way: Imagine that aliens landed their spaceship on earth and the first thing they saw was people trailing after dogs with pooper scoopers. Whom would they assume was master of the planet, dogs or us? It's a good point. So, are we the "paragon of animals," as Hamlet claimed, or is our intellectual power somewhere below that of the common housepet? Who's right here, Hamlet or Jerry?

Of course, humans are indeed the smartest beings on Earth. We have large brains, and it is our intelligence that has given us the evolutionary edge over all other species. But Hamlet was also wrong—he overestimated our intellectual abilities by a wide margin. Our faculties are not infinite. In fact, they are measurably finite; our brains only have about 1,500 cubic centimeters of processing capacity. Our five senses, however, are capable of taking in much more information than our brains are able to compute, so we need to simplify the information streaming in through our eyes and ears before we can use it. We cut corners and take shortcuts in our thinking to better handle the sensory load. Doing this means that we are not getting a direct readout on the world, so our thoughts and beliefs about the world are vulnerable to error. As it turns out, we make fairly predictable mistakes as we try to make sense of our world. Eight of these errors directly interfere with our resilience, with how we handle the setbacks and stresses in our daily lives.

The Eight Common Thinking Traps

Aaron Beck, the "father" of cognitive therapy, uncovered seven thinking traps that make people particularly vulnerable to depression.[1] Our work has demonstrated that these traps apply not only to depression but more generally to resilience. We've added an eighth trap, externalizing, a thinking style that actually protects people against depression. But externalizing saps resilience in other ways, by crimping our problem-solving ability and taxing our relationships.

As we share the thinking traps with you, try to recall the last time you fell into each trap yourself. While almost all of us have made all of the thinking errors at one time or another, each of us tends to be most vulnerable to two or three traps.

THINKING TRAP 1: JUMPING TO CONCLUSIONS

John is a junior employee who has worked in the same position for the same boss for the last six months. In that time they have developed a reasonably good working relationship. His manager has been evenhanded with her feedback in the past, giving concrete and detailed information on how she'd like certain aspects of his work performance to improve but equally forthcoming with praise when John meets or surpasses expectations. They work in a high-pressure environment, juggling several high-profile projects with tight deadlines. One morning John checks his e-mail and finds a one-line message from his boss: "Call me as soon as you can." He thinks, "I must have done something wrong."

Can you get a sense of the thinking error John made here? Without any data, he's assumed that his boss has e-mailed for negative reasons, that she's upset about some glitch or problem. This is not an outlandish assumption. The contemporary workplace is a pressure cooker—mistakes are bound to happen, problems occur frequently, and bosses often e-mail their employees to get things fixed. But it's an assumption nonetheless. The trouble with John's thinking is that he *automatically* believes, and believes with *certainty*, that his boss was e-mailing because something was wrong. He could be mistaken. There are other possibilities, right? His boss may simply wish to alert him to a new task or a new order of priorities for existing tasks.

The thinking trap of making assumptions without the relevant data is called *jumping to conclusions*. It's the umbrella error, really, since all of the thinking traps involve making an assumption of one kind or another. Did you notice that John jumps to a second conclusion? Not only does he presume that a problem has arisen, but he also instinctively believes that he must be the cause of it. Isn't it possible that, yes, there is a problem, but his boss is e-mailing him to fix someone else's mess, not to pin the blame on him? And yet John assumes it's his fault. We'll take a closer look at this trap, called personalizing, a little later in this chapter.

Let's see how John was affected after he jumped to a conclusion. Remember, as soon as he saw the "call me" e-mail, he said to himself, "I must have done something wrong." With your knowledge of the five B–C connections, how do you think John feels when he makes that assumption? Try to label the type of belief and then identify the emotions and behaviors that will follow. (Consult the B–C Connections chart on page 75 if you need to.)

"I must have done something wrong" is a loss belief—it implies that John is not as competent as he may have thought he was. We would expect him to feel a little sad and down. Most likely he'll also feel anxiety. Why? Ticker-tape beliefs rarely come in neat one-sentence packages. Most often they cascade from one to another. Once John has jumped to the conclusion that he has done something wrong, it's perfectly natural for him to make predictions about what will follow next. So his ticker tape is likely to be along the lines of "She's going to be really pissed at me, and I'm really gonna get it." These are future-threat beliefs, and future-threat beliefs lead to anxiety. John is not in control. He's not in control of his thinking, and so he's not in control of his emotions.

Let's say John does identify his "mistake"—perhaps he now assumes he miscalculated the budget figures on that latest project and that's why his boss is e-mailing him. He'll probably start rehearsing how to talk about it with her. He may plan his apology and work out possible solutions to his phantom problem. What if, instead, he can't find anything that he's done wrong? Now John feels more anxious and confused. "What did I do? What did I do?" He may delay getting back to his boss because he's nervous and doesn't want to speak with her until he feels prepared. Regardless of how this scenario plays out, one thing is certain: Because John jumped to conclusions about the meaning of the message and then acted as if his conclusions were certain, he's unable to respond effectively. Through self-fulfilling prophecy, John himself brings about the very outcome he most feared. Whether his assumption that he did something wrong is accurate or not, his Cs, his emotions and behaviors, make the assumption a losing proposition.

Can you remember a time when you fell into the thinking trap of jumping to conclusions? Think back, recall your ticker-tape beliefs (your Bs), and work through the emotional and behavioral consequences that ensued. Can you notice *when* you jump to conclusions? Do you make this mistake more often with certain people, in a certain domain of your life? Are there certain situations that make you most vulnerable to this trap— interaction with authority figures, as with John, or perhaps when others' opinions of you are on the line? John assumed that he was to blame, but perhaps your tendency is to blame others too quickly. John's conclusion brought on sadness and worry; if your tendency is to blame others, then you will often feel angry. The bottom line is that people who habitually jump to conclusions respond impulsively to situations because they act before they have full information.

In describing this thinking trap, we are not suggesting that intuition is a bad thing. The gut feelings we get about a situation, particularly those around danger, are often valuable. And there are some situations in which it makes sense to act first and think later. If you are walking alone to your car in a dark parking lot and you see a lone man approaching, the most resilient response is to trust the fear you are feeling and run away. Intuition can have survival value.

But most of the intuitions we have do not require immediate action. Most intuitions, just like assumptions, can benefit from gathering more information. In fact, we suggest that you treat intuitions and jumping to conclusions in the same way. That is, by all means take them seriously, but treat them as theories, not facts. They are hypotheses to be tested. And when we test our assumptions, it's valid to consider past experiences. If John's boss has a history of contacting him only to point out his mistakes, then it's reasonable for John to suspect that this is why she e-mailed this time. It's a thinking trap when there's little evidence to support the conclusion, or if John responds to his boss as if he were 100 percent certain that his assumption is true.

How might John respond more resiliently? He could spend a minute or two checking back mentally through yesterday's work to see if he may have slipped up somehow. But before he assumes a mistake occurred, he needs to gather more data. He should respond sooner rather than later to his boss's e-mail. But before he gets on the phone to his boss, he should say to himself "Okay, John, at this point, all you know for certain is that she wants you to call. If you assume you did something wrong, you won't be open-minded on the phone and you'll sound nervous. If it turns out you did make a mistake, the best thing you can do is to be calm and clear-headed." By counteracting the thinking trap, John gains control of his emotions and is less impulsive. He's in a much better position to respond resiliently to whatever comes his way.

THINKING TRAP 2: TUNNEL VISION

Sue is standing at the head of a long conference table. She's a middle-level manager in a financial services firm, presenting her team's progress on a project to a group of six manager peers and the director to whom they all report. Were Sue to have unlimited capacity to attend to and process all the sensory information before her, she would notice myriad behaviors in her colleagues at the meeting. Dave, Margaret, and Steve have held eye contact with her throughout. Margaret and another colleague, Brian, each ask questions indicating that they have paid attention to the content of her talk. Halfway through the meeting one of the managers, Rachel, answers her ringing cell phone and leaves the room, never to return. The other two managers, Jim and Trisha, exchange comments frequently as the meeting unfolds. The director listens throughout, often nodding her head or throwing in a comment or two. At one point she yawns. As she nears the three-quarter point in her presentation, Sue thinks, "This presentation is going so poorly."

Like the rest of us, Sue cannot process everything that happens around her. She is unable to attend to the entire sensory scene before her. Her mind automatically takes shortcuts by sampling select scenes and details from the environment, leading her to register only these samples. Doing this would serve her well if only she were an equal-opportunity sampler. But she's not. Sue tends to focus on the negative aspects of her environment. She selectively notices the clandestine conversation between Jim and Trisha and assumes their comments are derogatory. She dwells on Rachel's departure from the meeting and can't tear her eyes from her director's yawn. Sue systematically ignores the nods of agreement, the interested glances, the eye contact, and the informed questioning. Sue is a victim of *tunnel vision*. She sees only the negative aspects of a situation. Because she samples from her environment in such a biased way, she draws the incorrect conclusion that the presentation is going poorly.

How does this thinking trap drain Sue's resilience and prevent her from achieving her goals? She wants this meeting to go well. She's spent a lot of time preparing for it, and she realizes it's an excellent opportunity to prove her mettle to her manager. But when she concludes that the presentation is going poorly, she's quickly led to other ticker-tape beliefs that derail her: "This is going to do the exact opposite of what I want. Far from viewing me as competent, the director will think that I was unprepared and, worse, will conclude that I've been mismanaging this project. This will probably mean that I'll be overlooked next time important assignments come up." Consider the effect of these beliefs in the context of the ABC skill and the B–C connections. Sue is having future-threat beliefs, which are bound to produce anxiety. And anxiety of this degree almost invariably adversely affects performance. Sue's tunnel vision may bring about the very outcome she most fears.

Tunnel vision is most often directed toward negative outcomes, since being broadsided by an unexpected boon doesn't carry the same survival threat as an unanticipated adversity. But some people develop styles that tunnel their vision for the positive. And while ABC dictates that such people will avert negative emotions, such as the anxiety and sadness that Sue is likely to experience, positive tunnel visioning creates problems of its own. Take, for example, the case of Richard, a vice president in a Fortune 500 company. Richard is a very successful man whose energy and optimism afforded him a meteoric rise in the organization. He came to our executive coaching because he had been unable to solve a problem that had been recurring for the last several months. His company was undergoing enormous structural and procedural change to bring it into line with current business practice—teams were being reorganized by job function rather than geographic location, and hands-on procedures were becoming computerized. Richard knew he had to keep his directors apprised of developments and involved in decision making for this initiative to be successful. But the problem, as he saw it, was that while the directors all agreed to his proposals in the weekly meetings, many of them simply were not following through on the job. What was going wrong?

We spent some weeks talking with Richard in the abstract about those director meetings and could make no headway. We came to believe that we needed to see a meeting in action. As the meeting unfolded, it became clear why Richard was so successful. His presentation was precise and lucid, laying out his vision of the organization and what was needed to get the division in line. It was motivational and inspiring. When the meeting ended, as the last of the directors filed out, Richard turned to us and shrugged. "See what I mean?" he said. "I got great agreement in there, but I know that at least half of them will fail to act." We were impressed with his presentation, but, frankly, we did *not* see what he meant by "great agreement." It's true that four of his nine directors—those sitting closest to him at the conference table—had nodded and murmured agreement throughout the meeting. One or two others had taken notes to indicate that they were at least following the presentation. But had Richard failed to see the times when two or three directors had been staring vacantly out the window? Did he fail to see the two occasions when three or four of them were slowly and subtly shaking their heads? Or when two of the directors, separated by a third, eased back in their chairs to get each other's attention and rolled their eyes? No, he'd seen all those things. At least he'd seen them in the literal sense—light carrying that information had hit his retina and caused neurons in the visual system to fire. But due to his tunnel vision, he hadn't attended to these details, processed them, or stored them in his memory. Instead he had focused on those behaviors that meshed with his thinking, the nodding heads and the note taking. And while, thanks to his tunnel vision, his positive outlook and self-esteem were intact, his failure to see that his directors were generally not on board rendered it impossible for him to fix a situation that threatened the success of his division and his future in the company.

When we worked with Sue and Richard, we learned that they each had strong beliefs about themselves and their world. Sue believed that she was a borderline speaker who didn't command attention in presentations. Richard believed he was a persuasive presenter who could motivate his staff to follow his mission. And both Sue and Richard screened in the information that was consistent with their beliefs and ignored the data that could disconfirm them.

THINKING TRAP 3: MAGNIFYING AND MINIMIZING

We met Ellen in one of our parenting programs. During introductions she told us that her reserves of resilience were running at an all-time low. She had made the decision to be a stay-at-home mom and had left her middle-level management position in a security firm to care for her daughter, Annie, age four and a half, and her son, Max, who is almost two. We could hear the emotion in her voice, her sadness and frus-

Why Do We Tunnel to Certain Information?

What leads people to systematically ignore important information? Why do we tend to tunnel into only a fraction of the data available to us? This trap stems from our habit of preferring evidence that bolsters our theories about ourselves and the world around us.

Check out the following puzzle, first proposed by decision theorist P. C. Wason.[2] There are four cards presented. Each card has a letter on one side and a number on the other.

Your job is to decide how to test whether the following rule is true or not: If a card has a vowel on one side, then it has an even number on the other. Name the cards, and only those cards, that you would need to turn over to test the rule. What did you decide?

Most people asked to perform this task reply that they would turn over cards E and 4. Did you? What this neatly demonstrates is our penchant for evidence that can confirm our theories about the world. Turning over the E card is a good decision. If doing so reveals an odd number, we know the rule is incorrect, while evidence for the rule is bolstered if an even number is revealed. But turning over the 4 card cannot help us at all. Regardless of whether a vowel or consonant is revealed, the rule may still be true. (There's nothing in the rules that suggests that if a card has an even number on one side then it must have a vowel on the other.) But we want to see a vowel on the other side of that 4 card, to confirm that rule. Psychologists refer to this as the confirmation bias—our preference for evidence that confirms our theories about the world. What we should do, if we were good scientists, is to set out to prove the rule wrong, and the only way to do that is by turning over cards E and 7.

tration, as she told her story. She still considered leaving her job to be one of the best decisions of her life, but lately her day-to-day existence was taking its toll. She told us, "At the end of almost every day I feel like a failure. I've devoted so much of my time to raising my kids—it's my career and I can't get it right. More and more a typical day leaves me feeling down and empty. I dwell on the bad stuff—when Max threw his tantrum at the grocery store checkout, when I couldn't track down that book I wanted for Annie, or when Max tried to bite one of his playmates. It colors my whole day, and I find myself thinking 'I am so sick of being a mom.' It's only when I push myself really hard that I remember any of the good moments—like when Annie rushed to help Max when he fell over in the yard. Or when Max laughed and laughed at the story I read him. Sometimes it even takes a call from my mom to remind me that I'm doing a good job with this. Why can't I see things in a more balanced way? The good things get swallowed up by the failures, and it's making me miserable."

We were struck with Ellen's insight. Most people who magnify the negatives and minimize the positives in their lives are not aware that they are in a thinking trap. Unlike people with tunnel vision, magnifiers and minimizers have registered and can remember most of the events that have occurred, but they tend to overvalue some and undervalue others. As lecturers at Penn we've seen this with our students also. Some of our college seniors have confided that they think their chances of making it into graduate school are slim because of a C they received in, say, the first semester of their sophomore year. It's as if a telescope were suspended above that C on their transcript, for all the world to see, while their other, excellent grades are being viewed with the telescope reversed—as tiny images way off in the distance. And this was the trap into which Ellen had fallen. By overblowing the negative, the connections inherent in ABC pull for negative mood and compromised resilience.

Some people do the opposite—they magnify the good and minimize the bad. They might dismiss the importance of a negative event, such as a fight with a friend, saying to themselves something like "These things always blow over." They may shrug off a negative evaluation at work with "So I didn't meet my objectives this quarter. I've done well in the past and will again." Or they may blow off signs of ill health: "My blood pressure and cholesterol are high, but the important thing is that the doctor was happy with my weight." Those who magnify the positive and minimize the negative, just like Richard the tunnel visioner, may be underestimating real need for life change.

Think about your daily routine. As you drive home from work or talk about your day across the dinner table, do you recount more of the negative events than the positive? This thinking trap will undermine your success at work and in your relationships. Magnifying the negative and minimizing the positive will lead to negative emotions and will destroy your enthusiasm for the things you do in life. How could you be excited about work, your relationship, your new hobby, if all you focus on are the mishaps and problems? Negativity is a mood kill, and negative moods tend to sap energy and effectiveness.

If you fall into the maximizing and minimizing thinking trap often, your professional relationships will suffer. We've coached countless work teams, and one of the most common complaints we hear is about colleagues' negativity. People do not like to work with someone who is forever forecasting doom and gloom. Not only is it unpleasant, but negative moods slow creativity and problem solving, for both the individual experiencing them and for members of the team. People tend to think less clearly, less flexibly, and less effectively when they are angry or sad. Colleagues start to distance themselves from those who can't rein in that negativity. This thinking trap often leads to self-fulfilling prophecy.

Friendships also will be affected. Moods are contagious, so if you are sullen, angry, or sad much of the time, your friends will catch it. Or perhaps your friends will begin by trying to cheer you up, to help you to see more of the positive, but after repeated failures they give up and move on. This may be a wise decision on their part, because negative people often are self-absorbed and lack the empathy required to maintain close relationships with others. Imagine that a friend comes to you with a problem, and she starts to describe an argument she had with her husband. You'll be head-nodding right along. You'll be asking all the right questions to get her to think more and more about the specifics of the problem: what he said, how he said it, when he was like this before. Your friend will feel understood and appreciated. But then, as she tries to find a bit more balance in her understanding of the problem, when she tries to talk about the good moments—when he was understanding and loving, the fun they had together at dinner—that's when she'll lose you. You'll steer the conversation away from the good and back to the bad. That's not empathy. You don't do this to be mean—it doesn't happen at a conscious level—but your thinking bias will propel you to the negative like a moth to flame.

Maybe you don't magnify the negative but, instead, minimize it. Do you push the negative out of your awareness and focus exclusively on the good things that took place? The exclusive focus on the positive may leave you feeling cheery, but eventually your denial of reality will catch up with you. And when it does, you'll be unprepared. At work, you may find that you tend to downplay problems and setbacks, focusing your energy instead on the projects that are going well. Playing to your strengths is sensible, but not to the exclusion of correcting problems that exist. As one woman told us, "I got myself in trouble because I tended to minimize the importance of problems when they arose. Rather than focus on them, I'd try to keep moving forward on other fronts, but of course, this put me behind the eight ball. By dismissing the problems, I gave them the time they needed to grow from manageable setbacks into crises."

Magnifying the positive and minimizing the negative is equally destructive to your personal relationships and your health. Growth and change cannot happen unless you are able to take stock of a situation accurately. The man who is overweight and smokes a pack a day will have no impetus to quit if he minimizes the importance of these health risks. The woman who ignores her husband's concerns about their relationship and focuses only on the elements of the marriage that are working, is going to wake up one day to find the other side of the bed empty. Resilience rests on an accurate appraisal of one's life. Extreme pessimists and extreme optimists will suffer equally.

THINKING TRAP 4: PERSONALIZING

Joey's parents enrolled him in our children's resilience program in the Upper Darby School District on the outskirts of Philadelphia. As children sign up for the program, our researchers guide them through a battery of questionnaires that provide us with information about their explanatory styles, self-esteem, the nature of their ticker-tape beliefs, their anxiety, and their levels of depression. All the evidence indicated that Joey was at heightened risk for depression. At the age of eleven, Joey was already showing more depressive symptoms than most of his peers, and the bulk of his thinking was negative. According to his responses on a test for explanatory style, Joey was strongly "personal" in nature—he tended to blame himself for the adversities in his life.

What the questionnaires had revealed was confirmed as the program unfolded. Recall that we discussed explanatory style in Chapter 3—our habitual and reflexive way of explaining the events in our lives, and that a "personal" or "me" style was a known risk factor for depression. So it came as no surprise, given Joey's strong "me" style, that he was already experiencing high levels of depressive symptoms. One exercise in the program is designed to help the children identify their ticker-tape beliefs. In this exercise we outline hypothetical events and ask the children to practice capturing their why beliefs. For example, imagine that you agree to water your neighbors' plants while they're away on vacation and the plants die. Why did this happen? Some children will duck responsibility by reflexively blaming others or circumstances: "They gave me the wrong keys," "They didn't tell me how much water they needed," "They shouldn't have asked a kid to do this," or even "The plants should have been tougher." But Joey never did. His reflex was to automatically blame himself: "I didn't realize what a big job it would be" or "I spaced that I was supposed to do it." In fact, Joey seemed to attribute any problem not only to himself but to a deep character flaw within himself. The plants died because he couldn't be trusted. His sister got a bicycle for her birthday and he got a sweater for his because he's not nice like she is ("Everybody thinks that, even Mom and Dad"). He didn't do well in math because he's just "dumb."

The thinking trap that Joey found himself caught in is called personalizing—the reflex tendency to attribute problems to one's own doing. If we view this thinking trap through the lens of ABC and the B–C connections, we'll see why this style, with its typical beliefs about loss of self-worth, so often leads to sadness. In conflicts with friends or loved ones, personalizing will lead to beliefs of violating the rights of others and so to the emotion of guilt. Sadness and guilt—two emotions with which Joey was all too familiar.

It's important to acknowledge the adaptive edge to personalizing. In many cases, we think that if we attribute the cause of the problem to ourselves, then we grant ourselves the power to solve it. Two psychologists, Bernard Weiner and Julian Rotter, working independently, have contributed enormously to our understanding of personalizing and control. Rotter differentiates people on whether they perceive the control of their lives as coming from within or from some outside force, such as others, luck, or circumstances. Clearly those who see control coming from within will possess greater self-efficacy, resilience, and increased motivation to seek and act on solution strategies.

But does that mean it's always better, more resilient, to take responsibility for problems? Joey, at eleven, was not the picture of self-reliance and confidence. To the contrary, he was at great risk for depression. When faced with problems, he didn't work hard to solve them; instead, he would become passive and give up. How do we understand this? The answer is through accuracy. Resilience comes when you believe that you have the power to control the events in your life, the power to change what needs changing—*and* that belief is accurate.

There are two occasions when attributing the cause of a problem to oneself does not increase resilience. First, if you—like personalizers—*only* see the internal causes of a problem and systematically ignore the external causes, then your resilience will be lowered. Imagine that you work collaboratively with a colleague, let's call him Stewart, in the technical support department of a large company. You and Stewart are asked to write a proposal on methods for improving the company's Internet-based communications with clients. You present your proposal jointly, and it's not well received. Now imagine that we (but not you) have full knowledge of the problems, and they are:

- ✦ A section you wrote for the proposal did not provide enough evidence to support the conclusions you made.
- ✦ A section Stewart wrote lacked clarity, and readers found it hard to assess the bottom-line recommendation.
- ✦ In the oral presentation, you and Stewart interrupted each other several times, leaving the audience confused.

✦ The audience found Stewart to be dismissive of some of the concerns they raised.

Because you are a personalizer, your assessment of the situation will be skewed. You'll acknowledge that sections of the proposal that you wrote did not present your argument persuasively enough. You'll apologize to Stewart for interrupting him during the presentation. But you will be oblivious to Stewart's contribution to the problem—the lack of clarity of the sections *he* wrote and his dismissiveness. Your thinking-style bias will enable you to see your contribution to the situation but will blind you to his. Why is this a problem? Because an effective collaboration, and bouncing back after failure, requires a full and accurate analysis of what went wrong. Because you personalize, you'll miss those causes of the problem that are not due to you, and so you'll take no steps to correct them—for example, having an honest conversation with Stewart. Resilience requires accuracy.

Second, self-efficacy, and therefore resilience, hinges on whether you believe the internal causes of the problem are changeable or not. Whenever confronted with a problem, Joey looks inside himself, but what he sees as the causes of his problems are aspects of himself that are resistant to change. When Joey does poorly on a test, he doesn't focus on specific behaviors that he can alter, such as his study habits. Instead, he immediately and reflexively impugns his character: "I got a C because I'm dumb." Study habits are changeable; stupidity is hard to fix. If you tend to personalize, track your beliefs closely to see whether you also tend to attribute problems to behaviors that you can control and change or to deep-seated aspects of your character that are immutable. The combination of attributing problems to things about yourself that are unchangeable is a double whammy, and it's corrosive to resilience. It's the combination of personalizing with another thinking trap called overgeneralizing. We'll discuss overgeneralizing in more detail when we get to Thinking Trap 6. For now, keep paying attention to your ticker tape. It matters.

THINKING TRAP 5: EXTERNALIZING
Externalizing is the flipside of personalizing. Although personalizing undermines resilience, that doesn't mean you simply should blame others whenever something goes wrong. This thinking trap—externalizing—has a cost as well. We've worked for more than twelve years with sales forces

in several industries, and we observe a clear pattern in their thinking styles—problems are rarely their fault. "No one can sell in this market." "No one could sell this schlocky product." "If only the marketing division had a budget for glossy brochures." This style protects the sales agent's self-esteem and keeps the self-doubts at bay. And, certainly, self-doubts are especially destructive in sales. But knee-jerk externalizing also has a downside. Externalizers fail to locate those elements of an adversity that are genuinely of their doing and within their control. They may be failing to hone their pitch and approach or the client lists they generate, because they can see only how others are letting them down. And again, seen through the lens of ABC, while externalizers avoid sadness and guilt, they instead find themselves prone to anger.

THINKING TRAP 6: OVERGENERALIZING

Margaret and her teenage daughter, Samantha, have been arguing more lately. The issues are largely petty, at least in Margaret's eyes—what clothes Sam can wear to school, what time she must be back home from trips to her friends. But the fighting certainly has increased in intensity and frequency in the last few months. It culminated yesterday when Sam brought home a D in math. Margaret was furious. She had warned Sam repeatedly to hit those books to no avail. As a teacher herself, she believed that she had really let Sam down. It's true that when they were in the middle of the quarrel, Margaret felt angry with Sam for not working harder and for breaking her curfews. But all the time, running through her head like ticker tape, was the thought "I'm a bad parent."

Margaret explains her run-ins with her daughter as due to being a bad parent—a flawed character trait that is not quickly or easily remedied. In other words, she makes always and everything explanations about herself—the double whammy we referred to before. A more objective observer could find several possible explanations for the recent arguing. Some are less to do with Margaret and more to do with Sam: "Sam is entering those rebellious teen years, as all kids do," or "Sam has been moody lately." Some might place the responsibility squarely with Margaret, but on causes that affect only very specific aspects of their relationship: "Margaret loses patience with Sam when she underachieves at school," or "It really pushes Margaret's buttons when Sam defies her and stays out later than her curfew." Margaret fails to see these causes because of her style. Consider the ABC of this situation. The next time Margaret is called on to help Sam with homework, to discuss a thorny teenage issue, or to place limits on her freedom as parents of teenagers must, is she more or less likely to get involved, given her belief that she's a bad parent? And by withdrawing from her responsibilities, through self-fulfilling prophecy, she causes the very thing she most wishes to avoid—being a bad parent.

Of course, overgeneralizing is not limited to the self. While personalizers who overgeneralize assassinate their own character, externalizers who overgeneralize assassinate the character of others. When you and your significant other fight, would you be more likely to think "He's always so selfish" or "He didn't think about my needs"? When your employees don't complete a task on time, would you be more likely to think "They are lazy and unmotivated" or "They didn't manage their time well"? When your child argues with you, would you think "She's obnoxious" or "She's been in a foul mood lately"? If the former statements better capture your thinking style, then you externalize and overgeneralize; you attribute the causes of problems to other people's *character* rather than to their *behavior*. This is not a winning motivational strategy. When you overgeneralize to global characteristics in others, you've stripped them of control, at least in your mind, just as personalizers who overgeneralize strip themselves of control. Next time you catch yourself making one of these double whammies, ask yourself: Is there a behavior—either mine or someone else's—that could have caused this problem? If so, that's the behavior you're going to want to alter for your own good.

THINKING TRAP 7: MIND READING

In the summer of 1996 we worked with a Fortune 500 company in the computer industry, and in one of the workshops we ran we met Louise. What a delight she was. She was outspoken and opinionated, a genuine firebrand, and we became fond of her early on the first day. Before every workshop we ask all the prospective participants to complete a questionnaire about their perceived strengths and weaknesses as well as the adversities they encounter at work, at home, and in balancing the two. Louise's responses were memorable. Her answers were those of a strong, ambitious, and intelligent woman, making it all the more surprising that she was still in a low-level job after eight years in the company. During the workshop, while completing one of our worksheets, Louise disclosed her belief that prejudice was a roadblock to her progression in the organization. "I've applied for about five or six promotions in the time I've been here," she told us. "I know I'm qualified for the jobs I apply for, but there's no way they're going to promote an African American woman."

No one logs the kind of time we have in the corporate world without seeing prejudice. It is a real problem that needs a real solution. But we were also aware that African Americans had risen to very high ranks within this particular company. And so we asked her to tell us, as comprehensively as she could, how the typical interview unfolded and to pinpoint the beliefs that ran through her mind at each point in the process. In other words, we asked her to ABC her last interview. This is how she described it. "I went in very prepared. I recognized that it was going to be tough for me, as a black woman, so I made sure I knew every facet of the job so they couldn't fault me. I knew who was going to be on the interview committee, who was going to be sitting in that room, but somehow it still struck me just how 'white' the committee was. In the beginning the interview seemed to go well. My ticker tape was 'I think this time I'm going to break through,' and I felt like I could take on the world. But all of a sudden I started to think it was going off the rails." We asked Louise to try to recall exactly what was happening immediately prior to the perceived turning point. She replied, "Well, I guess it was when two members of the interview panel started whispering to each other. Yeah, that was it. Mike Simmons had asked me a question about what procedure to follow if a client lodges a complaint and as I was answering that question, I saw Rhonda Jenkins and Bob Cassamatis whispering to each other. I couldn't hear what they were saying, and they weren't looking at me so I couldn't see their faces. But I knew then that I was not going to get this job." We asked her how she could be so sure. "Because I know they were trying to come up with some way to rob me of the job—probably hatching some kind of impossible question to make me look bad. I know that all or most of that panel didn't want a black woman to have that job. They were all just going through the motions. They have to interview me—turning me down for an interview is too obviously racist even for this company. No, they agreed to interview all right, but there was no way I was going to get that job. I could just tell what they were thinking."

She continued. "When I first saw them whispering I started to feel anxious—I guess because I was thinking that I had no future with this company. Then I just thought what a monumental waste of time this whole thing was—and I felt helpless and unmotivated. I know after that I just coasted through a couple of questions. And then I started to think how unfair it was that these people held the key to my future. I felt myself getting very angry. In the end I just told them, 'Look, it's all there in my resume. Why even bother with these questions when it's all just a waste of time? Just read it in the resume.'"

We are not suggesting that racism isn't a factor in corporate promotion decisions. We know well that it can be. But notice the self-fulfilling prophecy that Louise has incurred. Her belief that this committee will not promote her due to racism leads, understandably, to anger toward the committee members, resentment toward the company, and the desire to make a statement, either by walking out of the interview or at least by sending the clear signal that she is aware of their racism. Of course, even if the committee members were completely blind to race and sex, even if they were acting in a fair and responsible manner, Louise's obvious anger guarantees that she will not get the job. Is her belief that they are racist correct? She may be right, but the data she has used to draw that conclusion is suspect—a whispered comment between two members of the panel that she was unable to hear. Louise believed she knew what they were thinking—that the members of the committee were thinking of ways to deny her the job. Louise was mind reading.

Many of us are mind readers. We believe we know what those around us are thinking and we act accordingly. Some mind readers expect others to know what they are thinking. How often have you come home after a long and arduous day at work and been frustrated with your spouse for not being more sympathetic? This is perhaps one of the most common thinking traps relationship partners fall into, especially those with children. "Why is he suggesting we go out for dinner? Can't he tell I've had a terrible day at work and all I want is a long, hot bath and a little peace and quiet?" Or "I don't believe she's suggesting I take the kids to the park. I've had the day from hell and she can't even give me a little time to relax before I'm sent on another chore. Doesn't she know that I'm exhausted and frustrated with the day at the office?" Well, no, she doesn't know you're frustrated and exhausted. No, he can't tell you've had a terrible day. People are not mind readers, but we often expect them to be.

Just as personalizing and overgeneralizing tend to co-occur, mind reading has a common partner. People who mind read tend to jump to conclusions. Gary's story illustrates how these two thinking traps work together to undermine his leadership. Gary is the business administrator in the psychiatry department of a medical school. He is directly responsible for seven full-time employees and three part-time employees. When work is calm, Gary is compassionate, warm, and fair. He's a good listener, and the people who work for him feel pleased to be part of his team. Work, of course, is not always calm. If you were to stop by Gary's office late in September, a few weeks before grant applications are due, the anxiety in the office would be so thick, you could touch it. The close of grant cycles is an adversity for Gary, and it brings out the worst in him.

Once Gary and his staff were working frenetically on twenty different budgets for twenty multimillion-dollar grants. Midday, Gary received an e-mail from the chair of the department notifying him that he needed some of the budget information by noon of the next day, a week and a half earlier than the original timetable. Gary needed to leave the office early to attend a meeting across campus, so he e-mailed specific instructions to each person in the office detailing what he wanted them to work on for the rest of the day. The next morning Gary arrived at the office and met individually with each employee to get status reports. When he met with Maria, she sheepishly told him that she had not completed any of the tasks on her list. Gary's immediate thought was "She knew the time crunch we were under, but she just didn't care. I can't believe her!" He became furious, his emotions were out of control, and it showed.

But did Maria know about the time urgency? Gary never told the staff of the change in timetable; it wasn't part of his e-mail message. He was angry at Marie for failing to read his mind. Once Gary fell into the thinking trap of mind reading, it was all too easy for him to jump to a conclusion. Gary's ticker tape continued: "If she didn't do what I asked, then she clearly is not committed to this office and that's not the kind of person I want working with me." Gary, usually a good listener, barely let Maria speak. When she tried to explain her actions, he saw it as a face-saving lie and dismissed her with obvious disgust. His thinking errors led him to act impulsively and in ways that undermined his authority.

Gary's thinking errors are unfair to Maria, and, as important, they interfere with his problem solving. Gary was angry and distrustful of Maria, so rather than have her work on getting the information, he delegated it to another staff member who was already overloaded. Had Gary slowed down and taken the time to find out what had gone wrong, he would have learned that Maria didn't complete the work because she had to leave early to pick up her son who had become ill at school. Maria was working under the assumption that she had a week and a half to complete the work and was planning on coming in over the weekend to catch up. She would have gladly stayed late to get as much done as possible, but because Gary delegated the work to someone else and had treated her so rudely, she left at five feeling misunderstood and unmotivated to be a team player.

Are there times when you fall into the trap of mind reading and treat others poorly or fail to rise to the occasion as a result? The next time you find yourself getting upset because someone failed to read your mind, or you believe you have read someone else's, slow yourself down and ask the other person a question that will help clarify where the communication breakdown has occurred. If Gary had simply asked, "Maria, I'm confused. Don't you understand the time pressure we're under?" the damage would have been controlled. Instead, it was compounded.

THINKING TRAP 8: EMOTIONAL REASONING

We met Wendy in one of our corporate seminars in the winter of 1999. At that time she was a manager in the marketing division of a major telecommunications company, and over the course of the training she told us of a recent and recurrent pattern in her job that was beginning to trouble her. Convincing others of the merits of her marketing proposals was her lifeblood. It was one of her greatest strengths. And her track record was impressive. Wendy could pitch a pitch (as we ourselves found when she successfully argued for an early end time to our first day of training together).

Wendy outlined the strategy she had developed in meetings with marketing directors and VPs; those making the decision on whose ideas to adopt. Usually it worked, but lately her approach had been failing her. "I'll leave the meeting thinking that I had won them over, I'll use my time going after other projects, and I'll find out later that I didn't get the project. When I confided in one of the directors recently that I was surprised they went with someone else, she told me that my supporters for that project were scarce on the ground. I was stunned." Wendy's question of us: "If this is all about thinking, then what's wrong with my thinking? Have I lost my touch?"

We first thought Wendy's problem was tunnel vision; perhaps she was falling into Richard's trap of failing to see the signs of disagreement. Or maybe magnification and minimization—she was registering the signs of disagreement but was undervaluing them compared with the nods and the murmured assents. But as we probed Wendy's thinking in the moment of these meetings, we realized that hers was a very different trap from Richard's or Ellen's.

The stakes had risen for Wendy recently. It was an open secret that she was being considered for a major promotion that would give her directorship over one of the company's largest advertising campaigns. Wendy wanted to nail the promotion down. She welcomed each presentation to the directors and the VP as an opportunity to hit a home run, but she also saw each presentation as a chance to strike out. She began getting anxious before the meetings; something she hadn't experienced since she was a rookie. But she was still very good at what she did—the presentations went well and as they drew to a close she knew that she had not struck out. In the wake of this realization she would feel a surge of relief, a positive glow, as the tension and anxiety ebbed away.

The telling question, the question that revealed the thinking trap, was when we asked Wendy why she felt good at the end of the meeting. "Because I thought I had won them over," she replied. "Because I believed I had the numbers." We were skeptical. We asked her to vividly recall the last time this occurred. We asked her to revisit the emotion and describe it to us, including its source. She locked eyes with us, smiled, and nodded. "You're right. I feel good because I'm just relieved it's over."

Wendy had experienced a positive emotion because she had avoided messing up. None of the directors had asked any difficult questions, there were no obvious signs of disinterest—in fact, she'd been able to marshal tangible excitement for her ideas among a few of those present. But she falsely attributed her good feeling to having achieved her objective of landing the project. Her thinking took the following form: "I'm feeling good so I must have convinced them that I was the person for the project." Notice the logical error here. Certainly if she had landed the project, she would feel good. But there are several possible pathways to feeling good in this scenario. Perhaps she was feeling good because she hadn't bombed. Wendy was drawing conclusions, false conclusions as it turns out, about the nature of the world based on her emotional state. We call this thinking trap *emotional reasoning*.

Perhaps a more illustrative example of emotional reasoning comes from personal experience. When Andrew was in college, one of his best friends, we'll call him Mark, was an enthusiastic skydiver. And he was good. Very good. He and the other three members of the Australian team had just won the world championship. To the unitiated, such as Andrew, their event was sheer lunacy—they threw themselves out of a plane together, formed patterns in the sky, were rated by judges on the creativity and degree of difficulty of their midair antics, and then, it was hoped, glided safely to earth. Mark often tried to entice Andrew out to the drop zone (which Andrew considered a very unfortunate name), and he always declined. You see, while Andrew's friends, including Mark, worked on their law degrees, he was pursuing a major in philosophy that could only lead to chronic unemployment. Andrew figured he was living dangerously enough. But one night, over a couple of convivial drinks, Mark did convince their mutual friend, Peter, to make his first jump. Plans were made for about a month hence.

Intrigued that Peter would acquiesce, Andrew asked him the obvious question: "Peter, what do you think the chances are that you'll die doing this?" Peter was unperturbed. He mulled it over for a moment and replied, "Well, I suppose that there are about 10 million jumps a year or so, and probably about one or two fatalities a year—so, maybe about one in 5 million or so." His logic was pretty impressive. About a month later, on the eve of the jump, the three friends happened to be together again. And of course, being a supportive and caring friend, Andrew asked the question: "Peter, what do you think the chances are that you'll die doing this tomorrow?" He responded earnestly, "Pretty small, I guess—about one in 10,000."

One in 10,000. One in 10,000—when a month earlier his estimate was one in 5 million. Had skydiving suddenly become so much more dangerous? Of course not. So, what led Peter to perceive that the threat had increased so dramatically? As we saw in Chapter 4, anxiety is often a direct consequence of beliefs about a future threat. Our estimate of the level of threat is determined by our perception of three aspects of the situation: how dangerous the threat is, the probability that it actually will occur, and how close in time it is to us. For example, while smokers are engaged in a very dangerous activity with a high probability of negative health consequences, the threat seems so distant in time that their anxiety is typically quite low—low enough to be an insufficient incentive to stop. Similarly, we send our children off to school in the morning despite our knowledge that school shootings do happen. There is no more sizable threat than the possible loss of a child, and it could be very close in time—it could happen that morning. But most of us recognize that the chances are very remote that a school shooting would happen in our school, to our child. So we are able to keep our anxiety in check. In Peter's case, the imminence of the threat had changed considerably, from one month distant to a matter of a few hours. The proximity in time led to a significant increase in his level of anxiety—and he allowed his heightened anxiety to falsely inform him that the threat was actually more likely. He had succumbed to emotional reasoning.

Andrew didn't accompany Mark and Peter to the drop zone, he didn't go up with them in the plane, but he's fantasized about being there. He imagines Peter hanging on to the wing strut while Mark kicks at his fingers, "encouraging" him to let go. Andrew imagines himself, from the safety of the plane, shouting above the roar of the wind to make himself heard: "Peter, what do you think the chances are you'll die doing this?" And Andrew imagines Peter's response as he hurtles to earth: "One in twooooooooooo."

Both Mark and Peter made it back safely.

Why Do We Fall into Thinking Traps?

In this chapter we've covered the eight thinking traps that most threaten our resilience. You are now well on the way to identifying the two or three traps to which you are most vulnerable. And in the next section we'll arm you with tactics to recognize these thoughts and with some questions that will help you out of the trap or even allow you to avoid it altogether. But before we introduce the skill of Avoiding Thinking Traps, let's consider how and why we fall prey to these traps.

We probably could avoid the traps if we were more logical, but research shows that humans are poor logicians.[3] Here's an example. Imagine that we know two facts, or premises, for certain:

> No Xs are Ys.
> All Ys are Zs.

What can we conclude about Xs and Zs? Most people jump to the conclusion that no Xs are Zs. Did you? From the perspective of formal logic, this is incorrect because the conclusion doesn't necessarily follow from the premises. This becomes more obvious if we put some real-world flesh on the bones of these Xs, Ys, and Zs.

This next example has the same structure as the one above but involves concepts we're more familiar with:

> No girls are boys.
> All boys wear clothes (or, more precisely, all boys are
>   clothes-wearing humans).
> Therefore, no girls wear clothes.

Now we can see the error we made when dealing with Xs and Zs. So why do so many of us jump to false conclusions? Why do most of us have such difficulty with logic? Because the basic process of logic is very different from the kind of processing we have to do in the real world and that we've evolved to perform. In formal logic, all the information is there at our disposal. Our task is to determine what conclusion must follow from the information provided to us. For example, in a classic syllogism that all students of logic encounter, we are first given a general rule: "All men are mortal." Next we are supplied with information that links a specific case, such as Socrates, to a general category, in this case: "Socrates is a man." Our task is a *deductive* one—to deduce what information must flow from what we already know. So it is that we arrive at "Socrates is mortal." In the deductive process we move from the general to the specific.

The problem is that life's not like that. We're rarely provided with general information about the world like that which we receive in formal-logic exercises. In fact, to understand the world, we usually have to piece together the general rules of how it operates by ourselves. Most of our thought processing involves using our intellects to detect patterns or rules about the world based on our experiences. This is a process of *induction*—of building general rules from an accumulation of specific examples.

Our predecessors had to be skilled at inductive reasoning to survive. General rules about what was safe and what was dangerous were crucial. When our cave dweller, Throgg, first encountered a saber-toothed tiger that tried to devour him, he quickly developed the rule: "Saber-toothed tigers are dangerous." He did not need to encounter all saber-toothed tigers to make that judgment, and a good thing too. The fewer close calls with a predator it took for us to develop the general rule that they are dangerous, the greater the chances we'd live to form that rule and to leave heirs. When it comes to inductive thinking, Hamlet was right—we are the paragon of animals. The problem is that we often apply inductive thinking to situations that require deductive reasoning. Here's an example:

Please take a moment to read the following brief passage about a fictional character named Linda:

Linda is thirty-one years old, single, outspoken, and very bright. She majored in philosophy. As a student, she was deeply concerned with issues of discrimination and social justice, and also participated in antinuclear demonstrations.

Now rank the following statements in order of probability. That is, put the number 1 against the statement you think is most likely, a 2 next to the statement you believe is second in probability, and so on:

1. Linda is a teacher in an elementary school.   _____
2. Linda works in a bookstore and takes yoga classes.   _____
3. Linda is active in the feminist movement.   _____
4. Linda is a psychiatric social worker.   _____
5. Linda is a member of the League of Women Voters.   _____
6. Linda is a bank teller.   _____
7. Linda is an insurance salesperson.   _____

8. Linda is a bank teller and is active in the feminist movement.   _____

This is a sample problem developed by two famous psychologists, Daniel Kahneman and Amos Tversky.[4] Take a look at your answers to items 6 and 8. Did you rate 8 as more likely than 6? If so, you are in good company—the majority of people do. But doing so breaks the rules of logic. Why? Because there cannot be more bank tellers who are active in the feminist movement than there are bank tellers, just as there cannot be more people with brown hair than there are people. We make this mistake again because we cannot shut down our inductive thinking. We build a mental picture of what Linda is like, which includes her political beliefs. And even though we're asked specifically to judge probability, we instead judge on the basis of how similar each description is to what we've already learned about Linda and the image we've formed of her. Being active in the feminist movement and a bank teller fits better with our image of who Linda is than her just being a bank teller.

Normally our inductive processes are useful—they are valuable rules of thumb, or heuristics. But as we've seen, we sometimes try to use them, inappropriately, in situations that call for deduction instead. And even when induction is the right process to apply, we often get it wrong.

Ask people whether sharks or lightning strikes kill more people each year, and most will answer "sharks." But even if we look at the two major "shark attack" states, California and Florida, it's clearly false—in the period 1959–1990, 331 people were killed by lightning in those states compared with only ten shark-related deaths. How do we build such a false picture of the world? The media pays much more attention to shark attacks because of the primeval interest we show in them. So when it comes time to make a judgment, we can recall many more victims of shark attacks than of lightning strikes. In a nutshell, our mistaken beliefs about the world may cause us to underestimate the probabilities of real threats, leading us to fail to act in adaptive, preventive ways.

This is what the thinking traps are all about. Over time, using induction, we develop general rules about the world and ourselves. When we jump to a conclusion, we are applying that rule to a new situation. Personalizers have as the rule of thumb that they themselves are generally to blame for problems. For externalizers, it's other people that cause them setbacks. And of course, overgeneralizing is exactly the trap we fall into when we take one of our inductive rules and apply it where it doesn't belong. We continue to fall into these traps because, by and large, induction is useful. But we should be more aware of our shortcomings—that we may not have all the information in our reach—and we should not be so confident that we have considered the problem comprehensively. Problems arise when we allocate our resources based on these mistaken judgments. Our resilience is diminished when we commit ourselves to action based on false belief.

This is where the skill of Avoiding Thinking Traps comes in. The skill doesn't deny that building theories about the world and ourselves through induction is useful. Rather, it helps us recognize the mistakes we make most often in the inductive process and to become better at it.

Using the Skill of Avoiding Thinking Traps in Your Own Life

We'll model the skill of Avoiding Thinking Traps by showing you how Gary, the mind-reading manager, applied it after the conflict with Maria. Most people begin the process of mastering these skills by using them after the fact, rather than in the moment of the adversity. As with any new skill, there is a learning curve. Often it's easier to practice the skills after your emotions have calmed and some time has passed. You wouldn't teach yourself to drive on a freeway during rush hour, and you shouldn't teach yourself these skills when you are overcome by emotion. Our recommendation is to try the skill in a post hoc manner half a dozen times and then start to apply it as soon after the adversity as possible. Within a few weeks, you'll find that you can identify your thinking traps almost immediately.

Most of the resilience skills begin by breaking the situation into A, B, and C. You can choose a recent adversity from your life and work it through as we model the skill with Gary. When you first start using the skills, you can use pen and paper. In Chapter 9 we show you how to master the skills in the moment, in your head. Back to Gary. He wrote:

ADVERSITY: I returned the next morning to the office and found out that Maria had not accomplished any of the work I had asked her to complete in my e-mail. [This is a good description of the A. It's objective and specific and is not infiltrated by his beliefs. Check to make sure you haven't exaggerated your adversity or let your beliefs alter the objective description of the situation.]

BELIEFS: Maria knew the time pressure we were under, but she clearly just didn't give a damn. I can't believe how irresponsible she is. She obviously has no integrity and is not committed to this office. She's not the kind of person I want working with me. [This is a good description of Gary's beliefs. It sounds real, not censored. Make sure your ticker-tape beliefs are what you actually said to yourself in the heat of the moment, not a sanitized version.]

CONSEQUENCES: I felt unbelievably angry and I cut her off each time she tried to offer an explanation. I could see that she was becoming more and more upset, but, frankly, I simply didn't care. After venting at her for about five minutes, I told her that I was going to give her work to Janice to complete. For the rest of the day I avoided her, but I could tell she was having a hard time and that everyone else in the office was siding with her. All in all, it was a really good example of really bad management. [Gary did a good job describing both his emotional and behavioral consequences. He also described how his beliefs affected the other people in the office. If you find it hard to recall exactly how you were feeling, use your knowledge of the B–C connections to help you ballpark your emotional consequences.]

After Gary finished analyzing the ABC of the situation, he was ready to look more closely at his beliefs. Gary checked his ticker tape against a list he'd made of thinking traps. As you practice this skill, you may want to have such a list handy. Most people, however, find that after using the skill for a few weeks, they know the two or three thinking traps they fall into most and just focus on those.

As Gary went through the list of thinking traps, he found that he had committed three. Can you identify them? Of course, he expected Maria to read his mind—we noted that earlier in the chapter. Maria didn't know about the new deadline because he didn't inform her, yet he expected her to act with this information in mind. We also discussed his jumping to a conclusion—when Maria failed to do the work, he concluded that she lacked integrity and was not committed to the office. You may have noticed that there is a third thinking trap embedded in his jump to a conclusion. Look closely at what he attributes Maria's behavior to: personality flaws, such as a lack of integrity and a lack of commitment. He did not consider specific, changeable causes, such as as poor time management or difficulty following instructions. At this point in the situation, Gary does not have any facts about what happened, but his mind automatically, reflexively assassinated her character. He overgeneralized. In your real-life example, what assumptions and judgments did you make automatically?

Simple Questions to Avoid Thinking Traps

You will learn later in the book how to correct these thinking errors by testing the accuracy of your beliefs and evaluating their usefulness. But even before you learn those skills, you can ask yourself some simple questions to climb out of the traps you fall into.

If you tend to jump to conclusions, you know that speed is your enemy. Your goal should be to slow down. Then ask yourself what evidence you've based your conclusion on. Are you certain, or are you guessing?

When reviewing moments when you're prone to tunnel vision, you need to refocus yourself on the big picture. Ask yourself: What is a fair assessment of the entire situation? What is the big picture? How important is this one aspect to the big picture? These questions will help you broaden your perspective beyond the tunnel.

If you find that you overgeneralize, you need to look more closely at the behaviors involved. Ask yourself: Is there a narrower explanation than the one I've assumed to be true? Is there a specific behavior that explains the situation? What does impugning my (or someone else's) character buy me? Is it logical to indict my (or another's) character and/or worth as a human based on this specific event?

Do you magnify the bad and minimize the good? If so, then you need to strive for balance. Ask yourself: Were there any good things that happened? Did I do anything well? Alternatively, if you tend to dismiss the negative, ask yourself: Am I overlooking any problems? Were there any negative elements that I am dismissing the importance of?

If you are a personalizer, you need to learn to look outward. Ask yourself: Did anyone or anything else contribute to this situation? How much of the problem is due to me and how much is due to others?

On the flip side, if you habitually externalize, you need to start holding yourself accountable. Ask yourself: What did I do to contribute to this situation? How much of the problem is due to others, and how much is due to me?

Mind readers need to learn to speak up and ask questions of others. But first, ask yourself: Did I make my beliefs or feelings known directly and clearly? Did I convey all of the pertinent information? Am I expecting the other person to work hard at figuring out my needs or goals?

Finally, if you lapse into emotional reasoning, you need to practice separating your feelings from the facts. Ask yourself: Have there been times when my feelings didn't accurately reflect the facts of a situation? What questions must I ask to know the facts?

Remember, you'll fall into thinking traps most often when you're dealing with a button-push adversity, so listen closely to your beliefs when you're faced with stressors you know you're susceptible to. For the next few weeks, set the goal of detecting patterns in your thinking and noticing what your thinking traps do to your mood and behavior. As you become better at detecting thinking traps, practice catching your thinking errors in real time and try to ask yourself some of the questions just noted as soon as you identify the trap you fell into. The better you are able to avoid these thinking traps, the easier it will be to hold yourself back from those inaccurate assumptions that are so costly to your resilience.

The Next Step

In this chapter we've detailed the eight major thinking traps that tax our resilience, helped you identify the two or three you make most often, and provided you with a few quick methods of getting out of the traps. We've looked closely at why people prefer inductive thinking, building general rules about the world, and how while this style usually serves us well in the world, it can lead us to fall into the thinking traps. We've looked at some specific examples of induction gone awry, respresentativeness and availability, and we've considered some of the factors that keep our thinking traps in place. Now it's time to move from the level of ticker-tape beliefs to the deeper beliefs and values that affect our emotions and behavior—and that may be placing a ceiling on your resilience.

CHAPTER SIX

Detecting
Icebergs

Have you ever had a time when your emotions seemed too intense—you felt horribly guilty rather than mildly so or deeply depressed rather than a little sad? Or have you ever been surprised by an emotion because it seemed to be the wrong one—you felt angry when the situation should have left you feeling guilty or were red-faced with embarrassment when you ought to have been red-faced with anger? Maybe there have been times when your *behavior* seemed overboard or out of line—a friend teases you in front of a group and you refuse to speak to her for days, or you blow up at your spouse for leaving his dishes in the sink—but you just couldn't help it?

Sometimes your ticker-tape beliefs don't explain the intensity of your reaction to a given situation. When that happens, it's a sign that you are being affected by an *underlying belief*—a deeply held belief about how the world ought to operate and how you feel you ought to operate within that world. Examples of underlying beliefs include "I should succeed at everything I put my mind to" or "Getting emotional is a sign of weakness." These deeper motivations and values often drive us and determine how we respond to adversity. And since these underlying beliefs—or icebergs, as we call them—are usually outside our awareness, deep beneath the surface of our consciousness, we need a special skill to detect them.

Mastering the skill of Detecting Icebergs is an important step in increasing your emotion regulation, empathy, and reaching out scores on your RQ profile. More important, it's a skill that will significantly improve your relationships. Most of the "personality" clashes that occur at work are due to differences in iceberg beliefs, and these beliefs are also responsible for many of the rifts between couples. By using the skill of Detecting Icebergs, you will better understand your core values and motivations and those of the significant others in your life.

Surface Beliefs versus Underlying Beliefs

We've explained that ticker-tape beliefs are your in-the-moment beliefs about an adversity and that they drive your emotions and behaviors. You can think of ticker-tape beliefs as *surface beliefs*, because they float on the surface of your awareness. Even though you may not be aware of your ticker-tape beliefs in any given moment, you can shift your attention to them with relative ease and identify what it is that you're saying to yourself. Don't confuse surface, however, with superficial or irrelevant; in most situations, your surface beliefs hold the key to why you react to things the way you do. But sometimes your ticker-tape beliefs *don't* explain your reactions. When that's the case, it means that you're responding not to your ticker-tape beliefs but to your underlying beliefs—fundamental, deep-rooted beliefs about who you are and your place in the world. Underlying beliefs are general rules about how the world ought to be and how you should operate within that world. Because they're general rules, they apply to many different adversities. And since they are general rules, once you've identified and challenged them, you'll become more resilient in many areas of your life.

You use Detecting Icebergs to bring your underlying beliefs to the surface so that you can evaluate them and, in essence, determine what's making you "tick." Once you've done that, you can decide whether these underlying beliefs still work for you, or if you'd be happier and more productive with a different, perhaps more useful worldview.

Iceberg Beliefs

Some underlying beliefs are adaptive; they help us to behave in ways that facilitate success and happiness. "It's important to treat others with respect and dignity," "Being honest matters to me," and "I will not give up as soon as something becomes difficult for me" are underlying beliefs that will serve you well. But not all underlying beliefs are helpful; many minimize our effectiveness in responding to adversity and may even bring on serious psychological disorders. Mark (a.k.a. "anger man") has a deep belief: "People can't be trusted. They'll take advantage of me at every opportunity." This underlying belief informs many of his surface beliefs by biasing his interpretation of events. We call these underlying beliefs iceberg beliefs because they are fixed, frozen beliefs that you don't often consciously think about and since they lurk beneath the surface of awareness, they can sink you. Iceberg beliefs tend to be general propositions or rules for living that apply to more than the situation at hand. "The world is a dangerous place," "People must respect me at all times," "Women should be kind and supportive," "A man doesn't let his emotions show" are examples of iceberg beliefs. In fact, many people have iceberg beliefs that fall into one of three general categories or themes: achievement, acceptance, and control.[1]

ACHIEVEMENT

Do any of these beliefs ring true for you: "Being successful is what matters most," "Failure is a sign of weakness," or "I must never give up"? If so, you're probably an achievement-oriented person. People who are achievement oriented tend to have an underlying belief that success is the most important thing in life. Naturally, they have a strong desire to succeed: They set high standards for themselves and are overly focused on their mistakes and imperfections. Stu, a regional branch manager we worked with, believed that "There is nothing worse than failure." This iceberg belief almost cost him his job because his desire to succeed at all costs actually made him a poor leader. As a regional branch manager, he was expected to model perseverance and initiative and to help those in the ranks develop their skills. Stu was supportive when his team was doing well, but when people struggled, his fear of failure got in his way. Rather than being encouraging and helping team members to understand what was going wrong and correct it, Stu became angry and critical. Instead of working with them, he would take over the project because that was the only way he knew to ensure success. But, of course, that strategy was incompatible with his job description—he wasn't helping his team develop and grow. Instead, he would step in and push people to the side. Stu was so threatened by failure that he doomed himself to fail as a leader.

Iceberg beliefs around perfectionism are also common for achievement-oriented people, and they often suffer from tunnel vision, one of the thinking traps. Laura, a college student we coached, believed "Anything less than perfect is a failure." Despite her ambition and desire to do well at Penn, she spent most of her time procrastinating and avoiding her studies and assignments. Even after beginning a project, her tendency toward tunnel vision made it hard for her to continue. If she didn't like the first draft of a paper she wrote, she would find it almost impossible to continue to work on it; all she could see was what wasn't working, and none of what was, so her impulse was to just throw in the towel. Not a formula for success. In fact, by the end of her sophomore year, she had two "incompletes" on her transcript because her perfectionism drove her to give up rather than persist in challenging courses. Laura was confused by her behavior and didn't understand why college had gone so badly for her. We asked Laura to tell us her ticker-tape beliefs as she set herself the task of beginning a history paper. Here's what she said: "I want to write a really great paper. I want to impress Professor Williams and write the best paper in the class." Laura couldn't see how those desires could lead to such intense anxiety that she'd do anything to avoid writing. (She told us that the only upside to her procrastination was that she had the best-organized closet on campus.) Laura was confused for good reason. Her surface beliefs—the ticker-tape beliefs—didn't explain her emotions and behaviors. We taught Laura to use the skill of Detecting Icebergs, and after becoming aware of her iceberg belief—"Anything less than perfect is a failure"—she could see what was paralyzing her. Armed with this understanding, Laura was in a position to take control of the problem.

ACCEPTANCE

How familiar are you with these beliefs: "What matters most in life is being loved," "It's my job to please people and make them happy," or "I want people to always think the best of me"? These beliefs revolve around the issue of acceptance, the need to be liked, accepted, praised, and included by others. People who are governed by an underlying need for acceptance are more likely to notice, and then overreact to, interpersonal slights and conflicts. Acceptance-oriented people tend to jump to conclusions and mind read. In ambiguous situations—a boss who doesn't say hello, a friend who doesn't return a call—they assume they've fallen from favor, which works to reinforce their iceberg belief.

James works in customer service and operates with the iceberg belief that, "If I'm not liked by someone, then that means there is something very wrong with me." Can you imagine a worse fit? A customer service representative who can't stand rejection is as disastrous as a professional athlete who shies away from competition. When a customer treats him poorly, James assumes he's done something wrong and wastes a lot of time trying to win the customer over. Because James is focused on being liked rather than on selling a service, his approach on the phone does not work. Customers initially enjoy his laid-back, personal style, but as he becomes more informal and inappropriate—joking with them in the hopes of winning their favor or asking personal questions to get to know them better—they lose patience and end the call. When colleagues are standoffish, he tries so hard to please them that he develops the reputation as a brown-noser. You can see the irony. His desperate need to be liked drives him to act in ways that cause people not to like him.

Carol, a chef, is driven by the underlying belief that "I deserve to be praised for what I do," which leads her to boast about her accomplishments and narcissistically focus on herself. When she was recruited to work at the hot new restaurant in town, Carol recounted every detail of the conversation to each of her friends. By Carol's account, they shared her excitement initially but then became jealous of her success and refused to talk about it anymore. From her friends' perspective, they were genuinely pleased for Carol but grew tired of her incessant repeating of the story. In a similar vein, Carol's relentless need for approval and praise taxes her relationships. When we met Carol, her live-in boyfriend was in the process of moving out. He told us, "She's warm and charismatic and it's obvious that she wants to make it work, but I simply can't give her what she needs. If I don't give her 100 percent of my attention, whenever she wants it, she sulks and withdraws. When our friends try to talk about themselves instead of just listening with rapt attention to 'The Carol Show,' she lashes out at them and accuses them of being jealous. She just doesn't see how her neediness is driving us all away." Carol's relationships tend not to last.

CONTROL

Do you hold these beliefs: "Only weak people can't solve their own problems," or "Asking for help shows that you're not in charge," or "If you're not in control then you're a weakling"? People who are control oriented have underlying beliefs about the importance of being in charge and in control of events. People who have strong iceberg beliefs around control tend to have a heightened sensitivity to experiences in which they are not in charge or are not able to change the course of outcomes. Although most people find it uncomfortable to feel out of control (except for short periods of time, like on a roller coaster or when making love), for "control freaks," as they're sometimes referred to, the experience is overwhelming because they ascribe lack of control to personal failure. A Philadelphia firefighter we spoke with described intense guilt for not having helped enough in the weeks after the Twin Towers fell. As we worked with him, two iceberg beliefs emerged that contributed to his guilt: "I must always be in charge" and "Being passive is a sign of weakness and cowardice." These iceberg beliefs motivated him in a variety of ways. Certainly his choice of profession was partly informed by his strong desire for control. By fighting fires, he's able to take charge and be in control in a situation that would leave most of us feeling helpless and powerless. Initially following the terrorism, his beliefs around control helped him organize other local firefighters to aid in the relief effort. But despite helping out at Ground Zero, he believed that he wasn't doing enough and that it indicated a flaw in his character. Like Laura, the firefighter felt confused by his reaction. Many of the people in his company were shaken by the tragedy and felt compelled to find ways to help. Many felt an underlying guilt when they left New York City. But for him, the guilt was pervasive and deep. It kept him up at night and interfered with his ability to concentrate. It consumed him. As is the case with most iceberg beliefs, the firefighter's were overly rigid and had begun to hurt him more than they helped him.

The cost-benefit ratio of iceberg beliefs is important to assess. Indeed, after you have identified your iceberg beliefs, the fundamental questions you must ask yourself are: What is this belief costing me? How is it helping me? and How can I change it so that I reduce the costs and increase the benefits? As these questions imply, not all iceberg beliefs are always counterproductive and harmful. Sometimes they serve you quite well in some areas of your life but hold you back in others. Jill, an office manager, is a good example of this. Jill keeps her office organized. Her iceberg belief, that "Disorder is a sign of bad character" serves her well, and she excels professionally because her job rewards the same behaviors that her iceberg belief produces. Then Jill landed a second job—motherhood. Dirty diapers. Finger painting. Routines that changed so quickly they could hardly be called routines. The mess and chaos that came with an infant clashed with Jill's iceberg beliefs about disorder, making the already tense and frantic few months of motherhood even harder. We helped Jill to tweak it rather than eliminate her value of orderliness. Does disorder really equate with bad character? Jill, like many control-oriented people, was falling into the thinking trap of overgeneralization. When she felt out of control, she acted as if being out of control indicated that she was a flawed human being. As we were helping Jill to evaluate the logic of her iceberg belief, we also helped her to articulate other values she holds, such as being a calm and loving mother, which may require a higher tolerance of mess. Jill was able to recast her value—reshape her iceberg belief—to "I like to keep things organized and orderly. I also like to feel relaxed and enjoy my children. So I will keep things reasonably, rather than perfectly, ordered." As we will ask of you, we challenged Jill to keep the baby but throw out the bath water.

What Is Your Theme?

How would you describe yourself? Are you more achievement oriented, acceptance oriented, or control oriented? When you find yourself shrinking from opportunities, is it out of a fear of failure, concerns over rejection, or worries about not being in control? When you have problems in your relationships, is it because you are so focused on your career that you don't make enough time for your personal life, or are you too needy or overly controlling? As a parent, do your child's successes and failures impact you as strongly as your own? Do your feelings get sorely hurt when your children say they hate you? Do the normal fluctuations in routine that come with family life cause you excessive anxiety or anger? Of course, these themes are not mutually exclusive, nor are they exhaustive. Some people are as focused on acceptance as achievement, and, as we will illustrate, problems can arise when two iceberg beliefs clash. Others may have iceberg beliefs specifically around gender roles. As we continue with the last of the know thyself skills, the challenge for you is to develop a fine-grained picture of yourself so that you can better understand what motivates you.

How Are Icebergs Formed?

Perhaps you are wondering where your iceberg beliefs come from. How are they formed, and why do you have control-oriented beliefs but your spouse has achievement-oriented ones? Both of us have met people with hypochondriasis—a disorder in which people believe that they're sick but show no signs of real medical illness. In every case that we have seen, these people had a specific, common history: Each of them grew up in households with sick relatives. Perhaps a terminally ill grandparent came to live with them. Perhaps one of their parents underwent an extensive series of medical tests over a prolonged period. They observed their parents constantly monitoring the symptoms of illness, scanning for any new development, and consequently, as adults, they constantly monitor their own physical health, so hyperaware of every twinge and ache that they detect symptoms that are not there.

Just as hypochondriacs learn their behavior from their parents, so do all of us, as children, develop iceberg beliefs from our families. There we learn, rather than inherit, the worldview—the core values—of our parents. Children absorb messages from those around them about how one should behave and how the world should be. Imagine that your parents were particularly focused on the issue of respect. They continually reinforced the importance of respecting your elders, and whenever you were the slightest bit disrespectful, you were punished. As a consequence, you might have developed a kind of "respect radar"—you scan the environment for examples of the violation of your right to be respected and feel angry each time you find one. Or perhaps you were privy to ongoing discussions about how best to care for an aging grandparent and sensed the heavy guilt that your parents felt because of the quality of care they could provide. As an adult, then, you might be overly sensitive to violating the rights of others and therefore experience a lot of guilt. Perhaps you often witnessed your father's frustration when he couldn't master something perfectly and thus developed the iceberg belief that unless something is done perfectly, it's a failure. Did you grow up in a household where you were told to put on clean underwear before you left the house, just in case you were in an accident and have to be rushed to the emergency room? If you were sent recurrent signals that the family name is to be protected at all times—that embarrassing the family was unforgivable—then it makes sense that you would emerge from your family with a heightened sensitivity for times when you did not measure up to other people. As a result, you may fail to take on opportunities for fear of failing and being embarrassed.

How Iceberg Beliefs Can Hurt You

Four problems can arise from iceberg beliefs, each of which will undermine your resilience:

- ✦ Iceberg beliefs can become activated at unexpected times, which leads to out-of-proportion emotions and reactions.
- ✦ Their activation might lead to emotions and behaviors that, although not extreme, are mismatched to the situation.

✦ Contradictory iceberg beliefs can make it hard to make decisions.
✦ Iceberg beliefs can become too rigid, which causes you to fall into the same emotional patterns over and over again.

PROBLEMS 1 AND 2: ICEBERG BELIEFS CAN LEAD TO B-C DISCONNECTS

"Your mug is on my table. Your wet mug is on my nice wood table. Didn't you see the pile of coasters sitting there? I don't get it, Guy. Help me to understand why you would put your wet mug on my wood table without using a coaster. Really, help me to understand this!" These lines were delivered with a snide inquisitiveness most often reserved for courtroom melodramas. The speaker was struggling to maintain composure, but she was galled. For his part, Guy was rendered mute by his fiancée's rabid attack. There is no polite way to say this, in that moment, Karen was off her rocker.

The infamous "coaster incident" happened ten years ago but remains one of our favorite examples of what we call a B–C disconnect—when your ticker tape cannot explain the intensity of your emotions and behaviors. In this situation, the adversity (A) was that Karen's soon-to-be husband had put down his coffee mug on top of her wood coffee table without using a coaster. When she saw this, she became irate and began an interrogation that left him speechless and worried. As she was haranguing her fiancée, at some level she felt equally dismayed and confused. According to the logic of ABC, her ticker tape ought to explain the consequences—her tirade. But when she listened to her ticker tape ("He knows I like people to use coasters. He sees the coasters but he still isn't using one. That's just wrong"), what she heard was too anemic—it didn't explain the intensity of her reaction. The ticker tape had a clear violation-of-rights essence, which should have led to irritation or annoyance, but it didn't explain ferocious anger.

In B–C disconnects, the emotions seem out of proportion, the behaviors seem inappropriate, and even after you've identified your ticker tape, you are still puzzled by your reactions. When this happens, it's because an iceberg belief has been activated and violated.

When we teach the skill of Detecting Icebergs in our corporate seminars, not surprisingly, some people are hesitant to share examples of when they behaved unreasonably. Fortunately, usually one person is willing to put him- or herself on the line, and once the first person offers their own "coaster incident," the stories flow. We had just gotten to that awkward moment in the workshop when John, a senior manager in a Fortune 500 consulting firm, filled the void. John is well educated, highly motivated, and accomplished, but he did have a persistent adversity that left him puzzled and frustrated. Occasionally his wife would ask him to do some handyman work around the house, such as fixing a leaky faucet or touching up a paint job. He'd don his tool belt and beam with enthusiasm like a little kid. But almost inevitably the smile would disappear and John would find himself becoming more and more frustrated with the job, with himself, and with his wife. John told us about a typical incident that had occurred the previous Sunday. "My wife asked me to tack up a couple of blinds in a guest room. Sounded easy. I set to work with the tape measure and level, carefully penciled in screw positions, and drilled away. When it was done, I climbed off the stepladder and took a couple of steps back to admire my handiwork just as my wife came into the room. Immediately I could see that the blinds weren't straight. The left side was considerably lower than the right, and I knew that she could see it too. She looked at me and smiled and told me it was a great job, but the expression on her face said it all. She was disappointed in the work and disappointed in me."

John's adversity was that the blinds were not level. We asked him to tell us about his ticker tape as he noticed his wife's expression. "I thought to myself, 'I don't need this. I'd much rather be relaxing then taking care of projects for her. She should at least have the courtesy to be grateful.' " What would you expect John to feel and do given this ticker tape? How would you categorize his beliefs in terms of the B–C connections? He believes that his wife is being ungrateful and discourteous, both of which are violation-of-rights beliefs. We'd expect, therefore, for him to be angry. But notice how John explains his reaction: "I work most Saturdays, so Sunday is the only day we really get time together. But I felt so down I couldn't face her. As soon as I saw the disappointment in her face, I just had to get out of there. I headed to the garage to tinker with an old car, and I spent the rest of the day avoiding her. I just couldn't get past the humiliation I felt."

In the "coaster incident," an iceberg belief—we haven't disclosed which one yet—was activated and led to a disconnect in terms of the intensity of Karen's reactions. In John's situation, an iceberg belief was activated and led to a disconnect between his ticker tape and the *quality* of emotion he experiences—he felt humiliation rather than anger. Detecting Icebergs is used to evaluate and avoid both of these situations.

PROBLEM 3: CLASHING ICEBERG BELIEFS CAN MAKE IT HARD TO MAKE DECISIONS

So far we have explored situations in which one iceberg belief is activated and negatively affects one's emotions and behaviors. Many times, however, a situation leads to the activation of more than one iceberg belief, and often they are in conflict. Jane provides an example of the decision-making paralysis that can result when an achievement-oriented iceberg belief clashes with an acceptance-oriented iceberg belief.

Jane is a high school principal in a large urban school district and has two young children. Jane asked for help because she had been unable to make an important decision and was starting to feel discouraged. We asked Jane to tell us about the situation.

"Our current superintendent is going to retire next year. I'm being encouraged to apply for the position. Everyone thought I would leap at the opportunity and so did I, but I just can't seem to make up my mind about whether I ought to apply. One morning I'm certain I will but by the end of the day I'm certain I won't. It's exhausting! And it's taking away energy I need for other problems that I have to deal with."

Initially Jane was unable to articulate what made this decision seem so complex. But as we worked with her, it became clear that two iceberg beliefs had been activated simultaneously. Jane had constructed her professional life around her core belief that women should seek out the same opportunities and develop their careers as fully as men. This was not a conscious force in her life, but as we explored her career decisions in the past and focused on the beliefs that informed her decisions, Jane discovered that the iceberg belief "Women should be as ambitious and successful as men" operated in most instances. She described how she grew up in a family of strong, career-minded women. Jane's mother was a successful biochemist who made a name for herself as a researcher. Her grandmother took over the family grocery business when her husband died unexpectedly. Under her grandmother's leadership, the grocery business grew from a corner store to several locations throughout the county. The women in Jane's family were a tight group, and the girls in the family, with the exception of one sister, learned that the surest way to shine was to do well at school and seek out opportunities that were nontraditional for women.

Jane's underlying belief about ambition explained not only her own career trajectory but also why at times she became hypercritical of her sister and close female friends who seemed content with either part-time work or work in traditionally female careers.

The activation of her iceberg belief regarding women and work explains the pull she feels to apply for the position of superintendent. What explains her hesitation? Jane described her great admiration for her mother and her grandmother and their success in traditionally male fields, but Jane also felt lonely as a child and deeply longed for more of her mother's time. She remembered walking her siblings home from school to their empty house. Jane's mother would always leave a note for Jane explaining how to heat the dinner and telling her what time she would be home, with little pictures on the bottom of a mother stick figure holding the hand of her stick-figure daughter. She would end the note by telling Jane how much she loved her and would describe something special they would do together on the weekend. Jane saved each note in a box. When she missed her mom, she would look at the stick-figure drawings and think about the fun they would have on Saturday. As she talked with us about these memories, another iceberg belief emerged: "My children should come first." Now we could understand her dilemma.

These two iceberg beliefs—"Women should be as ambitious and successful as men" and "My children should come first"—were activated simultaneously by the opportunity to apply for a prestigious job. The former belief led Jane to focus on the many exciting aspects of the job and the increased power she would have in shaping the direction of education. The latter belief led Jane to focus on the costs that her family, particularly her children, would incur if she became superintendent. Jane would have to work longer hours, travel more, and attend meetings that would take her out of the house in the evening. She understood that as a new superintendent she would feel a lot of stress, which would affect her parenting. Jane was unable to make a decision because it seemed to her that each decision would contradict one of her core values. Jane's clashing iceberg beliefs centered on beliefs about work versus family. This is one of the most common clashes we see, particularly, although not exclusively, for women.

PROBLEM 4: ICEBERG BELIEFS CAN CAUSE YOU TO OVEREXPERIENCE CERTAIN EMOTIONS

The final problem with iceberg beliefs is that they cause you to experience the same emotion over and over again—even in situations that don't warrant it. That is, iceberg beliefs cause you to overexperience certain emotions and underexperience others. Emotionally resilient people feel it all. They feel anger, sadness, loneliness, happiness, guilt, pride, embarrassment, joy, jealousy, excitement—but they feel these emotions at the appropriate time and to the appropriate degree. Less resilient people tend to get stuck in one emotion, and that compromises their ability to respond productively to adversity.

Mark gets angry far too often. He operates with the iceberg belief "You can't trust most people," which leads to ticker tapes that bring on anger. The angrier he is, the less effective he is at work and the harder it is for those who love him to continue to love him.

Following is a typical day for Mark. During breakfast he notices an unpaid bill that his wife was supposed to take care of. Perhaps because of a bad night of sleep, or residue from an earlier fight, Mark's "People cannot be trusted" belief is easily activated. It colors the way he interprets her oversight. He thinks, "I can't rely on her to do anything." Mark leaves for work feeling irritated. Once activated, his iceberg belief becomes a radar that scans the environment for other examples of violation. This doesn't happen at a conscious level—to the contrary, the radar's operation is subtle and stealthy.

Mark hits traffic on his way in and rushes to his office to make a 9:00 A.M. meeting with a colleague. He arrives at nine on the dot to find a voice mail from his colleague telling him that he got hung up across town and will be twenty minutes late. Mark's "People cannot be trusted" radar begins to beep. His ticker tape reads: "Here I am rushing around to be on time and he strolls in at his leisure. That's not right." On another day, Mark might see the delay as no big deal. Today, however, it registers as a clear violation because his iceberg belief, activated earlier, has primed him to interpret this trifling event as a motivated offense.

Why Is It So Hard to Turn Off Our Radar?

You might be wondering why Mark can't simply shut off his overactive "People can't be trusted" radar. Can't he just tell himself to stop being so negative and cynical? Well, the problem is that once a person's radar is activated, two processes—assimilation and the confirmation bias—make it very hard to deactivate it. Cognitive science has demonstrated that if someone's radar is on full alert, as Mark's is in this case, then even an event that the person normally would see as positive gets reinterpreted or distorted to make it fit his or her perception of the world. This process is known as assimilation.

How does assimilation affect Mark? Well, imagine that as Mark waits for his colleague to arrive, his assistant hands him a memo that outlines a new and improved company policy regarding flex-time. Mark had been vocal in expressing the need for more flexible work schedules and ought to view this policy as an improvement, as did most people in his office. Instead, Mark derides the policy as insubstantial change. He says to himself,

"This is just another example of them paying lip service to our concerns. They act as if they care about us, but it's clear that they really don't." Although he didn't do this on purpose, Mark interpreted what should have been a positive event in a way that kept his "People can't be trusted" belief activated rather than facilitating its deactivation.

The second process that makes it hard for us to turn off our radar, known as the confirmation bias, is the fact that all of us are much better at noticing and remembering evidence that confirms our beliefs than we are at noticing and remembering evidence that proves that our beliefs are wrong. We call this the Velcro-Teflon effect because we are Velcro for evidence that supports our beliefs—it sticks to us—but we are Teflon for evidence that contradicts them—it just slides right off. Here's an example of the confirmation bias at work.

Wanda's marriage ended a year ago despite the couple's best efforts at making it work. Although the divorce was a mutual decision and proceeded with civility, Wanda emerged from the experience deeply concerned that she would not be able to find another person with whom to share her life. When we met Wanda she had recently started dating, and from her perspective, it wasn't going very well. Wanda's iceberg beliefs were about acceptance; she believed that "When people really get to know me, they stop liking me." We asked Wanda to describe to us her latest dating experience. "I had gone out with Todd several times. We were spending a lot of time together, and we seemed to be getting along real well. But then he called and told me that he wanted to take a few days to get his head together, and the first thing that popped into my head was 'Here we go again. As soon as a man gets to know me, he runs away.' " We asked her what evidence she had that her beliefs were true. "It's pretty obvious. We'd been spending almost every day together, and then suddenly he tells me he wants to slow the pace down. I called him on Tuesday and he didn't call back until Wednesday night. Oh, and when I ran into him at a restaurant, he didn't ask me to join him and his friends."

If we accept Wanda's account at face value, then it does indeed look like her initial beliefs were accurate—at least in this case. In fact, if we had a video of her life, everything she described would be there. The tape, however, would also show:

✦ A few weeks ago Todd explained over coffee that he's just getting over a bad breakup and doesn't want to let his feelings about that interfere with getting to know her.

✦ He didn't return Wanda's call Tuesday night, but he e-mailed her on Tuesday as he does every day.

✦ Although he didn't ask her to join his friends at the restaurant, he did sit down at her table for fifteen minutes and looked genuinely delighted to have run into her.

Wanda only sees the evidence that supports her belief, so it continues to exert its hold on her. When we describe the confirmation bias to parents, teachers, and employers, often we are asked whether the person is aware that he or she is noticing only the evidence that agrees with the iceberg beliefs. Others suggest that the confirmation bias is a fancy term for what's more often described as contrariness, stubbornness, or manipulation. Parents describe stories of sulky children who steadfastly maintain that their teacher hates them despite what the parent sees as clear evidence to the contrary. Bosses offer accounts of aggressive employees who conveniently see hostility directed at them whenever they are aggressive toward others. It's important to remember that the confirmation bias is not happening at a conscious level. Certainly there are times when people set out to prove themselves correct, but the confirmation bias is not motivated or planned. It's unconscious, which is what makes it so difficult to overcome.

How to Detect Your Iceberg Beliefs

The goal of Detecting Icebergs is to make you aware of the iceberg beliefs that are:

✦ Unwittingly causing you to overreact or react in a way that is different from what your ticker tape would predict (like Karen)
✦ Undermining your decision making (like Jane)
✦ Causing you to overexperience a particular emotion (like Mark)

Why is it important to recognize these iceberg beliefs? Until you have identified the belief that is driving your behavior, you are helpless to evaluate it and, if necessary, change it. If you're concerned about the way you react to certain events, it makes no sense to apply the change skills to your ticker-tape beliefs if they are not the beliefs driving your reaction. It's impossible for you to gain control over your emotions and behaviors, and increase your resilience, until you have insight into what is causing your response. Remember, insight is our goal in the know thyself skills, but now we want to apply that insight toward effective change.

In this section, you're going to answer a series of questions that were designed to help bring your iceberg beliefs into awareness. The purpose of each question is to delve further beneath the surface than you did when analyzing your ABC connections. As you plunge deeper and deeper, you will find that the beliefs you uncover become bigger and broader, like an iceberg whose true size is invisible beneath the water's surface. At this level, your beliefs become less and less specific to the situation at hand and begin to sound like basic values, or rules for living. The questions don't challenge the accuracy of your beliefs, but rather they guide you in uncovering the meaning and importance of the beliefs to you. This is crucial. Later you will use Skills 4 and 5—Challenging Beliefs and Putting It in Perspective—to test the accuracy and usefulness of your iceberg beliefs; right now the goal is to clarify for yourself what your iceberg beliefs are.

We should warn you that Detecting Icebergs is one of the most challenging skills. In our seminar, we notice a lot of squirming and an increased need to check voice mail after we've explained the skill and set the participants the task of trying it out. In fact, when we ask the participants to tell us their ticker tape, we hear things like "I don't know if I want to know my iceberg belief," "Maybe I'm not aware of it for a reason and I should just let it stay down there." It is often unnerving to explore deeply held beliefs. Unnerving, but necessary. Despite initial reluctance, most participants in our workshops describe this as one of the most powerful skills they've learned. It helps them clarify their values, explore their fundamental beliefs about themselves and others, and finally understand personal behaviors that had confused them for a long time.

Think about the last time you really overreacted or allowed one small moment to ruin your entire day, and use the following analysis of the "coaster incident" as a model for your own self-evaluation. In reality, you'll perform this exercise as soon as you notice yourself starting to overreact and blow things out of proportion.

The first step when detecting iceberg beliefs is to describe the ABC. As with all of the skills, you have to begin by breaking down your experience into the facts of the situation, listing your ticker-tape beliefs, and identifying the in-the-moment emotions and behaviors. As usual, you should write this information down so you can keep track of your beliefs as they emerge. Here's what Karen would record:

Detecting Icebergs Worksheet

Part 1: Describe the Adversity, your Ticker-tape Beliefs, and the Consequences.

Adversity: Guy put his coffee mug on the table without using a coaster, even though the coasters were right in front of him.

Ticker-tape Beliefs: He knows I like people to use coasters. He sees the coasters but he still isn't using one. That's just wrong.

Consequences: I was as angry as I ever get. An 11 on a scale of 1 to 10. I ranted for about ten minutes and then left the apartment and walked around the city to calm down.

© Copyright Adaptiv Learning Systems

After you've mapped ABC, check the B–C connection. There are three issues to focus on:

1. Check whether your Cs are out of proportion to your Bs.
2. Check whether the quality of your C is mismatched with the category of your Bs. That is, you feel sad even though your ticker tape suggests anger, or you feel embarrassed although your ticker tape is about how you've harmed another person.
3. Check whether you are struggling to make a seemingly simple decision.

If any of these situations is present, then it is an appropriate time to use the Detecting Icebergs skill. If none of these situations is present, then you don't have to work at detecting iceberg beliefs because you already know why you're feeling and acting the way you do. In fact, the most common difficulty people run into when using this skill is that they try to uncover iceberg beliefs where there are no icebergs—their ticker tape adequately explains their reactions. If your Bs make sense of your Cs, then there is no need to look deeper.

Once you've established that you need to use the skill, begin by asking yourself these questions:

✦ What does that mean to me?
✦ What is the most upsetting part of that for me?
✦ What is the worst part of that for me?
✦ What does that say about me?
✦ What's so bad about that?

THE RESILIENCE FACTOR ♦ 140

You'll notice that these are all "what" questions, as opposed to "why" questions. "What" questions guide us to describe the meaning of our beliefs more fully. "Why" questions, in contrast, tend to make us defensive. Most of us, when asked why we feel a certain way or believe what we do, feel picked on or challenged. We end up fighting hard to defend our belief or emotion rather than working to understand it. To identify your iceberg beliefs, it's important to stay away from "why" questions and focus instead on "what" questions.

Begin with your ticker-tape beliefs, which in this case are "He knows I like people to use coasters. He sees the coasters but he still isn't using one. That's just wrong." Now you ask yourself one of the "what" questions. (The order of the questions doesn't matter, nor do you have to use them all. Choose one that feels right and explore.) We'll show you Karen's inner dialogue to give you an idea of how this should work.

QUESTION: *So, he didn't use a coaster, what does that mean to me?*
KAREN: *It means that he doesn't care whether I want him to use a coaster.*
QUESTION: *Well, so what if he doesn't care about my coaster need? What is so bad about that?*
KAREN: *Taking care of our things is important to me and he knows that. I know I'm a bit of a control freak, but by not using the coaster he is showing me that he isn't willing to respect my needs and put up with my quirks.*
QUESTION: *Assuming that's true, that he doesn't respect my needs and put up with my quirks, what is the worst part of that?*
KAREN: *The worst part is that we're about to get married. And I expect my husband to support me and understand me. If Guy can't even bother to use a coaster, how can I trust him to support me on the big issues?*
QUESTION: *Assuming that I can't trust him around the big issues, what does that mean to me?*
KAREN: *It means that I am about to make a huge mistake and that he isn't the person he said he was. It means that for all of his talk about loving me, flaws and all, when it comes down to it, he thinks I'm not okay the way I am and wants to change me.*
QUESTION: *What is the worst part of that?*
KAREN: *The worst part is that it means he's been taking me for a ride and that he has been manipulating me all along. I deserve to be loved for who I am, just the way I am.*

Aha! Karen was overwhelmed by anger not because Guy didn't use a coaster but because she interpreted this situation to mean that she was being denied her basic right to be loved for who she is. Her iceberg belief, "I deserve to be loved for who I am, just the way I am," was activated by his minor offense. Once activated, it produced emotion appropriate to a betrayal much larger than etiquette. Once we identify the underlying belief, Karen's reaction makes much more sense. Whether the belief is accurate and useful still must be determined, but we can do that now because the belief driving her reaction has been recognized.

When we teach this skill for the first time, participants work in pairs, one member of the pair guiding the other to uncover the iceberg belief. As you try this skill out, you may find it helpful to have a trusted friend ask you the questions, so that you can focus on exploring your answers without having to switch between roles. When first learning to use this skill, it's easy to get derailed and to start trying to justify your beliefs rather than to explore them more deeply. The next transcript is from the first time John tried this skill. We point out when he moves laterally rather than more deeply and show how his partner used "what" questions to get him back on track.

QUESTION: *What was your ticker-tape belief?*
JOHN: *It was "I don't need this. I'd much rather be relaxing than taking care of projects for her. She should at least have the courtesy to be grateful."*
QUESTION: *And how did you react?*
JOHN: *I felt humiliated and sad and avoided her for the rest of the day.*
QUESTION: *Okay, so let's grant you that she wasn't grateful; what makes that so upsetting for you?*
JOHN: *Because I'm busy and I took the time to do this for for her and I could tell she was disappointed in what I had done. [John is moving deeper. He identified that he believed his wife was disappointed.]*
QUESTION: *Are you sure she was disappointed? I bet she didn't even notice that they weren't perfectly straight. What makes you sure she noticed? [Notice how this question pulls John off track. It leads him to justify his perception rather than explore the meaning of it.]*
JOHN: *Oh, I'm sure she noticed. She is a perfectionist and holds herself and others to very high standards. I actually like that about her.*
QUESTION: *Well, assuming that she was disappointed, what does that mean to you? [This question helps John is get back on track.]*
JOHN: *It means that she believes that I can't do a simple job like hanging blinds.*
QUESTION: *Okay, let's say she does believe that, what is the worst part of that?*
JOHN: *The worst part is that it means my wife doesn't have have faith in my ability to take care of the things that need to get done around a house to keep it operating smoothly. It means that she can't rely on me to take care of things that a man is supposed to take care of. [John is getting closer to the iceberg belief.]*
QUESTION: *Come on, John. I bet you're just being too hard on on yourself. Why do*

you think she'd generalize from slightly crooked blinds to not being able to take care of things that a man should take care of? [This question encourages John to evaluate the accuracy of his belief, but it's premature because he hasn't yet made sense of his own reaction. At this point he needs to focus on his beliefs, not his wife's.]

JOHN: *You're right, she probably wouldn't. Maybe I am being too critical.*

QUESTION: *Okay, suppose your wife can't rely on you to take care of the things that you are supposed to take care of, what does that mean?*

JOHN: *It means that I am not the kind of man she thought I was when she married me and that I am not the kind of man I was raised to be. [John is moving deeper and is now focusing on his own expectations of himself, not just his wife's.]*

QUESTION: *What is the most upsetting part of that for you?*

JOHN: *In my family there are certain expectations placed on men. My father was the kind of man who could take care of any problem, big or small. He prided himself on never needing to hire someone to fix the car or the plumbing or electrical problems. And he raised me and my brothers to be the same. The clear message was that a good man—as clichéd as it sounds—a real man, takes care of his house. I guess this boils down to my belief that if I were a real man, I would have been able to hang the blinds straight. [This is John's iceberg belief.]*

The equation now makes sense. John felt humiliated and avoided his wife because he believed that his inability to hang the blinds straight exposed that he was not a real man. His ticker tape was about violation of rights, but his underlying belief was about loss—the loss of his self-respect—which his wife witnessed. This is what led to his humiliation and why he couldn't face his wife afterward.

One of the most commonly asked questions about this skill is "How do I know when to stop?" As you begin this process, it does indeed feel as if you could ask yourself questions forever; however, there is a clear end point. You will know when to stop when you have the aha! experience, when your reactions no longer seem out of proportion, when the quality of emotion makes sense, or when you understand why a decision has been so difficult to make.

Detecting Other People's Icebergs

Detecting icebergs is a useful skill to improve empathy and social connection. One Thursday evening, long, long ago, Andrew found himself facing down the barrel of a tight deadline. A grant application for research funding was due in Washington by 5:00 P.M. the next day and several hours of work remained—it would require all night to complete. He was already irritable and overcaffeinated, and the night was still young. Soon he heard the trash truck coming up the street, ever so slowly, with its squeaking brakes and noisy compacting hydraulics. Andrew's significant other, Veronica, heard it too. He knew she had because the next sound he heard was that of her footsteps coming up the stairs to the second-floor office followed by her barging in and angrily stating, "It's the trash truck. Your turn to take out the trash."

Andrew forced a smile and nodded but had no intention of moving from his desk. She left. His emotional response took him completely by surprise. He was furious, his anger at a 10 on a 1 to 10 scale. Veronica knew about his deadline, and she could have taken the trash out herself. Andrew used the skill of Detecting Icebergs to discover why he was so angry. As he worked through the questions, he realized that an iceberg belief had been fueling his response. For Andrew, it boiled down to an issue of respect. At a deep level, he believed that by interrupting him, Veronica was demonstrating that she did not respect his work. Since work is profoundly important to him, it meant that she didn't respect him. Now he understood his reaction. But he didn't understand hers.

Andrew knew that with all the pressure he was under and the tension in the house, it was probably a good idea to wait before talking it through with Veronica. The next evening, however, when things were a bit more relaxed, he opened up a conversation with her about it. The conversation went something like this:

ANDREW: *I got pretty upset last night when you told me to take out the trash. And I could tell how angry you were too. How come you didn't take the trash out yourself?*

VERONICA: *You're right, I was mad. I know that you were busy, but do you remember the agreement we came to a few months ago? Remember, you were reading that article, the one about women in the workforce and how, even though they work about the same hours as men, they're still expected to come home and do most of the chores. We both said that wouldn't happen with us. One of your jobs was supposed to be to take out the trash.*

ANDREW: *Yeah, I know. But I still don't get why that made you so mad.*

VERONICA: *Because I knew you could hear the trash truck too—but you didn't come down.*

ANDREW: *So, when I didn't come down, did you think I was just being a jerk?*

VERONICA: *Well, I thought you weren't sticking to our agreement.*

ANDREW: *So that's why you were pissed.*

VERONICA: *Yeah. It seemed like you expected me to do more than my share around here.*

ANDREW: *Now I get it. It was an issue of fairness.*
VERONICA: *Yeah, at some level, it felt like you didn't respect me.*

And that's why she was so angry—angry enough to march up the stairs. If they had only argued using their surface beliefs to guide them, the fight might have blown over, but the root cause of the fight would have still been there, waiting to resurface again over another seemingly minor event. Many relationships suffer because the couple never recognizes the iceberg beliefs that are causing them to clash.

Andrew told Veronica that he'd been feeling much the same, because he believed she wasn't respecting him or his work. They were able to compare notes on how quickly each of them had jumped to their violations-of-rights radar. And most important, they came up with a plan to satisfy both of them. Andrew conceded that even with the deadline, he had had time to take out the trash. He agreed to be more vigilant of ways he could contribute around the house. For her part, Veronica acknowledged that there would be times when work would come first for each of them and that she would not jump to the lack-of-respect conclusion if Andrew had to bury himself in work at times.

The Detecting Icebergs skill can help you to identify your core values so that you and your partner can discuss them openly and directly.

Conclusion

Detecting icebergs will help you to identify the deep beliefs that interfere with your ability to respond effectively to adversity. As you practice this skill, you probably will find that you have a core set of iceberg beliefs that affect your mood and behavior over and over again—across a variety of situations. Once you've identified what they are, it's time to shift out of insight mode and start changing the beliefs that are getting in your way.

CHAPTER SEVEN

Challenging Beliefs

Life Change Is Possible

If you've completed all of the exercises we've presented so far, you have undergone an intense, perhaps even painful, process of self-analysis. You should be proud of yourself. It takes courage to look at yourself and your life with such brutal honesty. Maybe your self-analysis showed you snapshots of your style, your personality, even your character that were rather unflattering. Don't get discouraged. An important part of becoming resilient is owning up to your weaknesses and your flaws. You've already accomplished that.

The next step is to determine what aspects of those weaknesses can be impacted, what can be improved. The skills of resilience give you a freedom to choose that you didn't have before. You can accept yourself as you are and continue down the same path you've been traveling. Or you can change. The next four skills are about how to create that change. Now that you know what kind of thinking styles you have, we will guide you through skills to change your thinking to view the world more accurately, to be a better problem solver, to be less at the mercy of your emotions and behaviors, to respond better when adversity strikes—in short, to be more resilient.

Beliefs matter, and any doubts you have about your capacity for change will place a ceiling on how much the change skills can help you. As you progress through the change skills, pay close attention to whether you have any ticker-tape beliefs about the futility or difficulty of change. What do you say to yourself when you try to learn something new or change an old behavior? If the adage "You can't teach an old dog new tricks" sounds reasonable to you, then you are setting yourself up for failure. Your beliefs about the possibility of change allow you to learn the change skills—or prevent you from learning them—and determine whether you persist in the pursuit of greater resilience or not.

The Change Skills

As we saw in Chapters 4 to 6, each of the know thyself skills is a powerful tool to increase resilience. But the self-analysis the skills encourage you to do is also the groundwork for the change skills. You can't change your beliefs until you detect what they are, whether by doing ABC to tune in to your ticker tape or by detecting your iceberg beliefs. Once you've uncovered all the beliefs that play a role in determining how you feel and behave in the wake of an adversity, the next step is to evaluate how accurate—how realistic—those beliefs are and to change to more accurate beliefs when necessary. We have developed four change skills. With *Challenging Beliefs*, you can analyze beliefs about the causes of the adversity. In *Putting It in Perspective*, you can better determine the future outcomes of adversity. *Calming and Focusing* works to impact the negative emotions directly or to push nonresilient beliefs out of your mind. *Real-time Resilience* enables you to do Challenging Beliefs and Putting It in Perspective at the moment an adversity strikes.

Problem Solving: Why We Ask "Why" When Adversity Hits

When adversity strikes, what's your first response? Research suggests that people generally react in predictable ways. For example, when confronted with a problem, people typically ask themselves "why" questions—questions that are concerned with the cause of the problem: "Why did that happen?" "Was it my fault?" "Can I control this?" These questions pop spontaneously into our heads. The answers we give ourselves are our why beliefs—our beliefs about the causes of the adversities we face.

We are most likely to have why beliefs following failure (losing a job, being turned down on a date), unexpected events (doing poorly on a task that you thought you would do well on, learning that someone you believed to be honest acted dishonestly), and interpersonal conflicts (fighting with a loved one). We don't tend to ask why following successes (getting a job, having your proposal for a date accepted) or expected outcomes (doing poorly on a task that you suspected you'd do poorly on, learning that someone you believed to be honest acted honestly).

Why do failures and unexpected outcomes trigger why beliefs while successes and expected outcomes do not? Probably because our survival rests on our ability to find a way to terminate or prevent negative situations, while how we respond to positive events is not so crucial. It was more important, in terms of survival, for Throgg to figure out why a hunt went poorly than it was for him to understand why a hunt went well. Our tendency to pay close attention to failure is an evolved response.

Evolution, by predisposing us to think about why adversity happens to us, has given us a terrific problem-solving mechanism. We can't solve problems without locating their causes. The faster we identify the true causes of the problem, the faster we generate a solution. And so we develop mental shortcuts, just as we saw with the thinking traps, that guide us to identify causes quickly, in fact, almost instantaneously. But as we saw with thinking traps, the mental shortcuts—heuristics—sometimes can

With Problem Solving, Sometimes You Get Lucky

We said that Challenging Beliefs helps you to improve your problem solving. And this is true. But, of course, there are times when you might get lucky—when your problem-solving attempts may work, even if you are responding impulsively, guided by the first why beliefs that pop into your head. Indeed, history is littered with examples. Imagine, if you will, that you are an early human in the Paleolithic era, some 20,000 to 30,000 years ago. You live in a cave in what is modern-day Peru. A friend of yours begins to act strangely—sudden mood changes, talking to imaginary people, seeing things that aren't there. How would you, a Paleolithic Peruvian, explain this odd behavior? Well, naturally, you'd chalk it up to possession by evil spirits. That's what our Stone Age counterparts believed when confronted with mental disorders. And based on that cause, they developed a solution—free the evil spirits by drilling holes in the afflicted person's skull. Anthropologists have documented this practice, known as trephining, and have demonstrated that at least some of the patients survived the procedure, since skeletal remains show evidence of healing around the wounds. It seems that trephining was in vogue for centuries, a fact that also suggests it must have produced positive results—if the abnormal behavior had continued, surely trephining would have ended. Of course, modern-day scientists are pretty sure it didn't work the way the ancients thought it did. It certainly didn't release animal spirits. What's more likely is that trephining represented the earliest frontal lobotomy. By destroying parts of the frontal lobe, the afflicted person's troublesome behavior—and probably a lot of other behavior too—ended. Our Stone Age predecessors settled on a cause that led to a logical solution. It was the wrong cause, and therefore the wrong solution, but they got lucky. Their solution happened to solve the problem—in a manner of speaking. But at what cost?

Our question to you is: How often is your problem solving like that of our early predecessors? How often do you stumble on a solution that, in retrospect, hurts you more than it helps you?[1]

lead us to make mistakes. And if we identify the wrong cause, we'll pursue the wrong solution.

The Seven Steps of Challenging Beliefs

Challenging your beliefs will help you to clarify your problems and find better, more permanent solutions to them.

You have to start at the beginning: ABC.

STEP 1. ABC AN ADVERSITY

Choose an ongoing adversity, one that you've been wrestling with for some time, for which you have a makeshift solution in place at best or at worst about which you are becoming helpless and hopeless. Perhaps it's that you've been passed over for promotion, watching younger, less experienced people given opportunities, projects, and positions that you think you deserved. Perhaps it's the daily power struggles you're having with a teenage son or daughter. Or it may be difficulty balancing work and home. Whatever it is, note it down on the activity sheet that follows. Remember, just the facts: the who, what, when, and where of the adversity, as you learned in ABC. Just get the A for now—we'll tackle the Bs and Cs soon. As we work through the seven steps with a client example, follow along with the example from your own life.

Keith was in a hotel room in the Midwest on a business trip when he found himself on the horns of the work-home dilemma. It was to be the final leg of an intensive stint of business travel that saw him crisscrossing the continent, from North Carolina to Oregon, from Toronto to Dallas. He had promised his wife, Felicia, that he'd spend the next week at home. Keith was doing what one does in a hotel room when on a business trip—admiring the view of the strip mall five floors below and asking himself what kind of person would actually *choose* these curtains and carpets—when he got a call from his boss.

The gist of the call was that an unexpected business opportunity had come up with a client in Toronto. But it was a window poised to close—someone had to get there fast, preferably the next week. Keith listened and said little. He could feel the anger rising, firing his cheeks red and causing his heart to race. It took all of his willpower to suppress the urge to shout angrily into the phone. He was in the throes of one of his button-push adversities.

Keith knew that the first resilient step in any thorough analysis of a problem is ABC. You should do the same. Define your problem objectively and dispassionately—just the who, what, when, and where. You may recall that in Chapter 4 you learned to leave the why question out of the objective description of the adversity, the A of ABC. For example, Keith could have described his adversity as "My boss is a jerk who doesn't respect my personal life," but that statement contains several assumptions. Here's a more objective description of the adversity:

ADVERSITY: My boss called to "ask" me to go out of town for a week when I've promised Felicia I'd spend time with her and the kids.

ABC Activity Sheet
Adversity:
Beliefs:
Consequences
Emotions:
Behaviors:

Next, recall the most recent time your adversity occurred—the last time you failed to secure a project you had your eyes on, your last argument with your child, the last time you found yourself stuck in the work-home balancing act with three or four balls in the air and one hand tied behind your back. Remember the ticker tape that ran through your mind when you last experienced the adversity. Note it down verbatim in the "Beliefs" space on the Activity Sheet. Keith's ticker-tape beliefs were:

Belief 1. I'm starting to get really angry now.
Belief 2. Felicia is going to be really angry about this.
Belief 3. My boss doesn't respect my private life.
Belief 4. Felicia expects too much of me.

Finally, list the emotional and behavioral consequences, the Cs of the episode. For Keith it was:

C (emotion): I was pretty angry—about a 6 or a 7 on a 1–10 scale.

C (behavior): Stalked around the hotel room in an angry funk, vacantly flipping through the TV channels

Now that you have noted the ABCs of your adversity, focus your attention on the Bs. As you know from Chapter 4, our ticker tape is composed of different kinds of beliefs. Keith's first ticker-tape belief is a description—a readout of his perception of his changing emotional state. The second is a what-next belief—a prediction of Felicia's reaction. Beliefs 3 and 4 are examples of why beliefs—each one is an explanation for the problem Keith is having balancing work and home. When we challenge our beliefs we focus on the why beliefs.

STEP 2. PIE CHART THE CAUSES

The second step in Challenging Beliefs helps you get a deeper understanding of your why beliefs and how they affect your problem solving. Go back to the Activity Sheet and examine those ticker-tape beliefs you experienced in the midst of your adversity. Isolate the why beliefs. Be sure they are, in fact, causal beliefs or explanations for the problem. Let's practice with a few examples.

The ticker tape of someone who learns that, yet again, an important project was given to a more junior colleague may sound like this: "I can't believe this. It looks like I've been passed over again and Tom has given the lead on this project to Lorraine. Lorraine has been here only half as long as me. This really bugs me." These are not why beliefs—they are descriptions of the adversity and the person's response to it. If we kept tracking this person's ticker tape, we might come across thoughts like these: "This is really going to hurt my career. Maybe my future isn't with this company. I've heard rumors of downsizing in this division, and being overlooked for this project probably means I'm on that hit list." Again, these aren't the thoughts we want to focus on in Challenging Beliefs. This ticker tape reflects what-next beliefs.

The beliefs we want to test when challenging our beliefs are those that are specifically about cause: "I didn't get this project because I just haven't been able to convince Tom that I have the goods. And that's because I'm just not good with people. Or maybe I'm okay with people, but I just can't be assertive around authority figures."

We can similarly categorize the ticker tape that's likely to run through a parent's mind during the latest of a series of fights with a teenage son.

"It makes me so sad that we're having this same old argument again (description). I hate it when he talks to me like that (description). I'm worried that he's headed for trouble (what-next belief). If he keeps messing up like this at school, he'll never make it into college and never get a decent job (what-next belief). He's just so unreasonable these days (why belief). He's become such an angry young man (why belief). I guess I've become less patient over time too, feeling the pressure at work and then coming home to have to deal with him (why belief)."

Locate your why beliefs for your adversity. (Although uncommon, some people don't have why beliefs as part of their ticker tape. If this is true of you, ask yourself point-blank what caused the problem, and record the first why beliefs that occur to you. Use these as your initial why beliefs as you proceed with this activity.)

Take another look at Keith's ticker tape. It includes two why beliefs— "My boss doesn't respect my private life" and "Felicia expects too much of me." What Keith probably doesn't realize in that moment is that he's subconsciously deciding which of these causes is most to blame for the problem. It's a process that all human beings go through when trying to solve a problem, another remarkably adaptive ability we've developed across eons of evolution. It makes intuitive sense that once we know the main cause of our problem, we should channel the majority of our energy toward fixing it. We estimate how much each identified cause contributes to the problem, and we can represent that with a pie chart, with the size of the slices indicating their relative contribution. Keith believed, in that

Step 2: Pie Chart the Why Beliefs

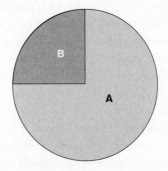

A. Boss doesn't respect my private life: 75%

B. Felicia expects too much of me: 25%

moment in the hotel room, that the major cause of his ongoing difficulties with work-home balance was his boss's attitude—about 75 percent of the problem. He believed his wife's excessive expectations contributed less— about 25 percent.

Use the following worksheet to create your own pie chart of your why beliefs.

The why beliefs you had in the moment of the adversity are your initial beliefs about its cause.

Pie chart how much each cause contributed to the adversity, according to how you saw the problem at the time. the percentages should add to 100%.

Decide whether each cause is not changeable (*), somewhat changeable (**), or highly changeable (***).

1 _____ %
2. _____ %
3. _____ %

Our intuitions about the Causes of an Adversity and how changeable they are determine what solutions we immediately pursue.

© 2002, Adaptiv Learning Systems

You've identified the why beliefs that first popped into your head and you've assigned them a percentage contribution to the problem. Trouble is, of course, that not all factors that contribute to a problem can be changed or fixed. When we're working on solving a problem, we are constantly asking ourselves subconsciously how much we really can do to change any of this. Keith may intuit, for example, that he has little chance of shifting his boss's single-minded work ethic—there's little Keith can do to change him. Instead, he may decide he has a better chance of shaping his wife's expectations, on the grounds that they are in a close relationship and therefore she may be a more receptive audience than his boss. Under these circumstances, it's best for Keith to focus his problem-solving attempts on the most changeable cause, although he believes it contributed less to the problem. Do this now for yourself. Refer back to your pie chart and asterisk those slices that you, in the moment of the adversity, believe are most amenable to change.

People's initial processing of adversity rapidly determines the trajectory of their problem solving—how they begin to solve the problem. Keith's first review of his adversity revealed two causes, one of which he perceives as being potentially changeable. This quick review dictates the solutions that occur to him. Based on his why beliefs, what he sees as the causes of his dilemma, he'd probably call Felicia from the bleak hotel room and give her the news that he'll be flying to Toronto next week, and ask her to cancel the dinners and other outings they had planned. Anticipating her disappointment and anger, he might also remind her, with a frustrated and angry edge creeping into his voice, that he doesn't like being on the road either but he's doing it for her—so that they can have the kind of life they both want. You can imagine the fight that would probably ensue.

Fortunately, Keith didn't act impulsively. Why? Because he knew that he may not have identified the *real* causes of his problem. He recognizes that he has an explanatory style that, like tunnel vision or magnifying and minimizing, draws him to certain possible causes but systematically filters other causes out. And so it is for you. You too have developed a style of explaining events that affects the way you perceive the problems you face and that influences the solutions you choose to pursue.

STEP 3. IDENTIFY YOUR EXPLANATORY STYLE

We introduced explanatory style in Chapters 1 and 3. As we've shown, explanatory style is our learned response to adversity, a pattern of ready-made explanations for the problems we experience. Remember that explanatory style can be described in three dimensions: "me–not me," "always–not always," "everything–not everything." Our explanatory style limits our problem solving. Our styles draw us to a subset of the real causes of the adversity, thereby making available only a subset of the possible solutions. The next step in the Challenging Beliefs process, then, is to map out how our explanatory style hurts our ability to solve our own problems. You'll now get a chance to practice using the three dimensions and, in the process, to decipher your explanatory style.

Me Versus Not Me

Do you usually see problems as being caused by you or by other people or circumstances? If you were walking down the hallway, saw your boss coming toward you, said "hi," and she didn't respond, how would you react? Would you put her silence down to something you had done: "I must have made a mistake in that last report I gave her, and she's angry with me"? This is a me belief. Or would you attribute it to her or to outside circumstances: "She must be having a bad day. Maybe she had an argument with someone" or "She's always in a world of her own on Monday mornings" not-me beliefs? Imagine another common adversity—you have left several voice mail messages on your best friend's home machine and she hasn't returned them. Why? A "me" response would be that "I haven't been a very good friend over the last few weeks. She's upset with me and that's why she isn't getting in touch." A "not-me" thought: "She has been so self-centered lately."

You may be thinking that your explanations don't follow a style, that they change depending on the situation, and, of course, you're right. There are times when we have clear information about the cause of the adversity. What if you were to walk down the hallway at work, say "hi" to your boss, and she were to scream, "Don't you 'hi' me! That report you submitted was full of holes. If I'd kicked that upstairs we'd all be the laughingstock of the department. What are we paying you for, anyway?" Given this information, and ignoring for the moment the fact that she was being unnecessarily harsh in public, all but the most strongly not-me person would probably settle on a me explanation. But you may be surprised at the degree to which our styles can blind us to explanations that to an objective person appear overwhelmingly true. At one time a young man came to therapy with a very strong "not-me, not-always, not-everything" style. During a session he spoke about a young woman he'd met at a party. She had given him her phone number, he'd put in several phone messages, but none of them was answered. Finally she called and left a message: "Please stop calling me. I don't want to talk with you, I don't want to go out with you. I'm sorry, but I'm just not interested in getting together and would appreciate it if you don't call here again." We don't really know why she wasn't interested in him, but most of us would agree that she certainly did not want to see him ever again. But the young man's "not-me/not-always" style made it difficult for him to acknowledge a "me" and "always" explanation, such as his personality. His question to the therapist was "So why do you think she said that on the machine? Do you think she's just stressed out right now and I should wait and call in a week or so?" In this case, his explanatory style biased how he interpreted the information available to him. Explanatory style also fills in the gap when the information is not available. That's the nature of a shortcut—we use it when the cause is ambiguous. Try to vividly imagine times when you've been in situations like these and recall the first belief that popped into your head at the time. Can you tell if your style is "me" or "not me"?

Always Versus Not Always

Are the causes you identify likely to be around for a long time, or are they relatively temporary? A salesperson pitches to important clients, and the meeting ends with their thanking her for her time but letting her know in no uncertain terms that they are not interested in buying. If she has an "always" explanatory style, she might think, "I don't have what it takes to connect with possible clients in face-to-face meetings." If she leans toward a "not-always" style, she may shrug and say to herself, "My pitch was off today. I guess I didn't get enough sleep last night." You are a project manager and the deliverable is overdue. An "always" explanation, in this case about a stable characteristic of the people you manage, would be "My team members are so lazy." Conversely, a "not-always" explanation, which is also a "not-me" explanation, is "My staff is not working hard these days. I guess they've burned out on the pace of things and need some down time." If you have a disagreement with a boss at work, what is your instant reaction? Is it an "always": "She's the expert; I must not be very good at this job"? Or is it a "not always": "I haven't been paying enough attention to her hints lately that my work priorities are out of order"? Notice that both are "me" explanations, but they vary on the "always–not always" dimension. Can you intuit, by looking across incidents in your life, whether your style is more "always" or "not always"?

Everything Versus Not Everything

This dimension of explanatory style assesses the degree to which you believe the cause of a particular problem will affect many areas of your life or just a few. When you're faced with a problem, do your ticker-tape why beliefs suggest that a wide variety of domains in your life will be affected—your work life, your marriage, your relationships with friends? Or do you typically envision a specific impact? A manager whose team failed to deliver a project on time could have an "everything" belief, such as "I'm irresponsible." This applies not only to the immediate issue but to all aspects of his work, to his recreational life, as well as to how he functions in relationships with friends, family, and significant others. An example of "not everything" would be "I've never been any good at this kind of project work. I just can't seem to learn it." Both these why beliefs, by the way, are "me" and "always." We have a friend who was having her kitchen remodeled and had hired a carpenter as part of the project. With only half the work done, her husband paid him in full. It took months to get the carpenter to return and finish the job. Our friend's explanation: "People can't be trusted." Not "This carpenter can't be trusted," or "Carpenters who get paid in full before a job is finished can't be trusted," or even "Carpenters can't be trusted." Her first instinct was to generalize from this event to all people—a highly "everything" belief since it affects all domains of her life, not just kitchen remodeling. Think about it: Are you more of an "everything" or a "not-everything" person?

It's important to understand your explanatory style because when an adversity strikes, the causal beliefs you generate will reflect this style. By preventing you from seeing the full range of causes of a problem, your explanatory style limits your ability to respond resiliently.

Coding the Explanatory Style

Let's go back to our friend Keith and take another look at the two why beliefs we identified earlier. We're now going to code each B on each dimension, using a scale of 1 to 7. We'll code extreme "me", "always", or "everything" beliefs as 1. We'll code extreme "not-me", "not-always", or "not-everything" beliefs as 7—and, of course, we can use the full scale. For example, a why belief can attribute the cause of the problem partly to the self and partly to other people, which would be a 4 on the 1 to 7 scale.[2] Let's try coding Keith's why beliefs:

WHY BELIEF #1: *"My boss doesn't respect my private life."*

Totally due to **me**	1 2 3 4 5 (6) 7	Totally due to **other people or circumstances**
Will **always** be present	1 (2) 3 4 5 6 7	Will **never again** be present
Influences **everything** in my life	(1) 2 3 4 5 6 7	Influences just **this one situation**

It's a "not-me" belief, and extremely so. There's no shared responsibility expressed, such as would be the case were he to suggest that "My boss doesn't respect my private life and I don't draw boundaries when he designates work." Let's rate it a 6. The belief is an "always"—Keith is attributing his problem to his boss's disposition toward work and home, which is likely to be a long-standing attitude formed over time and therefore highly resistant to change. Let's code it as a 2. Finally, it would seem to be an "everything" belief. The attitude of Keith's boss toward work-home balance affects the most important areas of Keith's life. It probably would fall on the scale as a 1.

WHY BELIEF #2: *"Felicia expects too much of me."*

Totally due to **me**	1 2 3 4 5 (6) 7	Totally due to **other people or circumstances**
Will **always** be present	1 2 (3) 4 5 6 7	Will **never again** be present
Influences **everything** in my life	1 2 (3) 4 5 6 7	Influences just **this one situation**

This is a "not-me" belief—there's no mention of Keith contributing to his partner's expectations. It too is a 6 at the "not-me" end of the continuum. It's an "always" in the same vein as the other causal belief. Expectations typically are constructed over time and so also take time to change. It would rate as a 3. Felicia's expectations here affect most of Keith's home life, as he perceives it, and intrudes somewhat on work, so he would rate this belief as a 3 on the "everything" dimension.

Both Keith's beliefs about cause are "not-me, always, and everything" beliefs. If he were to examine other incidents in his life, he probably would see this same pattern emerging as a general thinking style.

What Is Your Explanatory Style?

Code the explanatory style of the why beliefs you inserted on the pie chart on page 152 on the following activity sheet.

For each why belief from the pie chart, rate below the three dimensions of explanatory style. Write in the number from each dimension for each belief.

This process will provide you with a map of your explanations for this adversity–and also a "snapshot" of your explanatory style.

Please use the following scale:

Totally due to **me**	1 2 3 4 5 6 7	Totally due to **other people or circumstances**
Will **always** be present	1 2 3 4 5 6 7	Will **never again** be present
Influences **everything** in my life	1 2 3 4 5 6 7	Influences just this one situation

Write in your ratings below:

	Me/Not Me	Always/Not Always	Everything/Not Everything
Belief 1			
Belief 2			
Belief 3			

What did your ratings indicate about your explanatory style? Of course, to have a good representation of your explanatory style, you need to rate several why beliefs stemming from several situations. That's important because some people have one style when they encounter problems at work and a very different style when they encounter problems in their personal lives. For example, when something goes awry at work, a man may blame others, but when a problem arises in his personal life, the same person may tend to blame himself. To get a fair assessment of your style, work through at least ten negative events you've experienced, some having to do with work situations, some from your personal life, and then look for patterns. And, remember, 4s are a style too! If you find that whenever you're faced with a problem you neatly divide blame between yourself and others—right down the middle—then that is your style, just as the tendency to blame oneself or the tendency to blame others is a style.

What's the Right Explanatory Style?

Over the course of our consulting years, a lot of people have asked us what the right explanatory style to have is. Psychologists have been occupied with this question for the last twenty-five years. According to research, the short answer is that different styles have their own unique advantages and disadvantages, but any style is limiting. Our goal should be to think flexibly and accurately.

Thirty-five years ago, psychologists found that when people experienced adversities that were outside of their control, they quickly became helpless. And they tended to take that helplessness with them, even into adversities that were actually highly controllable. In 1978 Martin Seligman and his colleagues discovered why. It wasn't the type of adversity that determined who became helpless and who became resilient, it was how the person explained the adversity that mattered. The difference between resilience and helplessness was explanatory style. Pessimists—those people who explained their adversities with a "Me, Always, Everything" style—tended to become helpless and depressed. Optimists—those with a "not-me, not-always, not-everything" style—most often remained resilient and depression free.[3]

It was such a clear and definitive finding that the search began for other areas of life in which pessimism was a liability. And they were readily found. Pessimistic life insurance salespeople made significantly fewer sales and dropped out at higher rates than their optimistic peers. Pessimists got lower grades than optimists in college, even after controlling for their high school ranking and their SAT scores. Optimistic athletes tended to bounce back and perform better after a defeat, while their pessimistic teammates performed worse. Although Seligman advocated optimism *only* to the extent that reality permits, the presumption in the field became that pessimism was bad and optimism good.[4]

More recently, however, research has revealed that optimism also can be a liability. Our work and that of our colleagues has shown that *extreme* optimists actually have worse college grades than mildly optimistic students. Psychologists are coming to see that it's crucial to be flexible, to break out of our natural explanatory style. And it's equally clear that we need to be realistic—to accurately pinpoint the causes of the adversities we face. In Step 4 we'll guide you to be more flexible. In Step 5 we'll help you get more accurate.[5]

Len's Story—Flexibility and Accuracy

In November of 1999 we were invited to make a presentation to the National Leadership Conference of the American Society for Training and Development. There were about fifty people present at our talk, but we couldn't help notice one audience member in particular. He was a middle-aged man, distinguished in appearance, and impeccably tailored and coiffed. And he sat transfixed. Now, we're good speakers, but we almost never have that kind of effect on those who come to hear us. Toward the end of our talk, he became quite emotional—we could see the tears welling in his eyes, and he occasionally turned his face away from the others present. It was clear that something in our speech had deeply touched this man. At the end of the talk, when everyone else had gone, he came up to us, shook our hands, thanked us for the presentation, and then proceeded to relate one of the most poignant stories anyone has ever shared with us.

Len had risen meteorically in a Fortune 100 company, reaching vice-presidential ranks by his late thirties—a feat he attributed to his generous supply of self-efficacy. As Len explained, "I always knew what my recipe for success was, and I pushed it to the max. My greatest asset was my attitude; I never doubted that I could solve any problem that came along. I believed, no, I knew that everything was in my control. What separated me from those who didn't make it as far as I did in business was that I believed there was a solution to every problem, if I just looked long and hard enough—if I just put out that extra effort."

"To use the language you taught me today," he continued, "I was a very strong me, not-always, not-everything guy."

What had resonated so strongly with Len was our discussion of the importance of flexibility and accuracy. In the presentation we explained the impact of various explanatory styles on emotions and behavior, just as we have discussed them here. We argued that every style has its benefits and downsides, that any style is limiting, offering only a myopic view of the true causes of any adversity. We proposed that the key to resilience, therefore, was flexibility and accuracy. This is what had struck a chord with Len.

"I thought I had it nailed down. I thought I could solve everything," Len continued. "And so when I was diagnosed with multiple sclerosis, I thought I could beat that too. I was diagnosed in my midforties. I quit my job, liquidated a bunch of stock, and began the search for a cure. I saw doctors all over the world—the best in the world. It took me almost ten years before it sunk in—this was a disease without a cure. There was nothing much I could really do to solve this problem. I always knew I had an optimistic approach, an attitude that got me to the top of my company. Today I learned it was my explanatory style. Well, that style that fueled my career let me down when it came to dealing with my disease—the biggest adversity I've ever faced. It sent me on a fruitless search. I wish I could turn back time. I wish I had those ten years back to spend with my family."

STEP 4. BEING FLEXIBLE

If stupidity got us into this mess, then stupidity can get us out.

—WILL ROGERS

Ever noticed that you often try to solve the same old problem with the same tired strategy, only to fail in the same old way? We've all done that at one time or another. That's what relying on our explanatory style leads us to do: We're blind to most causes outside our explanatory style, we come up with tired old solutions that try to reverse those same old causes, and we fail at solving the problem yet again. To get out of this loop, we need to break out of our explanatory style, and that means getting more flexible.

It's something of a coincidence, but the two of us had an eerily similar experience in elementary school—all the stranger for the fact that we grew up on different continents, Karen in the United States, Andrew in Australia. Our art teachers had us working on a typical elementary-school art project—making collages with felt in one case, drawing with India ink in the other—and were wending their way around the room offering sage insights: "Susan, you're using too much ink, it's going to spill all over the desk." "John, hmmmm. What is that cow holding?" "Terry, I see that you've made your people bigger than the buildings?" "Andrew/Karen—you need to be more creative."

More creative. Probably accurate, but hardly advice. It's a diagnosis, but it's not a prescription. It's reminiscent of the phrase "to think outside the box." You've probably come across this expression before, perhaps in a corporate training, maybe in another self-help book. Indeed, it seems ubiquitous these days. Remember that even the fast food restaurant Taco Bell exhorted us in TV ads to be adventurous and try their new sandwich—in their words, "to think outside the bun." We're not fans of this phrase, and not just because we got Cs on our art project. You're entrenched in your thinking-style box, and it's going to take more than a command to think outside it to get you out. You've spent many years building that box, with help from your parents, teachers, even society. You've fallen into thinking traps and developed radar to scan the environment for violations of rights, for loss, and for future threat. And you've cemented the box with the confirmation bias, screening out information that contradicts the box and systematically filtering in that information that concurs. None of this is good, but each and every one of us has built a thinking-style box. How can anyone, then, expect you to be creative—to be flexible—just by telling you to be?

When it comes to why beliefs, the three dimensions of your explanatory style *is* the box you're stuck in. But now that you know how much of a "me/not-me, always/not-always, and everything/not-everything" person you are from Step 3, you can work around your style. Most of your adversities, especially the significant ones, are caused by many different factors. Typically, some of those factors have to do with you, and others are due to other people or circumstances. Some of the causes will be relatively intractable, others can be changed easily, still others could be changed through concerted effort. Some will have pervasive effects, others will apply only to a narrow and specific sector of your life. To be creative, to think outside the box, we have to use the three dimensions of explanatory style to code the why beliefs that first pop into our heads and generate some alternative reasons why an adversity has occurred.

And now back to Keith. We learned that both of Keith's why beliefs regarding his work-home balance problem are Not Me, Always, Everything, and we also know that these beliefs coincide with his explanatory style. Knowing this, Keith can use the three dimensions to come up with some other possible why beliefs. Why should he go to the trouble to do this? Because unless he does, he's seeing only some of the causes of his work-home balance adversity—those that his explanatory style lens "allows" him to see. If he sees only some of the causes, he's going to be able to solve only part of the problem. If he really wants to lick this problem for good, he needs to get a comprehensive view of the causes and direct his problem solving to those causes he can impact most.

Keith is an externalizer. There's no mention of his contribution to the adversity in the why beliefs that sprang to his mind in that hotel room. So a good start to getting more flexible, to thinking outside his explanatory style, is for him to come up with some me beliefs. To get real flexibility, he's also going to want to generate some not-always and not-everything beliefs as well. Remember, Keith's trying to think of more possible causes of the problem. At this stage it's important that he not screen out a possible alternative unless it's totally implausible. It will be difficult enough for him to think outside his explanatory style box without stifling his creativity. (He'll use Step 5, Being Accurate, to reject any why beliefs that don't stack up against reality.)

Keith was able to come up with some plausible me beliefs for his work-home balance problem—some ways he may be contributing to that problem. Notice that in the process of generating "me" beliefs, he's also got a sampling of the "always–not always" and "everything–not everything" dimensions.

ALTERNATIVE WHY BELIEF #1: *"I have a hard time saying no to my boss."*

Totally due to **me**	1 ②3 4 5 6 7	Totally due to **other people or circumstances**
Will **always** be present	1 2 3 4⑤6 7	Will **never again** be present
Influences **everything** in my life	1 2 3 ④5 6 7	Influences just **this one situation**

Is this a good alternative why belief? It is if it's outside of Keith's "not-me, always, everything" style. Is it? It's certainly a me belief—it's about how Keith may be contributing to the problem. It's probably middle of the range on the everything dimension. Keith's not claiming to be unassertive with everyone in his life—just with this one person. But his unassertiveness with his boss affects his work-home balance, which, since it cuts across life areas, seems to have more pervasive, or everything, effects. Keith rated this at a 4 on the everything scale.

Where does it rate on the "always" dimension? This may depend on some follow-up questions Keith needs to ask himself. Why is it difficult for him to say no to his boss? If his answer is "I'm weak," a stable character flaw, then it's more of an "always" belief. If, however, he sees his unassertiveness as due to, say, his lack of knowledge of how best to say no to this particular person to get the desired effect, then that's more of a "not-always" belief. For example, perhaps Keith is aware that a colleague has developed an effective strategy to set limits with the boss. Overcoming his unassertiveness may be as simple as conferring with that colleague about tactics. Keith decided that he wasn't generally unassertive but that he really didn't know how to approach his boss. He rated it a 5 on the "always/not always" scale.

Here's another alternative why belief that Keith came up with:

ALTERNATIVE WHY BELIEF #2: *"I'm bad at time management. If I could just plan out my week better, I wouldn't have to work so many weekends. I'd get more time to spend with Felicia, the kids, and our friends."*

Totally due to **me**	1②3 4 5 6 7	Totally due to **other people or circumstances**
Will **always** be present	1 2 3 4 5⑥7	Will **never again** be present
Influences **everything** in my life	1 2 3 4⑤6 7	Influences just **this one situation**

As Keith practiced coding his why beliefs, he became faster and more skilled at using the scales. He nailed this alternative why belief in a few moments: "It's obviously a 'me' belief," he told us. "It's mostly to do with me, maybe a little pressure from the work environment to rush from one crisis to the next without planning time, but most of it is me. I'd rate it a 2. Lack of time management skills really only applies at work, even though its effects may spill over into my personal life. I've given it a 5 on the 'everything' scale. It is a 'not-always belief' since I can learn to be better at managing my time—it's not like that's an ability you're either born with or without. I'd rate it a 6."

Keith did an excellent job of getting flexible—of getting outside his "not-me, always, everything" explanatory style. He first coded his initial why beliefs—those beliefs about cause he had in the moment of the adversity, in that badly decorated hotel room—on the three scales of explanatory style. And then he used those scales to get outside the box—to come up with other ways of seeing the cause of the problem that represented different places on the three scales. Then it was time for him to get accurate about his thinking.

STEP 5. BEING ACCURATE

We are not retreating. We are advancing in another direction.
—GENERAL DOUGLAS MACARTHUR

Getting more accurate in our why beliefs is an essential part of the Challenging Beliefs process. Without this step we are Pollyanna, susceptible to delusional positive spins like MacArthur's. Becoming an accurate thinker is like becoming a scientist, because your next step is to test both the why beliefs that popped into your head in the moment of the adversity and any alternatives you've generated against the solid evidence. You also could equate the process to being a good detective, as we do in our children's resilience program. When Sherlock Holmes arrives at the scene of a crime, he doesn't just go out and arrest the first person he sees. He approaches the crime more systematically than that. He recognizes that the first suspect is not always the real offender and puts together a list of suspects (or alternatives, as in Step 4), then looks for clues that establish who is the culprit (being more accurate).

The biggest obstacle to becoming more accurate is your confirmation bias, a mechanism we looked at closely in Chapter 5, which leads us to hold on to information that's consistent with our explanatory style while filtering out contrary evidence—details that don't fit neatly into our prepackaged perceptions. For this reason, you have to search deliberately for evidence both for and against each belief. Some people think of themselves as scientists or detectives or judges when they are doing this exercise; they are objectively sifting through the evidence to discover the true causes of the adversity. Others try to think of what their best friend would offer as evidence for and against each belief.

As we guide you through this process, you may find the following exercise sheet valuable in organizing the evidence for and against your why beliefs.

WHY BELIEFS	EVIDENCE FOR	EVIDENCE AGAINST
Belief 1		
Belief 2		
Belief 3		
Belief 4		

© 2002, Adaptiv Learning Systems

INITIAL BELIEF 1: *"My boss doesn't respect my private life."*
What evidence would count here? Perhaps if the boss were to insist repeatedly that Keith work weekends, travel on weekends, spend significant periods away from home, work overtime without giving extra time off, there would be sufficient evidence that he doesn't care about Keith's work-home balance. But when Keith thinks about it a little more, he finds evidence against his belief, like that time his boss sent a bottle of champagne to their hotel room when he and Felicia headed off for a weekend away. Or the time he insisted they go out to dinner on the company. There was also that time the boss disrupted his own vacation plans so that Keith and Felicia could schedule theirs. By writing down these examples, Keith can see that, while his boss is demanding, he also has proven at times to be respectful of Keith's personal life. There's some evidence for and some evidence against.
ALTERNATIVE 1: *"I have a hard time saying no to my boss."*
Have there been times when Keith's been able to say no to his boss?

Maybe he finds that he's perfectly comfortable opposing his boss on a business decision but not around his work hours. Notice how such evidence helps shape and modify his belief. Keith isn't globally unassertive with his boss, only when it comes to work-home issues—which makes it more of a "not-everything" cause. Knowing this, Keith then would want to explore whether this has emerged as a problem for him in previous jobs. If he finds that it has, now would be a perfect opportunity to try to detect the iceberg beliefs that must be somehow affecting his willingness or ability to stand up to authority figures when it comes to protecting his personal time.

Keith used the same kind of in-depth, objective questions to analyze all his initial and alternative beliefs.

STEP 6. NEW PIE CHART

As you engage in the process of becoming accurate, marshaling a list of evidence for and against each causal belief, you'll notice that you begin to build an intuitive sense of how important each cause is. The more evidence you find to support the belief, the more likely it contributes to the adversity. Of course, the reverse is true—the more evidence against the belief, the smaller the contribution; you may even find that some of the beliefs you came up with have no support at all. That's why we now want to draw a new pie chart. The process of being flexible opens up the possibility of more causes than were available for the first pie chart. The second pie chart should represent a more comprehensive and accurate analysis, one that surpasses our explanatory style–driven why beliefs.

Construct a new pie chart for your adversity. Include only those beliefs, either initial or alternative, that are supported by evidence. Based on his analysis, Keith came up with the following new pie chart. Notice that it includes all the beliefs he found evidence for, not just those we discussed.

Although originally Keith believed that Felicia's expectations contributed 25 percent to his problem, as on page 151, upon analysis he realized that there was no evidence to support this at all, so that slice didn't make it into the second pie chart. Keith did identify three new contributing factors, however.

Is your new pie chart different from your first? If not, your initial view was comprehensive and accurate. While the Challenging Beliefs process has not given you any additional information about the causes of your problem, by having gathered the evidence, you can be assured of the ac-

Step 6: Drawing a New Pie Chart

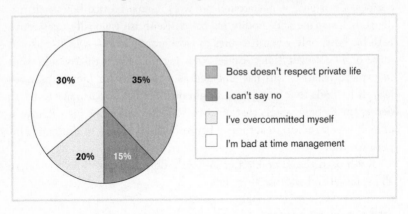

curacy of your initial view. However, in our experience, about 95 percent of people add new slices to their second pie chart. This means that about 95 percent of the people were able to identify evidence-based causes of the problem that they would not otherwise have considered had they launched into problem-solving based on their explanatory style–driven why beliefs. Each newly identified causal factor creates new problem-solving options. The more options you can pursue, the more likely it is that you will find a solution.

STEP 7. NEW SOLUTIONS

Now you want to rate the changeability of each of the slices of your new pie—how subject each cause is to change. Keith may still determine that he'll never be able to change his boss's attitude. But perhaps it has occurred to him that his boss tends to disregard *his* work-home balance more than that of his colleagues. So maybe the solution is to arrange a meeting to discuss a carefully planned list of topics about work-home boundaries. What other changes are possible? Keith clearly can take steps to improve his time management. He'll have to set time limits on the tasks he enjoys. Perhaps he should stagger the desirable and less desirable tasks, rewarding his completion of the onerous chores with a relished project. He can select a few staff members whom he most trusts and train them to perform some of the work he currently performs solo. Keith needs to come to terms with the beliefs that underpin his tendency to overcommit. He wants to determine what the activating situations that lead him to overextend himself are, so that he can be ready to challenge his beliefs in that moment, to maximize his resilience.

Notice how the process of Challenging Beliefs has dramatically changed Keith's solution landscape. Prior to the process, the only option he had was to challenge his wife about what he perceived to be her unreasonable expectations. Now several solutions are open to him. And more to the point, these solutions flow from a more comprehensive and accurate view of the adversity.

Conclusion

We have found that Challenging Beliefs is especially useful for people who wrestle with sadness, anger, guilt, and embarrassment. Those of you who experience anxiety, who focus on what-next beliefs, will appreciate the next skill—Putting It in Perspective.

CHAPTER EIGHT

Putting It in Perspective

I've had many catastrophes in my life, some of which actually happened.

—MARK TWAIN

When was the last time you woke up in the middle of the night, say 3:00 A.M., feeling apprehensive and anxious? Within a few minutes your mind was so revved up you'd given up any hope of getting back to sleep. Most people have had this experience, and when they explain why they have these sleepless nights, they say they couldn't get their brains to shut down—just couldn't stop thinking about work, an exam, their marriage, their kids, their mother's health . . .

For many people, their anxiety takes over and they catastrophize—they dwell on a current adversity and within a few minutes have imagined a chain of disastrous events stretching into the future. One of our clients was tormented by arguments she'd been having with her teenage son, ruminating on all the terrible things that could happen in the future because of their deteriorating relationship. "With all this fighting, he's going to pull away and start spending even more time with those misfit friends of his. Could he be using drugs? If he isn't now, he will be soon. What if he gets busted by the cops? There'll go all the dreams we had of college. He'll end up working at some fast food restaurant—that is, if he even manages to get a job. He'll be in and out of rehab so much that any job he does get will end up being short-lived. He'll blame us for all his problems and completely cut us out of his life." For many people, this chain of catastrophic beliefs and the intense anxiety they produce are a long, dark night of the soul.

Perhaps you catastrophize answers to these questions: In this economy, what'll happen if I lose my job? Will I ever find the right person? Will this marriage last? What will happen to my kids if I leave? What if we can't have kids? Other people catastrophize about their health. Every ache and vague symptom is a preface to major health problems. Difficulty remembering a name indicates the early stages of Alzheimer's. Shortness of breath while running for the bus is a sure sign of the beginnings of heart disease. That dog-tired fatigue means cancer.

If you tend to obsess or to blow things out of proportion, if anxiety is a major player in your life, your first task before reading any further is to write down what it is that causes you the most worry. Once you have a clear view of what troubles you, you'll be better equipped to put the skill of Putting It in Perspective to immediate use.

In Chapter 4, when we discussed the B–C connections of ABC, we noted that anxiety evolved to prepare us for a threat that's heading our way. But ironically, there are times when anxiety does anything but prepare us for threat. When you experience that early-morning wakening, when you find yourself obsessing over all the catastrophic events that could happen to you, do you feel physically, psychologically, and emotionally ready for action? No. You feel drained, your body is tired, and your thinking is distracted. You're in no position to respond resiliently to a problem or setback. Putting It in Perspective is a skill that, by changing your beliefs about future threat, brings your anxiety down to a manageable level—a level that is more in proportion with the real degree of threat. That's when you are best able to prepare for the most likely consequences of an adversity.

Like Challenging Beliefs, Putting It in Perspective is designed to guide us to more accurate thinking. But while Challenging Beliefs is applied to our why beliefs, our beliefs about the *causes* of adversity, Putting It in Perspective works with our beliefs about the *implications* of the adversity— what's going to happen in the future now that the adversity has struck. Challenging beliefs is often the skill people prefer to use when they are plagued by sadness, anger, or guilt. Our assessment of why an adversity happened will determine which of these specific emotions we experience. As usual, how we feel depends on the tone of our explanatory style. If we conclude that some personal flaw was responsible for the problem, we experience sadness. If we think we've done something to hurt others, we feel guilty. However, if we perceive that the adversity was not due to our own shortcomings but was caused by others, then the predominant emotion we feel will be anger. All of these emotions flow from our beliefs about the cause of the problem—our beliefs about something that has happened in the past. Putting It in Perspective is a parallel process to Challenging Beliefs, but it is designed to change our beliefs about the future.

Of course, there is a link between our explanatory style and our beliefs about the future—our what-next beliefs. People with always and everything explanatory styles are at risk for catastrophic what-next beliefs. If you have an "always" style, then you'll predict that the cause of this current problem also will play a role in your future life. If you also tend to have "everything-why" beliefs, then you are, in essence, saying to yourself not only that your problems will be around for a long time but that they will affect everything you do. A woman who attributes a failed relationship to "I just didn't click with him at all" is not making negative predictions about her future relationships, just this one. But if she believes that the relationship failed because "I'm just incapable of getting close to people," she is predicting a long future of bad relationships.[1]

People trained in Putting It in Perspective can use it in a multitude of ways. It can ease your anxiety and fear of embarrassment. It can teach you not to pounce on the first future threat belief that pops into your head as if it were necessarily true. By helping you to curb your worst-case fears, Putting It in Perspective can substantially increase your sense of optimism about the future. And with your fears in check, you will be freed up to reach out and take advantage of the myriad opportunities that come your way.

We've also worked with clients who underestimate their future risk. These people are not anxious enough. Putting It in Perspective helps them to identify genuine threats to their relationships, their careers, and their health. The skill replaces their unrealistic optimism with genuine optimism. Whether you use Putting It in Perspective to quell overwhelming anxiety or to stay alert to an actual threat, it will bring you greater resilience through superior emotion regulation, impulse control, and realistic optimism.

How Does Catastrophic Thinking Start?

Let's illustrate the major features of catastrophic thinking with a case study from some coaching we did with a highly successful salesperson whom we'll call Larry. Larry was generally quite resilient, very experienced in sales, and a top producer for his company. But one day Larry forgot to compile and mail sales brochures that he promised to an important prospective client. It had completely slipped his mind—until three-thirty the next morning, when he jolted awake with the realization that he'd made a huge mistake. To see how Larry begins to slide into catastrophic thinking, we have to ABC the adversity.

ADVERSITY: Forgot to send sales brochures advertising a key product to a very important prospective new client.

What follows are the ticker-tape beliefs that Larry reported to us. Notice how focused he is on what could go wrong in his future.

BELIEFS: Man, I cannot get to sleep and I've got to be up in three hours. Like I haven't got enough to do today without feeling lousy all day. Oh, crap—I forgot about those sales brochures! If I don't get that stuff out by five today, I'll lose the client. But if I work on putting those materials together, I'm gonna miss out on a good hour of sales calls. Once you start losing that time, it's over. Gotta get those calls in. No sales calls, no leads. No leads, no sales. No sales, no commission. It's the cardinal rule in selling. I'm going to end up getting squeezed out of this company. What'll I do then? Sales is all I know. I'll end up just squeaking by in a few other jobs—but the pay won't be the same and I'll be constantly looking for work on the side, just to cover the mortgage payments. And I could get fired again. What if we lose the house? Yeah, that'll help the marriage. Would she leave me? How can she sleep while our lives are falling apart?

Then Larry listed the consequences of his beliefs:

CONSEQUENCES (EMOTION): *Intense anxiety (10 on a 1 to 10 scale)*
CONSEQUENCES (BEHAVIOR): *Paced up and down in the living room for a couple of hours, woke up my wife, got into an argument with her, finally headed off to an unproductive day at work.*

It's your turn to start the skill of Putting It in Perspective. Recall the last time you found yourself catastrophizing. Write down your ABCs just as Larry did. The key elements are to describe the adversity objectively, to capture all your ticker-tape future-threat beliefs (which can also be called worst-case beliefs), and to identify how you felt, how strong the emotion was, and what you did.

Back to Larry for a moment. Larry's ticker-tape beliefs may seem a little ridiculous to an objective reader, but for Larry in that moment, at half-past three in the morning, the future-threat beliefs that rattled through his mind were not just speculations but certainties. And there was something else. He experienced a very strong, very persistent image of himself and his family on the sidewalk with all of their possessions, evicted from their home for defaulting on the mortgage. This image was very distressing, and it, along with the drone of his ticker tape, drove him out of bed. Eventually his wife, Elaine, came out to check on him. But recall his thoughts about her—he was frustrated that she was sleeping "while our lives are falling apart." And so when Elaine appeared on the scene, genuinely concerned about him, he was snide and confrontative. He briefly told her about the brochures and gave her a snapshot or two of his catastrophic beliefs. She tried to put his mind at ease by telling him that his beliefs were unfounded and that he was overreacting. But this only made him angrier—it was bad enough that she wasn't contributing to the solution, but to deny that the problem even existed was infuriating. They fought until Elaine gave up and went to bed. By the time Larry got into work, he was exhausted. He got the brochures together and mailed them, called the client to explain the oversight, and tried to fly under his sales manager's radar all day since he knew he would be angry. At three in the afternoon, on the pretext of calling on a client, Larry headed home and napped until dinner. Obviously these are very nonresilient consequences. Is there any way that Larry could have kept a grip on reality and better handled his anxiety? Of course—by Putting It In Perspective.

We'll model the five steps of Putting It in Perspective using Larry's problem and the following box to illustrate the process. Draw your own box with the adversity at the top and the following column headings: 1. Worst-Case Beliefs, 2. How Likely? 3. Best-Case Beliefs, 4. Most Likely Outcomes, and 5. Solutions. Use this box to follow along as you analyze the last time you succumbed to your catastrophic beliefs.

Step 1. Write Down the Ticker-Tape Chain

When looking back at that time, the first step is to write down your future-threat ticker-tape beliefs as they occurred, as each catastrophic belief chained into the next. Remember that for Larry, the adversity is that he forgot to mail out the sales brochures. From this emerge his future-threat beliefs—or worst-case beliefs—like so:

STEP 1: Worst-Case Beliefs	STEP 2: How Likely?	STEP 3: Best-Case Beliefs	STEP 4: Most Likely Outcomes	STEP 5: Solutions
Adversity = I forgot to send out the brochures to a prospective client				
I'll lose some calling time, so ▼				
Make no sales calls, so ▼				
Get no leads, so ▼				
Make no sales, so ▼				
Make no commission, so ▼				
Get starved out of this job, so ▼				
Will go through a succession of failed jobs, leaving some because I'll be unable to make enough money to get by, fired from others, so ▼				
Will not be able to pay the mortgage, so ▼				
Marriage gets placed under stress, so ▼				
Wife leaves me, so ▼				
Homeless, living on the streets				

Most of us would agree that Larry is catastrophizing. That is, we would recognize that a day's delay in sending out sales brochures does not mean he's going to spend the rest of his life living on the streets. We can see that Larry is making a mountain out of a molehill. Of course, it doesn't feel like catastrophizing to Larry. To him it feels like an accurate set of future predictions. And while none of us may have fallen into this specific catastrophic trap, every one of us has had times when our worst-case beliefs have run amok.

Larry's chain of beliefs illustrates well three noteworthy general features of catastrophizing. First, notice that all of his beliefs are projections into the future. Since these events have not yet occurred, they are not certain to happen—we can estimate how likely each link in the chain really is. Notice also that Larry is building a story, a prophecy, step by step and link by link. Each successive link represents a further reach into the future. No link in the chain can happen unless the link before it occurs, and although Larry doesn't realize it, the later a link appears in the chain, the less likely it is to occur.

Second, the jump from one link to the next is relatively minor. It's easy for us to see how Larry could believe that if he makes no commission, he'll get fired. Everyone knows that a salesman who makes no sales isn't worth having around. Larry also thinks, very logically, that if he's forced out of one job, it could happen again, and therefore it doesn't feel like such a reach to think that he could go through a succession of failed jobs. Of course, if that happens, it's not wildly unbelievable to think that he may not be able to pay the mortgage. And any reasonable person would understand how financial hardship like that could place stress on a marriage. Each step seems so small, so reasonable, and so logical that it's easy to see how Larry could get seduced into the chain. When we catastrophize, no single link requires us to make major leaps of faith or significantly suspend our disbelief, so we see no reason to doubt that the chain is reasonable and true.

The seductive nature of the catastrophic chain is compounded because elements of the chain *are* true, not in the sense that they are highly probable but that they flow logically one from the other. Parts of the chain are pure logic. Larry sells primarily through cold calling. If Larry makes no calls, ever, he will uncover no leads. And if he uncovers no leads, he will make no sales. If he makes no sales, he will make no commission. These statements are certainties—100 percent sure. These "patches" of logic in our catastrophic chain make it easier for people to glide over and accept the other parts of the chain. To make matters worse, as we create each link in the chain, our anxiety increases, and the increasing anxiety makes it even easier to believe the catastrophic picture that is emerging. The seductive nature of the chain coupled with your mounting anxiety is why your catastrophic beliefs seem so real when you're in the midst of them.

Obviously there are leaps in logic across the chain. Does it really mean no calls, no calls at all, if Larry spends a couple of hours putting the brochures together? No, probably not. Not unless Larry creates a self-fulfilling prophecy—if he gives up on making any calls because he falsely sees it as a fait accompli. It is more likely that Larry would lose *some* calling time—in fact, he'll lose as much time as it takes to get those brochures arranged and sent. A leap in logic, a thinking error spawned of his anxiety, leads Larry to the future-threat belief that he will make *no* calls. (When we asked Larry how likely he thought it was, when pacing up and down in his living room, that he'd end up in a Dumpster, he told us he reckoned about 60 percent!) What Larry needs, and anyone needs who tends to go straight for the worst-case scenario, is a tool to help him appreciate the real probabilities of his worst-case fears.

Step 2. Estimate the Probabilities of Your Worst-Case Fears

The key to ending your catastrophizing is, of course, to break free of the chain of future-threat beliefs. And the best way to do that is to underscore what you know as fact. The only thing of which Larry can be totally sure is that he forgot the sales brochures. The rest is guesswork and supposition. So let's use that fact to estimate just how likely it is that the events in Larry's chain actually will happen. What is the probability that Larry will lose some calling time the next day because he has to put the brochures together? Most of us would concede that it's pretty high. If he works a nine-hour day and he loses time assembling marketing materials, he *will* lose some of his call time. It's probably around 75 percent likely, or so. What is the probability that he will make *no* calls that day because he forgot the sales brochures? Most people would peg this as very low risk, unless of course his negative thinking and anxiety bring it about through self-fulfilling prophecy. It's probably about a one in 1,000 chance that he'll make no calls that day. But that's not all. He's also predicted that he'll make such a low commission that he'll get starved out of the company. Could this really happen after only one day of lost calling? It would take weeks of no calls, no leads, and no sales. So a more pertinent question is what is the probability that he'll make no calls, ever? Of course, it's very low. Some of you might say there's zero chance; others concede that it could happen but it's very unlikely. Most people in our training seminars estimate the chances at one in a million or less.

If making no calls at all is a one in a million prospect, then a succession of failed jobs is even lower in probability. This has to be so because those events that fall farther along the catastrophic chain have even smaller odds of coming true than one in a million. Larry estimated the probability for each link in his catastrophic chain, presented in the next box.

It may seem to you that Larry is being Pollyanna with his estimates. Isn't the divorce rate 50 percent of first-time marriages? But Larry's

Adversity = I forgot to send out the brochures to a prospective client

STEP 1: Worst-Case Beliefs	STEP 2: How Likely?	STEP 3: Best-Case Beliefs	STEP 4: Most Likely Outcomes	STEP 5: Solutions
I'll lose some calling time, so ▼	75%			
Make no sales calls, so ▼	1 in a million			
Get no leads, so ▼	1 in a million			
Make no sales, so ▼	1 in a million			
Make no commission, so ▼	1 in a million			
Get starved out of this job, so ▼	1 in a million			
Will go through a succession of failed jobs, leaving some because I'll be unable to make enough money to get by, fired from others, so ▼	1 in 2 million			
Will not be able to pay the mortgage, so ▼	1 in 3 million			
Marriage gets placed under stress, so ▼	1 in 3 million			
Wife leaves me, so ▼	1 in 5 million			
Homeless, living on the streets	1 in 10 million			

task is not to estimate the national averages for each of the events in his chain. His task is to estimate the real chances of future threat based on the adversity that has struck him. The relevant question is what are the chances that he and his wife will get divorced *because* he forgot the sales brochures. Go ahead and estimate the likelihood of your own chained events. But as you do, for each event in the chain, ask yourself what are the chances of this happening *because* your adversity has hit you.

Back to Larry. It's one in a million that he'll go through a succession of failed jobs because he forgot the sales brochures. It's one in 10 million that he'll end up homeless. Why should anyone spend so much time and energy on a one in 10 million, or even a one in a million long shot? The short answer is we shouldn't; it's not a resilient use of our emotional resources. Larry's catastrophizing leads him to waste his energy planning for highly improbable outcomes, leaving him dangerously exposed to the real threats that are likely to emerge from the brochure predicament—real threats that we'll home in on in Step 4. The more time he wastes ruminating on his inevitable joblessness, the less time he spends on figuring out the quickest way to get the brochures out and still make his calls. That's why it's in his best interest, and yours, to establish what's *most* likely to happen and take steps to prepare for it.

Step 3. Generate Best-Case Alternatives

Larry came to realize that the outcomes he initially thought had a 60 percent chance of coming true, like living in a Dumpster, were actually one in a million long shots. Surely that realization would be enough to get him back on track and able to identify most likely implications. Unfortunately, our experience suggests that it takes more than that. And just as exhorting someone to think outside the box or be creative is not sufficiently prescriptive, neither is it a useful strategy merely to tell someone to get real. So what does it take to climb out of a future-threat rut? You have to create best-case scenarios.

Constructing an equally low probability best-case scenario does two things. First, it forces you out of your worst-case scenario thinking. By spending two or three minutes developing an outlandishly fantastic and silly fantasy, you will be better able to think more clearly about the likely implications because you've switched off the doom-and-gloom part of your brain. Second, your best-case story will make you laugh. And there is nothing like a little humor to lower your anxiety and get you in a better place to deal with the real problems before you. In fact, if you don't find yourself chuckling at your best-case scenario, it's probably not outlandish enough so you should keep at it until the absurdity forces a grin.

Larry's Best-Case Scenario

Larry came up with a very creative best-case scenario. (It's clear that this exercise was from a training that predated the 2000–2001 tech stock crash.)

Larry's best-case scenario is amusing, but you'd probably agree that it would be a waste of time to channel significant resources toward making it happen. Just as it would not be resilient for Larry to prowl the streets looking for a well-stocked Dumpster, neither would it be resilient for him

Adversity = I forgot to send out the brochures to a prospective client

STEP 1: Worst-Case Beliefs	STEP 2: How Likely?	STEP 3: Best-Case Beliefs	STEP 4: Most Likely Outcomes	STEP 5: Solutions
I'll lose some calling time, so ▼	75%	I get fired, so ▼		
Make no sales calls, so ▼	1 in a million	I take my severance pay to Silicon Valley, and ▼		
Get no leads, so ▼	1 in a million			
Make no sales, so ▼	1 in a million	I start up a dot.-com designed to help people get their brochures together so that no one has to ever go through the ordeal I had to—I call the company sales-brochures.com, then ▼		
Make no commission, so ▼	1 in a million			
Get starved out of this job, so ▼	1 in a million			
Will go through a succession of failed jobs, leaving some because I'll be unable to make enough money to get by, fired from others, so ▼	1 in 2 million			
Will not be able to pay the mortgage, so ▼	1 in 3 million	I take salesbrochures.com IPO, and ▼		
Marriage gets placed under stress, so ▼	1 in 3 million	I become a multimillionaire ▼		
Wife leaves me, so ▼	1 in 5 million			
Homeless, living on the streets	1 in 10 million			

to spend calling time designing a logo for his start-up company. Resilience lies in detecting and problem solving the most likely outcomes, and our final step in Putting It In Perspective is designed to help us do that.

Step 4. Identify Most Likely Implications

Once Larry had the worst- and best-case scenarios in place as a frame, it was easy for him to locate the most likely outcomes. It's important to remember that this all began with an adversity, a negative event. So it's reasonable to expect that the most likely implications will be negative. We don't want anyone to sugarcoat the issues that are bothering them.

It was a week or so after he'd forgotten the sales brochures that we coached Larry on Putting It In Perspective—too late for him to fix this adversity. But let's wind back the clock and give Larry another shot. Let's move back to 3:30 A.M. and see how else he could have handled his anxiety. If he had known how to put it in perspective, he might have come to the following conclusion: "I know now that none of the catastrophes that I'm playing out in my mind is going to happen. Unfortunately, forgetting those brochures won't get me the key to the executive washroom. But getting fired for one small mistake is only about as likely as getting a fat IPO. So I forgot the brochures. Big deal. I'll have to spend some time getting that stuff together, and my best guess is that'll use up about one to two hours. I'll probably lose a couple of hours of calling time, but that's all. I'll still make some calls, and there are plenty more calls to be made in the days ahead. The client was expecting those brochures, but I'm betting that they're not sitting in their office holding their breath. The real problem will be explaining this to my boss. He'll rant and rave when he finds out." Larry's most likely outcomes are entered in the next box. You should do the same for your adversity, now that you have some worst-case/best-case scenario anchors in place.

Adversity = I forgot to send out the brochures to a prospective client

STEP 1: Worst-Case Beliefs	STEP 2: How Likely?	STEP 3: Best-Case Beliefs	STEP 4: Most Likely Outcomes	STEP 5: Solutions
I'll lose some calling time, so ▼	75%	I get fired, so ▼	Have to get the sales brochures ready tomorrow	
Make no sales calls, so ▼	1 in a million	I take my severance pay to Silicon Valley, and ▼		
Get no leads, so ▼	1 in a million			
Make no sales, so ▼	1 in a million	I start up a dot.com designed to help people get their brochures together so that no one has to ever go through the ordeal I had to—I call the company sales-brochures.com, then ▼	Lose 1–2 hours of calling time	
Make no commission, so ▼	1 in a million			
Get starved out of this job, so ▼	1 in a million		Boss will be unhappy when he finds out about the mistake and will rant and rave	
Will go through a succession of failed jobs, leaving some because I'll be unable to make enough money to get by, fired from others, so ▼	1 in 2 million			
Will not be able to pay the mortgage, so ▼	1 in 3 million	I take salesbrochures.com IPO, and ▼		
Marriage gets placed under stress, so ▼	1 in 3 million	I become a multimillionaire ▼		
Wife leaves me, so ▼	1 in 5 million			
Homeless, living on the streets	1 in 10 million			

After listing the most likely outcomes resulting from his mistake, Larry realizes he really has only two problems—finding time to get the brochures out while maintaining call time and managing his boss's anger. Now that Larry knows what the problems are, he can begin to solve them.

Step 5. Problem Solve the Most Likely

Now that Larry's equipped with the Putting It In Perspective skill, he'll be able to head off future catastrophizing episodes that someone with his future-threat style would otherwise inevitably experience. Had he been proficient in the skill at 3:30 A.M., had he been able to identify the most likely outcomes of his mistake, Larry concedes he would have acted very differently. He wrote down his solution strategies in the following box, and we ask you to do the same—come up with two or three ways that you could have fixed the real problems that stemmed from your adversity.

As Larry said to us, "I was reacting to my worst-case fears. If I'd zeroed in on the most likely outcome, the solution would have been as obvious to me as it was to you. I would've thought, 'Hey, I'm awake now anyway, why not head in to work early and get those brochures together and sent out.' I would have been done by 8:30 and ready to hit the phones at the regular time. I would've called the client and maybe even offered to drive the materials up to him. With this face-to-face time, I could have cemented a relationship with him and upped the ante on getting sales. Here's another thing I would have done differently if I'd had this skill at that time. Instead of avoiding my boss, I would have marched into his office and let him know what happened. 'Jim,' I would have said, 'I screwed up. I forgot those brochures yesterday. But here's what I've done to fix it.' I know this would go a long way with Jim." Now, that's good problem solving. Those are the actions of a resilient person.

"Killed in a Car Accident": Catastrophizing Without the Chain

Most chronic worriers catastrophize in a chain like Larry's. But we have come across many anxiety-prone folk who have a different catastrophizing process. We met Sandra in a teacher-certification training for our Children's Resiliency Program. As we taught her group the skill of Putting It In Perspective, we described the nature of the catastrophic chain and challenged each person to recall a time when they had found themselves in the

Adversity = I forgot to send out the brochures to a prospective client

STEP 1: Worst-Case Beliefs	STEP 2: How Likely?	STEP 3: Best-Case Beliefs	STEP 4: Most Likely Outcomes	STEP 5: Solutions
I'll lose some calling time, so ▼	75%	I get fired, so ▼	Have to get the sales brochures ready tomorrow	Get to work an hour or so early, prepare the brochures, and get them out before scheduled calling time
Make no sales calls, so ▼	1 in a million	I take my severance pay to Silicon Valley, and ▼		
Get no leads, so ▼	1 in a million			
Make no sales, so ▼	1 in a million	I start up a dot.com designed to help people get their brochures together so that no one has to ever go through the ordeal I had to—I call the company sales-brochures.com, then ▼	Lose 1–2 hours of calling time	
Make no commission, so ▼	1 in a million			
Get starved out of this job, so ▼	1 in a million		Boss will be unhappy when he finds out about the mistake and will rant and rave	Call the client and let them know there's been a delay. Smooth over the relationship. Offer to drive up and see them personally.
Will go through a succession of failed jobs, leaving some because I'll be unable to make enough money to get by, fired from others, so ▼	1 in 2 million			
Will not be able to pay the mortgage, so ▼	1 in 3 million	I take salesbrochures. com IPO, and ▼		
Marriage gets placed under stress, so ▼	1 in 3 million	I become a multimillionaire ▼		Tell boss preemptively of error and what steps taken to fix it.
Wife leaves me, so ▼	1 in 5 million			
Homeless, living on the streets	1 in 10 million			

grip of such a chain. All of them could, except Sandra. She certainly was no stranger to catastrophizing—Sandra immediately pegged herself as someone constantly on the lookout for future threats. She described a time when her husband and teenage son headed off together on an eighty-mile road trip to see the rock band U2 play in Philadelphia. Being a worrier, she made sure she knew everything about their itinerary—when the concert was slated to end and when they were expected home. Her anxiety started churning when they were thirty minutes late, but by the time an hour had elapsed, she was terrified and panic stricken. She assumed they'd been killed in a car accident. She paced up and down in her living room like a caged animal, and nothing could have convinced Sandra, in that moment, that her son and husband were safe and sound. When Sandra did ABC (the prelude to all the thorough skills of resilience), this is what she described:

ADVERSITY: My husband and son are one hour late returning from a concert.
BELIEFS: They've been killed in a terrible car accident and nobody has con-

tacted me yet because there was a terrible fire and the authorities are unable to identify the bodies.

CONSEQUENCES (EMOTIONAL): Terror and panic

CONSEQUENCES (BEHAVIORAL): Paced; turned on the TV to check for any car accidents; began calling area hospitals to check on admissions.

Sandra had clearly made it to a catastrophic end in her thoughts, but you'll notice that the rest of the chain, the earlier events that led up to the catastrophe, is missing. We pushed her a little harder to find other links. Nothing. In adversities such as these, where future-threat beliefs about the safety of her family were involved, Sandra knew only two "speeds": total calm and total anxiety.

Notice how "cleverly" her catastrophic belief is designed to block out any reassuring evidence to the contrary. An objective observer would remind Sandra that her husband and son were surely carrying IDs, and yet the authorities had not contacted her, so they were probably safe. But Sandra's future-threat radar was strong enough to account for that reassuring detail by adding in the "fire" component, which ensures that the catastrophic belief can remain unchallenged.

In chainless cases like Sandra's, we have to modify the worst-best/most-likely process to attain the best results. Asking Sandra to assess the probability that her loved ones were dead given that they are late will only serve to yield a falsely high estimate. That is the very nature of catastrophizing. We inflate the probabilities of terrible outcomes. When beliefs come as a chain, we can chip away at these false probabilities by forcing ourselves to estimate the likelihood of each link in the chain against the known adversity. It's by progressively getting more accurate with probabilities, link by link, that we get around the future-threat rut. If there's no chain, how can we apply Putting It in Perspective to help Sandra?

Instead of having her assess the probability of a disaster occurring, we encouraged Sandra to generate the best possible outcome she could muster. This is what she came up with: "They had such a great time together and the singer of U2, Bono, was touched by the father-and-son pair rocking away at his concert, so he invited them backstage. They sat around and chatted with the band for a couple of hours. It was such a bonding experience that their already close relationship becomes even closer and they were invited to tour with Bono and the band. They call me from the road and tell me to meet them at the airport because we're off to the Riviera for U2's next concert. I join Bono on stage at the concert, and the crowd loves me so much that I'm immediately signed to a multimillion-dollar deal with Sony." Not buying it? Neither was Sandra. But having devised the best-case fantasy, she was now laughing instead of worrying and was able to see things as they most likely were.

As it turns out, Sandra's son and husband didn't get to meet the band. In fact, traffic was a mess after the concert, and they decided to go grab a bite and wait for it to clear. This delayed them by a couple of hours, but eventually they arrived home very safe and very sound.

Unrealistic Optimism—Overly Positive Implications Beliefs

So far we've applied the skill of Putting It in Perspective only to helping severe worriers. The skill is also applicable, however, to people who do the opposite—who approach life with an unrealistic sense of optimism. This can set a person up for disaster as surely as catastrophizing. If you almost never get anxious, even mildly so; if you go through life believing that *everything* will *always* work out; if you've found yourself in a financial hole because you put your money into risky schemes; if you don't eat healthfully, don't exercise, and don't think that will affect your future health—then this may be the section for you.

The Nature of Positive Illusions

Many people underestimate risk. When smokers are asked to estimate their risk of getting lung disease, including cancer, they rate themselves significantly lower than what the national average indicates their risk to be. People engaged in high-risk behaviors see themselves as less at risk for HIV infection and contracting AIDS than the average risk for those who, like them, practice unsafe sex or share syringes. They are unrealistically optimistic—they fail to see that there's a problem to solve, much less that they should set about solving it.[2]

Wendy Middleton, Peter Harris, and Mark Surman, three British psychologists, decided to move their research on unrealistic optimism from the lab into the real world. They located a threat situation that met all the criteria for a thorough investigation of optimistic bias—a real, novel, and potentially life-threatening event. They found it in bungee jumping.

The UK Bungee Club estimates that as of 1996, when the study was done, about 100,000 people in Britain had tried this increasingly popular sport. One of the shortcomings of previous research into unrealistic optimism is that, for any given individual we interview about risk, we can never be sure that the person's optimism is unfounded. The person, for example, may be genetically robust against heart and lung disease in spite of a pack-a-day smoking habit. Particularly skilled drivers have genuinely lower risks on the roads. Likewise, in some dangerous activities, such as rock climbing and skydiving, some people may have natural abilities—excellent eye-hand coordination or leg and arm strength—which actually do place them at lower risk than the average Joe. But unlike rock climbing and skydiving, bungee jumping requires no skill, other than the ability to sign one's name on the indemnity form. There's nothing in the way a jumper throws himself from the platform that will affect level of risk. Injury, if and when it occurs, is always due to equipment failure.

Middleton, Harris, and Surman interviewed first-time bungee jumpers, as well as their family and friends who came to watch, some time between their signing up and being hoisted up to the platform. Respondents were asked to rate both how likely it was that *they* (or their friend or family member) would be injured during the jump. They also rated the risk to the typical jumper. The results were telling. The watchers, the people on the ground, saw no difference in the risk to their friend or family member and that of the typical jumper. Those respondents waiting to jump, however, believed that they were at significantly *lower* risk than the typical jumper. Clearly unrealistic optimism was at work in the minds of those willing to take the risk.[3]

It's clear that unrealistic optimism, since it underestimates risk, can lead us to engage in behaviors that are potentially harmful. So why do so many of us wear the rose-colored glasses? It turns out that it all comes back to beliefs. We all have beliefs about ourselves, about our strengths and abilities, our weaknesses and vulnerabilities. We also have beliefs about why people get involved in car accidents, have high cholesterol, get lung cancer, or get injured bungee jumping. As it turns out, unrealistic optimists believe that they lack the vulnerabilities, such as "cancer" genes, that put others at risk, or they think they have strengths to protect them that others lack—like exceptional driving skills. They distinguish themselves from the typical "victim," and in doing so they fail to see that, in many cases, they are also at genuine risk.

Researchers into positive illusions have noticed a certain egocentrism of unrealistic optimists. You know how some people come across as supremely arrogant or self-important, but once you get to know them, you find out that they're actually very insecure? The egocentrism of the unrealistic optimist is also often surface-level only. Some researchers believe that the positive illusions these people hold work to protect their fragile self-esteem when they're threatened. Not only do they set themselves above the risk-factor fray, but when adversity strikes others, they can blame the victim. They'll think, "Surely that person could have avoided that problem. I know *I* could have." This serves to ease their anxiety and to provide them with a sense of self-efficacy. But they've taken comfort in a false calm, a false sense of mastery, and a mistaken, inaccurate belief.

Applying Putting It in Perspective to Unrealistic Optimism

If you're an unrealistic optimist, you can use Putting It in Perspective too—but in reverse. You don't need to generate the most catastrophic outcomes, but it is important for you to come up with a list of possible negative implications of the adversity you're now facing. As always with these skills, the key is flexibility and accuracy. Be flexible enough to get outside your overly optimistic style so that you can identify potential problems and plan for them.

Conclusion

You've learned five skills that will help you build your resilience. Next you'll learn how to calm yourself and focus when your emotions have the better of you and how to use the skills of resilience in the heat of the moment, without needing a worksheet to see yourself through.

CHAPTER NINE

The Fast Skills: Calming and Focusing and Real-time Resilience

When You Need Speed

Challenging Beliefs and Putting It in Perspective are applicable in most situations, but they aren't the most effective skills when your emotions are so strong that you can't even think straight, when you don't have the luxury of fifteen minutes to process a situation, or when you need a simple but effective way to have a moment of calm amid the chaos. In these situations, you need something fast. We'll teach you two fast skills in this chapter that are used to change nonresilient emotions or actions as soon as they arise. Skill 6—Calming and Focusing—is a powerful tool that helps you to quiet your emotions when they are out of control, to focus your thoughts when they are intrusive, and to reduce the amount of stress you experience. Skill 7 is called Real-time Resilience, which takes the essential ingredients of Challenging Beliefs and Putting It in Perspective and uses them to fight back against counterproductive beliefs as they occur.

These two fast skills can stand alone but are often used together. Sometimes people find that once they have calmed their emotions and cleared their thoughts, they are able to move forward in that moment—for them, Calming and Focusing alone does the job. Later, when they have time to reflect, they can analyze the adversity and their beliefs about it, using one of the thorough skills. At other times, people are able to challenge their beliefs in the moment using Real-time Resilience. And then there are times when your emotions are so strong that you need Calming and Focusing to take the edge off before you can use Real-time Resilience. Both skills have a role in building your resilience, and we will point out the situations for which each is best suited.

Three People Who Need the Fast Skills

Everyone is always telling Warren to slow down. From the moment he wakes up in the morning until he falls asleep that night, he acts like he's playing "beat the clock." He drinks his morning coffee while he shaves. He eats his breakfast while he drives. He works long hours at the office, then, after his family is asleep, he works well past midnight at home. Typically, he gets no more than five hours of sleep at night. He used to enjoy the frenetic pace and thought the adage "If you need to get something done, ask a busy person" was right on the money, but lately the stress has been getting to him. He's been sick more in the last year than in the last five. Even when he isn't sick, his body never feels quite right. And his attitude has changed from upbeat to moody. Warren complains about the amount of stress in his life, but he doesn't know what to do about it.

Then there's Jeremy—the hothead. His emotions go from zero to sixty faster than most sports cars. His colleagues complain that he's a loose cannon. His wife and children are uneasy whenever he's around, afraid to do something that will set him off. He's hostile and aggressive in situations that most of us would see as innocuous—not finding a parking spot, being interrupted by a child, the video store not having the film he wants to see. When Jeremy is not seeing red, he's able to step back and see that he's overreacting, but he feels at a loss to get control. The only thing he knows how to do is to wait it out until his emotions release him.

Katherine's problem is that she's got too much internal chatter—she's a worrier. As an account manager of an advertising agency, Katherine's responsibilities are diverse. She has to be an attentive listener and a persuasive talker. Often, however, she finds it hard to tune out her own internal monologue. During an important presentation, she worries, "Am I going to be able to convince them we're the right agency to do their ads? Am I being strong enough? Did I answer them clearly? Do I look okay?" Afterward she ruminates, "I wasn't clear. I know it. I'm feeling really bad about this. Why can't I ever pull it together?" All this self-doubt causes Katherine to lose her edge, and she doesn't know how to regain her concentration and focus.

Which Story Did You Resonate With?

These three problems—losing your calm, losing your head, and losing your focus—drain your reserves of resilience. They cause you to waste valuable time in your professional life, they can deeply wound your relationships, and they even can make you physically sick. Consider the amount of stress you feel. Did Warren's story resonate with you? Have you noticed new aches and pains but haven't made the time to get to the doctor? Is your concentration and memory worse than usual? Do you have trouble sleeping? These are all signs of stress. If you don't learn how to reduce them, you may be heading toward serious health problems. In this chapter we teach you how to minimize the amount of stress in your life so that it doesn't rob you of resilience.

How about Jeremy's story—did you recognize yourself in it? Think about the past couple of weeks. Have there been times when you flew off the handle or felt engulfed in fear? Does your family walk on eggshells lately when you're around? Have you been told that you need to "get a grip"? When these emotions pass, do you see the situation differently and become aware of critical information that you were blind to while caught in the emotional storm? If you answered yes, you may have experienced what we described in Chapter 4 as an amygdala hijack, or you may have responded to iceberg beliefs about violation of rights. In either case, we'll teach you how to find your bearings in these moments and how to quiet your emotions so that you can start thinking straight again.

Maybe you can't recall a time when your emotions were out of control. Can you, however, think of times when you felt scattered and had a hard time focusing on the task at hand? Like Katherine, is your ticker tape filled with worry? Are you like a cow chewing its cud—reliving every experience, churning every detail around and around—but never actually finding a solution to the problem? Do you worry a lot about your work, health, or relationships? Do "off-topic" thoughts—thoughts that are unrelated to the task before you—cause you to feel anxious, lose your train of thought, or lead you to bury simple ideas under mountains of convolution? Perhaps your thoughts cause you to procrastinate? Sometimes our ticker-tape beliefs lead to too much anxiety and make it hard to enjoy the present. We'll teach you how to refocus your thoughts so that you can concentrate.

Let's begin by taking a closer look at the effects of stress on resilience.

Stress

The more you practice Calming and Focusing and the more you increase your Real-time Resilience, the more resistant to stress you will become. And that's important because stress is a serious threat to your emotional and physical health. Regardless of what your job is, or how many children in diapers live in your home, or how old you are, one thing is certain: You experience stress. In fact, you encounter stress on a daily basis—it's an unavoidable part of life. And that's okay, because some stress is actually a good thing; it stimulates us and motivates us to meet the challenges that we face. One consequence of stress is anxiety, and anxiety in manageable doses is a great motivator. Would you be as likely to put in the extra hours to prepare for an important meeting if you didn't feel a bit anxious about it? Would you be as likely to practice your golf swing, over and over again, if you weren't anxious about winning? Stress becomes a problem only when we don't control it and it begins to overwhelm us.

What is your health like these days? When someone in your office is sick, are you certain to get sick too? Well, according to the research, it might be due to too much stress in your life. In one study, researchers tested whether stress played a role in contracting the common cold. The researchers had about four hundred healthy people complete a number of questionnaires to assess the amount of stress they currently were experiencing. Then each person was given nasal drops that contained an infectious dose of one of five common respiratory viruses. For the next seven days the participants were quarantined so that the researchers could assess any symptoms of illness (including counting the number of tissues each person used). This study showed that the people who scored in the highest range of stress were almost twice as likely as those who scored in the lowest range of stress to have caught the cold.[1]

Colds are unpleasant, but they're certainly not life threatening. Coronary artery disease is. The medical community is increasingly recognizing the link between stress and cardiovascular disorders. Acute stress has been shown to trigger decreases in blood flow to the heart, known as myocardial ischemia, in people with coronary artery disease. In fact, stress was as strong a predictor of ischemia as intense physical activity.[2] Additionally, clinical depression (often a consequence of chronic stress) is an indicator of poorer prognosis for patients with coronary artery disease. Put simply, patients with coronary artery disease who are also depressed die sooner than those who are depression free.[3]

How is it that stress makes us more susceptible to illness or disease?

When you're stressed, you're likely to think inaccurately. You may see healthful behaviors as being futile—what's the point of changing your diet when your father and grandfather both died of heart attacks in their fifties? This is a clear example of Bs leading to nonresilient Cs. Research also shows that when people are stressed, their natural killer cell activity (cells that provide defense against virus-infected cells and cancer cells) is weakened. Put another way, stress compromises your immune system, and a compromised immune system means that you'll get sick more often.[4]

So, what causes stress? It is important to distinguish between *stress* and *stressors*. Stress is what happens to your body and your mind when exposed to stressful situations. Body aches, fatigue, compromised immune functioning, depression, and anxiety are a subset of the symptoms of chronic stress. Stressors, in contrast, are the events or situations that elicit stress in individuals. Stressors can range from mild (forgetting to pick up your dry cleaning, missing the train, spilling coffee on your new suit) to extreme, like the death of a loved one, a natural disaster, or being the victim of violence. Stressors usually are external events, things that happen to us. But they also can be internal "events," such as feeling angry at your significant other, thinking pessimistically, or suffering long-standing anxiety. You may be surprised to learn that stressors also can be positive events. As anyone who has ever planned a wedding or brought home a newborn child knows, the experiences of life that bring us the most happiness also can bring us the most stress. What stress researchers have found is that change, whether positive or negative, is a stressor.[5] And change is here to stay.

When confronted with a stressor—such as imminent danger—your body has what is called a stress reaction, in which there is an outpouring of adrenaline and cortisol. And the power that comes from the adrenaline is necessary when true dangers are present. It is what enabled our early ancestors to save themselves from the saber-toothed tiger, it's what makes it easier for emergency service personnel to do their jobs, and it's what enabled Donna, a 110-pound woman from Boston, to lift the family van off her husband, who had become trapped beneath it. But the stress we feel each day rarely comes from situations in which our literal survival will be determined by the quickness of our response. Making deadlines is important. Getting the kids to school on time matters. Peaceful family dinners are worth striving for. But in none of these situations does the success of our genetic lineage lie in the balance. Yet in spite of the dramatic change in the nature of stressors that most humans regularly encounter, the stress response has remained unchanged. Whether you are Throgg leaving the campfire in search of food or Tom leaving the boardroom in search of clients, once the fight-or-flight response begins, the unfolding is identical.

Some People Are Overwhelmed by Stress More Quickly Than Others

Research shows that how you interpret stressors and how you respond to stressors contribute significantly to how much stress you will feel. This sounds an awful lot like ABC, doesn't it? Dr. Suzanne Kobasa, a psychologist at the City University of New York, has been studying why some people who have lives that are rich in stressors fare better (that is, experience less stress and burnout and get ill less often) than others in the same occupation. Kobasa has worked with thousands of executives and managers and has found that there are three critical factors—*control, commitment*, and *challenge*—that differentiate those who are resilient to stress from those who are more vulnerable.[6]

✦ Resilient people believe they can directly influence the events that occur in their lives and translate their beliefs into actions—in other words, they believe they are in control. If you lack the ability to control what is happening in your life, or if you *believe* you lack the ability, you will feel more stress when faced with an adversity. Put simply, people who are powerless, even if it is just a matter of their beliefs, become victims, and victims get overwhelmed by stress. In contrast, people who take charge over the aspects of their lives that are controllable thrive despite real-life problems and difficulties.

✦ Resilient people also score higher on measures of engagement or commitment to what they are doing. For them, work is not just work—it's a source of meaning in their lives.

✦ And they are more likely to see change as an opportunity for growth rather than as a stressor.

Kobasa's research points out the importance of thinking style in dealing with stressors. There are some events over which we have no control—such as the death of a loved one or natural disasters. Nearly everyone would find such events extremely stressful, regardless of their thinking style. Most stressors, however, fall into the gray area in terms of control. We can shape and change some elements of these stressors, while other areas are immutable. For most of the daily hassles of life—project deadlines, travel, cranky children, and the like—whether we believe we have control, and then how we go about handling the situation, matter a great deal in terms of the amount of stress we will experience.

Using Calming Techniques to Minimize Stress

To be more resilient, you need to be able to handle stress well. You can learn to prevent or minimize the amount of stress you experience by changing the way you think when confronted with stressors. But let's face it, you're not going to be able to avoid stress completely, so you also need a way to calm yourself down once stress overtakes you. That's where the calming techniques come into play.

As you would expect, most of the stress-busting techniques hinge on increasing your ability to control how your body and mind responds to stress by teaching you how to bring yourself back into a state of relaxation. The power of relaxation is quite simple: The body cannot simultaneously be in a state of relaxation and in a state of stress—they're incompatible. So, if you learn how to relax, you will be able to control the amount of stress you experience.

As you read, it's important to remember that you don't have to use each technique to see improvement in how you respond to stressors. View these techniques as a menu from which you can sample. Some techniques will work better for you than others.

CONTROLLED BREATHING

When you are feeling stressed and the anxiety is building, what happens to your breathing? Most people find that they begin to take shallow, quick breaths. When this happens, you are breathing from your chest instead of from your diaphragm (the dome-shaped muscle at the bottom of your lungs), which means that only the topmost part of your lungs is filling with air. Because you are bringing in less oxygen to your lungs, less oxygen is being circulated through your bloodstream. The change in oxygen level sends off a warning alarm in your brain, causing more adrenaline to be released, which leads to even more anxiety, further shallow breathing, further oxygen depletion—a vicious cycle.

When you breathe from your diaphragm, your body feels different.

The breaths are deeper, slower, and fuller. The breaths feel cleansing. As you inhale your abdomen rises, and as you exhale your abdomen falls. Most people find the best way to determine whether they are breathing from their chest or abdomen is to lie on their back on the floor. When you do this, you can put your hand on your abdomen to help you notice whether it is rising and falling as you breathe. If your abdomen is still, then you are not breathing from your diaphragm.

There are a variety of deep-breathing exercises, but following is the one that we've found most useful. Once you have the basic technique down, experiment with variations in pacing until you find the one that brings you into the most fully relaxed state. It is important that you practice these techniques at least once a day.

EXERCISE

+ Sit straight in a chair without arm rests, feet flat on the floor. Put your hands comfortably in your lap.
+ Inhale through your nose until you can feel your abdomen expand.
+ As you take a slow, controlled breath, picture your lungs filling with air. As you inhale, count very slowly from one to four. Some people find it helpful to imagine a balloon expanding as they fill their lungs with oxygen. Be sure your stomach and shoulders stay relaxed.
+ Exhale slowly through your nose so that it takes to the count of four to exhale completely.
+ Continue this process of slow, deep breathing in and out for at least three minutes.
+ Focus your thoughts on your breathing. Notice how your shoulders and back, belly and legs feel. If your thoughts start to wander, consciously shift your attention back to your breathing. This step is often the most difficult, so be patient. As you get more comfortable with the breathing exercise, it will be easier for you to concentrate on the pattern of your breaths.

PROGRESSIVE MUSCLE RELAXATION

Another relaxation strategy that you can use in combination with controlled breathing when you start to feel stressed is to systematically relax the muscles throughout your body. When you are feeling stress, your body becomes tight. You may notice an ache in your lower back. Your neck may feel stiff. Some people find that their muscles twitch. Progressive muscle relaxation (PMR) is a process of tensing, then relaxing, individual muscle groups. It helps you to identify what your muscles feel like when they're tense compared to relaxed.

EXERCISE

+ Find a comfortable position, either lying on the floor or sitting in a chair with your back straight, feet flat on the floor, arms resting comfortably in your lap.

+ Close your eyes and follow the steps for controlled breathing for two minutes.

+ Begin with your lower arms and hands. Keep your mind as clear as possible. As you breathe in, make fists and tense your hands and lower arms. Do your best to isolate the tension just to the lower arm and hand rather than tensing your full arm or other parts of your body. Your muscles should feel tight but not painful. Keep the muscles tensed for fifteen seconds.

+ As you continue with the controlled breathing, focus on the feeling of tension in your hands and lower arms. Which part of the muscle feels most tight? When that muscle is tight, how do the muscles around it feel? Keep your muscles tight for the count of fifteen.

+ As you exhale, let the tension go from your hands and lower arms. Relax the muscles quickly and concentrate on the feeling of relaxation in those muscles. When you release the tension in the muscle, what do you notice about your breathing and your heart rate? Keep breathing, and after two or three breaths you should notice that the muscles feel completely relaxed. Try to keep the muscles fully relaxed for thirty seconds. You can now start the process over again, concentrating on the same muscles.

+ After you've practiced tensing and relaxing your hands and lower arms twice, take a one-minute break and then move on to the next muscle group. Continue to use your controlled breathing as you progress through the muscle groups.

+ For each muscle group, repeat the process you used with your hands and lower arms. Tense the muscles for fifteen seconds, then relax them for thirty seconds. Try to tense them as you breathe in and release them after a few breaths, while you exhale. For each muscle group, try to concentrate on the feeling of the tensed muscle and do your best to tense only the muscles you are targeting. When you relax the muscles, pay attention to how they feel and try to relax them as fully as possible.

✦ After each muscle group, take one-minute break before continuing to the next muscle group.

This entire process will take about twenty minutes. We recommend that you work through your entire body the first two weeks (practicing PMR at least once a day). Afterward you can target those specific muscle groups that are giving you trouble.

People run into three common difficulties when first learning and practicing PMR.[7] First, many people find it hard to isolate the muscles of one muscle group—this is normal. Unless you practice yoga or have a well-developed stretching routine, you probably haven't tried to isolate various muscles. As you practice PMR, you will see gradual improvement and you will become more attuned to the interconnections of your muscles.

A second problem people experience is an ironic effect of relaxation. For some people, the first few times they practice PMR and other relaxation strategies, they find themselves becoming more and more tense. In fact, just thinking about relaxing makes their heart rate increase and causes their breathing to grow shallow. Drs. David Barlow and Ron Rappe—two experts on using PMR to reduce anxiety—have found that this ironic effect is most common for people who have a strong need to be in control and in people who are prone to anxiety. The experience of relaxing, even simply closing their eyes, may feel uncomfortable because they interpreted it, through their beliefs, as relinquishing control. And for people who are prone to anxiety disorders, being told to "relax" may lead to more symptoms of anxiety—it even has a name: "relaxation-induced anxiety." As one man we worked with described, "As soon as I am told to 'relax,' my ticker tape starts with 'What if I can't relax? What if they see that everyone else is relaxed but I'm obviously becoming more and more anxious? What if they notice how fast I am breathing?' " If this happens to you, first put your catastrophic what-if thoughts in perspective. Once they are taken care of, you'll be able to use PMR successfully. You also may find it helpful to keep your eyes open during PMR and focus on a spot on the wall or floor.

The final problem that some people experience as they work to master PMR is that after a few minutes, they fall asleep. If this is true, you're probably overtired and could benefit from more sleep at night. (Couldn't we all?) Although a twenty-minute catnap will feel great, obviously, if you fall asleep every time you try to relax, you will not learn how to do PMR effectively. And there are many situations when you use can PMR—when you're stuck in traffic, before an important work event, before making love—in which it is beneficial to become more relaxed yet problematic to fall asleep.

Once you feel comfortable with PMR and are noticing changes in your relaxation level, you can move ahead to "advanced" relaxation, to help you to reach high levels of relaxation in difficult situations and to do so in the shortest period of time possible. It's one thing to be able to relax in the privacy of your own home after twenty minutes of controlled practice; it's quite another to be able to do so in the five minutes you have to gulp down your lunch in the crowded company cafeteria.

To increase the portability of PMR, you need to practice getting to the same level of relaxation using shorter and shorter exercises. After you feel comfortable tensing and relaxing all of your muscles, begin to cut back on the number of muscles you tense. A smart way to approach this is to rank the muscle groups in terms of how much stress you tend to feel in each. Then cut out the muscle groups where you experience the least stress and practice PMR on those that are most often tense. Try to shorten the time from twenty minutes down to fifteen or ten. After about two weeks, most people find that they can reach the same level of relaxation during the abbreviated PMR as they did when working through all their muscle groups. After you've mastered the abbreviated version, you will find that you can notice slight changes in tension and can immediately release those muscles without first having to isolate and tense them.

You also need to become skilled at relaxing even when there are significant distractions in the environment. For some, that means practicing PMR while the kids are chasing the dog through the house. For others, it means practicing PMR while sitting at the desk in a noisy office. To do this, list a few places that are distracting for you. Practice PMR first in the easiest location, building up to the hardest. For one woman we worked with, that meant first practicing PMR in her home while loud music played on the radio. Then she practiced while she ate dinner at the mall with her three teenage daughters, and finally she used PMR as she attended a stressful staff meeting.

POSITIVE IMAGERY

The third calming exercise is positive imagery. You can use it in all the same situations where you use controlled breathing or PMR. Try this now by closing your eyes and imagining a calming, relaxing scene—a place where you feel completely at ease, comfortable, and happy. Spend two or three minutes creating and then relaxing in the image you've created.

Now read the following two descriptions and decide which is more like the image you created—not in terms of the specific details, but in terms of the level of detail and vividness of the image.

SCENE 1

I'm on the beach. The sun is warm, but not too hot. I'm lying on a towel listening to the ocean waves crash on the beach.

SCENE 2

I'm on the beach. The sun is warm and I feel its rays spread across my body. I am lying on a towel listening to the ocean waves crash on the beach. I can see the waves off in the distance, building slowly as they approach the shore. I hear a faint and gentle whisper when they are out on the horizon. As they get closer to shore, I hear a growing tumbling sound and then a rhythmic crash as they break upon the sand. As I listen to the soothing sounds of the ocean, I can hear birds flying overhead and the air is rich with the smells of suntan lotion, warm rain, and cut grass.

Which image was more like the one you created? If your image contained the same level of detail as scene 1, then you need to practice constructing a more vivid image. (A quick read of a travel magazine, or even a romance novel, may do the trick.) Why is this important? Because the more detailed and vivid your visualization is, the more powerful it will be in helping you to relax. The following tips will help.

✦ Begin to relax yourself by using controlled breathing.
✦ Keeping your eyes closed, imagine that you are the set director on a film and your job is to create a soothing experience that is as real as possible. Start by focusing on major elements of the scene. Where are you? Many people find beach scenes or mountain scenes soothing. A place that includes the sound of running water is usually calming.
✦ Begin to fill in the details by focusing on each of your senses. What can

you see? What do you hear? What do you smell? How does it feel to your touch? The more detailed you can imagine the scene, the better.

✦ After you have a peaceful, vivid portrait in mind, repeat a positive phrase to yourself, such as "I feel calm" or "I feel at ease and at peace." Alternatively, you can visualize the stress flowing out of you. Some people find this step hokey. If you do, skip it.

Visualization exercises like this one are powerful tools when used regularly. The more you practice visualization, the easier it becomes because your mind begins to associate the imagined scene with being in a state of relaxation. You are, in fact, conditioning your body to relax in association with the image. After using the technique for several weeks, you may find that your body begins to relax as soon as you begin to think about the scene you have created.

A different positive imagery technique can be used to help you prepare for an upcoming stressful situation. In this way, the technique is used preventively, rather than to lower stress once it has occurred. You begin the same way, with controlled breathing, but instead of conjuring an imaginary scene, bring to mind the stressor that you must soon face and visualize yourself handling the situation with confidence and skill.

The process of visualizing yourself in upcoming stressful situations works best if you practice on several occasions before the actual event; the more detailed you are, the better. Try to visualize yourself performing the specific tasks that you'll need to do when the event actually happens. If the situation you are preparing yourself for is interpersonal—an interview, a difficult conversation with an employee or friend—practice the actual words you will say and see yourself responding to the other person with confident speech and body language.

Keeping your body calm despite the chaos that surrounds you is an important part of being resilient, so we encourage you to use the calming techniques whenever you feel stress spread through your body. The more you use them, the easier it will be for you to stop stress from taking control of your life.

Intrusive Thoughts

For some of you (a lucky few), stress may not be a big problem, but intrusive thoughts are. Remember Katherine? She found it hard to concentrate on the tasks before her because she was constantly interrupted by her own thoughts. Imagine yourself sitting at your desk or kitchen table, concentrating on the task before you—perhaps filling out forms, writing a report, or talking with someone over the phone. How long do you typically stay focused, fully attentive to what you are doing, before your mind starts to wander? One minute? Three minutes? Perhaps ten minutes? Okay, you might argue, my mind wanders in those activities because I don't really like doing those things. And sure, the less compelling we find a task, the more likely it is that our minds will wander. But most people's minds wander even during activities they greatly enjoy. One of the biggest problems for athletes, whether it's making a free throw, making a putt, or hitting a pitch, is a lack of concentration. And lots of women complain that they are thinking about other things (such as work they must complete, groceries they need to pick up, etc.) while they're making love. Naturally, these thoughts interfere with their pleasure.

These intrusive thoughts undermine your resilience in three ways.

1. They often center on negative experiences and cause your mood to turn sour.

2. They may lead you to obsess and obsessing interferes with problem solving.

3. They waste your time.

PROBLEM 1: INTRUSIVE THOUGHTS ARE OFTEN NEGATIVE AND CATASTROPHIC

Indulge us in an activity. Try your best to clear your mind. Do your best to keep your head empty of any thoughts—trust us, you won't be able to do it for very long. When a thought finally breaks through, notice what it is that has grabbed your attention. Chances are it will be something to do with a chore you need to finish, a person you need to talk to, or some other nagging issue that needs to be resolved. Here's what a woman we worked with reported. She sat quietly and tried to clear her mind and remain as open and relaxed as possible. We asked her to speak aloud her ticker-tape thoughts as they came: "The lights are humming. I hope they don't burn out. How long am I supposed to do this for? I'm tired. My back hurts. It feels too tight and achy. I've been feeling pretty run down lately. Jeff is right about me overextending myself. But I don't see how I can do any less. We need the money and my work is important to me. I don't think he really understands how much I *need* to work. I love being with the kids, but if I don't get out of the house then I'm way too impatient when I'm with them. Why can't he understand that? He expects me to love every second of my time with the kids, and that's just not realistic.

I'd like to see him spend the amount of time I do with them. We need to talk about this because it's really getting on my nerves."

What do you notice about this woman's chain of thoughts? When most people try this activity, they notice two things, both of which are true of the example: It's quite hard to clear one's mind—in fact, many people we've asked this of were not able to do this first step; they notice that their thoughts travel around aimlessly for a while but ultimately rest on something negative or problematic—our thinking style fills the void.

For the woman in the example, her attention was first grabbed by the sound of the lights. This "externally focused" thought didn't hold her attention. Gradually her mind shifted away from stimuli in the environment to internal stimuli. First, she notices the ache in her back. Then she starts to think about her hectic life and ultimately settles on the topic of the difficulty, but importance, of working and raising her children. As she thinks more about this, her thoughts lead her to a conflict with her husband and what she perceives as his inability to understand her need to work. How do you think she starts to feel as she continues down this path of thought? She becomes annoyed at her husband and the more she thinks about it, the angrier she becomes.

Now, you might say, "I understand your point, but my intrusive thoughts aren't about real problems. They're just ceaseless what-ifs that send me into a nosedive of anxiety." And you're right—our internal sentinels often warn us of dangers that are not present.

Although focusing on our intrusive thoughts can help us identify problems, it is helpful only when the problems we identify are real. When your intrusive thoughts bring your mental energy to bear on what-if situations, your mind is working against you and you minimize your effectiveness in dealing with a real problem or setback.

Do you see the problems of your life accurately, or do you create problems where they don't exist? In Chapter 8 we showed you how to use Putting It in Perspective to stop yourself from catastrophizing by considering all of the worst, best, and most likely implications. In this chapter we show you how to get to the same end point, but you'll learn how to stop the what-ifs dead in their tracks.

PROBLEM 2: YOU WON'T SOLVE YOUR PROBLEMS BY OBSESSING

Let's assume for a moment that your intrusive thoughts are about actual problems in your life. Once a problem grabs your attention, two very different styles of thinking arise—one that is useful, and one that is not. Read the next two examples and notice the different style of each.

Todd and Mary are planning their wedding—but it's not going smoothly. They spent the last twenty minutes arguing over whether the wild mushroom tartlets should be one of their twelve butlered hors d'oeuvres. Here is what they are saying to themselves.

Todd: "They can eat pigs in a blanket for all I care. Maybe we should take a break and just go out and have some fun. We had a blast that time we went bowling—maybe I'll suggest that—then we can get back to the all-important hors d'oeuvres list later tonight after we've had a chance to relax."

Now here's what Mary is thinking: "It's a stupid hors d'oeuvres list. Why can't we agree? This isn't good. I mean, we've got much bigger decisions to make, and I don't want to ruin the wedding because we're fighting over every little thing. I want to be happy. This should be fun. I'm really, really upset. There must be something wrong with us."

How would you categorize the difference between the two chains of thought? Todd is problem solving. Mary is obsessing. Let's start with obsessing—or rumination, as psychologists call it. Ruminators are like cows chewing their cud. They turn the same pieces of information over and over and over again, without generating planful actions or strategies for improving the situation. When people ruminate they tend to focus on their feelings, the causes of their feelings, and the meaning and consequences of those feelings. Ruminators, in fact, may be quite good at ABC because they spend a lot of time focused on their emotions and behaviors. The problem, however, is that they do nothing constructive with the information. Rather than use their self-awareness as the first step toward problem solving, they get stuck monitoring their thoughts, feelings, and behaviors.

Although the intention of ruminators is often to cope with and manage their moods, the process of rumination, unfortunately, has the exact opposite effect: Persistently focusing on one's mood worsens it rather than alleviates it. The problems with rumination have been extensively studied in the area of depression. Ask yourself this: When you start to feel sad, what do you tend to do? Do you sit and think about your feelings, or do you get up and do something? Dr. Susan Nolen-Hoeksema has proposed the "response-style" theory of depression, and she has found that your response style is important in determining how long your sad mood will last.[8] According to response-style theory, when men and women start to get depressed, on average they do two very different things. Men often distract themselves. They shoot hoops. They grab a beer.[9] They watch television or go bowling. Women, in contrast, ruminate. When they get sad, they call their friends and talk about how they are feeling. Women tend to focus on why they feel the way they do. They look for and notice subtle shifts in their emotions.

Research about response styles and depression suggests that distraction is a better strategy for clearing away self-destructive thoughts. And with a few important exceptions, we agree. Calming and focusing are "distraction" techniques. They are designed to help you to distract your attention away from counterproductive beliefs—beliefs that will serve only to increase your anxiety, sadness, or anger—so that you can bring yourself into a more productive frame of mind. But we want to be very clear about the distraction response style in general: Many of the ways people distract themselves, although they may decrease depression, are shortsighted at best, dangerous at worst. Reaching for a beer (or cocaine, or chocolate) is not a resilient way to manage your mood. Going to the gym every time you feel upset is better than sitting at home, wallowing in your symptoms, but pumping iron will not change what is causing you to feel depressed. Distraction is a short-term solution. It gets you out of your depressed mood, but unless you *do something* about the problem, the mood is likely to return.

Healthy distraction is step 1. Step 2 is problem solving. In one study, researchers compared dysphoric people (dysphoria is low-level depression) who were encouraged to ruminate to similar dysphoric people who were encouraged to engage in distracting activities to examine how rumination affected people's ability to problem solve.[10] By comparing groups that were equally dysphoric, any differences in their problem-solving capabilities could be attributed to their different response styles, not their depression. The results indicated that people who ruminate show nonresilient thinking in four areas that severely undermine their ability to solve problems. First, ruminators rated the problems they faced, such as conflicts with friends, as more severe and less solveable than did the distractors. But when independent judges were brought in to analyze these people's problems, they didn't see the ruminators' problems as any more severe or less solvable than those of the distractors. The ruminators also were significantly more self-critical than the distractors and were much more likely to see themselves as the cause of their problems. That is, when faced with problems, the ruminators tended to have a "me" explanatory style. Their "me" style coupled with their perception that the problems were severe and unsolvable—which are "always" beliefs—sapped any motivation they might have had to solve the problem. Third, not only were the ruminators more self-blaming, but they were also much more pessimistic and less confident in their ability to solve the problem even if they did try. Finally, the ruminators saw themselves as having much less control over the problems in their lives and said that they were less willing to actually attempt to implement solutions to their problems. In fact, when the participants were given problems to solve, such as how they would deal with a friend who was avoiding them, reseachers rated the ruminators' solutions as much less effective than those of the distractors.

When we put this all together, we see a clear picture of why it's so important to learn not to dwell on your feelings. Ruminators are poor problem solvers because they see the problems in their lives as uncontrollable and severe, and they see themselves as the cause. Even when they think they know how to solve the problem, because of their negativism they are unlikely to follow through on their idea. And, of course, by not solving the underlying problem, ruminators reinforce their negative views of themselves and the situation, creating a vicious cycle among rumination, depression, and decreased problem solving. Learning the fast skills will enable you to break this cycle.

PROBLEM 3: INTRUSIVE THOUGHTS WASTE YOUR TIME

Surely you know what it's like to be desperate to finish a task, only to be thrown off course repeatedly by thoughts that just won't go away. A teacher might have a pile of student papers she needs to read and comment on for class the next day. She picks up the first paper and starts reading. She reads for two minutes before she realizes, "Shoot! I forgot to return Jane's call. I hope it wasn't something important." She's able to ignore this thought and refocus, but then after a page and a half, she's interrupted by "Aaron was awfully cranky tonight. I hope he isn't getting sick." This train of thought costs her about fifteen minutes because once she starts thinking about her child's health, she decides to go and check on him. This leads to a stop in the kitchen, a quick spin around the TV dial, and then back to work (which meant starting that paper over again because by this point she's forgotten what she had previously read).

Wasting time is the third problem with intrusive thoughts. Even if you do not get caught up in rumination and your off-task thoughts are only a few seconds, once you are off task, it can take minutes to refocus and get back to work. Tomorrow, when you settle into your work—whether it is at an office or in your home—pay attention to the number of intrusive thoughts you have. Mark down on a piece of paper each time your thoughts pull you away from what you are doing. Most people are startled by the number of marks they accumulate by the end of the day and are astounded to learn how much of their total time was spent reengaging in their work after their mind pulled them off task.

Using the Focusing Techniques to Combat Intrusive Thoughts

So, how do you stop counterproductive thoughts from making you lose your focus? It's actually fairly simple. A number of techniques are quite powerful in stopping thoughts that are pulling you off task or causing you to ruminate. We call these techniques focusing techniques. Just like the calming techniques, we encourage you to try all of them and then stick with those that work best for you.

MENTAL GAMES

The purpose of mental games is to shift your attention away from the non-resilient beliefs so that you can continue with the task before you. For these games to work, they need to be challenging but not so difficult that you become frustrated and negative. They also should be fun so that your mood shifts from anxiety, anger, or sadness to a more pleasant emotion. Finally, they need to be relatively quick. The length of the mental games depends, to some extent, on the situation—a game needs to be quite brief if you are standing at a podium but can be slightly longer if you are waiting to be called in for an interview or sitting at your desk trying to get work done. Keep the mental games to under two minutes. Once you get the hang of them, feel free to make up some of your own.

✦ **THE ALPHABET GAME.** Work your way through the alphabet, naming someone for each pair of initials (e.g., AB—Annette Benning, BC—Bob
   Costas, CD—Charles Darwin, etc.). After a few times, the game may
   become too easy so you can restrict yourself to a particular category to
   make it more challenging. For example, try to name sports figures, au-
   thors, or movie stars for each pair of initials.

- **CATEGORIES.** Choose a category and name as many items in the category as possible within two minutes. Examples of categories are: vegetables, ski resorts, bones in the body, books written by Charles Dickens, Oscar-winning movies. Make the game more challenging by naming items within a category in alphabetical order (vegetables: asparagus, bok choy, carrots, etc.).

- **RHYMING.** Select a word and see how many rhymes you can come up with in two minutes. Cat is easy. Dour is harder.

- **MATHEMATICS.** Count back from 1,000 by sevens or rehearse the multiplication tables.

- **MEMORY.** Name all your school teachers, starting with kindergarten. Or mentally walk through your childhood home. Recall the layout of the furniture, the decorations on the walls, the celebrity posters hanging on your bedroom wall. (Obviously, this activity is not appropriate if thinking about your childhood upsets you.)

- **SONG LYRICS.** This is a great way to shift your mood. Recite lyrics from your favorite songs (stay away from depressing country and western songs and the blues). We recommend Motown songs or the Beach Boys.

- **POETRY.** Memorize an uplifting poem and then recite it when you need to refocus.

Using Calming and Focusing Techniques to Regain Control of Your Emotions

In Chapter 4 we told you the story of Barb and "Jim" and an errant glass of wine. Barb mistook a stranger for her cheating ex-fiancé and, in a fit of rage, doused him with wine. Not prone to those moments of drama, Barb was caught off guard by the suddenness of her anger and the irresistibility of her impulse. A lot of people have had Barb's experience. They've had moments when they lost control, when their emotions and actions seemed to flow even before they had fully registered the situation. This is normal, and if the moments are few and far between, they won't compromise your resilience. But for other people, these moments are not so few and the distance between them is not so far. If, like Jeremy, described at the start of the chapter, you often lose control and feel overwhelmed by your emotions, then your resilience is severely compromised. You will have significant problems in your interpersonal relationships, and you may have a reputation at work as being "difficult." For you, learning the Calming and Focusing techniques is crucial.

In moments when your emotions are so strong that rational thought is too difficult—you've just gotten bad news, you're afraid, you're trying to control yourself when your kid stumbles into the house obviously drunk—the calming techniques are the perfect ones to use. Most people find that calming themselves takes the edge off their emotions so that they can begin to think rationally. Once your emotions are less intense, you can use the appropriate skill to better understand what caused such an intense reaction. This often means using Detecting Icebergs to understand which beliefs were triggered and caused you to react so strongly, and then challenging your beliefs to determine whether the belief is accurate and worth holding on to or is causing you more harm than good.

If you favor focusing techniques over the calming techniques, use the strategy of reciting song lyrics; it is one of the easiest focusing techniques to do, and hearing the song in your head can have a big impact on your mood.

Jeremy learned how to use controlled breathing to relax as soon as he sensed his anger building. Often this was enough to keep his anger from becoming too strong. But sometimes—usually because he didn't use the calming techniques soon enough—he needed to follow the controlled breathing with Real-time Resilience, the final of the seven skills. Let's turn to it now.

Skill 7. Real-time Resilience

The value of Calming and Focusing are that they are fast, portable, and powerful. But the techniques do not challenge the beliefs that contributed to the stress, intruded on your work, or triggered the flood of emotion. In this way, Skill 6 is a stopgap—it will get you through the moment, but it will not prevent the thoughts from recurring. Skill 7, Real-time Resilience, is as fast as Calming and Focusing but it works by changing your counterproductive beliefs the moment that they occur. As you develop your skill, you'll notice that you have fewer counterproductive thoughts and that, when they do pop up, they are less potent.

You can use Real-time Resilience in the same situations that you would use the focusing techniques. In fact, ultimately most people find Real-time Resilience more powerful. Like Jeremy, you also can use it after you have relaxed using the calming techniques. It is particularly helpful in situations when your emotions are so strong that they threaten to overwhelm you.

Real-time Resilience works by taking the key ingredients of Challenging Beliefs and Putting It in Perspective and packaging them in a way that allows you to use them immediately. Because Real-time Resilience is dependent on challenging your beliefs and putting things in perspective, the more you practice those skills, the better you'll become at this one. The power of Skills 4 and 5 is that they give you a deep understanding of the complexity of a situation. With this understanding you can plan a course of action to deal with the situation and its implications. But the skills are used to process what has happened in the midst of a complicated and ongoing adversity. Real-time Resilience is used the moment that the adversity first strikes—that's why it's such a powerful tool.

When you do this skill, you are going to have an internal dialogue. Every time you think a counterproductive thought, you are going to attack it with a Real-time Resilience response. Real-time Resilience is not replacing negative thoughts with positive ones. Just like with Challenging Beliefs and Putting It in Perspective, the goal is accuracy. The mission is to change your nonresilient thoughts so that they are more accurate and powerful enough to send the counterproductive beliefs packing.

HOW TO USE REAL-TIME RESILIENCE: THREE TAG LINES

You can use three tag lines to help structure your responses as you learn Real-time Resilience. Once you've mastered the skill, you won't need them anymore.

ALTERNATIVES: A MORE ACCURATE WAY OF SEEING THIS IS . . .

When challenging your beliefs, the goal is to generate a variety of alternative beliefs that span the three dimensions of explanatory style—Me, Always, Everything—which enables you to get outside of your habitual way of explaining problems. In Real-time Resilience, the goal is to come up with just one other way of explaining the situation that is more accurate than your initial belief. The phrase *A more accurate way of seeing this is* . . . will help structure your thinking.

For example, if your negative thought is "I'm so nervous I'm going to sound like a blithering idiot and this date will be a total fiasco" you can respond with "A more accurate way of seeing this is that I'll probably sound a little nervous for the first few minutes—and he may too—but then we'll both relax and have an okay time."

EVIDENCE: THAT'S NOT TRUE BECAUSE . . .

Using evidence to test out the accuracy of your beliefs is the second strategy. In Challenging Beliefs, the goal is to find as much evidence as possible that points to the real causes of the adversity and to be evenhanded in your evidence gathering. But you know that the confirmation bias is going to make it easier for you to find the confirmatory evidence. That is why we recommend that you help focus your thinking and fight the confirmation bias by starting your response with *"That's not true because . . ."* The goal is to be as specific and detailed as possible. The more concrete your evidence, the more effective your response.

If your nonresilient thought is "My kids don't appreciate anything I do for them," you can respond with "That's not true because yesterday my daughter told me that the way I explained how to add fractions helped her a lot."

IMPLICATIONS: A MORE LIKELY OUTCOME IS . . . AND I CAN . . . TO DEAL WITH IT

Remember, Putting It in Perspective has three steps. First you list each worst-case belief. Then you list the best-case outcomes. Finally you identify the most likely outcomes and plan a way to deal with those.

In Real-time Resilience, all you need to do is identify one of the most likely outcomes and one step you can take to deal with it. This is easier if you start your response with *"A more likely outcome is . . . and I can. . . ."*

If your negative thought is "I'm going to get fired and I'll never find another job I like," you can respond with "A more likely outcome is that my boss will be annoyed that I didn't get the project done on time and I can apologize and ask her to help me prioritize the projects I'm juggling."

These tag lines are a great way to practice Real-time Resilience, but as you become more adept at the skill, you won't need them anymore. We'll illustrate the "advanced" use of the skill by showing you how Kirsten, a working mother, uses it to keep her mind focused on an important meeting.

Kirsten, a mother of two young boys, has a Ph.D. in education, works as a researcher at a university, and also serves as a consultant to a number of educational institutions. She's good at what she does and has had a lot of professional successes. As you can imagine, maintaining a balance between her professional life and her family is an issue that Kirsten struggles with daily.

What follows is Kirsten's internal dialogue as she and her colleague, Jacob, are driving to an important meeting. It's early in the morning and

Kirsten is upset because her children have fevers and stomachaches. Jacob and Kirsten planned to use the car time to discuss some issues related to the meeting, but Kirsten is distracted by thoughts of her sons. After a few attempts to engage her, Jacob, in a supportive voice, says, "Kirsten, I know you're upset about the kids and that you'd rather be home. But we do need to talk over some things for this morning. Is there anything I can do to help you feel better so that you can concentrate on work for a few minutes?" Following is what is going on in Kirsten's head after his question. As you read her ticker tape, notice when she falls into one of the thinking traps. We'll point them out in parentheses. And, when you read her responses, see if you can identify whether she is generating a more accurate alternative belief, using evidence to show why the belief is false, or putting in perspective the implications of the belief. We'll point that out as well.

KIRSTEN'S TICKER TAPE: *How can he expect me to concentrate on work when I'm upset about my kids? What a thoughtless jerk. (Overgeneralizing: She's attributing his statement to a character flaw.)*

KIRSTEN'S REAL-TIME RESILIENCE RESPONSE: *He's not being a jerk. He spent fifteen minutes talking with me about how I was feeling. (Evidence: She is using a concrete example from his recent behavior to prove why the belief was wrong.) That's because he cares about me and the boys. He knows that the work has to get done for this meeting to be a success, and we both want that. (Alternative: She is offering a more accurate interpretation of his behavior.)*

KIRSTEN'S TICKER TAPE: *But I just can't concentrate. It's not possible. I'm just way too upset about having to be here instead of at home. I'm going to ruin this meeting for Jacob, and he'll never let me forget it (catastrophizing).*

KIRSTEN'S REAL-TIME RESILIENCE RESPONSE: *It's a shame that I can't be home right now. But this isn't the first time that I've had to work when one of the kids was sick. We still have twenty minutes before we get there. If I spend a few more minutes fighting back against these thoughts, then I'll be able to concentrate and we'll get our work done. (Putting It in Perspective: She is identifying a more likely outcome and pointing out what she needs to do to make that outcome happen.) And of course Jacob will forgive me—he's forgiven me for stuff much worse than this! Like the time I failed to organize a research team and we got stuck doing all the work ourselves. (Evidence: She's using Jacob's past behavior as evidence for why he will forgive her.)*

KIRSTEN'S TICKER TAPE: *Still, what kind of mother am I? I talk a good game, but when it really counts, I always put my career first. (Tunnel vision: She's remembering only the times when she chose work over family and not remembering the* *times when she chose family over work.) The boys are going to be crying for me all day (catastrophizing), and I'm sure they think I don't love them (mind reading).*

KIRSTEN'S REAL-TIME RESILIENCE RESPONSE: *Hold on a second. First of all, there are plenty of times when I say no to work opportunities because I want to be with my children. Like last week when I turned down a chance to present in San Francisco because I didn't want to be away for three nights. (Evidence that she put her children first.) They may be upset at times; Eli will probably get really cranky when he wants to nap (Putting It in Perspective: She is being more accurate about how upset he will be), but my mother is with them and they love her (evidence that they will be okay) and I can call at nap time and sing Eli his favorite song. (Putting It in Perspective: She is identifying one thing that she can do to handle the actual implications of the situation.) Anyway, I know they love me—I mean, last night Eli asked me to marry him. What more could I want?*

KIRSTEN'S TICKER-TAPE BELIEF: *Blah, blah, blah! The bottom line is that I'm trying to have it all and I'm not doing any of it well (magnifying the problems and minimizing the positive aspects). Jacob has got to be sick of hearing me bellyache about my kids (mind reading), and I bet all these new collaborations he's got going are because he's looking to work with people who are more committed to their careers (jumping to conclusions). And what about my poor husband? I can't even remember when we had any time to ourselves. I'll be lucky if the marriage lasts through the year (catastrophizing).*

KIRSTEN'S REAL-TIME RESILIENCE RESPONSE: *Relax. I'm doing a lot of things well. The grant application I wrote got funded. The talk I gave last week was well received. The kids are happy and we have a lot of fun together (evidence). Jacob cares about my kids and likes to hear about them (a more accurate alternative). I mean, he talks about his dogs almost as much as I talk about my boys! And just because he's collaborating with other people that doesn't mean he wants to stop working with me. Just a few days ago he brought up the subject of writing another grant together (evidence). It's true that Dave and I have very little time alone, but Mom's going to start watching the kids once a week so that we can have more time to ourselves. (She's Putting It in Perspective by reminding herself of the plan she has for spending more time with her husband.)*

This process took Kirsten a few minutes. Once she had disputed her thoughts, her anxiety lessened and she was able to use the remaining time to work on her presentation with Jacob.

Mistakes You Will Make as You Practice Real-time Resilience

When we first describe Real-time Resilience to educators, parents, and managers, we are often met with a dose of skepticism. Some person inevitably shoots up a hand and says, "Aren't you just teaching people how to be better rationalizers and to let themselves off the hook when there are real problems to confront?" Parents and educators will often take it one step further and say: "This sounds like a really bad idea to me. The last thing we need is to help kids be better at shirking their responsibility. I'm worried that this skill may actually be doing harm."

Much to their surprise, our response is "You're right." And, with one proviso, they are. When people are first learning this skill, they make certain systematic mistakes, that if uncorrected, do indeed facilitate illusions of blamelessness and deny any cares or concerns. But once people are alerted to these common pitfalls and are taught how to correct them, the mistakes are short-lived and the skill leads to dramatic shifts in resilience. As with every skill in this book, knowing when to use it and how to use it correctly is essential. And we should point out that although people sometimes raise this concern when first hearing about the skill, after they have practiced it, they understand why it is such a crucial skill to know.

MISTAKE 1. USING POLLYANNA OPTIMISM

One of the most common beginner errors is to fall into the trap of Pollyanna optimism, when you replace your negative thought with an *unrealistically* optimistic belief. This mistake occurs most often when you are trying to come up with a more accurate alternative belief. Pollyanna responses sound glib and empty, and they are not tied to the facts of the situation. Tina, the head of a sales team, noticed that she often made this error as she was mastering the skill. For example, when she thought, "These people are so lazy and whiny—I just can't take another minute of them!" she responded with "A more accurate belief is that I don't have any problems with them. In fact, I really love our time together!" Whom is she kidding? Certainly not herself. "Happy" thoughts are not necessarily resilient thoughts.

As you practice Real-time Resilience, remind yourself that the goal is accuracy, not optimism. If you sound like Stuart Smalley of *Saturday Night Live* fame ("I'm smart enough. I'm good enough and doggone it, people like me"), try to craft a response that is optimistic but still in line with the facts of the situation. When your response is real, you'll feel it in your gut.

MISTAKE 2. DISMISSING THE GRAIN OF TRUTH

Another common pitfall is to dismiss the grain of truth in your counter-productive beliefs. This mistake occurs most often when you are trying to use evidence to refute your nonresilient beliefs. Although our nonresilient ticker-tape beliefs are often rich in hyperbole, buried beneath the exaggeration may lie a morsel of truth. If you don't acknowledge the truth in your response, it will lack credibility and the belief will come back. Why? Because you have not dealt with the underlying concern. For example, it's true that Kirsten does not get to spend much time with her husband. If she responded to her thought "Poor Dave—I can't think of the last time we had any time to ourselves" with "That's not true because Dave and I have plenty of time together" she would be dismissing the truth in her initial thought. And, by dismissing the truth, she constructed a response that she simply won't believe. The challenge is to acknowledge the truth and then to offer yourself a strategy for changing it for the better.

MISTAKE 3. THE BLAME GAME

The blame game is the error that people who fall into the thinking trap of personalizing or externalizing tend to play. It is a more specific variety of dismissing the grain of truth. By definition, the ticker-tape beliefs of personalizers—people whose explanatory style always points to "me"—contain a great deal of self-blame, and the ticker-tape beliefs of externalizers—people whose explanatory styles is usually "not me"—are rife with examples of how other people have caused their problems. If either is true of you, pay close attention to how you respond to your negative beliefs. A common beginner's mistake is to refute a belief by simply changing the direction of the pointing finger. For example, if you tend to point the finger at yourself, you instead point it at others. If you tend to point it at others, you point it at yourself. Mindlessly redirecting blame won't help you take control of the situation.

MISTAKE 4. MINIMIZING

Minimizing is a common mistake that people make when they are learning how to use Putting It in Perspective as part of Skill 7. When Putting It in Perspective is done correctly, you identify a more likely outcome and then at least one thing you can do to deal with it in a resilient way. What you don't want to do is simply minimize the importance of the situation. For example, imagine that your boss tells you that your work has been significantly below his expectations. You think, "That's it. I'm canned. He's going to fire me." It would be a minimization of the situation if you were to respond with "So what if he's mad at me? That doesn't matter. And if I get fired, big deal. Jobs are easy to come by." This response will not success-fully disarm the thought because it's dismissing the reality of the problem. As you are practicing the Putting It In Perspective response, take a second to check whether it is making light of an important situation and whether you have replaced a worst-case outcome with an equally improbable best-case outcome. Remember, the goal is to figure out what's most likely, and then save your energy for coping with that scenario.

Pointers for Using Real-time Resilience in Your Own Life

As with each of the resilience skills, the more you practice, the better they will work for you. It's important that you set realistic expectations for your use of this skill because it is the most difficult one to master. The following tips are helpful in guiding people's development of Real-time Resilience.

✦ **PRACTICE SKILLS 4 AND 5 FIRST.** Don't use Real-time Resilience until you feel comfortable with Challenging Beliefs and Putting It in Perspec-tive. To use Skill 7 effectively, you must be able to generate alterna-tives, effectively marshal evidence, and accurately identify more likely outcomes.

✦ **USE THE TAG LINES.** For the first few weeks, use the tag lines to structure your responses. They will help you to construct powerful replies.

✦ **BE DETAILED AND CONCRETE.** One specific piece of evidence is more pow-erful than sentences of generalities. Remind yourself that you must *prove* to yourself why the belief is false. Hand-waving won't work.

✦ **STICK WITH WHAT WORKS BEST.** Sample among the three tag lines, then stick with those that work best. You don't need to use each of the three types of responses.

✦ **CHECK FOR THE MISTAKES.** Anticipate that you will make some of the four mistakes. For the first few weeks using the skill, pause after each re-sponse and check it for mistakes. If you identify one, try again.

✦ **EFFECTIVENESS OVER SPEED.** Ultimately, you want your responses to flow as quickly as your initial nonresilient thoughts. But don't sacrifice ef-fectiveness for speed. While you are learning the skill, it is much bet-ter to view this as an art form in which you have to craft and re-craft your reply until you construct one that has the power to dispel the nonresilient belief. As you become more skilled at using the tag lines, the speed with which you reply will naturally build.

✦ **PRACTICE DAILY.** The difference between people who master the skill and those who do not is simply a matter of time spent practicing. Set aside ten minutes every day to practice this skill. Try to use it in the moment, but if you don't catch your nonresilient thoughts as they are happening, make up some negative beliefs and practice responding to those.

Remember, Fast Is Not Always Better

As you become proficient at Skills 6 and 7, you may find that you rely on them to the exclusion of the other skills. We live in a quick-fix culture that places a premium on speed. And when your counterproductive beliefs are preventing you from focusing on the task before you, when your emotions are so strong that thinking clearly is not possible, and when the amount of stress you are experiencing is overwhelming, then, yes, using the fast skills makes good sense. But most of the problems we face day-to-day do not require immediate responses. In fact, the majority of the challenges in our lives require thorough and thoughtful analysis, considered solutions, and planning. Understanding what is going wrong in a relationship and how to fix it, deciding whether to change jobs, identifying the root cause of a team's poor performance require analysis and time.

If you find that you are using Skills 6 and 7 and have stopped using the other skills, ask yourself whether there is something that you're avoiding or if you are missing important information. Resilience sometimes requires immediate action, but often it does not.

Putting It Together

You have now learned seven skills that will improve your ability to rise to life's challenges and deal with life's daily hassles. The more you practice the skills, the more you will find that you are better prepared and recover more quickly when adversity strikes. You will face situations that once left you confused and off balance with clarity and certainty. You will feel more confident and poised. You will have the inner strength to create the life you want for yourself.

Part Three focuses on handling major life challenges in all of the important areas in your life: relationships, parenting, work, and reaching out.

Applying

the

Skills

CHAPTER TEN

Resilience in Marriage and Long-term Relationships

W hat is it that you want from your relationship? If you are like most people, you want closeness and companionship, acceptance and love. You want to be understood and sexually fulfilled. You want to create a life rich in meaning and purpose, and you want to feel like you are doing it together. You probably find being in a relationship deeply rewarding but also frightfully challenging—perhaps, at times, downright exhausting. And you probably have a list of complaints. These are the ones we hear most frequently:

- ✦ We take each other for granted and don't make the relationship a priority.
- ✦ We don't seem to talk anymore. If we weren't married, I'm not sure we'd be friends.
- ✦ We're in a rut. We do the same old things over and over again.
- ✦ We seem to fight a lot these days and it often gets nasty.
- ✦ Sex? What's that?

There is an abundance of research about relationships—what makes them thrive and what makes them fail—and throughout the research, two themes recur over and over again. The two most common problems in relationships—problems that destroy the very foundation of the relationship— are poor communication and destructive fighting. All couples must struggle to understand the hopes, fears, and desires of each partner—and many couples run into difficulty when it comes to communicating with each other honestly and effectively. And no matter how strong your relationship is, you and your partner will disagree at times. Arguments—minor disagreements to full-blown shouting matches—are a normal part of sharing your life with someone, but *how* you fight with each other matters a lot. In this chapter we show you how to use the seven resilience skills to communicate more effectively and fight more constructively so that your relationship remains strong. But of course, as you well know, just because you communicate openly and have healthy fights, doesn't necessarily mean that you feel *close* to each other. So we'll also show you how to use the skills of resilience to reach out to each other and deepen your friendship.

Sometimes, however, despite a couple's best attempts, the relationship ends. At times the decision is mutual; often it's not. The end of a relationship is painful, sometimes devastating, whether it is a marriage, a long-term live-in relationship, or what you thought was a burgeoning love—and no amount of resilience is going to take away all of the pain. It makes sense to feel sad and mourn the loss of an important part of your life. But the resilience skills *will* make it easier for you to recover from the breakup and, when the time is right, to start dating again. We'll show you how to use the resilience skills to bounce back and move on so that you can reach out to others and try again.

Is Your Relationship at Risk?

Some of you might be wondering "Hmm . . . do I really need to read this chapter? Sure we fight at times, but I think we're doing okay." And, of course, some of you are doing better than okay in your relationships; you feel fulfilled, connected, and deeply happy. But the statistics are clear. Among young couples marrying today, almost 50 percent will divorce, and half of those divorces will occur in the first seven years of marriage. Second marriages have an even higher divorce rate than first marriages. If you're not married, it's important to know that many of the factors that lead to divorce also lead to the dissolution of long-term relationships. Many of the predictors of divorce or the dissolution of a relationship are things you can't control or change, such as being the child of divorced parents, having different religious backgrounds, or marrying at a very young age. Once these events have occurred, you can't undo them. But many of the factors that put your relationship at risk *are* changeable, if you know how.[1]

For example, you may have a negative style of fighting. When a disagreement occurs, you attribute it to your partner's character—overgeneralizing, which leads you to harshly criticize him or her. Or you may have unrealistically high expectations of your partner. When he or she lets you down, you begin to question the value of the relationship. You catastrophize when things aren't perfect and overreact to seemingly small offenses. Maybe you don't communicate with each other openly. When something is bothering you, you keep it to yourself until you can't take it anymore and then you explode. When your partner is talking with you about his or her feelings, perhaps you feel like you just don't "get" what your partner is trying to express. Silence has killed many relationships.

Read On

Perhaps after looking at this you've realized that you're not having problems in these areas. Your style of fighting seems healthy, you communicate well, and your expectations are reasonable and clear. Our hats are off to you. It took a lot of skill and work to build your strong relationship and you should be proud. But (you knew there was a "but," didn't you?), we still think this chapter will be of interest to you. We use the term "unconsciously competent" to describe people who are naturally able in some of the skills of resilience. And this may apply to you. Most people who are "naturally" resilient have learned the skills over a lifetime—maybe through trial and error, maybe by modeling themselves after others—and while they are great at dealing with problems and adversity, if you ask them how it is that they do it so well, they can't really put it into words. We have found that even these people can benefit by becoming more conscious of how it is that they do what they do. By having a common language, you and your partner will be in a better position to apply the skills even in the most stressful of situations. You can remind each other to challenge your thinking traps or to put it into perspective when a problem catches you off guard. And by having labels for the skills and knowing when to use each, you can help those around you, your friends, and your family to increase their relationship resilience. So, read on!

Closeness and Communication

Sara is a forty-year-old woman we met in one of our parenting programs. She signed up for the workshop because she wanted to learn how to be a better parent, but like many of the parents we meet, she spent a lot of time talking about her marriage. "I still love him and I know he loves me, but we don't seem to understand each other anymore."

Sara describes a typical miscommunication. She and her husband both work long hours, and by Friday night, they're just exhausted. One night, against their better judgment, they had agreed that their teenage son could have two of his friends come for dinner and then spend the night. When Sara's husband comes home, she says:

SARA: *What were we thinking? We just should have said no. He could have had his friends over tomorrow night instead.*
BILL: *Hey, you were just as willing to have this happen as I was. Don't blame me.*
SARA: *Relax, Bill. I didn't blame you. I said, "we," didn't I? Why are you twisting my words?*
BILL: *Well, being negative about it isn't going to make it go any better. It's not such a big deal.*
SARA: *I didn't say it was a big deal. I just wish the kids were coming on a different night. I forgot, we're not allowed to complain about anything. I'm just exhausted, that's all.*
BILL: *Yeah, you're just exhausted.*

Huh? Why did this conversation go so poorly? Sara didn't understand it, and we doubt her husband did either. This conversation got derailed because of what relationship expert Dr. Howard Markman calls "filters."[2] Think of filters as your beliefs and the emotions that follow. They bias how we understand what our partner says to us; they distort the message and make it difficult to communicate clearly. There are four basic filters, and each can be minimized by applying the skills of resilience.

✦ **DISTRACTING THOUGHTS.** The most basic filter is simply your level of attention to what your partner is saying. Sometimes the distraction might be caused by factors in the environment—the season finale of *The West Wing*, noisy kids running about—but your ticker-tape beliefs also can distract you from what your partner is saying. For example, your spouse is telling you about the cheap airfare he found so you can take a vacation together, but you're thinking about work that you need to complete or a disagreement that you had with a colleague, or you're replaying an earlier conversation with your partner that continues to upset you. Calming and Focusing are great ways to get your mind back on track whenever you realize you're being distracted by your thoughts or are having difficulty concentrating on what your partner has to say.

✦ **BELIEFS.** A second filter is your beliefs. Every conversation with your partner doesn't begin with a clean slate. You bring to the conversation beliefs from prévious conversations or experiences you've had earlier in the day. And, as you know by now, these beliefs can affect how you interpret your partner's statements. What Sara didn't know when she griped about the sleepover was that just as Bill was leaving his office, his boss—none too diplomatically—criticized him in front of a group of his colleagues. This set off Bill's violation-of-rights radar and made him angry. Then, when he got home, the radar—now on red alert—caused Bill to interpret Sara's initial statement as a criticism, that she was blaming him for the problem, not just expressing her frustration at the situation. But, unfortunately, Bill didn't test out the accuracy of his interpretation; instead, he just barreled forward and snapped at Sara. Challenging Beliefs is essential for accurate communication between partners. Sometimes, too, the problem arises because of one's thinking traps. If you tend to jump to conclusions or mind read, you will have a harder time hearing what your partner is really saying. That's why it's imperative that you look for errors in your thinking and learn how to override them.

✦ **EMOTIONS.** If you are already highly emotional when your partner broaches a topic, or if a strong emotion takes over as soon as you start talking together, it will probably distort what you hear. Bill was predisposed to get angry in this conversation because of events earlier in the day. Once angry, his anger affected how he heard each additional statement. One of the most effective strategies is simply to call for a time-out and then use that time-out to get a handle on your emotions—the calming techniques coupled with Real-time Resilience is a powerful combination.

✦ **DIFFERENCES IN COMMUNICATION STYLES.** Maybe you are comfortable sharing your thoughts and feelings and your partner is not. Perhaps your partner expresses feelings through actions rather than words. Your communication style often is determined by iceberg beliefs ("It's wrong for me to express anger" or "Men don't talk, they act"), and unless you acknowledge these beliefs, you will be doomed to miscommunicating and misunderstanding your partner, who likely has a different style from you. We'll show you how to detect icebergs beliefs as a couple so that you can understand what is fueling your misunderstanding.

Applying Skills of Resilience for Better Communication

Let's backtrack with Sara and Bill and see how the resilience skills could have helped them to communicate more effectively. Remember, they have agreed to let their son have friends over, but they are both feeling exhausted and Sara tries to talk with Bill about how she's feeling. We'll begin by exploring what they actually think to themselves—their ticker-tape beliefs—in contrast to what is being said. Each partner's ticker-tape beliefs are listed below, and you can see how these thoughts are fueling what they say.

SARA SAYS: *What were we thinking? We just should have said no. He could have had his friends over tomorrow night instead.*

BILL'S TICKER TAPE: I'm in the door all of one minute and already she's picking a fight. She agreed to this, too.

BILL SAYS: *Hey, you were just as willing to have this happen as I was. Don't go blaming me.*

SARA'S TICKER TAPE: What's with him? Already he's defensive. He never listens to what I say.

SARA SAYS: *Relax, Bill. I didn't blame you. I said "we," didn't I? Don't twist my words.*

BILL'S TICKER TAPE: She's always so negative. It's a few kids hanging out at our house, not a dinner party for the president. I can't stand how everything is a big deal with her.

BILL SAYS: *Well, being negative about it isn't going to make it go any better. It's not such a big deal.*

SARA'S TICKER TAPE: Why can't he ever acknowledge when he makes a mistake? He always has to act as if everything is fine, and then he gets on my case when I say I wish things were different.

SARA SAYS: *I didn't say it was a big deal. I just wish the kids were coming over on a different night. I forgot, we're not allowed to complain about anything. I'm just exhausted, that's all.*

BILL'S TICKER TAPE: Who is she kidding? She complains about everything! Everything is always a catastrophe with her.

BILL SAYS: *Yeah, you're just exhausted.*

It's no longer a mystery as to why Bill and Sara's conversation went so badly, is it? We'll show you how different the tone could have been had Bill used just three of the seven skills: ABC, Thinking Traps, and Challenging Beliefs.

Bill first has to notice that his initial reaction doesn't make sense. After all, Sara's initial statement is innocuous enough, and yet he immediately gets annoyed. Something must have pushed his buttons. Once Bill notices this, he could begin by asking for a time-out so that he could get a better handle on what's really going on. Then he could use ABC to figure out why he's getting so angry. Here is how it might go.

BILL: *Sorry, Sara. I'm not sure why I'm getting so annoyed. Give me a minute, okay? I just walked in the door and I don't think I'm thinking straight.*
TO HIMSELF: Okay, hang on. All she said was that she wished we hadn't said the kids could come over tonight. Why am I getting so mad? I guess it's because I assumed what she really meant was that I shouldn't have said yes.

Bill has identified the adversity—the statement his wife made—and the consequence—that he was mad. Next he captured his beliefs.

BILL CONTINUES: It seems like I might be jumping to conclusions about what she meant. I think I've let my bad mood from work color how I'm interpreting her comment. I mean, she didn't blame me, she did say "we." But I guess I was the one that said they could sleep over. She was definitely more ambivalent. Maybe she is blaming me. I better check it out with her.

Bill has identified the thinking trap and then continues by generating alternatives and citing evidence to test out the accuracy of his beliefs.

BILL TO SARA: *Hey, look, I'm sorry for getting on your case. I'm upset about something that happened at work and I think I may have misinterpreted what you said. Are you saying "we" to be nice but are really annoyed with me for agreeing to this? I know you probably would have said no if it had been totally up to you.*
SARA: *Oh, no, not at all. I really meant we. I'm just so tired from work that what I really want is some peace and quiet. I'm just not up for the testosterone-fest tonight. That's all.*
BILL: *Yeah, I know what you mean. Maybe we can lock them in the basement.*
SARA: *(laughing) You're bucking for Father of the Year, aren't you? So, what happened at work?*
BILL: *Oh, you'll love this. Just as I'm about to head out, Jack comes to my office and says . . .*

What a different conversation! In just a few minutes, Bill was able to identify his ticker-tape beliefs (ABC), label a thinking error (Avoiding Thinking Traps), and then test it out for accuracy (Challenging Beliefs). And by taking responsibility for his emotion and slowing himself down, Bill dramatically changed the direction of the conversation. Instead of feeling angry and isolated, Bill and Sara have commiserated with each other and feel close. Even though they're still going to be overrun with teenagers, at least now they're on the same team and can wait out the onslaught together.

Building Better Communication Through Empathy

Bill took responsibility for his mood and used the skills of resilience to communicate more directly with his wife. When he shifted his mood, Sara followed suit and the conversation took on a different tone. But let's face it, not all conversations go this well. Even after you use the skills, your partner still might feel misunderstood and be unable to shake his mood so quickly. Perhaps your partner doesn't know why he's feeling the way he does, or maybe he needs to know that you really understand his feelings before he can move on. You can use your knowledge of the B–C connections and Detecting Icebergs to empathize and connect with your partner.

Imagine that it's now Sunday evening. Bill and Sara are having a glass of wine, gearing themselves up for the upcoming week. Sara starts to run through their week and divvies up the chauffering responsibilities.

SARA: *Okay, let's see. Mike has a basketball game Tuesday at seven and Joey's mother said he can have dinner there on Wednesday 'cause they're finishing up their video project. Laney has dance until seven-thirty on Tuesday and something—I'm blanking on what—Thursday. Gosh, my mind . . . oh, right, Thursday is her mediation meeting at school. I can do Mike's game and Laney's dance. How 'bout you pick up Mike from Joey's and take Laney on Thursday?*

BILL: *Jeez, Sara. Slow down, all right? This was supposed to be a relaxing glass of wine, not the Olympics of Time Management.*

SARA: *Sorry. Sorry. It's got to get done though. If we don't talk about it tonight it won't get done and we'll be scrambling all week.*

BILL: *Whatever. Just write it down for me and I'll do whatever you say. (He leaves the room.)*

SARA: *(muttering as he leaves) Oh, sure, what am I, your secretary?*

BILL: *You mean my boss, don't you?*

So much for a little quiet time together. Bill is angry. Sara feels put-upon. Neither quite gets what the other is experiencing. But by talking together and using their understanding of B–C connections and the skill of Detecting Icebergs, they can work through this conflict. Let's fast-forward ten minutes.

BILL: *Look, Sara, you just can't talk like that to me. You really have to work on it.*

SARA: *I know I was irritating you, but to be honest, I don't get it. Did it seem like I was taking over?*

Sara knows that people's anger flows from a belief about their rights being violated, so she tries to find out if that's what Bill thought.

BILL: *Taking charge? You were handing me my orders without even letting me say a word. I've got to put up with that attitude at work, but I certainly don't have to tolerate it here.*

Bill is still angry.

SARA: *I'd be mad if I thought you were ordering me around, too, but you seem really angry—too angry. I'm not trying to pick a fight, I just want to understand why you're so mad.*

Sara handles this quite well. She doesn't challenge the accuracy of his interpretation. If she did that, Bill would probably get defensive. Instead, she notices that there is a disconnect between his ticker-tape beliefs—he is being ordered around—and the intensity of his anger. She begins to suspect that they have run into an iceberg belief.

BILL: *Well, like I said, I have to put up with that attitude at work and I just don't want more of the same at home. I'm not your lackey to order around.*
SARA: *I know that would really piss you off. Do you want to keep talking about this? It seems like something I said hit a nerve.*

Sara acknowledges his feelings and then opens the door to look deeper. She waits for his permission before continuing.

BILL: *Sure. I'm not trying to be cryptic. It's just that something about the way you were telling me which days I needed to cover really got under my skin.*
SARA: *Well, suppose I was giving you orders, what makes that so annoying?*

Sara asks questions to help him identify the deeper meaning.

BILL: *Like I said, I have to put up with that from Jack, and I don't want more of the same at home.*
SARA: *Okay, but assume that you do get more of the same at home, what's so bad about that?*

Again, Sara asks another "what" question to guide Bill toward looking deeper.

BILL: *I just can't stand being treated like an underling, like I'm somebody's servant or something.*
SARA: *I know what you mean. But what's the worst part about being treated like that?*

Sara keeps the focus on uncovering more beliefs.

BILL: *It makes me feel like a fool. Like I'm being disrespected and I'm just taking it.*
SARA: *So, at some level, it seemed like I was trying to put you down. Do you think that's why it got you so angry?*
BILL: *Yeah, you know, I just don't know what to do about Jack. He has this way of talking at me—it's like he's barking out orders. And it's really tricky, because*

he's not the easiest guy to approach, so I don't know how to talk to him about it. But I want it to stop.

Notice that Bill doesn't even feel the need to talk more about his interaction with Sara. Now that he's identified his iceberg belief—that he's a fool if he tolerates someone being disrespectful—Bill's focus naturally shifts to the true source of his anger. How did this happen? Bill felt as if Sara understood him and empathized with his feelings. She didn't have to say a lot of "I hear you saying . . ." statements that many therapists encourage their patients to use (but which feel awkward and phony for many people). Instead, by asking the questions, she communicated that she was interested in what he was thinking and feeling and that his experience was beginning to make sense to her. That is a clear communication of empathy.

Of course, Sara might have her own iceberg beliefs in this situation. Bill now feels understood, but Sara might not. If that's the case, they can come back to Sara's experience and try to understand it better. Some couples might want to do that right away; others might be comfortable coming back to it later or even letting it slide altogether—often the connection they feel after having worked through the process once as a team mitigates the need to go back and apply it again. That's not to say that one partner should always focus on the other, which does happen—particularly if one partner is more comfortable in the "guiding" role than the other. Although we don't recommend keeping a scorecard, if you notice an imbalance in how often your "stuff" versus your partner's gets talked about, that might be worth discussing.

We're well aware that reading dialogue in a book makes the process seem easier than it actually is. These conversations—at least initially—have fits and starts. The first handful of times you try this, it may not go well at all or it may feel stilted and uncomfortable. That's okay. In fact, that makes a lot of sense. How could trying something new not feel a little uncomfortable at first? But our experience shows that if you hang in there and keep practicing, Detecting Icebergs gradually will become more comfortable and you will find the language and pacing that works for you.

Fighting Resiliently

Learning how to build empathy, communicate more effectively, and really *hear* what it is that your partner is saying is a great step forward. But let's be honest, even if you communicate effectively, your relationship isn't going to be perfect. In fact, there is one thing you can be certain of: Conflicts will arise in your relationship. And research shows that *how* you fight is of critical importance. By the way, when we use the word "fight" we mean verbal arguments, not physical violence. If you are in a physically or emotionally abusive relationship, both you and your partner need to seek counseling immediately. You can begin by contacting the National Domestic Violence Hotline at 1–800–799–SAFE (7233) or 1–800–787–3224 (TDD).

Read the following fights and ask yourself which one is most similar to how you and your partner argue.

"WHAT IS IT WITH YOU?"

Julie and Rich are midway through their chaotic morning routine. Rich gets two of the three kids dressed for school while Julie showers and dresses for work. Julie puts on the kids' socks and shoes while he showers and sends an early morning e-mail. At seven-fifteen, when Rich gets downstairs, the kids are eating their breakfast in front of the television while Julie is packing lunches for the school-bound kids and leaving a note for the babysitter about a play date for the youngest.

It's breakfast in front of the TV that triggers the fight.

RICH: *What is it with you? Why are they eating breakfast in front of the TV? I thought we agreed.*

JULIE: *Because I can't be late again, okay, I just can't be late again. Please don't start with me this morning. I'm too tired to fight.*

RICH: *It's just idiotic. It doesn't even save us any time. We've been over this twenty times already. We agreed that they'd eat at the table.*

JULIE: *Fine. You want them to eat at the table? Great. Go for it. From now on, you're in charge. You get them dressed, pack their lunches, get their breakfast, make sure they've peed, get them in the car, really, go for it. Have fun.*

RICH: *I don't get it, Julie. Mothers all across America are getting their children breakfasted and off to school, and as far as I can tell, they don't think of themselves as martyrs. Why's it such a big deal for you?*

"WHOSE SIDE ARE YOU ON?"

Meg and Joe have been living together for a year and half. Joe's mother, who doesn't approve of them living together, is coming to visit for the weekend, and Meg is not looking forward to it. Joe's mother has a history of being critical and negative, and it often leads to fights between Meg and Joe. Meg wants Joe to stick up for their relationship and make clear to his mother that some topics are off limits.

MEG: *Any chance you can talk to your mom before she comes and tell her not to comment about us living together? It would be just so much easier for me if I didn't have to worry all weekend about when "the conversation" was going to happen.*

JOE: *Come on, Meg. Cut her a break. She's from a different generation. She just doesn't agree with what we're doing. You can't expect her not to say anything. Just shrug it off. It's not like her opinion is going to change anything between us.*

MEG: *That's not the point. I just don't want to be tense all weekend, and if you told her that the topic was off limits, I might be able to relax and enjoy the visit. It just seems like you don't want to defend our choices to her, and I find that a real problem. Whose side are you on?*

JOE: *Listen to you. She's just coming for the weekend, Meg. One weekend. I wish you could keep a little perspective. You're making it sound like I'm always siding with her over you. We haven't even seen her in six months.*

MEG: *I know it's just one weekend, but let's be honest, there have been a lot of times when you've let her talk about us in ways that you wouldn't put up with if it came from anyone else. Are you forgetting the you're-going-to-serve-dinner-on-those-plates conversation? I just want to feel like I'm your primary concern. Is that too much to ask?*

JOE: *You are my primary concern. It's just not so easy with her. You see what she's like. She can suck the air out of a room. Wasn't it good that I told her that she could only come for the weekend? She wanted to stay for a week, remember? I deserve points for that.*

MEG: *Yeah, you're right, that was great. Just promise me that you'll change the conversation if she brings up our living together. Really. Promise me. I need you to do that for me.*

JOE: *Okay. I will. I promise.*

HOW DO YOU FIGHT?

Two different styles of fighting. Rich and Julie are caustic and sarcastic with each other. Meg and Joe make their complaints clear and keep them specific. The research on relationships shows that *how* you fight with your partner—whether you are married or not—matters a lot more in terms of the longevity and health of your relationship than *if* you fight with your partner.[3] Every relationship requires work; every relationship will go through tough times, all couples will disagree and argue, but some couples, like Rich and Julie, have a style of fighting that is toxic, whereas other couples, like Meg and Joe have a healthy, resilient style of fighting.

Fighting Styles

Dr. John Gottman, one of the leading relationship and marriage experts, and his colleagues have been able to pinpoint the specific styles of fighting that lead to the demise of a relationship. In fact, across a series of studies, Gottman's team was able to accurately predict in over 90 percent of the cases which couples would stay together and which would ultimately split up. They found that caustic beginnings and character assassination mangle relationships.[4]

CAUSTIC BEGINNINGS

When Rich sees the kids eating their Cheerios in front of the television, his first comment to his wife is "What is it with you?" Researchers call this a "harsh start-up" because comments like these are critical and demeaning, and they lead the other person to respond in kind. The couple then gets entrenched in an escalating battle of meanness that leaves no room for empathy or constructive problem solving. Caustic beginnings shift the focus of the argument away from solving the problem and make the implicit goal hurting the other person. When Rich and Julie fight, the goal almost immediately changes from wanting to voice a complaint and resolve a conflict to wanting to inflict harm and humiliate. Listen to how Julie brings up the "breakfast fight" later than evening.

JULIE: *I really didn't appreciate the way you attacked me this morning. You're always so high and mighty with me like you're just the absolute best father in the world . . . give me a break!*

Even if Rich wanted to discuss their fight from the morning openly and honestly, it would be very hard for him to do so. Her tone reeks with insult. Statements such as "always" and "you're such an X" are like a red cape to a bull—they're nearly impossible to resist. That's why the opening gambit of a fight is so important. It sets the tone of the interaction. If begun with sarcasm and contempt, it makes it very hard to continue in a productive manner.

The escalation in Rich and Julie's fights is sometimes hard to miss, but perhaps in your fights it's more difficult to see. In fact, there are times when Rich and Julie don't raise their voices and their insults are subtle. Here's an example.

RICH: *The pan you used to make the stir-fry is still dirty.*
JULIE: *I know. I cooked the dinner, right?*
RICH: *Right. So you should finish what you started.*
JULIE: *That would be nice for you, wouldn't it? Then you'd get to relax and watch the news.*
RICH: *Does it always have to be quid pro quo? I forgot to check the "household division of labor" contract, so sue me.*
JULIE: *It can just sit there. I'm not touching it.*

They didn't shout and there was no nasty language, but the message was still clear. Julie feels burdened and thinks Rich should do more around the house. Rich thinks the division of labor has obliterated a spirit of generosity. They might both be right. Who knows? But one thing is certain: This conversation did nothing to bring them closer, and it did not help them to talk about the underlying problem.

How do your fights begin? Start paying close attention to how you and your partner broach a conflict. If you or your partner tend to start out with sarcasm and contempt, you are most certainly doing more harm than good. Often these harsh beginnings are fueled by ticker-tape beliefs such as "If I don't paint a really negative picture, he'll just ignore what I have to say and blow it off altogether" or "She's much better at arguing than I am so I have to make my point really strong." The problem, of course, is that these beliefs lead to destructive comments that take the fight far away from the real problem. By challenging the ticker-tape beliefs that fuel your caustic style, you will be in a better position to argue fairly and constructively.

BLAMING CHARACTER INSTEAD OF BEHAVIOR

Part of what makes Rich and Julie's beginnings so harsh is that they attack each other's character instead of their behavior. When Julie forgets to pay a bill, Rich accuses her of being "oblivious." When Rich leaves his gym clothes strewn across the bedroom floor, he's a "pig." Rich and Julie do not keep their complaints focused on the behavior; instead they fall into the thinking trap of overgeneralizing and see every slight and mistake as an indication of the other person's flawed character. We refer to overgeneralizing as "character assassination" because that's exactly how it feels. It's as if you're calling into question the person's fundamental worth as a human being. Being on the receiving end of such questioning is never pleasant.

To practice constructive criticism, re-craft each of the following overgeneralizations into a more specific complaint. The goal is to point out the specific behavior that you're upset about and avoid attacking your partner's character. We'll do the first one for you.

Your partner gives you a kitchen appliance for your tenth anniversary.

Overgeneralized complaint: You don't have a romantic bone in your body.

Constructive complaint: *The toaster-oven is great, but I'd really like getting romantic presents on our anniversary.*

Your spouse decides to attend a conference and leaves you alone with two sick kids.

Overgeneralized complaint: Some parent you are! All you care about is your career.

Specific complaint: _____

Your partner has put on weight and is in the process of taking a second slice of cake.

Overgeneralized complaint: I thought you were trying to lose weight. You've got zero self-control.

Specific complaint: _____

The tendency to overgeneralize reflects a distinct explanatory style. Read the following pairs of comments that Jon says to his partner, Jess, and decide whether each is more me or not me; always or not always; and everything or not everything.

Situation 1: Jon and Jess get lost while driving to a new restaurant.
Jon says:

A: *Your spatial skills aren't exactly your strong suit.*
B. *The directions were really bad.*

Situation 2: Jon and Jess have been squabbling on and off all day.
Jon says:

A: *What's with you? You're always so defensive and moody.*
B: *What's with you? You've been picking fights all day.*

In each situation, response "A" reflects a more Me, Always, Everything explanation about Jess. That is, in these statements, Jon attributes the problem to Jess rather than to external factors. He sees the cause as global ("you're so defensive and moody") and unlikely to change ("your spatial skills aren't exactly your strong suit'). The "B" responses, in contrast, were often personal, but focused on a specific and changeable attribute. When problems arise in your relationship, do you habitually blame your partner? When you blame him or her, do you blame a specific behavior, or do you blame his or her character or personality?

The difference between behavior versus character blame is telling. Couples who blame each other's character are much less happy and satisfied in the relationship than couples who keep the complaint focused on a specific, changeable behavior. While many couples blame each other's characters at times, the real problem emerges when this style of criticism becomes contemptuous—which it very often does.

Using the Skills of Resilience to Change the Way You Fight

Which skills of resilience you use depends on what you and your partner fight about. The relationship research shows that what couples fight about can be broken down into two broad categories. Solveable problems versus perpetual problems.[5] Some of the problems that lead to fights are solvable. The fights are about a specific, controllable event, and, if your style of fighting is healthy, you usually can find a solution to the problem. You and your partner can work out whose turn it is to go to the market, where you should go on vacation, whether to get your friends a soup tureen or the martini shaker as a wedding gift. Other problems are much more difficult to solve because they aren't about a specific situation; instead, they center on basic differences in personality between you and your partner, and, in most cases, these basic differences aren't going to change. Perhaps you like things orderly and believe everything has its place (alphabetizing is your way of life) but your partner sees this as a disease and argues that an overly clean house is a symptom . . . of what he's not yet sure. Or perhaps you are gregarious and love a full house. Old college friends, old girlfriends, family you've never met are always welcome. Your partner, in contrast, loves "family time" and relishes quiet evenings at home playing board games and watching videos. Maybe the basic difference between the two of you is about money—one of you is a saver, the other is guided by the motto "It's good for the economy"—or about sex—once a week is seen as "frequent" to one and "infrequent" to the other.

Whatever the difference, Gottman has dubbed these issues "perpetual problems" because they tend to recur over and over again throughout a relationship, often resulting in what he calls "gridlock." Gridlock occurs when you talk and talk but make no headway—usually because your thinking styles are fueling the same old patterns. Instead, it feels like you're going around in circles, saying the same old things to the same old effect. According to Gottman's research, most of the problems that couples face are of the perpetual variety. It's when couples get stuck in gridlock that the relationship begins to seriously suffer.

You'll need to learn how to avoid gridlock so that even when the same old problems arise, you'll not get stuck in the same old, ineffective patterns.

Using Resilience with Solvable Problems

Our first example is about a solvable problem. We'll model the use of Learning Your ABCs, Avoiding Thinking Traps, and Challenging Beliefs.

THE WEEKEND BATTLE

Remember Meg and Joe and their fight over Joe's mother? They have a recurrent problem—not a big problem, but it gets in their way almost every weekend. Meg and Joe have recently bought a house. It's a rambling house with wide hallways, leaded windows, charming window seats, but it needs a lot of work. Walls need to be stripped and painted. Floors need to be sanded. Fixtures need to be replaced. Their "dream house" doesn't look so dreamy right now, and the fantasy of working side by side like Steve and Norm from *This Old House* has turned out to be just that—a fantasy.

They both work high-pressure jobs—Meg as a lawyer, Joe as an investment banker—and are used to working long hours. Occasionally one will have to work on a weekend, but for the most part, their weekends are free—sort of. That is where the conflict arises. Joe wants to spend weekends relaxing with Meg, visiting friends, hiking, biking, enjoying downtime. Meg sees weekends as the chance to make headway on the growing list of house projects that need to get done. Friday nights are pleasant and quiet, but, almost without fail, conflict erupts on Saturday morning.

To get to the bottom of the problem, we asked Meg to describe the fight that had occurred the previous Saturday and to be as specific as possible about what was said and how it was said. Here's what we learned.

Saturday morning, eight-fifteen. Meg, already dressed, brings Joe a cup of coffee and gently wakes him up.

MEG: *Hey, sleepyhead. Time to get up. The day's a-wasting.*
JOE: *(looking out the window) Looks like a great day for a ride. How about I fix us breakfast and we take the bikes to Valley Green?*
MEG: *You know, I was hoping you could finish up the steps. We've haven't gotten around to sanding them, and they need to be sealed and the railing needs a second coat of paint. If you do that, I thought I'd do the base coat in the guest room.*
JOE: *You're kidding, right? Let's do it tonight. I don't want to spend the day on house stuff. Come on . . . Me, you, our bikes . . . the great outdoors . . .*
MEG: *I was thinking me, you, the sander . . . the great indoors . . .*

Their conversation starts out friendly enough but quickly sours. Joe accuses Meg of being a taskmaster and not wanting to spend time with him. Meg counters that he doesn't follow through on stuff and doesn't care what shape the house is in. She tells him that she would never have agreed to buy a fixer-upper if she knew he was going to let the fixing-up part drag on for so long. She says she feels duped.

This is not a new fight for them. Afterward, they usually steer clear of each other for a while, Meg halfheartedly piddles on a house project, and Joe takes the dog out for an extra-long walk. When they reconvene a few hours later, they feel distant and regret that the same old fight has gotten in the way of having fun together.

We began our work with Meg by asking her to identify her ABCs. We asked Meg to pretend that it was last Saturday and to capture what was going on for her as the fight developed. Here's what Meg told us.

ADVERSITY: Most weekends Joe wants to go someplace and doesn't want to work on the house. So, on that Saturday, I wake him up and in a playful way I suggest we work on the stairs. Joe says that he'd rather go biking and then we start to argue.

MEG'S BELIEFS DURING THE FIGHT: He's Mr. Go Get 'Em at the office, but then he comes home and turns into a slug. He says he wants to spend time with me, but really he just wants to avoid the projects around the house. If he didn't want to fix up the house, then he should have been honest about it and we could have bought one that didn't require so much work. I knew he didn't really want this house, but I pushed and pushed until I got my way. Now everything is a mess.

MEG'S CONSEQUENCES: I was really mad at Joe and felt let down. I just wanted to avoid him for the rest of the morning. I also felt kind of bad about myself. Like I was too aggressive about getting the house and didn't pay enough attention to his concerns.

After mapping out her ABC, Meg checked for the B–C connections.

By the way, Meg's example shows why it's a good idea to work with pen and paper when doing these skills—there was a lot going on for Meg, and it would have been difficult for her to keep track of it all in her head.

Next, Meg needed to check for thinking traps. Instead of accepting her ticker-tape beliefs as a factual readout of the situation, Meg asks herself whether she is falling into any of the eight thinking traps and records them in the appropriate column.

BELIEFS	TYPE OF BELIEF	THINKING TRAPS	CONSEQUENCES
1. He's Mr. Go Get 'Em at the office, but then he comes home and turns into a slug.	Violation of rights		Angry
2. He says he wants to spend time with me, but really he just wants to avoid the projects around the house.	Violation of rights and loss		Angry Sad
3. If he didn't want to work on the house, then he should have been honest about it and we could have bought one that didn't require so much work.	Violation of rights		Angry
4. I knew he didn't really want this house, but I pushed and pushed until I got my way. Now everything is a total mess.	Violation of his rights and loss of self-worth		Guilty Sad

Meg found three thinking traps in her ticker-tape beliefs, so she asked herself a series of straightforward questions to help her challenge these thinking errors. In belief 1, she was overgeneralizing. Does not wanting to spend Saturday morning sanding the steps make Joe a slug? Are there times when he is helpful around the house? In belief 2, Meg realized she was mind reading. How does she know what Joe was thinking when he said he wanted to spend time with her? What grounds does she have for doubting the sincerity of the statement? In belief 3, she realized that she was using tunnel vision. Is it true that Joe *never* finishes what he starts, or is she selectively focusing on only some of the information? Meg decides that the last two beliefs did not contain any thinking traps, but she acknowledges that they aren't necessarily accurate either.

Meg then needed to decide whether to use Challenging Beliefs or Putting It in Perspective. Remember, Challenging Beliefs is used to test the accuracy of why beliefs—beliefs about the cause of the problem—and Putting It in Perspective is used to test whether your what-next beliefs are catastrophic, and, if so, to instead identify the most likely outcomes. When Meg looked over her ticker-tape beliefs, she realized that most of

BELIEFS	TYPE OF BELIEF	THINKING TRAPS	CONSEQUENCES
1. He's Mr. Go Get 'Em at the office, but then he comes home and turns into a slug.	Violation of rights	Overgeneralization	Angry
2. He says he wants to spend time with me, but really he just wants to avoid the projects around the house.	Violation of rights and loss	Mind reading	Angry Sad
3. He never finishes what he starts and I'm sick of it.	Violation of rights	Tunnel vision	Angry
4. If he didn't want to work on the house, then he should have been honest about it and we could have bought one that didn't require so much work.	Violation of rights		Angry
5. I knew he didn't really want this house, but I pushed and pushed until I got my way. Now everything is a total mess.	Violation of his rights and loss of self-worth		Guilty Sad

them were about the cause of her ongoing conflict with Joe, so she rightly chose to use Challenging Beliefs.

Meg used the dimensions of explanatory style to generate some alternative explanations to the problem. Since many of her initial beliefs were external (blaming Joe) and pervasive, she tried to generate some alternatives that were more specific and shared responsibility for the problem, such as "Joe doesn't mind living in the house the way it is and he does mind never getting a chance to relax and have fun," and "We have different ideas of fun. I see working on the house together as fun and he doesn't."

Notice how different these alternatives are from her ticker-tape beliefs. The very spirit of them has changed from finger-pointing to a more generous understanding of their motives. Meg was now ready to weigh up the evidence, which she decided could best be accomplished by sitting down with Joe and talking with him about his thoughts and feelings about the problem, and sharing hers with him.

When we next spoke with Meg, she told us that she and Joe had had their first fun weekend in months. They had a good, honest talk and realized that the two biggest factors causing their Saturday morning fights were that Meg actually enjoyed the house tasks and didn't look forward to early-morning adventures and Joe felt the reverse; and Joe was worried that Meg would be critical (and indeed there was evidence for this) when he didn't do a project just right. Once they had identified the causes of the problem, the various solutions became clear.

Meg called us a few months later to let us know how things were going. She said that weekends were no longer a battle. "It's clear that the skills have helped us deal with problems better, but I think there has been a more fundamental change in our relationship. It just seems like we're on the same team more of the time now."

Using the Detecting Icebergs Technique and Putting It in Perspective with Chronic Problems

Joe and Meg used the skills of resilience to find a workable solution to an ongoing conflict. But what about when the problems are not so easily solved? As we suggested before, many of the conflicts that couples face boil down to differences in personality that aren't going to change: You're a neat freak and your spouse is happy when your house looks lived in; promptness is a religion for you but not your partner; you're a saver and your partner is a spender; you're indulgent with the kids and your spouse is a strict disciplinarian.

What are the perpetual problems in your relationship? Every relationship has them, and the sooner you recognize that some of the conflicts that you encounter are simply not going to go away, the better off you will be. But don't get us wrong. That doesn't mean that there is nothing you can do to minimize the effect of these conflicts. To the contrary, healthy relationships are able to keep the conflicts in perspective and don't get stuck in gridlock. John Gottman describes the hallmarks of gridlock as:[6]

+ The conflict leads you to feel rejected by your partner.
+ You and your partner say the same old things over and over again.
+ You and your partner are unwilling to compromise around the conflict.
+ As time goes on, you and your partner exaggerate the differences in your perspectives so that they become caricatures of the real difference.
+ You can't muster up any generosity or humor and instead feel hostile or worn out.

We have found that there are two powerful skills for overcoming grid-lock and keeping these differences from ruining your relationship:

1. Detecting Icebergs to prevent gridlock
2. Using Putting It in Perspective to pave the way to acceptance

DETECTING ICEBERGS TO PREVENT GRIDLOCK

Gus and Carla have been married for nine years. They have two young children. Carla chose to put her teaching career on hold until her children were in school so she is now home full time. Gus works as a computer programmer. In Gus's words, "We're basically happily married. We'd do it over again, but it sure would be nice to find a way to smooth out the edges."

Despite their success in many areas, there is one perpetual problem that they have not been able to get around. In fact, they have been grid-locked for a long time. As it turned out, it wasn't until they discovered that they each held hidden iceberg beliefs that they were able to break free.

The Nest-Egg Scene

Humor is big for Carla. She is witty, silly, and has an irreverent streak that can shock people at times. She fancies herself one part Dave Barry and two parts David Sedaris. Gus loves to talk; he's up for just about any topic, but he's not a particularly funny man, nor does he value humor the way Carla does. When she's doing her shtick, Gus enjoys it, but he just can't do it himself.

Perhaps this doesn't seem like a major conflict, and for many couples it wouldn't be a conflict at all. But for Carla and Gus, it is the source of ongoing tension and disappointment, and they just didn't get why it led to so much ill feeling between them. For them, "How can you not think that's funny?" would inevitably trigger fights that left them both confused. They were able to identify their ticker-tape beliefs, but the beliefs didn't explain the intensity of their reactions. A classic example is what they refer to as "the nest-egg scene."

The nest-egg scene is from the movie *Lost in America* starring Albert Brooks and Julie Hagerty. Briefly, Brooks and Hagerty play a married couple who quit their jobs to explore America in their RV. When they get to Las Vegas, the wife gambles away all of their money. The next day the husband, shocked and enraged, berates her for losing their nest egg. Carla has seen the movie at least thirty times, she worships Albert Brooks, she knows the words of this scene by heart, and each time, it makes her laugh until her sides hurt. Once she laughed so hard it triggered an asthma attack.

If Gus is in a particularly zany mood, the nest-egg scene will evoke a smile.

Carla self-medicates with *Lost in America* and watched it a few nights ago after a bad day with the kids. She called Gus over to watch the nest-egg scene with her. This is the conversation that ensued after the scene ended.

CARLA: *Wow, I think I almost saw you smile that time. It's getting to you, isn't it?*
GUS: *It's funny. I guess it's funny. It just doesn't do it for me. That's all. We're not really going to have this conversation again, are we?*
CARLA: *I just don't get it. It's probably one of the funniest scenes of all time and you don't even laugh. I know people have different tastes when it comes to humor, but my God, how can you not find that funny?*
GUS: *Yes, Carla, I'll admit it. I do not think Albert Brooks is funny. I know. I know. It's blasphemy. But there you have it. Now, please, let's just let it drop.*
CARLA: *I wish I could. Really, I do. Everyone else I know loves the movie and even if they don't love the movie, they at least laugh out loud during that scene. What is it with you?*

This is where the conversation becomes gridlocked. From this point on Carla and Gus will try to dissect "humor" and argue whether certain lines are "universally" funny. From there the conversation inevitably moves to Cindy, an ex-wife of a friend who, like Gus, just didn't find the scene the least bit funny. Carla starts to point to other unflattering similarities between Cindy and Gus, and then, within a few minutes, Gus has had enough and leaves the room. Neither understands why this issue pushes so many buttons.

We asked them to use Detecting Icebergs to try to uncover the deeper meaning of this conflict. They decided to start by looking for Carla's iceberg beliefs since, according to both of them, Carla was the one who pushed the issue. (After all, she could watch the movie alone, but instead she calls Gus over each and every time the scene plays.) As always, we had them start by capturing Carla's ABCs.

CARLA'S ADVERSITY: I think the nest-egg scene is comic genius, and it makes me laugh every time I watch it. Gus doesn't think it's funny.
CARLA'S BELIEFS: What's wrong with him? How can he not laugh at this? It is objectively funny stuff, and he is not laughing. I don't get him.

CARLA'S CONSEQUENCES: I usually start off feeling angry at Gus, but by the end of the conversation I feel really sad, almost lonely.

Neither Carla nor Gus understands why she feels sad and lonely, so Gus begins to ask her the iceberg questions. Gus knows that sadness comes from beliefs about loss, so he's going to be exploring this theme.

GUS: *Okay, so you think the movie is funny and I don't. What does that mean to you?*
CARLA: *If you don't think it's funny, then you must not think anything is funny.*
GUS: *Assuming that I don't think anything is funny, what makes that so upsetting?*

Notice that Gus isn't challenging Carla's belief as he continues to ask her questions.

CARLA: *Laughing and joking are important to me, but they're not important to you.*
GUS: *What makes that so upsetting?*
CARLA: *It upsets me because in my family, we get close to each other through humor. We develop shticks and laugh at things, and that's how we connect. I share that with my family and with my friend, Doug, but I don't share that with you.*
GUS: *And let's assume that it's true that you don't share this with me and you do with your family and Doug, what is the worst part of that for you?*
CARLA: *I love my family and I love Doug, but I want to feel closer to you than I do to them. And if we don't share this basic part of who I am—one of the parts of who I am that I most like—then I don't think we'll ever be as close as I want us to be.*

Aha! (Remember—we told you that you'd know you'd hit the iceberg belief when you experienced the aha!) The problem isn't whether Gus thinks the nest-egg scene is funny, the problem is that Carla wants to share her joy of humor with Gus and can't.

Identifying the real issue is the critical first step. But now that they understand why they keeping running into this conflict, what comes next?

This is a perpetual problem, and there is no clear solution. Gus can't pretend to enjoy Albert Brooks. No matter how hard he tries, he won't suddenly secretly yearn to be a stand-up comic like Carla does, he won't replay funny lines in his head and call up his family and friends to try them out. It's just not who he is. But they can talk more about the different ways in which their families expressed closeness and connected with each other—for Carla's family it was around humor, for Gus's family it was around discussing "painful" topics. And they can learn to accept this difference and avoid this particular gridlock. And isn't maintaining a loving, healthy marriage hard enough without throwing fights about Albert Brooks into the mix?

USING PUTTING IT IN PERSPECTIVE TO PAVE THE WAY TO ACCEPTANCE

To accept this fundamental difference, Gus and Carla need to keep the implications of that difference in perspective. Like many of us, both of them catastrophize the meaning of the unchangeable difference between them. (Ironic how we often get into a relationship with another person because we are attracted to some of the differences—"His sense of adventure inspires me," "Her sociability helps bring me out of my shell"— but once the relationship is established, they threaten us.)

Since we illustrated the use of Detecting Icebergs with Carla, we'll demonstrate how Gus used Putting It in Perspective to identify his greatest fears and find a way to break free of them.

This is how Gus described what he said to himself after he and Carla identified her iceberg beliefs.

"I was proud of us both for hanging in there and getting to the bottom of things. But later that night I started to worry. Humor is so important to her, and it's just not to me. She even said that it's how she feels close to people. She's really sad and feels lonely because I can't give her what she needs. Now when she's feeling silly she'll feel even more justified in calling Doug. The two of them always have so much fun together. She must feel closer to him than she does to me. That's just going to continue and eventually she'll start turning to him for other things as well. The closer she gets to Doug, the more distant she'll feel from me. Our relationship is going to get worse and worse, and I bet she'll finally decide that I'm not the right man for her." On and on it went. Gus's middle-of-night fantasy ended with him living alone, never seeing his children, and being ridiculed by all their friends and family.

Gus isn't crazy for worrying about what this difference could lead to. But by catastrophizing, he is wasting emotional energy and time worrying about the wrong things. He and Carla have work to do, and it requires both of them to be resilient.

We'll show you how Gus used Putting It in Perspective to prevent his anxiety from getting the better of him. He recorded his worst-case, best-case, and most likely outcomes that could result due to their difference. Recording the worst-case implications was a no-brainer, but when he got to the best-case outcomes, he had to remind himself that it should be as unlikely as the worst case. (It's important to create worst-case and best-

WORST CASE	MOST LIKELY	BEST CASE
Carla plays *Lost in America* and I don't laugh during the nest-egg scene.	Carla continues to enjoy humor and be funny, and I continue to not enjoy it as much and not be funny.	Carla plays *Lost in America* and I laugh uncontrollably during the nest-egg scene. I laugh so hard I wet my pants.
Carla feels lonely and sad.	Carla connects with other people around this but not with me.	Suddenly, everything that she thinks is funny, I think is funny too.
She calls Doug and invites him over to watch it. They laugh for hours.	She feels some disappointment and sadness.	I start doing stand-up and draw the attention of Jerry Seinfeld.
They start spending hours together on the phone.	Carla stops asking me to watch the nest-egg scene since it just leads to fights.	Seinfeld invites me to tour with him, and Carla and the kids come along.
She starts spending less and less time with me.	We spend more time enjoying the things we share—loving our kids, gardening, reading true crime, etc.	While touring, Carla and I develop a routine and we try it out during open mike night.
She begins to despise me and decides to leave me and takes the kids.	I will occasionally feel threatened by Carla's relationship with Doug.	Albert Brooks is in the audience and gives us a standing ovation.
I'm left alone and never see the kids because they side with Carla and see me as a stick in the mud.		Seinfeld and Brooks beg us to write a screenplay and they pay us $10 million for it.
All our family and friends turn their back on me and start calling me "the bore."		We give up our jobs and devote ourselves full time to writing and performing.
		I become the hero of our family and friends, and they start calling me "funny man."

case scenarios; often it is difficult to hit upon the likely outcomes until you first create the two poles.)

After Gus used the skill of Putting It in Perspective, he and Carla came up with a plan for dealing with the likely outcomes of this basic difference between them. Carla recognized that it made no sense to continue to "test" Gus on the nest-egg scene. They created a list of the top five things that make them feel close and taped it to their bedroom mirror (talking about the kids, reading books out loud in bed, making love, planning fantasy vacations, catching up at the end of the day). Gus anticipated feeling threatened by Doug, and they agreed that when he felt this way, he would tell Carla and she would either spend less time with Doug or find another way to reassure Gus. By acknowledging the underlying issue and then being realistic about its implications, Carla and Gus were able to keep this perpetual problem from undermining their relationship.

Other Ways to Enhance Your Relationship: Reaching Out

We have discussed two basic issues in relationships—empathic communication and healthy fighting—and we hope you have learned how you can apply the skills of resilience so that you and your partner communicate openly and deal with conflicts productively. But if you are like most couples, you want more than healthy communication and constructive fighting. You want to do new things together, have fun, and create a life that is meaningful.

There are many simple steps you can take to have a more intimate, deeper connection to each other. You can set up a date night every week. You can work on incorporating traditions into your relationship, like lighting candles at dinner every Friday night or taking photos of yourselves every summer wearing the same silly hats. Why not shake things up a bit in your relationship? Arrange for babysitting and show up at your spouse's office with tickets to the theater. Agree to something you have been resisting for a long time (dinner at that tacky new restaurant, canoeing with her college friends, wearing the Mary Ann costume that your partner "jokingly" brought home last Halloween). Have you ever written your partner a letter? We mean a real letter, stamp and all. Why not make it a tradition to mail one to each other?

You can reach out to your partner and deepen your friendship in an endless number of ways. And, let's face it, the hard part is not coming up with these ideas, the hard part is *doing* the ideas you come up with. That is where resilience comes in to play. Most often what stops couples from building and tending to their friendship is their ticker-tape beliefs: "I don't have time to go out tonight"; "If I give him a massage, he'll expect sex"; "She would be annoyed if I showed up at her office unannounced." . . . On and on go our beliefs. If you want to reach out to your partner so that your relationship is deeper and more fulfilling, you need to challenge the beliefs that are standing in your way. The seven resilience skills equip you to do just that.

When It Doesn't Work Out: Using the Skills of Resilience to Bounce Back from a Breakup

Sometimes, despite your best effort, the relationship doesn't work out. Or perhaps it was working for one of you but not the other. All of us have experienced the end of an important relationship—and many of us will go through a divorce. Resilience doesn't make the experience pain-free, but it will help you to openly mourn the end of the relationship, honestly confront why it didn't work, and gradually heal and move on.

When they decided to separate, Angela and Tony had been married for thirteen years. Their children, Michael and Ashley, were seven and six. Tony works for the city and Angela worked for an insurance company, but she stopped working when Michael was born. Tony is very ambitious and devoted to his career. He works long hours and, when he's not working, he enjoys tinkering with his many projects in the basement. He's never been much into socializing, nor does he have many friends—and frankly, he doesn't feel like he's missing out. Angela, in contrast, is a "people person." She enjoyed working, and part of what made it so rewarding for her was the friendships she formed with her clients and colleagues. Angela, as the wife, was in charge of their social calendar. Most of the time she felt like Tony would have been happier if they had just stayed at home.

The biggest difference, however, was in how they dealt with problems. Angela and Tony faced many challenges across their thirteen years together, and their styles of dealing with these challenges were incompatible. Angela tried to turn to Tony for support. She wanted to tell him how she was feeling and know what he was feeling as well. Tony's style, however, was to shut down and throw himself harder into his work and hobbies. In fact, the more Angela approached, the more Tony withdrew. Several times throughout their marriage, Angela suggested they go for counseling, and although Tony went, it was never of much use. Fundamentally, it seemed that Angela wanted to work on things, but Tony was more comfortable with the relationship staying as is. Each year they grew more distant from each other, and eventually Angela stopped trying to make things better.

As Angela describes it, there was no single incident that led to her decision to suggest divorce. "It was about a month before my fortieth birthday and I was sitting in our bedroom—Tony was somewhere else—and I remember thinking to myself that if we didn't get a divorce, I'd spend the rest of my life in a lonely marriage—never feeling truly loved, not having intimacy, not being able to share myself with someone. And I knew that I couldn't do that to myself." As she sat alone in their bedroom, Angela decided that if she was ever going to have a loving, successful marriage, she had to face that this one had failed.

Tony didn't put up a fight, and one month after her fortieth birthday, he moved out. Many people think that when a relationship ends, the one who initiated the split has an easier time adjusting than the other person. And certainly that's sometimes true. But, for Angela, as for many women who precipitate the divorce, the months after Tony moved out were the hardest challenge she had ever confronted. Two emotions were causing Angela the greatest problems, depleting her energy and resourcefulness. Angela expected to feel guilty—but its intensity came as a surprise. At night she would lie in bed and ruminate about how selfish she was and how much her children would suffer. By morning she was exhausted and was so overly vigilant about how her kids were feeling moment to moment that they started to feel like they were under a microscope.

The guilt, at least, was expected; she was simply unprepared for the amount of anger that she felt. She was angry with herself for being foolish enough to marry him in the first place and then naive enough to think she could change him. She was angry at him for all the years he didn't do more for her, for having to go back to work, for having to be the one to deal with the kids' sadness and anger every day. She was frustrated that she didn't get divorced earlier—before she had turned into a middle-aged, graying, heavy-hipped mother of two. She was angry that Tony didn't even seem bothered that she had kept all the best CDs and books and left him with all the chipped plates and mismatched cutlery. He deprived her of that pleasure as well.

Some guilt and anger make sense, but Angela was becoming immobilized by it, and that was making it even harder on the kids.

After Tony moved out, Angela knew she had to go back to work, but as the weeks wore on, she couldn't get herself to start the process. She wasn't particularly anxious about job hunting—she was confident that she'd find something, but she just couldn't break free of the hodgepodge of emotions she was feeling and wasn't even sure what was getting in her way. We'll show you how Angela used ABC and Real-time Resilience to understand what was interfering with her ability to get moving on the job search.

One morning, after getting the kids off to school, she sat at her computer—supposedly doing an Internet search for job openings—and decided to work through her ABCs to see if she could get a better understanding of what was going on for her.

Angela's ABC Worksheet

Adversity: I have to go back to work but I can't get myself started on the process. Every time I'm supposed to be working on my resume or looking at the help wanted section, I end up just sitting there doing nothing or else I find something "more important" that needs to get done immediately.

BELIEFS	CONSEQUENCES
I love being with my kids and planned to be at home until they were much, much older. I don't want to go back to work.	Sadness
If I hadn't put my needs first and gotten a divorce, I could have stayed home with them and been the kind of mother they deserve.	Sadness Guilt
It's bad enough that their dad moved out, now they're going to see less of me too. They need more of my time, not less of it.	Guilt
If I'm not here for them to help them through this, they're going to end up even more screwed up and might really get into trouble when they're older.	Guilt Anxiety

© Copyright Adaptiv Learning Systems

By mapping out her ABCs, Angela discovered that the emotions she was experiencing were actually a mixture of sadness, anxiety, and a lot of guilt. Her ticker-tape beliefs centered on the loss of her identity as a mother and her fears that she had harmed her children—and would harm them even more by going back to work. Once she identified the beliefs that were interfering with her ability to start job hunting, she decided to use Real-time Resilience to challenge her beliefs and find more resilient ways to think about the situation. Angela began by repeating the ticker-tape beliefs she identified through ABC. As she worked through those, other beliefs emerged as well. Here's how it unfolded.

TICKER-TAPE BELIEFS: *I love being with my kids and planned to be at home until they were much, much older. I don't want to go back to work.*
REAL-TIME RESILIENCE RESPONSE: *That's true, this isn't how I imagined my life going. I don't want to go back to work, but I need to. I can find a job that enables me to get home by dinner, and I can make sure that I spend extra time with the kids in the evening and on weekends.*

TICKER-TAPE BELIEFS: *If I hadn't put my needs first and gotten a divorce, I could have stayed home with them and been the kind of mother they deserve.*

REAL-TIME RESILIENCE RESPONSE: *It's true—I did put my needs first, but I didn't make this decision lightly. I tried for years to make the marriage work. But let's face it—it wasn't good for them to grow up in a house with so much tension and to constantly hear their parents arguing like we did. I hope I marry again some-day, but even if I don't remarry, at least they won't see a bad example of mar-riage every day of their lives, and they'll have two loving parents who aren't always angry and disappointed in each other.*

TICKER-TAPE BELIEFS: *Listen to me! I'm just making excuse after excuse. The truth is that by getting this divorce, I've permanently damaged my kids and no amount of sugarcoating is going to change that.*

REAL-TIME RESILIENCE RESPONSE: *Hang on. The divorce has harmed them— that's true. But let's face it, we're divorced, and we're certainly not getting back together. I'm not doing my kids any good by obsessing about how much I have ruined their lives. If I want to help them through this, then I need to stop drowning myself in guilt. All that does is make it harder for me to see what they're really feeling and how I can best help them cope with this situa-tion.*

TICKER-TAPE BELIEFS: *Yeah, but the divorce was hard enough on them, now I'm go-ing to abandon them again by going back to work. I should find a way to be home with them.*

REAL-TIME RESILIENCE RESPONSE: *It'd be great if I could stay at home, but we sim-ply need the money. I'll find a way to be at home with them as much as possible, and I'll make sure that the person who watches them after school is someone that I really trust. Unfortunately, that's the best I can do.*

After responding to her beliefs, Angela didn't suddenly leap at the "opportunity" to go back to work. She was still worried about her kids and was sad that she wouldn't be there when they got home from school. But by fighting back against her nonresilient beliefs, she was able to move for-ward and begin the process of finding a job that would afford her the most flexibility—she was able to start constructing the best life she could for herself and her kids.

For the first few months, Angela used Real-time Resilience daily— sometimes hourly. She used the skill so that she could stay calm and con-structive when talking with Tony about issues they needed to resolve. She used the skill to stop herself from catastrophizing whenever the kids were angry at her and complained that their lives were ruined—and, by doing so, she was in a much better position to comfort them and respond to their needs. Gradually the beliefs that led to her sadness, anger, and guilt shifted fundamentally—she still got angry and worried about her children, but her emotions did not prevent her from doing the things she needed to do in order to get their lives back on track.

Using the Resilience Skills to Recover after a Relationship Ends

Angela found Real-time Resilience was a powerful tool for battling the negative beliefs that were interfering with her ability to begin the next phase of her life. Many other people find Putting It in Perspective prevents them from getting lost in their worst-case fantasies so they can focus their energy on the real problems before them. We've put together a list of common emotions that ensue after a relationship ends. Then we present the skills that will be most helpful in dealing with those emotions. Common emotions include:

✦ Sadness and depression
✦ Guilt
✦ Anger
✦ Anxiety
✦ Shame and embarrassment

SADNESS AND DEPRESSION

The end of a relationship is a loss, and it makes sense to feel sad or down. If your sadness is getting in your way of functioning at work, home, or school, or is getting in your way of taking care of your responsibilities, then you may want to use the skill of doing your ABCs to identify the beliefs that are causing the sadness or depression. We know from the B–C connections that they will be about loss, but pay attention to them—are you saying overly negative things to yourself, such as "It's all my fault. I ruin every relationship I'm in" or "This proves that there's something really wrong with me. Maybe I'm just incapable of loving someone"? When you identify your beliefs, check them for thinking errors and make sure that you are not personalizing ("It's all my fault. I ruin every relationship I'm in"), overgeneralizing ("There must be something really wrong with me"), or using emotional reasoning ("I feel so horrible—I'm never going to get over him"). If your ticker-tape beliefs don't account for the intensity of your sadness, check for iceberg beliefs. Perhaps this breakup has tapped into a larger issue that you struggle with—particularly beliefs around acceptance and the importance of being in a relationship.

Once you have identified the beliefs that are accounting for your feelings, you can use Challenging Beliefs to test whether they are fully accurate. This is an important step because often in the weeks or months following a divorce or breakup, people become more pessimistic than they usually are—so even if your beliefs are typically fairly accurate, don't assume they are in this particular situation. Another reason to break free from the beliefs that are bringing on excessive sadness is that the beliefs often cause us to withdraw from our friends and family—we feel passive and helpless, and believe that we're just crummy company—but getting support from those who love you is absolutely necessary.

GUILT

Many people feel guilty after the end of a relationship, often because they were the one who chose to end it or because they are worried about the effects on their children. Feeling a little guilt is not a bad thing—you may have hurt the other person, and feeling guilty about that means you're a caring person—but excessive guilt probably stems from biased beliefs rather than the actual facts of the situation, and it may interfere with your ability to heal. As always, begin with ABC. Identify the ticker-tape beliefs or the iceberg beliefs that are fueling your guilt. You can expect that they'll be about having harmed someone you care about. Do a quick check to make sure you are not personalizing and taking full responsibility for something that was mutual. People often feel excessive guilt when they catastrophize how other people are going to respond to a divorce or breakup. For example, the beliefs "Our kids are going to be devastated and won't ever get over it" or "She thought we'd be together forever. This is going to destroy her" are about harm, but they are also catastrophic and are blowing the consequences out of proportion. If your beliefs are similar to these, then the skill of Putting It in Perspective will help you to assess more accurately the consequences of the breakup on those you care about. And that's important, because you're not doing anyone any good by making a bad situation even worse.

ANGER

Anger results when you believe your rights have been violated. No matter who precipitated the breakup, anger is a normal response. But, just as with sadness and guilt, if your anger is excessive and interfering with your healing, then it's time to try to get a better handle on it. This is particularly important if you have children, because although your marriage may have ended, your relationship hasn't. After most divorces, the parents continue to have contact. Your anger at your ex can be more destructive to your child than the actual divorce. Even if children are not an issue, anger can consume you and make it nearly impossible to move forward in a new relationship. (How many of us have ever been on a date with someone who is clearly still really angry at his or her ex? It's not a turn-on.) After you've identified your Bs, check for externalizing to make sure that you're not blaming your ex for everything and denying any contribution to the failed relationship. Another thinking trap that can bring on excessive anger is magnifying and minimizing—in which you rewrite the history of your relationship to include only the horrible things your ex did to you and none of the positive things. This may be a fun activity for the first few weeks after the breakup, but eventually you want to have an honest and accurate understanding of your relationship because, without it, you'll be unable to learn from it. After you've identified the beliefs, challenge their accuracy. The goal is not to convince yourself that you have nothing to be angry about but to make sure that your anger is reasonable. Eventually you may decide that forgiving your partner will help you to move on, and forgiveness will be easier if your anger is under control. The calming techniques can help you to lower your anger when it threatens to overwhelm you—if you need to hash out custody issues or a settlement—because anger that is too intense will make you less effective in your negotiations.

ANXIETY

The anxiety that people feel after the end of a relationship can center on many different issues. Perhaps you're anxious about taking over responsibilities that your ex used to help with—taking care of the kids, paying the bills, fixing things around the house—or maybe you're worried about being alone, having to date again, or how to make ends meet with less money. Probably more than any other emotion, out-of-control anxiety can be downright paralyzing. Simple decisions seem hard. Hard decisions are too daunting to even think about. Many challenges must be confronted when a relationship ends, but your anxiety may cause you to want to bury your head in the sand. The goal is not to avoid all anxiety but to keep your anxiety manageable. The most effective skills for lowering your anxiety are the Calming and Focusing techniques and Putting It in Perspective. If the very thought of taking over the finances makes you sick to your stomach, use the calming techniques to relax yourself so that you can begin to study your portfolio and educate yourself about the issues. If you decide that you're ready to date again but keep finding yourself lost in dates-from-hell fantasies, use Putting It in Perspective to identify and plan for the more likely dating scenarios (like boning up on current events to get the conversation rolling again when it inevitably lulls). Anxiety can convince you that you're completely ill-prepared to handle the adversities in your life, but if you begin to take control where you can, your anxiety will slowly and steadily recede.

SHAME AND EMBARRASSMENT

Some people become embarrassed or ashamed when their relationship ends—they see it as an indication of a deep, personal failure, and they're certain that others see it that way as well. It might be a bit uncomfortable or awkward to explain over and over again that you're now single, but are you too quick to assume that others are thinking ill of you? Check to see if you're mind reading when you hear yourself thinking "There's that look. I can tell she's feeling sorry for me" or "I bet they think that it's no surprise we split up. They always thought we were a bad match." If you feel a sense of shame, look for iceberg beliefs that may have been activated. What messages did you learn as a child about marriage and divorce or commitment and forbearance? Deep down, do you believe that a failed relationship means that you're unworthy of love or damaged in some fundamental way? Once you've brought the iceberg belief to the surface, ask yourself whether it's accurate and whether it's a useful guiding force in your life. If it isn't, see if you can reframe the belief so that you keep what you value but get rid of elements that are doing you more harm than good. You can use Real-time Resilience to keep the embarrassment and shame-eliciting beliefs in check so that they don't prevent you from moving forward in your life.

The Importance of Practice

One of the messages that we've repeated throughout this book is the importance of practicing these skills. This is doubly true when it comes to applying the skills of resilience to your relationships. Sometimes relationships bring out the best in us, and sometimes the worst. So, as you practice these skills, remember you don't have to use them perfectly—good enough is good enough. The more you practice them, the more resilient you will become. You'll feel more intimate with those you love and, if a relationship doesn't work out, you'll recover more quickly from the breakup.

CHAPTER ELEVEN

Resilience in Parenting

As a parent today, you must confront challenges that your grandparents did not face when raising their children. In past generations, drinking on prom night might have been a concern, and perhaps a real "troubled" child smoked pot, but today the picture is quite different. In a national study conducted by the Centers for Disease Control, over 15,000 students in grades 9 to 12 completed confidential surveys regarding drug use, sexual activity, cigarette smoking as well as a host of other risky behaviors.[1] The picture is far from positive.

✦ In the thirty days preceding the survey, 33 percent of the students had ridden in a car with a driver who had been drinking alcohol, and 13 percent had themselves driven a car after drinking alcohol.

✦ 17 percent of students had carried a weapon at least once in the thirty days prior to the survey.

✦ 13 percent of female students had been forced to have sexual intercourse.

✦ 28 percent of students reported feeling hopeless for at least two weeks; for females it was 35 percent.

✦ 8 percent of the students had attempted suicide once in the past twelve months.

✦ 33 percent of students reported smoking cigarettes, cigars, or using smokeless tobacco.

✦ 27 percent of students had used marijuana at least once during the last thirty days and 11 percent had tried it by the time they were thirteen years old.

✦ Half of the students had already had intercourse; 8 percent reported having intercourse by the time they were thirteen. Sixteen percent had already had four or more sex partners, and only 58 percent used a condom during the last time they had intercourse.

Although these are just numbers from a survey, we have seen firsthand the problems that arise when children are not taught how to solve their problems and cope with the stress. We've met eleven-year-olds who abuse alcohol. We've met thirteen-year-olds who skip school and commit crimes. We've met fifteen-year-olds who have attempted suicide once and are planning to try it again. And we've met seventeen-year-olds who have lost hope and no longer look forward to their future. We know that for children to live productive, meaningful, and happy lives, they need more than to learn how to read and write. They need more than to learn how to drive a car, find a job, and balance a checkbook. Today's children, perhaps more than ever, need to learn how to solve problems, negotiate relationships, and persevere in the face of adversity. They need to be taught resilience.

The High Cost of Depression

How many times have you wished for the carefree days of your youth? For a very long time, people—psychologists among them—believed that children and adolescents did not become depressed. Sure, children get sad and adolescents are known for their moodiness, but depression—severe, crippling depression—was thought to be a disorder of adulthood. Well, the fantasy of a footloose and fancy-free childhood is truly a fantasy. Your child is at greater risk of depression in her lifetime than you are in yours.

Children are experiencing pessimism and depression on an unprecedented scale. As many as one in five adolescents suffer a major depressive episode before the end of their high school years. For many depressed youth, the future seems foreshortened and bleak—a pervasive sense of hopelessness casts a long shadow. And suicide, the ultimate expression of this hopelessness, is far too common. More than 8 percent of high school students in this country attempt suicide each year, and approximately 13 in every 100,000 American adolescents ages fifteen through nineteen do kill themselves.[2]

These numbers are alarming. All the more so because once you've had a first bout of depression, you have a 50 percent chance of having it recur at least once—often repeatedly—in your lifetime. And the younger you are when depression first hits, the greater the likelihood that it will recur.

As if this isn't bad enough, once a child becomes depressed, a whole host of other negative situations arise.[3] The symptoms of depression—lethargy, difficulty concentrating, intrusive negative thoughts—make it hard to focus and participate in school so grades often deteriorate, and as school becomes more difficult, depressed kids often begin to cut classes or skip school altogether. Depressed children and adolescents are also more likely to smoke cigarettes and to abuse drugs and alcohol, perhaps in a misguided attempt to self-medicate. As they begin to participate in more antisocial activities, depressed children often withdraw from their old friends and the activities they once enjoyed and start forming friendships with children who have more behavioral problems. These new friendships often serve to introduce the adolescent into more and more delinquent activities—truancy, petty crime, more severe drug use.

The picture of depression in adolescence is frightening. Depressed adolescents find themselves on a life trajectory that, once begun, is often hard to reverse. The depression itself is highly treatable through either cognitive therapy or medication, but treating the depression is the easy part. Once the depression goes away, the more intractable problems often remain. Overcoming addiction, reconnecting with healthier friends, dealing with the consequences of having committed a crime are not so easy.

We know that today's children are at greater risk for depression than you were at their age, but we don't know why this is true. Many theories have been offered: increased rates of divorce, greater access to illegal drugs, more children born to single mothers, the list goes on. Most likely, all of these factors (and many not named) contribute to the problem. Although we do not know for certain the root cause, one solution is clear: If we teach children how to be more resilient, they will have a better shot at overcoming the risk of depression and the myriad of other challenges that adolescence brings.

Teaching Children to Have High Self-esteem Is Not the Answer

As the data about depression in youth became known and the problems associated with depression mounted, educators and parents searched for ways to help. For many, the search led to "self-esteem programs." If depressed children feel bad about themselves, the thinking went, then if we can teach them to feel good about themselves, they ought to get better. This straightforward and seemingly obvious statement led schools to adopt programs designed to improve self-esteem. Here are a few of the self-esteem–enhancing activities we saw in schools across the country:

✦ Children pass a mirror around the room. When the mirror reaches them, they look into it and say three things they like about themselves.
✦ Each child takes a turn on the "love throne." As they sit on the chair (draped in red velvet cloth), they describe what they love about themselves.
✦ Each child repeats "If I can dream it, I can be it, and I dream . . ." and then fills in the blank.
✦ Before dismissing for lunch, the class repeats together, "I am like a snowflake, I am special and unique. There is no one just like me."

Of course, self-esteem enhancement is not just the mission of schools. Parents as well as teachers have been persuaded that making sure their child feels good about herself is of the greatest importance.

Emma is a fifth grader at Hilltop Elementary School. She is smart, quick-witted, hardworking, and artistic. Emma likes school and is doing well. She has two close friends from whom she's inseparable. Her parents, however, are worried about her because Emma is overweight. Next year Emma will be going to middle school, and her parents are concerned that she'll be tormented because of her size. One day at Emma's house, her friend Laurel tells Emma that she has decided to join the school dance club and wants Emma to do it with her. Emma, aware that she is not particularly coordinated and was not blessed with grace, tells Laurel that she just agreed to sing the school song, buck naked, at the next assembly, so, unfortunately, she'll be busy preparing for *that* humiliation and just won't have the time. Emma's mother, who overheard the conversation, brings it up after dinner. Her parents tell her that they think the dance club would be a lot of fun and it would help her to slim down a bit as well. When Emma talks about her lack of talent and says that she doesn't really want to learn to dance, her father counters with, "Come on, Em. What kind of attitude is that? You can do anything you set your mind to. You'll just need to work hard. We believe in you and you should believe in yourself." After much cajoling, Emma's parents convince her to join the club.

Like a trooper, Emma goes to dance every Tuesday and Thursday. Laurel and the other girls tap, twirl, and sashay with delight. Emma feels lucky if she manages to stay on her feet. At the end of the semester, the dance club puts on a recital for the school. Emma is filled with dread. She has worked hard and has improved some, but the thought of dancing before her peers is horrifying. On the night of the big event, Emma's mother whispers to her, "Imagine yourself as a graceful ballerina and you'll *be* a graceful ballerina."

In the ballet number, Laurel floats across the stage; Emma bumps into the fake swan. In the tap number, Laurel throws her cane and catches it without missing a beat; Emma's cane almost impales the conductor, and she trips as she scrambles to retrieve it. In the modern dance performance, all the girls end up on stage right and Emma, breathing heavily on stage left, scrambles to join them. When it comes time for the final curtsy, all the girls beam proudly and bask in the applause; Emma secretly prays that the ground will open up and swallow her whole.

After the performance, Emma's mother says, "Sweetheart, you were beautiful. You did a wonderful job. You looked so graceful and strong. I knew this would be a wonderful experience." Emma, looking at her mother as if she were a raving lunatic, says, "What are you talking about? This was the most embarrassing night of my life. Laurel looked beautiful, graceful, and strong, I looked like a stampeding circus elephant and everyone knows it."

Her mother, not wanting Emma to feel bad, says, "Oh, that's crazy. I'm sure everyone thought you did a fantastic job. Don't put yourself down like that. You danced beautifully, you really did." Emma rolls her eyes and walks away.

What is wrong with this story? Perhaps the mother was a bit overly cheery, but she didn't want her daughter to feel bad—where's the crime in that? And some of you may think that the school programs we described sound valuable and are probably making a difference. Others may think that although the school programs may not be doing any good, and while Emma might not really believe her parents, it's all harmless enough, so why worry about it? We disagree. We believe these programs and "self-esteem parenting" actually may be doing harm. Here's why.

Two Parts to Self-esteem: Feeling Good and Doing Well

Healthy self-esteem has a clear formula: Do well in the world and you will feel good about yourself. Get good grades, make friends, hit the ball, write a poem, solve a problem, and you will feel proud of your accomplishment and yourself. The feeling-good part of self-esteem is the result of doing well. The way, then, to increase a child's self-esteem is not to feed her empty phrases or to praise her for accomplishments that are not real but to teach her skills for doing well. If we teach children how to study effectively, how to join groups and mend broken friendships, how to identify their talents—whatever they may be—and give them the opportunity to pursue them, then as they succeed, they will develop a healthy and reality-based view of themselves.

The research on self-esteem is actually quite clear. It is true that many adolescents who use drugs feel bad about themselves; kids who drop out from school and commit crimes often report self-loathing; pregnant teenagers describe feeling unworthy. But we have to be careful not to confuse cause with effect. Most people believe that low self-esteem causes these problems. The research, however indicates the opposite. Low self-esteem is the effect, not the cause.[4]

How can this be? Hundreds of research papers about self-esteem and performance report that children who do well in school have high self-esteem, children who are truant have low self-esteem, and on and on. The problem, however, is that almost all of these studies are correlational; that is, they tell us that low self-esteem and doing poorly go together and high self-esteem and doing well go together, but they do not address which came first. To determine the direction of causality, the research must be longitudinal. That is, the same group of children must be followed across time, measuring self-esteem at the beginning of the study and measuring the presumed outcomes, such as grades, friendships, drug use, depression at the beginning, and then again at the end of the study. If self-esteem affects a child's performance, then if we looked at the kids with the same grades at the beginning of the study, those with higher self-esteem ought to have better grades at the end of the study than those who have lower self-esteem.

The longitudinal research tells us that self-esteem is not a cause—not of grades, drug use, or depression—and it points out the grave problem with trying to pump up a child's self-esteem directly. Psychologist Roy Baumeister and his colleagues reviewed the literature on self-esteem and violence and contend that contrary to what is often suggested, low esteem is not the cause of violence and aggression. In the many studies they reviewed, they found compelling evidence that people with high self-esteem were far more likely to commit violent acts. Put simply, people who are aggressive and violent tend to think themselves superior, not inferior.[5]

Emma knows that she is not a graceful dancer. Her parents' enthusiasm doesn't change the facts. She can plié for three hours a day and dance will still not be an area in which she excels. Her parents' pep talks have served one purpose only: They have undermined their credibility. The next time they praise Emma, she will be skeptical. And worse, by relying on pep talks and positive thinking, they are falling short when it comes to teaching Emma skills that she can use to do well. Wouldn't it have been more valuable if they had helped Emma to identify why she didn't want to dance, to test those beliefs out for accuracy, and then to help her find another activity that she would have enjoyed and excelled in? Research tells us that doing well helps you to feel good about yourself, and this straightforward finding makes our mission clear. By teaching children how to be more resilient, they can solve problems and do well in their life. Their self-esteem—and more important, their successes—will increase on their own. Slogans are unnecessary.

We want to provide you with two perspectives on parenting and resilience. First, we discuss the parenting style that increases resilience in children. You can use this information to guide your general approach to parenting and to create an environment in your family that fosters resilience. We'll give you examples of how to use the skills you have learned to stay resilient and constructive when dealing with a crisis with your child. Second, we show you how to teach your child the core resilience skills that our research shows prevent depression.

How to Promote Resilience in Your Children

Jonathan is eight weeks old. His mother, Jennifer, cradles him in her arms. They are looking intently at each other and are responding to each with great precision. Jonathan raises an eyebrow, his mother cocks her eyebrow in return. Jonathan smiles at her, and she smiles and coos. His smile broadens and his eyes shine as he imitates his mother's sounds. She coos again, and now Jonathan wriggles his arms and legs in delight. The mother feels a sense of euphoria and awe, and she communicates these feelings to her infant through her face, body, and voice. At a fundamental level, Jonathan has experienced the beginning of self-efficacy: He successfully communicated to his mother and elicited communication in return.

The ballet between an infant and his mother is intimately choreographed. It is a lively social interaction that serves a vital role in the infant's development. We often think of infants as helpless when, in fact, they have considerable power to summon help from others, particularly their parents. They can elicit cuddles and soothing sounds by crying and wriggling. They can elicit smiles and laughter through their smiles and laughter. And, of course, they can get food by making sucking motions and turning their head toward the mother's breast. Jonathan, like most infants, has a caregiver who responds when he communicates. Sometimes Jennifer may misunderstand his cues, but as if playing charades, she keeps guessing until he shows her that she got it right. This game of charades is essential for Jonathan. His cries, coos, smiles, and wriggles are the only methods he has for asking for help and learning about the world. These early communications provide infants with help negotiating the challenges of their environment, in regulating their emotion, and in building skills that will become necessary in mastering later developmental tasks. Developmental psychologists describe this responsive relationship between an infant and the mother as a secure attachment.[6]

The secure base that attachment provides confers a wide range of advantages that extend through childhood and adolescence. Researchers found that those with a secure attachment as infants were better problem solvers as toddlers and got along better with their peers as ten and twelve year olds.[7] They were less likely to use drugs as adolescents and had better relationships as adults. When children are young, attentive parents and a secure attachment lay the groundwork for the development of self-efficacy, emotion regulation, and impulse control each of which contributes to resilience.

The basic challenge, then, is to provide a secure base from which the child can increasingly venture farther and farther away. To build independence, the child must feel confident that her parents will welcome her back and help her navigate the psychological complexities independence requires. What style of parenting does this best?

Psychologists have described three general styles of parenting.[8] An authoritarian parenting style is restrictive and cold. A permissive parenting style is indulgent and sometimes neglectful. An authoritative parenting style is warm and sets limits. Hundreds of studies have investigated the effects of these styles. The consensus is that an authoritative style of parenting is most effective in promoting competent, successful, resilient children. Let's take a closer look at each of these styles of parenting and their effects on children.

BECAUSE-I-SAID-SO PARENTING

Do you parent with a tight fist? Do you impose lots of demands on your child and expect strict obedience? Is the phrase "because I am your mother/father, and I said so" something you say often? Do you think your child should learn to "tough it out" and that expressing emotion, particularly sadness, is a sign of weakness? These are hallmarks of the authoritarian parent. Following is a dialogue between a seven-year-old boy who wants to go with a friend to the park across the street and his authoritarian mother.

BOY: *Can I go to the park, just me and John, and you stay home?*
MOM: *You know the rule. You have to have either me or Dad with you.*
BOY: *Please? I'll be right on the baseball field and I won't go anywhere else. I promise.*
MOM: *You know the rule.*
BOY: *Why, Mom? Why can't I go with John? We won't go anywhere but the ball field, and I'll come back exactly when you tell me to. Really, I will. You can trust me.*
MOM: *I said no and that's final. I don't want to hear another word.*

Rules and control are very important to authoritarian parents. They are demanding and have strict and inflexible expectations for their children. Expressions of empathy are infrequent, and helping children express their emotions is not a priority. Authoritarian parents do little to encourage their children to pay attention to their beliefs and feelings nor do they help their children to think flexibly about solutions to problems. In the dialogue above, the mother shows no empathy for her son's desire for greater autonomy. She does not explain the reasoning behind her decision, nor does she help him to think through other solutions to the problem. Compromise and negotiation are not common practice for authoritarian parents.

Authoritarian parents tend to have children who are more fearful, nervous, and moody than children of authoritative parents. As preschoolers, they are more vulnerable to stress, they move about the classroom more aimlessly, and they are more sulky and unfriendly with peers.[9] Studies show that adolescents who are frequent drug users had parents who were more critical and unresponsive when they were young children.[10] Although authoritarian parents may believe they are teaching their children right from wrong and are raising them to make good decisions, they're actually having the opposite effect on their kids.

LAISSEZ-FAIRE PARENTING

Do you see yourself more as your child's friend than as her parent? Do you make few demands on your child? Do you grant your child a lot of leeway in terms of decision making? Are you often unsure of whom your child is with and where they are? Does your child spend a lot of time unsupervised in the home as well as outside it? These are indications of a permissive parenting style. Permissive parents abdicate responsibility. Many are warm, loving, and accepting of their children, but to a fault. They value emotional expression yet they often fail to help children develop skills for regulating their emotions. It is common to hear an adolescent of permissive parents yell profanities at them or throw angry tantrums when he does not get his way. Rather than help the child to express himself with more control, permissive parents tend to allow their children to vent their emotions in whatever form they take. These parents rarely exert firm control. They do not set many rules, nor do they supervise or monitor their children closely. Permissive parents tend to fall into one of two different categories: Indulgent parents demand little from their children but are responsive to their emotional needs; indifferent parents neglect to set limits for their children, and they are uninvolved in their emotional lives. Below is a dialogue between a seven-year-old boy and his indulgent mother.

BOY: *Can I go to the park, just me and John, and you stay home?*
MOM: *Oh, I don't know. I think it would be better if I came with you.*
BOY: *Oh, Mom. I don't need you to come with me. You act like I'm such a baby. I can do what I want and you can't stop me. I don't have to listen to you.*
MOM: *Okay, okay. I guess you can go. Just be careful and stay out of trouble, okay?*
BOY: *Okay. Bye.*

Many permissive parents convince themselves that their style of parenting helps develop independence and that their willingness to tolerate any expression of emotion shows their children that it is okay to be expressive. They also believe that by not monitoring and supervising their children, they communicate that they trust their children and believe in their ability to negotiate the world autonomously. Regardless of the messages that permissive parents believe they send, laissez-faire parenting is not good for children.

Research indicates that permissive parents tend to have children who are more rebellious, impulsive, and lacking in self-reliance and self-control.[11] They tend to be aggressive and domineering with friends and don't do as well in school as peers who were raised in an authoritative manner. Adolescents of permissive parents are more likely to be heavy drug users. The lack of structure, the poor monitoring and supervision foster acting out and poor control, not healthy autonomy.

RESILIENT PARENTING

Authoritative parenting engenders the most resilience. These children clearly do best in terms of academic and social competence. As preschoolers, they show better social and cognitive skills. They are more self-reliant and self-controlled. They cope well with stress and approach problems with curiosity and a sense of purpose. With their peers, they are more cheerful and friendly. With adults they are cooperative and expressive. As adolescents, children with authoritative parents are less likely to use drugs. In general, authoritative parenting increases the very characteristics that promote resilience.[12]

What does an authoritative parenting style look like? There are four key areas of importance:

1. The parents monitor and supervise.
2. They provide consistent discipline.
3. They are supportive and communicative.
4. They help their children to develop emotional awareness, expressiveness, and control.

Authoritative parents set clear limits and then monitor and supervise their children to make sure the rules are followed. Unlike permissive parents, they are closely involved in the daily lives of their children, even when their children become adolescents and spend more time away from the family. These parents are involved at their children's school and know the families of their children's friends because they understand that friends influence their children's behavior and attitudes. Whereas authoritarian parents expect strict obedience, authoritative parents are more flexible and provide explanations for the rules and limits that are set. It's not strict obedience that is valued; instead, these parents want their children to understand the "why" behind the rules and to develop the ability to question and negotiate when it is appropriate to do so. When rules are broken, authoritative parents enforce rules appropriately and consistently. They are neither indulgent nor punitive or coercive. Additionally, authoritative parents communicate openly and warmly with their children. These parents value give-and-take in family discussions and want the input of their children when making family decisions. But don't get the wrong idea. These parents are not "touchy-feely" people for whom every rule is negotiable, every behavior is excusable so long as an explanation for it can be offered—they are not slaves to the child's wishes and whims. It's just that the authoritative parent understands that development of responsibility, autonomy, and respect is a gradual, interactive process.

Finally, authoritative parents value emotions and become emotional coaches for their children. They help them to differentiate among the emotions children and adolescents feel because they understand that "I feel 'bad' " might actually mean sad, angry, guilty, or embarrassed, and they know that each of these emotions is brought on by different beliefs. They also guide their children in expressing their emotions in healthy and controlled ways. Here is how an authoritative mother might respond to her seven-year-old's request.

BOY: *Can I go to the park, just me and John, and you stay home?*
MOM: *Oh, I don't know. I think seven-year-olds should have a parent with them with they go to the park. When you're older, you'll be able to go alone.*
BOY: *Oh, Mom. I'm not a little kid anymore. You still treat me like I'm a baby. If I'm old enough to go to first grade, then why aren't I old enough to go to the park without you? We're just going to play baseball. We won't go anywhere else.*
MOM: *Hold on a sec. Let's see if we can work this out. You're right, you are older now, and you do a lot of things without me and Dad. That's great. What I'm worried about is the street. It's such a busy corner and the drivers sometimes don't even look.*
BOY: *Well, you could walk us across the street and then go right back home.*
MOM: *How would I know when to come to cross you back?*
BOY: *We could pick a time and you could come over then and we could walk back together. Like in two hours.*
MOM: *One hour. Sounds like a great plan.*

When parents have high expectations for their children, provide supervision, set clear and appropriate limits, respond with warmth and consistency when rules are broken, engage their children in problem solving, and help their children to express and control their emotions, children do well. They succeed in school and are liked by their peers. They are ethical and socially responsible. And they respond to stress and adversity with hardiness. In short, authoritative parenting increases resilience.

In our workshops with parents, we talk about the importance of monitoring, supervision, consistent discipline, and open communication. Yet for most parents these "best practices" are not enough. They want more specific techniques for promoting resilience in their children. And we agree that to instill resilience in your children, the prescription needs to be more detailed. You've already learned in Chapters 4 to 9 how to use the skills in your own life. Now we'll show you how those skills can get you through the most difficult parenting moments. Because parents also must learn how to be "resilience coaches," we'll teach you how to model resilience and coach your children so that they can respond resiliently even when you're not around.

Using the Skills of Resilience When You're Feeling Anything But

Let's face it. Although most of the time being a parent is a great joy and a blessing, sometimes it can be a real drag. If you've got young children, you probably have moments when you feel overwhelmed by your kids, when you would love nothing more than to have just one of your "kid-free" days again—sleeping late, sipping coffee, and nibbling a warm crois-sant while reading the Sunday paper (cover to cover), watching television shows and movies that aren't animated or have theme songs sung by high-pitched fuzzy animals. Worse are the moments when—yes, it's okay to ad-mit it—we feel like we don't even like our children that much. Teenagers are tough, and it's perfectly normal for them to get on your nerves—when they argue every point with you, rolling their eyes at every comment or suggestion, endlessly questioning every rule. Sometimes the blessing feels more like a curse.

Hope is a single mother of two teenage daughters, Farrah and Faith. She's a middle school science teacher and does private tutoring two evenings a week to make extra money. The "three mouseketeers," as they refer to themselves, get along well and clearly have a deep love for each other. When Hope was debating about taking on extra tutoring hours, her daughters were supportive and offered to do more around the house so that she wouldn't have to come home to a mess. The girls are old enough to cook themselves dinner on the nights Hope works late, and often they surprise her with a warm meal when she gets home from work.

Gradually, however, things have changed. Farrah, the older daughter, has become less communicative and is sullen and cranky. Without asking, she got her tongue pierced and has replaced her Gap wardrobe with black, baggy outfits that cause constant battles with her mother. When Hope tries to talk with her about what's going on, Farrah mutters, "I'm fine" and makes a quick retreat to her bedroom. Even Faith is beginning to worry. She confides to her mother that she sees Farrah hanging out with "scary-looking" girls at school. Hope is scared that Farrah might be using drugs but has no proof.

Like many parents of teenage children, Hope begins to feel lost. She doesn't know how to connect with her daughter, and she's deeply concerned about the changes in Farrah's personality and behavior. Finally, one day while the girls are at school, Hope searches Farrah's bedroom. She looks through drawers, under the beds, in the back of the closet. She feels guilty about invading her daughter's privacy, but she needs to know what's going on. By the end of the search, Hope has found things that leave her shaken: cigarettes, rolling papers, birth control pills. She's upset and confused but doesn't want to blow it when she talks with her daughter about what she's found.

Hope's first step is to use the calming techniques to get control over her emotions. She spends ten minutes doing controlled breathing and then sits down at the kitchen table with a cup of coffee to map out her ABCs. Not surprisingly, there's a lot going on.

Hope's ABC Worksheet

Adversity: My fifteen-year-old daughter is apparently smoking, using drugs, and having sex.

BELIEFS	CONSEQUENCES
Oh my God—my daughter is a drug addict. What if she has AIDS?	Anxiety
How could this have been going on without me knowing it? Here I thought we had a really good relationship, but all the time she was off smoking pot and doing who knows what. It's my fault for working so much when I should have been home with them.	Sadness Anxiety
I'm gonna kill her. Who the hell does she think she is? I am absolutely going to level that girl when she gets home.	Anger

© Copyright Adaptiv Learning Systems

Getting it down on paper, in and of itself, is a help. Seeing her beliefs on paper gives Hope enough distance to begin to think more clearly. Since many of her beliefs are causing her to feel intense anxiety—and the cata-

THE RESILIENCE FACTOR ✦ 266

strophic thoughts just kept on coming—she decides that she should first try to gain a little perspective so that she can better plan out how to respond.

Hope uses Putting It in Perspective to make sure she isn't allowing herself to catastrophize—the situation is bad enough without letting her imagination run wild. She spends ten minutes balancing her worst-case scenario with a best-case scenario and then identifies the most likely outcomes.

WORST CASE	MOST LIKELY	BEST CASE
My daughter's a drug addict.	She's having sex.	The cigarettes, pot, and birth control pills belong to a friend.
She has AIDS.	She's smoking pot and cigarettes.	She took them from her friend because she's trying to get her cleaned up.
When I confront her, she's going to deny it and leave home for good.	She's going to deny it initially when I raise the topic.	20/20 does a special on "kids helping kids" and features Farrah.
She'll end up living on the streets and will become a prostitute to pay for her drugs.	She's going to be angry at me and try to focus on the fact that I snooped in her room rather than deal with the real issues.	
I'll won't see her for years and then one night I'll see her interviewed on a 20/20 segment about "lost children," and she'll be horribly malnourished and will blame me for all her problems.		

It isn't easy for Hope to generate the best-case outcomes because her mind keeps generating more and more catastrophic beliefs. But by the end of the ten minutes, she is able to identify the most likely outcomes. Although they aren't pleasant, her anxiety has decreased enough that she feels prepared to think through how to best deal with each outcome and is operating with realistic expectations. Hope decides that since her daughter probably will initially react with anger and denials, she'll view the conversation as a two-part process. Her goal for the first part is to tell her daughter what she has found and to not get sucked into an argument about how she has destroyed Farrah's trust by violating the sanctity of her bedroom. Hope plans for the first conversation to be brief and will talk more about it in the morning.

Hope works out a plan for the follow-up conversation in which she'll ask her daughter more specific questions about drugs and sex and will tell her that she's made an appointment with a counselor for them to see together. She also decides it's important to acknowledge that, although she's upset that her daughter's having sex, she's glad she's using birth control pills.

Of course, when Farrah gets home, it doesn't go as smoothly as Hope had hoped, and she finds herself losing control of her anger. Hope uses the calming techniques to get better control of her anger and Real-time Resilience to respond to her negative beliefs, which are undermining her ability to stay calm and clear-headed in the midst of this difficult conversation.

HOPE'S TICKER-TAPE BELIEF: *I can't believe she has the audacity to sit there and tell me a bold-faced lie. It's bad enough that she's gotten herself involved in all this crap. I ought to just kick her out.*

HOPE'S REAL-TIME RESILIENCE RESPONSE: *Slow down a second. She's lying because she's scared. I've got to stay focused on the real issue and not let her behavior right now sidetrack me. She's gotten herself into trouble, and I've got to help her figure this all out.*

HOPE'S TICKER-TAPE BELIEF: *Trouble? That's putting it mildly. I've worked my ass off so that she could have the clothes she wants and go out with her friends and have money for college, and she's blown every chance I've given her. She'll be lucky if she makes it through high school with the s**t she's been pulling.*

HOPE'S REAL-TIME RESILIENCE RESPONSE: *It's true that I've been working hard to make sure the girls have the kind of life I wished I'd had, and Farrah certainly seems to have gotten herself into a mess. But it's not going to help to blow this way out of proportion. I still don't know what the real story is—and how long this has been going on—and the only way I'm going to figure it out is by staying calm and giving her the chance to talk. If I lose my temper, I'm only going to make things worse.*

HOPE'S TICKER-TAPE BELIEF: *The cigarettes I can understand—I tried smoking for a while when I was a kid too—but the pot and sleeping around—that I simply can't understand. I raised her better than that. With all the diseases she could get . . . how could she be so stupid?*

HOPE'S REAL-TIME RESILIENCE RESPONSE: *This is a big problem, and we're going to have to spend a lot of time figuring out why she made the decisions she's made. But I should also remember that she at least had the sense to go on the pill. If she had the sense to do that, maybe she had the sense to use condoms. She's a good kid—that hasn't changed—but something has clearly gone wrong for her, and it's my job to help her make it right again.*

By using Real-time Resilience, Hope is able to keep her anger—and anxiety, sadness, and embarrassment—from preventing her from starting a constructive conversation with her daughter. Her resilience enables her to keep focused on the real issues and not to be derailed by her negative thoughts and emotions. All parents will have experiences like Hope's—perhaps the issue won't be sex or drugs, but there will be some issue—and to help our children through whatever crisis they face, we must be able to control our emotions so that we can think clearly and respond appropriately.

Teaching the Skills of Resilience to Your Children

Knowing how to stay resilient during the hardest moments of being a parent is, in and of itself, a great benefit to your child. But most parents want to do more—they want to teach their children the skills of resilience so that their kids can use the skills as they confront the everyday challenges of growing up.

In this section we describe the key issues you will need to grapple with as you teach the core resilience skills to your child. Readers who would like a detailed description of how to teach the skills to their children most effectively are encouraged to read *The Optimistic Child*, which describes our work with children in greater depth.[13]

LAYING THE GROUNDWORK

Before you get started, there are a few points to keep in mind.

1. If you are pedantic and overly rigid when you present the skills, your kids will not like it, and they will not learn the skills. It will work best if you can keep the tone engaging and fun.

2. Your child will need to feel safe and supported—which means don't try this when your child is angry with you—and it is important for him to feel comfortable joking around as he learns the skills.

3. Don't become too rigid about the amount of time you spend practicing the skills—if it feels like homework, your child will tune out.

INSTILL CURIOSITY

Start out spending about fifteen minutes on a skill and work toward increasing the amount of time to thirty minutes. Although your immediate goal will be to help your child to become more resilient, more generally, you want to instill in her a curiosity about herself, her thoughts and feelings. The best way to do this is to show her that you are curious about your own thoughts, emotions, and behaviors. Imagine that you're driving your daughter to a friend's house, and you find yourself becoming unreasonably irritated by the elderly man driving very slowly in front of you. Work through the ABCs of this situation aloud so your child can hear how you analyze your thoughts. Don't do it in a formal way—you don't want to precipitate a bout of dismissive eye rolling—but say what your belief was and the feeling it generated: "This is really making me angry, and I don't like getting angry when I drive. I guess I'm feeling angry because what I'm saying to myself is 'If he can't drive the speed limit, he shouldn't be on the road. He's making me late and I'm already stressed enough as it is.' " If you show curiosity in knowing how *your* mind works, your children will learn to be curious too.

WHEN TEACHING YOUR CHILD BECOMES AN ADVERSITY

Finally, it's important to acknowledge the inherent difficulties in teaching your child the resilience skills. You see this as an important endeavor, but your child may not. You probably already have had some ticker-tape beliefs about teaching these skills to your child—"I hope he understands how much this can help him" or "I haven't gotten more than a one-word grunt out of my son in the last six months—there's no way he's going to tell me what he's thinking." It is crucial that you ask yourself a few questions and answer them honestly before you get started.

✦ *How well do* you *know the skills? Have you practiced them daily?* Until you are comfortable using the skills in your own life, you should not begin to teach them to your child. If you're confident using the skills, you will convey authority and your child will be more likely to invest the time.

✦ *Do you usually talk with your child about your feelings and thoughts or theirs?* What is your relationship like with your child these days? Are you comfortable talking with each other about your feelings, behaviors, and thoughts? If you don't easily talk about emotions and thoughts, or if you talk about them only rarely, then it's important to set realistic expectations. First you must build trust and comfort. Then you can teach the skills. You might begin by spending the first few weeks simply asking your child more about his life and sharing more of yours. Once this becomes relatively comfortable, you can begin to teach the skills.

✦ *Who is the best person to teach your child the skills?* If your child has a closer relationship with one parent than the other, you may want to have the parent she feels closer to teach the skills. Of course, this is a great opportunity for the other parent to develop more closeness; just adjust your expectations about how quickly the process will go.

✦ *How do you express your disappointment and frustration?* When your child does not learn something as quickly as you hoped, or gives you a hard time, how do you express your disappointment and frustration? If you get easily irritated or, alternatively, shut down and give up, you will have to work hard at using the skills of resilience yourself as you teach them to your child. Throughout this process you will be modeling resilience or a lack of resilience—whether you mean to or not— and these informal "teaching" moments will have a great impact. So, whenever possible, model the use of the skills.

✦ *Are you expecting these skills to replace the need for more intensive therapy?* The skills of resilience will benefit all children, but if your child is in the middle of a crisis—is struggling with addiction, failing school, clinically depressed or suicidal, engaging in delinquent behaviors—these skills will not replace immediate professional help.

The Four Key Resilience Skills for Children and Adolescents

There are four essential skills for you to teach your children. The first is ABC. Your children can't cope with challenges and adversity unless they first understand how their beliefs affect their mood and behavior. Next, your children need to learn how to test whether their beliefs are accurate by using Challenging Beliefs. Catastrophizing is a common problem for children and adolescents, and it causes overwhelming anxiety. Putting It in Perspective will teach them how to control their worries and anxiety. Finally, it's important for you to teach your children how to fight back against their nonresilient beliefs in real time, using Real-time Resilience.

ABC: ADVERSITIES CHILDREN FACE

In order for children to respond with resilience, they must first learn the connection between their thoughts and their feelings and behaviors. It is as important for children as it is for you because children have as many adversities in their lives as adults do. When we talk with children about the adversities they face, the same issues come up over and over again: conflicts at home, fights with peers, interaction with authority figures, awkward social situations, and peer pressure. They also may be struggling with identity situations—feeling uncomfortable with their looks (being too fat, too thin, too tall, too short) or feeling worried about their religion, race, or sexual orientation.

When we talk with parents, we're often surprised by their tendency to downplay the seriousness and importance of what a child struggles with. One parent described that his daughter was upset all day about a fight she had on the playground with a group of girls at school. It started over a disagreement about who should be on whose team and ended with a shoving match between his daughter and two other girls. The father told us that his daughter couldn't concentrate in her classes, was moody for the rest of the day, didn't eat dinner, and couldn't focus on her homework. He just didn't see why one fight would leave her out of sorts for so long. We asked the father to imagine that he decided to eat his lunch in a park across from his office and, while lunching, two other men came over and started shouting slurs and shoving him around. When he got back to his office, we asked, did he think he'd be able to concentrate on his work? Whenever you find yourself dismissing your child's problems as unimportant or find it difficult to empathize, try to recast the problem in its adult form. For those of you with young children, a child's need to have his favorite blue cup, his favorite striped shirt, his favorite meal over and over again is often the source of frustration. And you simply can't understand why he gets upset when he doesn't get his way. But adults are like this too. Whenever Karen finds herself becoming annoyed by these seemingly capricious needs, she has learned to ask herself how she would feel if her husband refused to give her the coffee in her "writing" mug. Ask yourself how you would feel if the new suit you had planned to wear to an important meeting disappeared from the closet? These aren't traumas, but they are real disappointments for you—and for your child as well.

As you begin the process of teaching the skills of resilience, it's important to focus on adversities that are meaningful for your child.

ABC: SELF-TALK

With children, the best way to teach the skill of ABC is to first focus on their self-talk—what we called ticker-tape beliefs. This may take a little while because most of us are in the habit of asking our children A ques-

THE RESILIENCE FACTOR + 272

tions (What did you do today? Who did you sit with at lunch?) and C questions (How did you feel when that happened? What did you do when she said that?). We don't often ask the B questions (What were you thinking when she said that? What did you say to yourself when that happened?). The problem is that by asking only A and C questions, we convey that only *that* information is worth discussing. For our children to become more resilient, we need them to pay attention to their beliefs and to value those beliefs as highly as how they feel and act.

Remember, even if children do not immediately know what you mean when you explain self-talk, the beliefs are there; your challenge is to help them to identify those beliefs. One way to help children get better at this is to ask what they are thinking the next time you notice a sudden shift in their mood. Of course, if you're the subject of the child's self-talk, it's important that you don't challenge what she is thinking. At this point, you just want to reinforce her for being able to capture what it is that she says to herself during adversity.

Once your child is able to capture his self-talk, you are ready to introduce the ABC model. The key point is that his feelings and behaviors don't come out of the blue, and they are not wholly determined by the things that happen to him. Instead, it is what he says to himself—his self-talk—when problems arise that cause him to feel and act the way he does. Ask for an example of a time when he felt sad, angry, embarrassed, or guilty and acted in a way that he didn't like—was mean to a friend or didn't try something he really wanted to do. It's important that your child doesn't think that ABC applies only when something horrible happens. You want him to use this skill to handle the daily challenges of life, not just major setbacks. After you've identified a situation, guide him in capturing his self-talk and the emotions and behaviors that followed. Try to work through at least three situations this way. As your child practices this, there are five things you should be listening for.

1. **IS YOUR CHILD DESCRIBING THE SITUATION OBJECTIVELY—STATING JUST THE WHO, WHAT, WHEN, AND WHERE WITHOUT EXAGGERATION?** If the description includes exaggeration ("Sally never lets me sit next to her" instead of "Sally didn't let me sit next to her today"), help him to restate it with greater precision.

2. **DO THE B'S MAKE SENSE OF THE C'S?** As your child learns this skill, he may describe beliefs that don't seem to fit with the consequences. Use your B–C Connections chart (on page 75) to check out whether the Bs are of the right variety. If they aren't, it's usually because there are more beliefs present that the child was not able to identify. Ask: Is there anything else you were thinking? Did the situation remind you of

something else? Some kids are more visual than verbal, and their "beliefs" may take the form of mental pictures. Ask your child to describe the mental picture; by doing so, he will convey his beliefs.

3. **ARE THE C'S OUT OF PROPORTION TO THE B'S?** We don't teach detecting iceberg beliefs to children because usually they cannot implement this skill effectively. However, if your child's reactions seem out of proportion to his beliefs, ask questions to help him identify whether there were any deeper beliefs activated in the situation. Use the same questions described in Chapter 6. If you can help him to identify one or two more general beliefs, such as "I've got to be liked by all the kids" or "It's not okay to fail," then you have done a good job.

4. **DOES YOUR CHILD HAVE BOTH WHY AND WHAT-NEXT BELIEFS?** Resilience requires him to think about the causes of problems and to determine which causes he can control. It also requires him to think about the future so that he can develop a plan to handle the most likely outcomes. If your child tends to have only why beliefs, ask: "Now that it happened, what do you think might happen next?" If your child tends to have only what-next beliefs, ask: "Why do you think that happened? What do you think caused the problem?" By asking these questions, you will help your child to have a more balanced style of thinking about adversity.

5. **IS YOUR CHILD ABLE TO SEE THE SELF-FULFILLING PROPHECIES?** Most children don't see the self-fulfilling prophecies that their belief causes. It is important to help them understand that not only can their beliefs make them feel bad, but beliefs actually can bring on things they don't want to happen. For example, if a child says to herself, "I'm so stupid. There's no way I'm going to do well on this test," she will be less likely to study hard and so is more likely to do poorly on the test. Of course, by doing poorly, the negative belief is reinforced and is even harder to shake the next time.

Here's an example of what ABC sounds like when done by a twelve-year-old.

ADVERSITY: Yesterday I had a bunch of friends over and my dad was going to show us this really cool plane collection he has. We were psyched because he was going to let us fly some of them with the remote. When he came down from his office, he kept calling me "squirt" in front of everybody. I told him the other day that I don't like when he calls me that, but he did it anyway.

BELIEFS: He's always trying to embarrass me in front of my friends. He thinks it's funny so he's going to keep calling me that even though I told him I hate it.

CONSEQUENCES: I got so mad that my face turned red and I told him in a really mean voice that I wanted to have privacy with my friends and he should just leave. Everyone was kind of upset because they wanted to fly the planes, but I just wanted to get as far away from him as possible.

Once your child is able to work through an ABC sequence, like this one, with little prompting from you, you can move on to Challenging Beliefs.

Teaching Your Children to Challenge Beliefs

STEP 1: GENERATE ALTERNATIVES

The first part of generating alternatives is to teach your child the dimensions of explanatory style and to help her to notice how she tends to explain the causes of problems. Help her to begin to judge whether she is more optimistic or pessimistic by focusing on the three dimensions of explanatory style. Ask your child to describe an adversity and to tell you the first thought she has about why it happened. Then help her to label whether the belief was more of a me or not-me belief, always or not always, everything or not everything. You'll need to work through several examples before your child can accurately label her beliefs.

Once your child has gotten the hang of it, look for patterns in her explanatory style and point out any similarities to your own. Although one's explanatory style may be partially genetic, it's mostly learned by listening to how one's parents explain the good and bad events in their lives and in their children's lives. For this reason, it's very important that you model a more flexible explanatory style for your child. When you catch yourself attributing a problem totally to yourself or completely to other people or circumstances, generate more resilient alternatives aloud. By modeling a more flexible thinking style, you help your children have an easier time learning the skill for themselves.

It's also crucial that you begin to listen to how you reprimand your child. Children listen to how adults (parents, teachers, coaches) criticize them and absorb the style of the criticism as well as the substance. When your child does something wrong, are you more likely to attribute it to her behavior or her character? For example, imagine that your child's room is a mess. Are you more likely to say "You are such a slob. Why can't you ever keep this room clean?" Or would you say "You didn't clean up your room. It's too messy today"? Imagine that your child has been picking fights with his sibling for the last hour; are you more likely to say "You are such a troublemaker" or "You've been in a bad mood since lunchtime"? The first example in each situation illustrates "character criticism" because you are attributing the problem to something stable and pervasive about your child's character. The second example illustrates "behavioral criticism" because you are attributing the problem to specific, changeable behaviors. If you tend to blame your child's character, you are doing more harm than good because your child learns that you believe that it's stable and unchangeable attributes in his personality that are causing him problems.

Don't misunderstand: It's perfectly healthy to reprimand your child. As we discussed earlier, authoritative parents hold their children accountable when they break rules or act inappropriately. Parents who are overly permissive with their children are teaching them to let themselves off the hook and that it's okay to act any way they want—clearly, this leads to problems. But while holding your child accountable is a good thing, how you do it matters. There are two general rules to follow:

1. Be accurate. Exaggerated blame leads to guilt and shame that are out of proportion to the situation. When these emotions are out of proportion, rather than helping the child to change his behavior, they lead to depression and passivity.

2. As much as reality will allow, attribute the causes of problems to *behaviors* rather than your child's character. A child can learn to clean up his room, change his mood, and study more effectively. It's much more difficult for a child to learn how to stop being a slob or troublemaker. Behavioral criticism points to problem solving; character criticism stymies it.

Once your child has a sense of her explanatory style, you're ready to move on to the next step and help her generate alternatives. Just as our goal as adults is to identify the true causes of problems, accuracy is equally important for children. Before they can think more accurately, however, they need to get outside of their thinking-style rut. We must help them to be more creative and generate a variety of possible causes to the problem by using the dimensions of explanatory style.

STEP 2: TEACHING YOUR CHILDREN HOW TO LOOK FOR EVIDENCE

Even though most children are skilled disputers when someone else accuses them of something ("I am not stupid, I didn't know the test covered stuff about Lincoln"), when the accusation originates in their own mind, they act as if it must be fact. So, even if your child argues back whenever you criticize him, don't be surprised if he has difficulty mastering the step of using evidence to test out the accuracy of his own beliefs. Once your child has learned how to challenge his beliefs, he will be protected from failure and rejection. It's not that bad things will suddenly stop happening—he'll still get turned down on dates, not get into his first-choice school, be passed over for promotions—but if he knows how to fight back against his nonresilient beliefs, these setbacks will not set him back for long.

As you teach your child this step, let the evidence guide his thinking. If your child is simply replacing negative thoughts with great big smiley face thoughts, he won't become more resilient. We find that the detective is a good metaphor for this process because good detectives do two things:

✦ They generate a list of suspects. (They generate alternatives.)
✦ They look for clues to figure out which suspect committed the act. (They use evidence.)

Tell your child that instead of believing the first thought that pops into his head, you want him to be a detective and look for evidence so that he can figure out whether or not the thought is accurate. Explain that it doesn't make any sense for us to feel sad, angry, embarrassed, or guilty if the reason we are feeling bad isn't even true.

Before you get started, it's important to remember that the confirmation bias (the tendency to remember evidence that fits our beliefs and forget evidence that doesn't confirm our beliefs) will make it difficult for your child to gather evidence in an evenhanded way. So begin by explaining this bias to your child. We refer to it as the Velcro-Teflon effect: Evidence that proves that our first belief is true sticks to us like Velcro, and evidence that proves that our first belief is false slides right off of us as if we were coated in Teflon. Your child can prevent the confirmation bias from interfering with accuracy in three ways:

✦ **ASK YOURSELF WHAT YOUR BEST FRIEND WOULD SAY.** Usually, by helping your child to shift his perspective, he is able to see evidence that normally would elude him.
✦ **LOOK FOR CLUES.** Ask your child what clues a detective would look for and then help him to look for those clues in his own life.
✦ **PROVE THE BELIEF FALSE.** Since we know the tendency will be to see more of the supporting evidence, ask your child to start out by looking for evidence that proves the belief is false. Once he has made a list of that evidence, he can go back and find the evidence that supports his initial belief.

Once your child understands the Velcro-Teflon effect, work through an example from his life. Begin by asking him to identify a recent adversity, say, one he used before when practicing generating alternatives. As always, first get the ABC down. After he's identified his initial belief, ask him to generate two plausible alternatives that get around his explanatory style and then look for evidence for each belief. Here's an example from a fifteen-year-old.

ADVERSITY: My mother and father split up two years ago and now my mother is dating. The other night she had her "boyfriend" over for dinner. She was so ga-ga over him that she basically ignored me the whole night. I had to ask her three different times just to pass me the stupid chicken.

BELIEFS: Great. It's bad enough that I'm trying to date. I certainly don't need my mother dating also. She is so selfish and caught up in her own little world that she isn't even thinking about how weird this is for me. This is going to be even worse than when they first split up.

CONSEQUENCES: I was so mad. I nearly left the table three times. Instead I just sat there and didn't say a word, and as soon as dinner was over I went to my room and blasted the music.

CHALLENGING BELIEFS: It does kind of suck to have a mom who is dating, but I guess I'd rather her be happy than never have another man in her life. It's probably not fair to say that she doesn't care how I feel. I think she was probably just nervous and was doing her best to make an awkward situation okay (alternative: Not Me, Not Always, Not Everything). I mean, she did talk with me about it before he came over and asked me how I felt about her dating (evidence). She said that she wanted to date but that she also wanted me to be comfortable so we should think of the dinner as a test case (evidence).

Once you and your child have worked through the steps of Challenging Beliefs, you are ready to focus your energy on problem solving. Begin by crossing off any beliefs that are inaccurate. Then help your child to identify which of the true causes of the problem he has control over. This is important because often children overestimate what they can control. Alternatively, depressed children may underestimate what they can control and believe that there is nothing they can do to correct the situation. Finally, work with your child to identify two or three concrete ideas about how he might solve the problem.

Putting It in Perspective

Now that your child has practiced thinking more accurately about the causes of problems, she is ready to test out the accuracy of her predictions for the future. Catastrophizing is one of the most common problems we see with children and adolescents. It's difficult for them to maintain a sense of perspective about the future, so the skill of Putting It in Perspective is quite important.

Begin by asking your child to come up with a time when she catastrophized. Tell her that just as it's important to be accurate about the causes of problems, it's also important to be accurate about what is going to happen next, once a problem has occurred. Otherwise, she'll waste a lot of energy and time worrying about all sorts of horrible things that actually will never happen. Use the following questions about the situation she described to help her to see the effects of catastrophizing on her mood and behavior.

✦ *How did you feel when you were imagining all of those bad things?* Most children feel a combination of anxiety and sadness. Ask her to rate on a 1 to 10 scale how strong the emotions were.

✦ *How much did you believe those bad things were going to happen?* While they are catastrophizing, most children believe that the negative implications are highly likely. Later the beliefs may seem silly and unlikely, but you want her to understand that while the situation is happening, the beliefs seem highly probable.

✦ *Do you think you were more likely or less likely to deal with the problem when you were thinking all of the negative beliefs?* Most children feel drained and overwhelmed when they catastrophize and feel helpless to deal with the situation.

The child version of this skill is almost identical to the version you learned. The first step is to generate the worst-case beliefs. Then you help the child to generate equally improbable best-case beliefs. Finally, using the worst and best as poles on a continuum, you help her to identify the likely outcomes of the situation and a plan of attack for dealing with the situation.

Larry, a seventh grader, said, "I used to always think the worst in every situation. I was like the Energizer Bunny of crazy thoughts. But now I know how to stop myself from doing it. I'm real good at coming up with these wild and funny best-case scenarios that always makes me laugh, and once I start laughing, it's a lot easier to see the situation like it really is instead of all the crazy things I imagine. My dad says my face looks more relaxed now—whatever that means. For me, the big change is that I just don't feel so lousy."

Real-time Resilience for Children

The final resilience skill for kids is Real-time Resilience. Children first must be able to generate alternatives, find evidence, and identify likely outcomes before they can use this skill effectively. Don't rush it. It may take a few weeks of practicing the other skills before a child is ready for this one.

But don't skip Real-time Resilience. The kids who have gone through our program tell us that this is the skill, more than any other, that they use to keep themselves thinking clearly so that they can handle the problems they encounter. In fact, in 1995, when we were featured on *Oprah*, we asked a group of students who had recently been through our program: "What skills do you want to show Oprah and the world?" (Oprah has a lot of clout with adolescents, and being on her show did more to increase our credibility in their eyes than anything we could have said.) Real-time Resilience was the unanimous answer.

Begin by explaining to your children that there are some situations in which they have to fight back against their thoughts as they are happening to stay focused on the task at hand. In these situations, it's not possible to take out a worksheet and list all the evidence for and against a variety of beliefs, so they need to develop a skill that they can do in their head, the moment the negative belief occurs. Help your child to list situations where it would be helpful to fight back against negative thoughts in real time: immediately before or during a test or a class presentation, while you're asking someone to play with you or on a date, while playing a sport.

Make clear that the time to use this skill is when children need to disarm counterproductive thoughts so that they can get back to the task at hand. It is not appropriate when the situation is complex or when there is time to think the problem through in a thorough manner.

Your child will use the same three tag lines (slightly reworded) that you practiced as you were mastering this skill. They are:

✦ *Evidence:* That can't be true because . . .
✦ *Alternatives:* Another way to see this is . . .

✦ *Putting It in Perspective:* The most likely thing is . . . and I can . . . to deal with that.

Demonstrate how to use each of these phrases with a simple example. For example, you are about to take a math test and you think, "I am so stupid. I won't get any problems right." You can fight back against this thought by saying "That's not true because on the last test I got a lot of the answers correct." Or "Another way to see this is that I'm smart enough to solve these problems." Or "The most likely thing is that I'll get an okay grade and I can study even harder next time if I want a better grade." Then explain each of the pitfalls to your child—we've simplified them for kids.

✦ *Happy Thoughts.* Explain that the goal is not to replace every negative thought with a "happy thought." They can't just make up evidence. The evidence has to be real.
✦ *The Blame Game.* Explain that the goal is not to simply switch who is at fault. If their initial belief is about them having done something wrong, they can't just blame someone else instead.
✦ *So, Who Cares?* Finally, when the problem is important, it is not okay simply to dismiss it. For example, if a child's parents are divorcing and the belief is "I'm going to be sad for the rest of my life," it is not appropriate to replace that thought with "Divorce is no big deal. So who cares if I don't see my dad much? That doesn't matter."

After you've explained how to avoid making the common mistakes, you're ready to guide the children through the first practice. An easy way to teach this skill is to write down a few common adversities and two or three negative beliefs for each. Then read the beliefs, one at a time, to your child, and ask him to use one of the tag lines to come up with a more resilient response. It's crucial that you emphasize accuracy over speed. In fact, don't worry about how quickly your child can generate the responses until he has practiced the skill for several weeks. Once he masters the skill, the speed with come naturally.

Benjamin is ten and uses Real-time Resilience whenever he starts to worry before a test.

BEN'S BELIEF: I'm so nervous I could throw up. There's no way I'm going to remember how to wire a circuit. I might as well forget the whole thing.

BEN'S REAL-TIME RESPONSE: I was nervous before the last test too, and if I take a deep breath and tell myself that I've done well on all of my other tests, I can do well on this one too.

BEN'S BELIEF: Yeah, but this stuff is much harder. Science is not my best subject. I'll be lucky if I don't fail.

BEN'S REAL-TIME RESPONSE: This electricity stuff is harder, but Mom quizzed me last night and I got all but one right. I've never failed a test and I'm not going to fail this one either.

Conclusion

We all want the best for our children. We want them to be successful at school, accepted and liked by their peers, fair-minded and moral. We want them to make good decisions and be kind to others. We want them to have high expectations for their future and have the tools to meet those expectations. Wanting these things is the easy part; equipping our children with the abilities to achieve them is harder. By using the resilience skills as you navigate the difficult road of parenting, you will experience more moments of joy and fewer moments of hair-pulling frustration. And if the tough moments don't throw you, you will have an easier time instilling in your children the values that you want them to embrace. If you also teach your children the resilience skills, you will give them a great gift. Life is going to throw all sorts of problems in their paths, but you can feel confident that they'll have the tools to overcome them.

CHAPTER TWELVE

Resilience at Work

In June of 2001, over a thousand American adults were polled about their work and recreational activities. The poll revealed that Americans work an average of fifty hours per week—two-and-a-half times the number of hours they spend on their relaxation pursuits. (In 1973, the ratio of job time to downtime was only one and a half.)[1] For many of us, work has come to dominate our lives. Therefore, one of the biggest boosts in our resilience may come from applying the seven skills to the adversities we encounter on the job.

In our research and training roles with our company, Adaptiv Learning Systems, we've taken the resilience skills to a wide variety of organizations: from small not-for-profit agencies, government departments, through Fortune 500 companies. And regardless of the size of the organization and its mission, the same five major obstacles to success at work emerge. People want help dealing with stress in the wake of corporate restructuring and the demand to be more productive with fewer resources. They want to know how they, as individuals, can impact a corporate culture that's interfering with their success. They want guidance on how to cope with and overcome prejudice in their workplace. They want help bouncing back from the loss of a job. And they want to know how they can find a balance between work and home.

Some of these problems are so chronic and so systemic that a solution may be beyond our reach. But we'll show you how we've worked with people to help them think more accurately about their adversities—free of their thinking styles—and how, armed with a more flexible and accurate view, they've exerted as much control as they possibly can. For most people, that's gained them enough leverage on their problem so that their work lives become transformed—they're able to change their workplace enough that they feel energized and reconnected to their jobs. For others, even after they've done flexible and accurate problem solving, their jobs are still not what they are seeking—and they've moved on. In either case, the skills have enabled them to be as resilient as they can be at work.

Why We Need Resilience at Work

Pick up a copy of *Time* or *Newsweek*, pretty much any week will do, and you're likely to come across an article on the new economy. The face of industry is rapidly changing, with high-tech and service organizations replacing the manufacturing base. The corporate landscape is in daily flux with mergers and acquisitions, and the market is becoming global.

What has this meant for the average corporate employee? Business is now often conducted at a distance; we find ourselves in teams with colleagues we have never, or rarely, met except via telephone and e-mail—with all the accompanying communication problems and potential for misinterpretations that these media present. There's constant pressure to produce more with fewer resources. As corporate ranks are cut through downsizing, we're required to serve several functions within the organization. Our job descriptions and roles have become malleable and unstable, on the premise that this will provide the corporate flexibility required to survive in an ever-changing marketplace. Many of us are floundering through role confusion, work-home imbalance, and the constant threat of job loss. We are stressed.

Workplace Stress

We talked about stress in Chapter 9 and how your thinking style makes you more or less vulnerable. U.S. industry loses an estimated 280 million workdays each year through absenteeism due to on-the-job stress. And it's not just an American phenomenon. At the global level, stress-related illness is a major financial drain on corporations—as much as $200 billion is spent each year on the treatment of disorders to which stress contributes, such as gastrointestinal problems, mental disorders, substance abuse, and hypertension. In fact, there are one-and-a-half times as many insurance claims for stress as for physical injuries. (This is especially remarkable given the estimate that somewhere between 60 and 80 percent of on-the-job accidents that lead to physical injury are stress-related.)[2] The take-home message: Stress is pervasive, and its epidemic proportions are due to massive changes in the workplace. But these figures are a little over-whelming. Let's place a more human face on this.

We met Rick in a client workshop in North Carolina. He'd been referred to us through his employee assistance program (EAP) to help him deal with the persistent anxiety he was experiencing and the depression with which he'd wrestled for the last nine months. Rick, who was then in his mid-forties, traced his problems back to a time when the nature of his job changed dramatically.

"I wouldn't describe myself as a 'company man.' I was only a junior manager, pretty low level, had three people who reported to me. Never had been very ambitious, but I was kinda proud of what I did, you know. We provided a contract maintenance service for the telephone lines that the big long-distance companies own and operate. Each weekend when my kids called their grandparents long distance, I felt good that I'd played a small part in making that possible—that I had helped them and thousands of other families get connected.

"About two years ago there was a takeover, and our company with its 1,500 employees was swallowed up by a huge telecommunications corporation with 40,000 people. Everything changed. *Everything.* I was picked to head up a multisite team to decentralize accounting operations. All of a sudden I had eight people reporting to me, scattered across five sites all around the country. Every day I'd get to work to find my e-mail jammed with their questions. I seemed to spend most of the day answering e-mails and phone calls. For the first time in my career I started missing deadlines. Work just kept falling through the cracks.

"I guess the first sign that it was getting to me was the migraine headaches. Every morning before I went to work it would start. It felt like my brain was tearing in two. My gut was in knots before the morning was done, and I was popping antacid pills like candy. I started getting dizzy spells, and often I could feel my heart beating through my shirt. I dreamed about the stupid job. Nightmares, really. Remember that scene from *I Love Lucy* where she can't keep up with the chocolates on the con-veyor belt and she starts stuffing them in her mouth? That's what the dreams were like—all this work coming at me and no way I could keep up."

Using the Skills of Resilience to Steer Through Work-related Stress

The situation came to a head one day when Rick's boss asked him to take on another project. Rick felt his anxiety skyrocket immediately. The ticker-tape belief he identified—I'll never get this project in on time—simply couldn't explain the intensity of his anxiety. That was one sure sign that iceberg beliefs were fueling the emotion. So he used the skill of Detecting Icebergs.

TICKER-TAPE BELIEF: I'll never get this project in on time.

QUESTION: What's so upsetting about that for me?

RICK: It's never been like that for me before. I've always been able to take care of business.

QUESTION: And what does it mean to me that I'm struggling now, for the first time, to get things done?

RICK: It means I'm dropping the ball and letting people down.

QUESTION: What's the worst part of that for me?

RICK: Well, I've disappointed people who really matter to me. First, there's my boss in the old company who really pushed hard to get me this job when the takeover happened. But mostly I feel like I've really let my wife and kids down. If I lose this job we're in big trouble financially.

QUESTION: Assuming that's true, what's the worst part of that for me?

RICK: Everyone knows about my stress and anxiety and about how I haven't been coping well—the people I work with know, my family, my kids, my neighbors, the people at my church. I feel really embarrassed.

QUESTION: What's so embarrassing about what I've experienced?

RICK: I should be able to handle anything that comes my way.

Aha! As we've seen, many iceberg beliefs, like Rick's, are about how we *should* be in the world. You can't use Challenging Beliefs on these icebergs, because it makes no sense to ask what evidence you have that you should or should not do something. This kind of iceberg belief represents a value, which resides outside the world of facts. Rick can ask himself, however, if keeping this belief is *useful* to him. He probably formed this iceberg belief early in life, and it may not be relevant to his life today. In his current world this iceberg belief may just be a museum piece—an anachronistic influence on his emotions and behavior.

Rick asked himself what this belief was buying and costing him in his life. For one thing, it was costing him a lot of stress. Second, it just wasn't realistic in the modern corporate world, where everyone is expected to do more with less and where very few people are able to complete everything that comes into their in box—or if they do, it's at the expense of quality. As he had constructed the situation in his mind, there was an enormous amount at stake in this new job. If he failed to keep up, he was violating his basic rule about the kind of person he should be. Who wouldn't feel pressured if they held that belief and found themselves slipping behind at work? At the first sign that work was falling through the cracks, Rick panicked, because, as he had cast it subconsciously, his integrity as a person was at stake. And that intense level of anxiety, in turn, adversely affected his performance. It was a self-fulfilling prophecy. As the automotive magnate Henry Ford once said, "Whether you think you can or you can't, you're probably right."

Once Rick proved to himself that his iceberg belief was not useful, much of his anxiety subsided. He became a master at the calming techniques. When he felt the stress mounting at work, he took thirty seconds out to use positive imagery, imagining himself and his family at the beach in the Outer Banks of North Carolina. He practiced controlled breathing and progressive muscle relaxation at his desk without anyone ever noticing.

Now that his anxiety was at a manageable level, Rick was able to use Challenging Beliefs to tackle the real problem—not whether he was a good person or not, but his difficulty coping with the workload. Given the nature of Rick's iceberg belief, we wouldn't be surprised to find he has a "Me, Always, Everything" explanatory style. The why belief that popped into his mind whenever he failed to get work done was "I don't have what it takes to do this new job." We guided Rick first to flexible thinking—generating alternative beliefs using the three dimensions of explanatory style—and then to accuracy. He came to realize that other factors contributed to his problem. He wasn't managing his time well. He allowed himself to spend inflated amounts of time on projects he enjoyed—a luxury he could afford in his old company but one that now led to missed deadlines on less interesting work. He also wasn't delegating work well. The eight people who reported to him were productive, but he was not fully utilizing their time. His style of management, of heading up every project, worked well in the old job with a staff of three and much less to do, but it failed under these new job conditions. And Rick recognized that he'd never really talked to his new boss about how best to prioritize his work, to ensure that the critical projects were triaged for greater attention.

Prioritizing is essential in corporate environments where workload exceeds resources, but so many people still adopt a first in, first out approach. Now, with some "not always" and "not everything" why beliefs in place, new solutions opened up for Rick, and he began to take control of what he could.

Rick used Real-time Resilience whenever the work seemed overwhelming, to remind himself that this was not a test of his quality as a human being. He focused on what he could control: "I may not be able to complete this project on time along with all the other work I have to do. But one thing I can do is to get clear priorities from my boss, then manage the amount of time I spend on each project. It may mean that the quality of each deliverable is not what I'd like it to be, but I have to be realistic about what's achievable here." Rick called us five months after we'd worked with him, just to let us know that he was off the antianxiety medication and that things were working out well.

Using Resilience to Change Corporate Culture

For years an intriguing story circulated among corporate consultants.[3] Four monkeys were introduced to a novel environment—a penned enclosure in the center of which stood a long pole. Atop the pole was monkey "treasure," a bunch of the sweetest, juiciest-looking bananas a monkey had ever clapped eyes on. Very tempting indeed. The monkeys began clambering up as quickly as they could. But a nasty surprise awaited them. As they neared the top, the experimenters doused them with an avalanche of water—anathema to our adventurous four. (Monkeys like water only slightly less than cats.) The monkeys shimmied down and huddled together at the farthest corner of the pen, never venturing near the pole or the bananas again. The experimenters removed three of the monkeys, leaving only one. (We like to think those three were given a veritable banana feast in reward.) Three new monkeys were led into the pen, and they also responded to the bananas immediately, throwing themselves up the pole. Of course, they hadn't witnessed the waterfall, but the fourth monkey had. And he did everything he could to save the newcomers from an uncomfortable dousing. He grabbed them by the legs and pulled them down. He bared his teeth, growled, and successfully kept them at bay. They never made it up the pole, and they didn't get wet. In the final stage of the study, two of the newcomer monkeys were removed, as was the original monkey who had himself been soaked, and three new monkeys were introduced. Note that not one of these monkeys had been doused with water. In fact, none of them had even witnessed the event. Only one of them had been stopped from climbing the pole, but presumably he had no idea why. What did he do? He pulled the newcomers down, bared his teeth, growled, and prevented them from climbing up. We'd heard this story years ago and hadn't thought much about it since—until we did consulting with an organization in the summer of 1999.

At that time we conducted a two-day panel with fourteen top executives in a manufacturing company. The organization was a major player in its industry, but it was an industry in major decline. In 1975 the firm employed 40,000 workers. When we met them there were only 12,000 on payroll. We kicked off the roundtable discussion with introductions. The first person to our right began with "I'm Robert Greenwood, VP of production for the Northeast, and last year I closed a plant that employed 5,000." The gentleman to his right followed: "Hal Jenkins, VP of production for the Midwest. Three years ago I oversaw the closing of our Indiana factory, and I must have done a good job, because they asked me to help Bob in shutting down Pittsburgh." And so it continued, an eerie litany of the big hits their industry had taken over the last decade.

The adversity was clear—they were hemorrhaging money, losing millions of dollars each year, which led to several plant closings, making it even more difficult to generate revenue. Of the fourteen people in the group, only two took part in the discussion about what was going wrong. Donna, a young and talented executive in her mid-thirties, offered a solution. "We're stuck in our old ideas about what this company does. We need to think about how we can diversify for new markets. Everyone, us and our competitors, has lost enormous dollars on the old products. This is not just market slippage on our part, there's no company on earth expanding these old lines of product." Donna moved into solution mode, as resilient people tend to do: "With minimal expenditure we could overhaul our existing plants to manufacture products that are growth areas. We need to shift away from the thinking that the old products are what we do. That doesn't have to be our fate."

The others in the group sat stony-faced and silent. Only Kenny was nodding as Donna spoke. Kenny stepped in. "I agree. We need to shift our focus to new products. But we also haven't taken a good look at our marketing and sales practices in twenty years. We still have lone-wolf salespeople operating out there, trying to sell at all costs. They're too aggressive and they don't care about maintaining existing clients as long as they get the commission. That's not what our clients want anymore. They want to build a relationship with our salesperson. We need to restructure the sales force into teams, with a point person who is good at managing the client and the rest of the team there to support his or her efforts."

There was quiet in the room but no peace. The tension was palpable. Donna and Kenny were in the minority. Everyone else in the room showed all the nonverbal signs of strong disapproval, if not disgust, at what the two had suggested. The silence and head-shaking continued until one of the senior VPs spoke. "What you're suggesting has been talked about before. But it makes no sense. We've never built the kinds of products you're talking about. We've never adopted the kind of sales strategies you're presenting. You two have been a part of this organization for, what, five or ten years. Many of us in this room have been in this organization for thirty or more years. We know a little more about this company than you. We know what works and what doesn't work. We know what the employees will go for and what they won't. We know what the board and the investors want. Your ideas just won't fly and they just won't work. This company was around a long time before I started on the factory floor decades ago. We've never done things that way and we never will."

At that moment we remembered the monkey story and we had to suppress smiles. Kenny and Donna were trying to save their organization by using good problem solving. But their peers and superiors were figuratively grabbing them by the legs and pulling them back down. When they tried to scale the pole again, they were barked at. No one could articulate why their ideas were "foolish," why they wouldn't work, just as none of the monkeys in the final stage of the story had ever actually seen the water cascade down. They just "knew" climbing to the goal wouldn't fly.

This is, in essence, the power of a corporate culture. A methodology is put down years before that may have been adaptive at the time. The trajectory is then set, and momentum builds. In many ways this process mirrors the development of underlying beliefs and icebergs. We build beliefs about how the world is that are often incomplete and inaccurate. But these beliefs then become our "reality"; they take on a life of their own. The irony in our work with this company lay in the fact that the fourteen people present represented some of the highest-ranking executives in the organization. If they didn't have the power to change their culture, then no one in their company did.

We wish this story had a happy ending, but it doesn't. Kenny and Donna stayed with the organization between three to six months after our meeting and then, when it was clear their innovative thinking would never be adopted, they did what resilient people do as a last resort: They cut their losses, resigned, and moved on to high-level management jobs in other industries. Toward the end of 2001 we learned that the organization had filed for bankruptcy.

Using the Resilience Skills to Change Corporate Culture

So, how can people challenge the corporate cultures in which they find themselves? In any organization, you see informal leaders and innovators emerge, and we've had the privilege of training many of them in the skills of resilience. Through our discussions with them, we've learned how they're able to bring about significant change to their departments and divisions, even though they may lack the formal power that comes with rank, title, or seniority. They begin by helping their colleagues see that current practice is not a fixed reality.

When we first met Carl, he was in his third month of a new job—as director of the grants division in a large not-for-profit agency that channels services to at-risk youth. When he took the job he anticipated working with a group of self-motivated and optimistic people—the kind of people he assumed would be attracted to an organization like this. He was wrong. After the honeymoon period was over, the real culture of the organization emerged. Many of the people were burned out and pessimistic about really changing the lives of the kids they served. And Carl's attempts to rejuvenate their enthusiasm were met with cynicism.

Carl knew that he had to control his own emotions before he could bring about change in his team. The first step for him was to put in perspective the catastrophic beliefs that plagued him when he realized that this new position was not what he'd expected: "I won't be able to motivate my staff and I'll have to leave this job or burn out. If I quit this job less than six months after starting it, it'll look really bad on my resume. With a flawed resume in this economy, it's going to be impossible to find another job. We won't be able to pay the bills and we'll have to move to a small apartment across town where the school districts are bad—our kids' educations will be hurt. My wife will never forgive me for this. I've already asked her to give up a lot with the pay cut that came with this job, and this will just add stress to our marriage." After Putting It in Perspective, Carl came to see that his position was nowhere near as dire as his worst-case outcomes suggested. Sure, there'd be a hiccup in his resume, but his employment history before this was solid and he had marketable skills that eventually would land him a good job if this position didn't work out. One thing he could do was to keep his ear to the ground for opportunities opening up elsewhere—in case he was unable to carry off the plan he was assembling to jumpstart his division.

Carl realized that he may have fallen into the thinking trap of overgeneralizing by painting *all* of his employees with the same brush: "They're all cynical, pessimistic, and unmotivated." When he thought more carefully about the people in his team, he recognized that two who reported directly to him were less jaded than the rest and seemed to be informal leaders in the group. As part of his plan Carl met with these two to gather information. Why was the team so demoralized? What were the biggest stumbling blocks to the division successfully applying for grant money? He learned that most of his employees believed that the quality of their grant submissions didn't matter. His staff shared the belief that the city's budget decisions were beyond their control: "Every so often the council will throw some money our way, if there's a budget surplus, but we're not a priority and so, in lean years, regardless of how well we present our case in the grant application, no money will be forthcoming." This led them to submit poorly written and uncompelling grants because "Well, it doesn't matter anyway."

Carl telephoned the city department responsible for the services his agency provided and, through his persistence, arranged for a council representative to speak to his group on the funding process. In that talk it became clear that each grant was reviewed extensively and that each year money was allocated to some agency—which one depended on the merits of their applications. Carl scheduled individual meetings with his staff, to ask each of them why they had joined the agency and what they each hoped to achieve for themselves and their division over the next year. Together they wrote a mission statement with all of their ambitions represented and a copy was posted at every desk.

Carl knew that "negative people" were a button-push for him—an adversity that fueled his nonresilient thinking. He prepared a Real-time Resilience script for himself to use whenever he encountered "whining" from his team: "It's not that these are bad people. They're unmotivated because they can't see a way out. It's my job to give them that solution. Don't overgeneralize. Stay focused on the quality of the grant, not the character of the grant writer. Worst-case scenario—I leave the job. But that's a last resort, and there's plenty I can do to lead these people. Once we get a grant application successfully funded, they'll have more hope."

The climate of Carl's division didn't change overnight. But, over time, Carl was able to shift his staff's attention from what they couldn't control, such as city politics and budget constraints, to what they could control—the quality of their work. Last time we spoke to Carl, his division had been awarded city grants each quarter they'd applied, and he'd convinced his team that the time was right to seek federal funds. At that point he was in the third year of his directorship.

Prejudice in the Workplace—Issues of Race, Sex, and Age

The demographics of the American workforce have changed dramatically over the last thirty years and continue to do so. In 1970 women represented only 38 percent of the working population. By 1990 the figure had grown to 45 percent, and it's predicted that between 1990 and 2005, the number of jobs will have risen by 26 million, almost two-thirds of which will be filled by women. In addition, racial and ethnic minorities have expanded their roles in the corporate sphere and are expected to increase their workplace presence even more over the next five years. It's anticipated that in the period between 1990 and 2040, the number of Asian Americans will rise by 500 percent, the number of Hispanics will triple, and the number of African Americans in the workforce will rise by 50 percent. As this rapid growth occurs among minorities, the number of Caucasian workers is predicted to increase by only about 13 percent. And as we all know, our population is aging. Our already diverse workforce will become significantly more so, by sex, race, and age—challenging organizations to better understand, embrace, and manage diversity.[4]

Our ability to address racial problems in the workplace came about as a result of an earlier study Andrew conducted at the University of Pennsylvania. That research, and our work since, has demonstrated that the skills of resilience can build bridges across racial divides.

In May of 1994, Andrew was talking with Lani Guinier, a very prominent professor of law at Penn, about whether racial stereotypes could be changed. That conversation led to a three-year agenda of research investigating how the cognitive skills could be applied to issues of race. Along with Guinier's collaborator, Susan Sturm, Andrew and his colleagues, Esteban Cardemil and Veronica Rice, set to work to assemble and test a cognitive program designed to guide people to a greater understanding of their beliefs about race and how those beliefs affect their interactions with others. In their study, racially diverse groups met to discuss community issues that were traditionally divisive along race lines. Participants met in one of three programs: a collaborative intervention that represented then state-of-the-art diversity training; a no-intervention control; and a cognitive program that contained many of the resilience skills, including ABC, Avoiding Thinking Traps, and Detecting Icebergs. Each group met for their discussion a week before and a week after the four-session program. At the end of each discussion session, the participants rated how much progress they'd made on the issue, how many solutions had been generated by the group, and how much they agreed with the solutions, and predicted how many more hours would be required before they would reach agreement. On all criteria, students who had participated in the cognitive skills program proved significantly more effective in problem solving than the others. When we saw these results, we knew that the skills in this book could be applied to issues of race and prejudice.

The study showed that prejudice interferes with people's ability to work effectively as a team. Do you remember Louise, the mind reader from Chapter 5? Louise was still in a low-level position after eight years in a Fortune 500 company, having applied unsuccessfully for five or six higher-level positions. Louise was clearly bright and energetic, and we too were surprised that her career hadn't advanced further. Louise, an African American woman, put it down to racism, and as we've said, you don't log as many hours as we have in the corporate arena without witnessing how prejudice factors into hiring practices, whether on the basis of race, sex, or age. But we also knew that African Americans had made it to several key positions within the organization, including Louise's division. It turned out that at least part of the problem for Louise was her mind reading. In the middle of a job interview she would assume that the panel members were looking for ways to deny the job to an African American. This made her understandably angry, and she would derail the interview. Louise may have been a mind reader, but does this mean that racism was not playing a role in her succession of interview failures? Not at all. It's very possible that both factors were contributing.

Our research has shown that people develop styles around explaining racial issues just as they develop general explanatory styles. In one study, we presented African American, Asian American, and white students with a series of anecdotes depicting interactions between people of different races. In each case the situation ended badly for the "minority" actor, and we asked the students to decide why. For example, imagine that you're an objective observer at a store, watching as several people head toward a sales counter to make their purchases. You notice that a young African American woman arrives before a middle-aged white man. You also see that the clerk, a white male, serves the man first. How do people explain the clerk's behavior? Is it racism, sexism, ageism, or is it just that the clerk didn't notice who got there first? It turns out that the race of the students was important in predicting whether they put it down to racism or not. But there were also substantial individual differences within each race. People develop styles of explaining racial issues.

Just as in real life, in this anecdote we're not privy to the beliefs and motivations of the clerk. And as we discussed with Louise, the same is true in a job interview. The situation is ambiguous. Unless the prejudice is overt—a racist comment, for example—it's difficult to be sure whether it's present or not. It's in exactly these conditions of uncertainty that our thinking styles kick in—to fill in the missing information with our assumptions and beliefs. Louise's style was to assume racism, and as we've seen, that wasn't a resilient strategy for her. It got her caught up in anger when she needed to be clear-headed. It caused her performance in the interview to nosedive. And it probably wasn't accurate. Other people's style may be to assume that it's not due to racism, and that's not resilient either. That assumption also sends people down the wrong problem-solving path. Getting job training, overhauling your resume, and putting in extra work hours probably won't get you that executive position if a glass ceiling is firmly in place for minority groups in your organization. Prejudice does exist, and if it's operating in your workplace, you need to know and you need to take steps to deal with it.

So how did Louise use the skills to boost her resilience? She recognized that she tended to mind read. She also recognized that she tended to jump to conclusions—assuming, for example, that when managers dumped work on her desk or were on her back about a project deadline, they were riding her especially hard because of her race. When she found herself caught in these thinking traps, she used Focusing to keep on track. Her favorite technique was to mentally walk through her childhood home, thinking about each room and the fun she had playing with her brothers and sisters when they were kids. The Calming and Focusing skill came in especially handy in her next interview for a junior management position. She got the job.

Louise was successfully avoiding her thinking traps, but how did she attempt to tackle the real prejudice that existed in her company? She used Challenging Beliefs to examine why the racism was there and came up with a couple of possible solutions. Louise familiarized herself with the regulations that guaranteed equal employment opportunities in the work-place. She and her director organized a series of seminars on diversity and nondiscrimination policies for the people in her division. Challenging Be-liefs helped her locate the factors she could potentially change.

We spoke to Louise a few years ago, and she told us, "I needed to get a handle on my beliefs about race first, and Detecting Icebergs was a great skill for that. I've learned that there are a lot of white people who are not racist. Some of them say some insensitive things at times, and when that happens I say to myself, 'Louise, these are not bad people. They've got iceberg beliefs just like you do.' Sometimes I'll talk to them about what they said and how it made me feel. Sometimes that leads us to get a much better understanding of each other. Sometimes it doesn't. And then there are some people in my company who I think really don't like African Americans. I've learned that other than the diversity seminars, there's not a lot I can do to change their attitudes. But I can hold them accountable if they behave in prejudiced ways—I've got the law on my side."

Louise told us, "I'm not Dr. King. I can't change the world. But I can bring about some change at my work. I feel comfortable with my job now. I'm not reacting to everything I see or hear, but I'm not allowing people to walk on me either. I'm holding my own here." Louise had learned the central tenet of resilience: Change what you can and, when possible, come to peace with what you cannot.

Coping with Unemployment

Literally hundreds of research articles have been published on the emo-tional and psychological effects of unemployment. Our ability to support our families through work and, in the process, to contribute to our soci-ety is a core part of the meaning we seek in our lives. For that reason, be-ing fired or downsized is a particularly threatening adversity. It hits up against big iceberg beliefs and is likely to produce major catastrophizing.

Before Andrew came to America, he worked for some time in Australia's Department of Social Security. It was his responsibility to interview people who'd been fired or downsized and assess their entitlement to unemployment benefits. The times were tough economically, and a constant stream of people came through the office.

Andrew was working with other interviewers who'd been in the job much longer than he, and after a few months he asked to sit in on an interview with a more experienced colleague. The client was a man in his late forties who'd lost his middle-level management position due to a companywide downsizing. He was articulate and bright. He talked about his employment history and how much he wanted to get back to work as soon as possible. He wore a suit—so many of those interviewed showed up in jeans and T-shirts, showed patchy job histories, and demonstrated no desire to hurry back into the workforce. This client was clearly motivated, and Andrew was thinking that he'd be off their books in a very short time, back in the saddle of full-time employment. So he was surprised when, after the interview was over, his workmate turned to him and said, "We'll be paying that guy benefits for a long while." Andrew disagreed. "No way. With his motivation, educational credentials, and his smarts, he'll get another job in no time." But six months later he was still unemployed. About that time Andrew saw him when he came in to pick up his check. His clothes were wrinkled, his hair unkempt, and he clearly hadn't shaved in days.

How could Andrew's colleagues so accurately predict who would easily get back on their feet and who would not? It turned out that their secret was to pay close attention to the why beliefs the interviewees voiced—their beliefs about why they were fired or downsized. It seemed that, as we've seen before, those who remained resilient were flexible and accurate in their thinking. The resilient among them recognized that part of the reason they'd lost their jobs was the economic downturn. They didn't personalize the issue, and so they didn't fall into helpless depression. They did, however, scrutinize what they'd contributed to the problem and took action to remedy it. Taken together, their flexibility and accuracy kept them in problem-solving mode longer and got them back to work.

Stephen, one of our executive coaching clients, was referred to us by his employment agency when it was clear that his resilience was flagging. He'd been downsized a month earlier from a project manager job he'd held for five years with a corporate consulting company that was going through some hard times. The company had experienced phenomenal growth in the prior two years and had made more than a hundred new hires. But now it needed to scale back, and Stephen was one of the casualties. The outplacement specialists from the employment agency had noticed that Stephen seemed very stressed and anxious and that he hadn't followed through on any of the job leads they'd set up for him.

Stephen was in his early thirties, married, with a two-year-old son. As he became more comfortable with us, he opened up about what was really troubling him. "I've never felt so down in all my life," he told us. "It's not as if I wanted to be in that job forever or even with that company, for that matter. But I didn't expect to get fired either." We helped him look at the situation clearly using ABC.

ADVERSITY: I was downsized from my job.
BELIEF: This job was contributing $45,000 a year to our income. My wife makes about the same, and we've got savings. But this job was important to us financially, especially with the baby. You know, there were a lot of people who joined the company after me who kept their jobs. I must have really screwed up.
CONSEQUENCES (EMOTIONAL): Intense depression (a 9 or 10 on a 1 to 10 scale).
CONSEQUENCES (BEHAVIORAL): Passivity, helplessness, and hopelessness. Avoidance of further job opportunities.

As we taught Stephen the B–C connections, we asked him whether he thought the Cs he was experiencing seemed appropriate in light of the Bs he had detected. It's possible to entertain the belief that you "screwed up," and yet continue to seek another job. Stephen's belief, "I must have really screwed up," is a loss of self-worth belief, and depression could be expected. But even Stephen agreed that his emotional response was greater than his ticker tape warranted. It was time for him to use Detecting Icebergs.

TICKER-TAPE BELIEF: *I really screwed up.*
QUESTION: *What's the most upsetting part of that for me?*
STEPHEN: *Well, I was downsized when a lot of people who joined the company after me were kept on. That means I really must have dropped the ball. I must have been targeted. I must have been seen as really incompetent.*
QUESTION: *What does that mean to me?*
STEPHEN: *I know I was never the most ambitious guy there and not the hardest working either, probably. But I cared about that job and the company, and I thought I was pretty good at what I did. This layoff came as a surprise to me.*

Notice that in this last response, Stephen has uncovered more of the surface beliefs about his loss of sense of self-worth. But this has not driven him deeper to detect the iceberg beliefs floating below the conscious level. It's a lateral move, not a downward one, and we encouraged him to use one of the four questions to dig deeper.

QUESTION: *What's the worst part of all this for me?*
STEPHEN: *That's sort of the minimal requirement, right? To hold a job, I mean. You may not rise to the top of the company, and you may not bring home the biggest paycheck in the world, but you should at least be able to hold a job.*
QUESTION: *What do I mean when I say "should"? Why should I be able to hold a job?*
STEPHEN: *I'm not a kid anymore. It may be okay to burn through jobs when you're a kid, but this was supposed to be my career. My wife has a good job. It's not as if I'm stuck in some* Leave It to Beaver *thing where I have to bring home all the bacon. But we have a kid. We're a family. I should be contributing. My wife and son should be able to rely on me to support them.*
QUESTION: *What would it say about me if I couldn't help support my family?*
STEPHEN: *I haven't been a parent very long, but it's the most important thing in the world to me. I'd like to think I could be the kind of father to my child that my dad was to me. He was always there for us. You could rely on him, you could trust him, you could depend on him. He worked for the same company from the day he graduated from high school to the time he retired, fifty years later.*
QUESTION: *And what does it mean that he worked in the same company all that time, and I won't?*
STEPHEN: *I guess that's it, isn't it? I'm never going to be as good a father as my dad. There's nothing I'll ever be able to do to make this up. Now there's no way that I can be a good father to my son.*

Stephen got the aha! when he uncovered that final, deep belief. Losing your sense of competence around a job is one thing. But Stephen attached a much deeper meaning to the job loss than that. For him it meant that he was not, and never could be, a good parent. That's the kind of major "loss" belief that could explain the intense depression he felt. And, of course, if his esteem can never be redeemed, then what's the point in trying to get another job? Any rejection he experiences as the job search unfolds will simply serve to further crush his self-esteem—so it's better to avoid job interviews, right?

Of course not. That's not resilient at all. Stephen's situation is a perfect illustration of how our beliefs can undermine our resilience. In fact, through self-fulfilling prophecy, Stephen's beliefs were driving him toward the very antithesis of his goals—to get a new job and support his family.

The next step Stephen took was to analyze his why beliefs with Challenging Beliefs. His first pie chart was taken up by one belief: "I'm incompetent." His second pie chart, reflecting greater flexibility and accuracy about the causes of his layoff, looked like this:

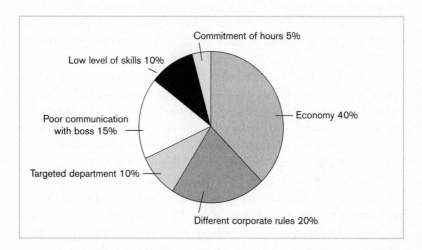

The economic downturn, Stephen admitted, was a major reason why his company resorted to the downsizing. It's also true that corporations today play by different rules—they're no longer willing, or able, to ride out economic recessions and keep a full contingent of staff. In the modern economy, companies sacrifice loyalty to their employees to minimize the impact on the bottom line and to keep investors happy. But Stephen had to face facts: People more junior in the company were kept on while he was let go. During the evidence segment of Challenging Beliefs, Stephen examined why he was selected for the cut. Part of the reason had nothing to do with his competence and performance. It was simply that many of the people who kept their jobs worked in areas of the company considered more crucial to generating revenue than Stephen's. However, it's still undeniable that some people within his department, hired after Stephen, were kept on. Why?

To put it down to "incompetence" is not useful. The concept of incompetence is too diffuse, too nebulous, and not solvable. We encouraged Stephen to get concrete—to break down exactly what he may have contributed to the adversity. He concluded that he hadn't worked on keeping his skills up to date. Others in his department had sought out training and developed skills in focal areas of the company's operation. Stephen was not ambitious, and he tended to be a nine-to-fiver. Perhaps if he'd put a little more time in, he would have been seen as more indispensable to the company. And finally, while Stephen had had some successes over time, he hadn't communicated them to his boss. Stephen was guilty of mind reading when he assumed that he'd be seen as a valuable employee.

Challenging beliefs provided the groundwork to change Stephen's beliefs. But what proved most powerful for him were the fast skills, especially Real-time Resilience. When Stephen attended sessions at the outplacement center, he found that he bombarded himself with nonresilient beliefs. "I'm such a loser. Look at these people sitting here listening to this guy talk about preparing a resume. We're all losers. None of us can hold down a job." As we've seen, for Stephen, these thoughts were tied to deeper beliefs—iceberg beliefs—that caused him great sadness and hopelessness. As a result, he'd avoid anything to do with outplacement. Stephen came up with some powerful real-time responses to use when the nonresilient beliefs hit him: "It's not that I'm a loser, it's that I'm in a very different world from that of my dad's. In this new economy, there are ebbs and flows in hiring and firing. Almost no one is immune. Getting downsized doesn't mean I'm not reliable and dependable. The real test here is how hard I try to get another job. What matters now is that when I get that next job, I don't make the same mistakes I made before. Plenty of people get downsized, and almost all of them find work again." Six weeks later Stephen landed another job.

Balancing Work and Home

Carol Gilligan, a sociologist at Harvard, has identified important differences in how boys and girls are traditionally raised.[5] Typically, little boys are encouraged to be competitive and to achieve. Just as often, little girls are discouraged from such pursuits. Instead they are reinforced for establishing friendships. Better that they sacrifice their own success than hurt a relationship. This learning stays with us as adults, shaping the very beliefs we hold of what it means to be a man or a woman—which in turn is a focal part of our self-image. For this reason, men often are hit harder when they face unemployment. It hits them in the achievement domain—the place many of them have learned over time to prize most. But we also live in changing times. Women have entered the workforce in record numbers, and they too have developed beliefs about the importance of work—it's become an essential element in their self-image. The early learning remains, however, coded in our underlying beliefs. Unemployment tends to hit men harder, but work-home balance, pitting career against family relationships, is particularly problematic for women.

In 1974, 60 percent of women stated that they preferred to stay at home. By 2001 the figure had dropped to 53 percent. But as ambitious as they are, many women are torn between work and home—and more so than men. Almost twice as many women as men would prefer to stay at home and take care of the family.[6] Many women are caught between their drive for achievement and their desire to nurture their family.

In our work with a large sales division in a Fortune 500 organization, we had the chance to meet Andrea. We always ask participants at the beginning of our workshop what they hope to achieve in our time together. Andrea was adamant. "I need your help or I'm gonna go crazy. I am just not coping right now," she confided. "I've been in this job for six years, and I really like it. People can't believe that but it's true." Andrea worked in cold-calling sales. It was her job to call business offices without any kind of in, find her way to a decision maker within the company, and convince him or her to buy advertising space. It was a tough job, and the low retention rate was evidence of that. "I know it's the kind of job that's not for everyone. But I love talking to people, and I love the challenge of seeing just how long I can keep someone on the phone before they say no. And then I want to change that no to a yes." Andrea was very good at what she did. She'd been the highest producer in her office of thirty salespeople twice in the last four years. And yet she told us, "I don't want to, but I'm thinking of quitting."

Andrea went on to explain the big issue in her life. "With this job, I just don't get enough time with my kids. It was okay a few years ago when they were smaller, but now they need me to do things for them and I haven't been able to. I want to drive them to soccer, but I'm in here every Saturday morning trying to catch those potential leads that trade on weekends. The other day my kid got sick. I asked my sales manager if I could take half a day to be with him. She told me no—that since I hadn't made my figures that month, I couldn't go. I got into a battle of wills. She's got the power—she won. I had to ask my mom to take him to the doctor. I was heartbroken."

We asked Andrea to vividly imagine she was back in that situation, on that day, and to describe the adversity, tap into her ticker tape, and identify the emotional and behavioral consequences:

ADVERSITY: My kid is sick and needs to go to the doctor. My manager tells me I can't have time off.

BELIEFS: I know this is nothing serious with my kid, just a flu. But this kind of thing has been happening a lot lately, being caught between work and home responsibilities. It's because they treat us like machines here. Gotta make the numbers, gotta make the numbers, like we're just stupid machines with no life outside of this place.

CONSEQUENCES (EMOTIONAL): Anger at a 5 on a 1 to 10 scale. Sadness at a 9 on a 1 to 10 scale.

CONSEQUENCES (BEHAVIORAL): I just went through the motions for the rest of the day. Didn't make a single sale.

Andrea's causal belief, her explanation for why she is unable to manage work and home, is that her manager treats her like a machine. This is clearly a violation-of-rights belief, which could account for the anger she felt. But what about the sadness? What can explain that? Detecting icebergs can help us when we have a strong emotion and cannot locate a belief that could explain it. Andrea decided to use that skill, and went through the process aloud so we could help guide her.

QUESTION: *They just treat us like machines here. What is the worst part of that for me?*

ANDREA: *They don't respect us as people. They don't see us as whole people with lives outside of our jobs here. It's as if we don't exist outside this office—like we just melt away when we clock out and get reconstituted when we clock in the next day. Well, it's not like that. I have a family that's more important to me than this stupid job.*

Notice how this line of questioning is only leading further down the violations-of-rights and anger path rather than shedding light on the "loss" beliefs that must be present if someone experiences sadness. Andrea changed tack.

QUESTION: *This has been happening to me a lot lately. What does that mean to me?*

ANDREA: *It means that I can't cope with being a good mother and doing this job well at the same time.*

QUESTION: *What does being a "good mother" mean to me?*

ANDREA: *A good mother is always there for her kids. A good mother is always there at mealtimes, always prepares dinner—none of that takeout stuff. A good mother drops everything when one of her kids is sick. A good mother should be at home—*

Andrea stopped midsentence, looked at us, her mouth agape. "Oh my God. I don't believe that came out of my mouth. That's got to be my mother speaking. You know, my mom was the traditional stay-home mom. Packed our lunches every morning, always there when we got back from school, that sort of thing. That's *not* how my sister and I wanted our lives to be. We both work, and even though Mom doesn't say anything directly to us, we've always suspected that she doesn't approve."

KAREN: *So, what is a good mother?*
ANDREA: *A good mother loves and cares for her kids. She's there when they're sick, but she doesn't have to be a stay-home mom. A good mother also can be someone who contributes financially to the household. That's why I'm in this job, you know. Just so I can help my kids.*
ANDREW: *We're not offering, but if we were to pay you your salary and commission to stay home, would you?*
ANDREA: *(Smiling) Probably not.*
KAREN: *So, what would be the worst part of having to make a choice between work and home?*
ANDREA: *I'm good at what I do here at work. I don't want to give that up. Every day I get out of bed and hit the floor running because I want to get to work. When I'm spending time with my kids, I know I can hold my head high because I contribute financially and because I'm good at something out there in the world. It gives me confidence. I have a daughter, and I want to show her that women can do anything in this life if they want to.*
ANDREW: *So, what's the worst part of making a decision between keeping the job and being a full-time mom?*
ANDREA: *Either way I lose. I want this job, but I want to be a good mom. I can't have both.*

Now we can understand her sadness. Andrea had set this up as a decision. And not just a decision between work and home, but a decision between all that that represented to her, as coded in her deep beliefs. As she presented it to herself, a good mother is able to be there when her kids are sick or when they need things done for them. And this job didn't allow for that. However, a good mother is also someone who contributes financially, is a whole, confident person with her kids, and is a quality role model. If she chose to stick with her current job, she, by her own definition, was a bad mother. If she chose to give up the job, by her criteria, she was a bad mother. Enormous loss was inevitable, and the high level of sadness inexorably followed.

We guided Andrea through challenging her beliefs, helping her to generate alternatives to the single causal belief she had initially detected. With her icebergs clearly uncovered, she recognized that there was a possible solution here. What if she spoke to the sales director about working more flexible hours? Maybe if she had to run out and be with one of her kids, she could make up that time later. Sounded good to us, but the answer from management was no. Resilient people are able to steer through these kinds of setbacks, and Andrea tried another approach and asked to be put on half-time status, thinking again that this would help her satisfy both roles in her life. The answer: no. After more coaching, more prodding with Challenging Beliefs, Andrea decided (and for what's it's worth, we agreed) that she was not going to get what she wanted from the company she was in.

Andrea used the skill of Challenging Beliefs to regroup and problem-solve in the face of rejection. Nine times out of ten that process will lead to the desired change. One time out of ten this process will also dead end. But resilient people know they did all they could to achieve their goal. They recognize that not everything is in their control. And they wrest control where they can. For Andrea that meant applying for other sales positions outside her organization. She got several offers, and with each company she considered, her priority was to establish what its attitudes toward time off were. She found one that was a great fit.

Conclusion

We've seen how the skills of resilience can be used with adversities that arise in the workplace. In our final chapter, we apply the skills to the larger issues in our lives—to help us through a national disaster like the events of September 11, to guide us through bereavement, and to lead us to reach out and create meaning in our lives.

CHAPTER THIRTEEN

Resilience
for Life

*Ours is essentially a tragic age, so we refuse to take it tragically. The cata-
clysm has happened, we are among the ruins, we start to build up new little
habitats, to have new little hopes. It is rather hard work: there is now no
smooth road into the future: but we go round, or scramble over the obstacles.
We've got to live, no matter how many skies have fallen.*

How September 11 Changed Us All

The passage just quoted was written in 1928 by D. H. Lawrence, but it
could be a description of our lives since September 11, 2001. All of us
were affected by the events of that day in myriad ways. Some of us lost
people we love. Others lost colleagues and acquaintances. Most of us in
America did not personally know anyone who was killed, and yet we lost
something too. Commentators and pundits suggested we'd lost our inno-
cence, and while that resonated for some of us, it didn't for others. We are
not a naive people. We've been through turbulent times before, economically and politically. We were not innocent. And yet we did lose something,
and it's something precious. We lost our sense of justice. We lost our sense
of safety. And we were very suddenly alerted to our own mortality.

The events of September 11 and their aftermath drew back the curtains
on our lives. We began to examine them closely—many of us for the first
time. We paused and took stock. We asked ourselves the big questions: What
kind of person am I? What are my priorities? Am I really spending time on
what's important? Why do I allow my work to come before those I love so
often? What meaning is there for me in this life? And, of course, we realized
that these are the questions we should have been asking ourselves all along.

You can use the skills of resilience to answer these big questions. As we've seen, resilience enables you to overcome childhood obstacles, steer through day-to-day adversities, and bounce back from extraordinary trauma. Resilience will help us through the aftermath of September 11. What September 11 reminded us is that we must reach out and connect with our loved ones—that life can be all too brief, so we must reach out for opportunities when they present themselves. To do this, you need to better understand the kind of person you are and take control of the forces that, even now, are shaping the future "you." Armed with the knowledge of who you are and who you want to be, you can create meaning in your life. You can do this by using the resilience skills to develop more intimacy with those you love, to fill your life with purpose and meaning via your work on involvement in the community. You also can use the skills to take on new challenges.

Creating Yourself: Understand Who You Are and Who You Want to Be

Since the flower power days of the 1960s, many people have been obsessed with the idea of "finding themselves." In fact, a lot of self-help books are designed to guide you on that journey. Don't get us wrong: Self-exploration is an essential part of being resilient. (It represents the first three know thyself skills.) But to paraphrase George Bernard Shaw, identity is not "found" like a coin on the sidewalk. It is created—shaped by the experiences of a lifetime.

How can you apply the skills of resilience to reach out and become the kind of person you want to be? First you must become aware of the kind of person you *are*, and that means examining your deep beliefs and values about yourself, your world, and your place in it. You must understand what beliefs are leading you to behave in the old, tired ways that you don't like as well as the thinking that's holding you back from reaching your ideal. And you must challenge those beliefs. You now know the skills that are designed to help you through this process from ABC to Real-time Resilience. Armed with these skills, you can shape your own identity.

Allen is a high-level account executive for a major advertising firm in New York. He came to our executive coaching for help with a specific issue—controlling his aggression. Allen was the picture of success: mid-forties, very much in love with his wife of eighteen years, three great kids, and a wonder at his job. He'd always seen his aggressive behavior as his strong suit. "I have the biggest book of business in the company. That doesn't happen to nice guys. I banged away at potential clients until they left our competitors. I yelled down the phone at the office manager until I got the support staff I needed. And you know why I've got the biggest office on the floor? Because I stood toe-to-toe with the district manager and told him if he didn't give it to me, I was gone."

But lately Allen's aggression seemed to be holding him back from his real ambitions and desires. His boss didn't take him seriously when he asked to mentor the new recruit to the organization. "I'm at the point in my career where I want to give back. But a lot of people in my company think, probably correctly, that I just have the wrong temperament to mentor. They don't want me 'corrupting' the next generation of ad men." Allen continued, "And it's not just at work. I really care about my wife—she's a great person—but I think a lot of times I stifle her with my personality. I'm a domineering guy, and I'm worried that one day she'll come to resent it. And I always seem to be angry with my kids. I never hit them, but I yell at them a lot, and the other day I saw my little boy cower slightly just because I was walking toward him. That could have been me in the Twin Towers on September 11. If I had died that morning, what memories would my family, my friends, my colleagues have of me? Probably of a big guy with an angry red face poking his finger at them. I don't want to be like this. I don't like the person I've become."

In the first couple of sessions with Allen, he detailed several incidents in which he "lost it"—at work, with his wife, his kids, with a neighbor, at a PTA meeting, and at a ball game. When a single emotion, in this case anger, shows itself so frequently and across the gamut of life areas, you can be certain that an iceberg belief is causing it. Clearly a job for Detecting Icebergs, once he'd captured the ABCs:

ADVERSITY: Went to a PTA meeting where another parent presented his fundraising ideas for the school. I disagreed with him and said so, loudly and publicly. The PTA voted to approve his plan.
BELIEF: I know a lot about marketing and this idea will never work. I can't believe they voted with that bozo instead of me.
CONSEQUENCES: Intense anger. But by the time I got home I felt very ashamed. I stormed out of the room in disgust, slamming the door on the way out.

It's a classic example of how Allen was burning bridges—burning connections with people in all parts of his life. He was able to detect his own iceberg:

ALLEN'S QUESTION: *I was thinking that they should have listened to me instead of him. Why is that so upsetting to me?*

ALLEN'S ANSWER: *Because I'm the one with the expertise, not him. Don't they appreciate that I'm one of the best at what I do?*

QUESTION: *Let's assume that's true—that they don't appreciate what I do. What's the worst part of that for me?*

ANSWER: *They don't respect or want my knowledge, and they don't respect me. People should be pleased to have my kind of expertise, especially when I'm giving it for free.*

QUESTION: *What does it mean to me when people don't respect my expertise?*

ANSWER: *It means they don't respect me. They should respect me no matter whether I'm talking about marketing or not. I'm a survivor, and I know more about life than the vast majority of people. They should listen to what I have to say. No—it's not just that they should listen to my advice, they should take it.*

Allen uncovered the violation-of-rights iceberg beliefs that were causing him so much anger. Through Challenging Beliefs, Allen came to see that his iceberg beliefs were not accurate—that it's not true that people should hang on his every word and always follow his advice. He recognized that he wasn't entitled to unlimited perks at the office and that if his manager said no to one of his requests, it was not necessarily a violation of his rights. But, while Allen was motivated to avoid his icebergs, he struggled to use Real-time Resilience. "When I'm in that moment, when I feel like I'm being screwed, the anger seems to take over. Part of it too is that anger works for me—it's always proven to be a useful way for me to get what I want."

Allen needed a fast skill that didn't involve too much effort—anger came too easily to him and overwhelmed his attempts to uncover and dispute the violation-of-rights beliefs. Many of his angry outbursts happened in his office, over the phone. Allen believed that if he could only remind himself of his goal to be a better person, he could avoid the anger. He chose to go with some calming skills. He stuck a big letter A by his phone to remind himself that he tended to be "Anger Man." On the top of his computer he pasted a small sign with the letters RIP—a reminder of how he wanted to be remembered after he had passed on. And he strategically placed a photograph of his family at eye level on a bookshelf—his loved ones were the major motivation for his desire to change.

His tactics worked. A few months after we completed Allen's coaching, we received a letter from his wife. She wrote that Allen was a changed man—that he rarely got angry and, when he did, it was justified. By being less aggressive, he had proven to himself that he didn't need aggression to succeed. He saw the positive changes in his relationships with family and colleagues, and their responses led him to want to be even better. Eventually his iceberg disappeared. By being less angry, fewer people actually *were* out to get him.

Like Allen, you can use the skills of resilience to reinvent the kind of person you are. Then you can reach out to create meaning in your life— meaning that comes from intimate connections with others or from grasping new opportunities in life.

Loss of Meaning and the Existential Paradox

The events of September 11 reminded us of our own mortality. But the research shows that, even before September 11, we had become progressively more preoccupied with death over the last seventy years. Some psychologists attribute this to our waning attachment to things bigger and more important than ourselves. They argue that we have become increasingly individualistic and at the same time have lost faith in the grand institutions that extend beyond our lives. Belief in religion has diminished. Trust in our political assemblies tanked dramatically after the Nixon years. In the large urban centers across America, our communities have disintegrated. All such institutions bridge the existential gap—they existed before we arrived, and they will exist after we leave. But church, community, society, and even extended family are no longer the source of connection they once were. We have foundered. We have lost meaning in our lives.

Our mortality results in a paradox—it leads us to want both to reach out and to shrink back from risk. We have a finite time in this world, and we can never be certain of the consequences of our actions. We may be very fearful of an upcoming plane trip and be injured in a car accident on the way to the airport. Life has no guarantees. We just never know. And this makes us vulnerable to making very costly errors. Of course, were we immortal, we would have an eternity to make mistakes and recover from them. But we are not immortal, and that makes every decision at least a little daunting. Our mortality and our fallibility press us to avoid risks, even calculated ones. They lead us to be cautious in life—to keep us defensive instead of willing us to reach out.

It's our mortality that makes time precious. Our knowledge that we have only one life, with no dress rehearsals, and that the show is brief is what coaxes us out into the world. It motivates us to develop our talents, test our limits, and reach out to others. Our mortality reins us in, but it also releases us with purpose. And that's the paradox. When we create meaning, we must challenge those beliefs that hold us back as well as harness those impulses to connect to things that are bigger than us.

Creating Meaning Through Reaching Out

He was prisoner number 119,104 in a Nazi death camp. Like millions of others, number 119,104 was forced to live and labor under the most unimaginably horrible conditions. And like almost all prisoners, his world shrank to miniature proportions. He had once been a successful psychiatrist who lectured to hundreds of students and addressed scholarly conferences. But his world now consisted of gathering tattered clothing, of finding the next meal, of surviving. All his mental energy was focused on the lowliest decisions—whether to trade his last cigarette for soup, how he could locate a piece of wire to use as a shoelace.

After the war, prisoner number 119,104 wrote of his experiences. He wrote of one day that transformed his life:

I became disgusted with the state of affairs which compelled me, daily and hourly, to think of only such trivial things. I forced my thoughts to turn to another subject. Suddenly I saw myself standing on the platform of a well-lit, warm and pleasant lecture room. In front of me sat an attentive audience on comfortable upholstered seats. I was giving a lecture on the psychology of the concentration camp! All that oppressed me at that moment became objective, seen and described from the remote viewpoint of science. By this method I succeeded somehow in rising above the situation, above the sufferings of the moment, and I observed them as if they were already of the past. Both I and my troubles became the object of an interesting psychoscientific study undertaken by myself. What does Spinoza say in his *Ethics*? . . . Emotion, which is suffering, ceases to be suffering as soon as we form a clear picture of it.

Prisoner number 119,104 was Dr. Viktor Frankl, an eminent psychiatrist who founded a form of therapy known as logotherapy—an existential analysis. The goal of logotherapy is to extract the patient's central sense of meaning and to set the person back on that trajectory. What Viktor Frankl's life demonstrates most powerfully is that the search for meaning is central to our existence. Without it we are as lost as those prisoners who gave up hope. Imbued with meaning we can endure even the worst conditions—we will be resilient. Most of the prisoners learned to overcome, to bounce back, and to steer through, but it wasn't enough. True salvation, as Frankl came to learn, comes by reaching out, by creating meaning in our lives. Our circumstances are not the tragic experiences of Dr. Frankl, but we too can achieve significant meaning by reaching out. We can reach out in our intimate relationships with others, and we can reach out to new opportunities, to our community, or to create meaning in our work.[1]

Creating Meaning by Reaching Out to Others

Many people struggle with intimacy. Perhaps you're wondering whether to commit to a long-term partner and are having fears and doubts. Perhaps as a child you experienced the divorce of your parents, which you have never fully "overcome," and now, when things get tough in your marriage, your impulse is to flee. Or maybe you have realized that although your work is going well and your marriage is fine, you don't seem to have close friends and you miss that kind of connection. The skill of detecting iceberg beliefs can help you to uncover the beliefs you have built about love and commitment and to evaluate whether they are getting in the way of having the kinds of relationships you want.

We build underlying beliefs of relationships and intimacy, the foundations of which are often laid down by our perception of our parents' relationship—and these beliefs come to take on a life of their own. The only way to test these icebergs adequately is to look objectively at the evidence. Gordon, a forty-year-old man, struggles with intimacy. Whenever he begins to feel close to a woman, he starts to behave badly and inevitably drives the woman away. After she's gone, he feels lonely and sad and wants to try again. But usually it's too late. Gordon used the skill of Detecting Icebergs to identify his deep beliefs about intimacy and to see why he was stuck in this destructive pattern. As he worked through the skill, he realized that one of his core beliefs was "Being vulnerable is a sign of weakness," and he was able to trace the development of this belief to messages he learned from his father. Gordon knew that he needed to find a new way to understand the meaning of vulnerability if he was ever going to have the kind of relationship he wanted. He used the skill of Challenging Beliefs to prove to himself that vulnerability need not be equated with weakness. In fact, many of the men he most admired were men who were expressive—not the weeping-at-the-made-for-TV-movie kind of expressiveness, but emotionally honest and able to talk about what they feel and listen to their partners. By identifying and then challenging this deep belief, Gordon was able to change the way he approached relationships. He no longer needed to sabotage his relationship when he started to feel close to a woman, and so his relationships now had a fighting chance.

Just like Gordon, if you are struggling with intimacy, you must recognize your patterns of thought and emotion and the thinking traps to which you are most vulnerable. Use the Detecting Icebergs skill, a powerful self-awareness tool, to understand the kind of person you are—your strengths as well as your button-push weaknesses. And this above all: Recognize that your perceptions are not reality. Once you have challenged the beliefs that are holding you back, you will be able to relax in your relationship and create the kind of connection you want.

Creating Meaning by Reaching Out at Work

Another way to reach out in your life is by taking on new challenges at work. Opportunities come in many forms—interesting projects, leadership duties, higher-level jobs, lateral moves to new and exciting divisions within your organization, leaving for another company, or even beginning a totally new career. If you are tempted by challenges such as these but find yourself shrinking back, tap into your ticker tape as you weigh your decision. We have found in our work with corporate employees, in training and executive coaching, that at choice points such as these, profound underlying beliefs will come into play. Some are iceberg beliefs around autonomy: "I don't have what it takes to handle the responsibility of a higher position." Some, of course, are related to initiative and motivation: "This will require too much work. If I take this promotion I'll be a slave to the organization, at their beck and call. I'm better off staying in this lower job where I'm my own person." We've seen icebergs about identity impede reaching out. One client with whom we worked was considering leaving her management job of fifteen years to apply for law school. At that time Sharon was thirty-eight. She told us, "I've never wanted to do anything this much before. It's all I can think about. I dream about being in law school all the time. I feel strongly that being a lawyer is what I want to do with the rest of my life, but I can't. It's as if I just can't bring myself to break loose from where I am now. I took the LSATs and did really well. I sent off applications and I got accepted to a local school that I think is a great match for me. But as it gets closer I'm really struggling. I don't know what's hold-ing me back, but I keep telling myself to keep my job and play it safe."

Sharon realized that her ticker tape in the moment of indecision was "I've got a good thing here. I shouldn't rock the boat. Some things are just not meant to be." We used this as the launching point for Detecting Ice-bergs.

As Sharon went through the process of identifying her core values, she realized that she was worried about taking risks. As she put it, "If you're doing okay, why would you risk that? If you're in a bad situation, then sure, go ahead and take the risk—what do you have to lose? But I've got a lot to lose and it would be foolish to give it up."

It was clear that Sharon did not like taking chances and that she had conceptualized this choice accordingly. She saw the law degree as risky. But would she really be taking a big chance if she were to go to law school? It would be one thing if she gave up work to study for the LSATs—that is, without knowing her chances of being accepted. But she's been admitted. The question is: Will she graduate? We asked Sharon to inquire about the completion rate at the school she had chosen. She found the odds were very much in her favor. But even with this evidence at her fingertips, we continued to funnel through the layers of beliefs in an attempt to get to the heart of the issue for her. As it turned out, she was also concerned about loss of her identity and her ability to give back to the world.

As she continued to uncover her deep beliefs, she told us that if she went to law school and it didn't work out, she would feel so stupid. She was able to connect this fear to messages she heard growing up. "My dad always said I'd never amount to anything. I shut him up when I got pro-moted to this manager's job. He would have a field day if I messed this up." She also realized that part of her ambivalence was fueled by beliefs about respect. She had earned the respect of her colleagues, but she wor-ried about starting over and having to claw her way to the top again—hav-ing to prove herself to get the respect that is so important to her identity.

After working her way through the questions, Sharon was able to iden-tify the root cause of her indecisiveness. "I can't afford to mess this up. I want to do the best I can in this life. That's always been my motto. I'm not married and, at thirty-eight and single, I don't think kids are in my fu-ture. One of the reasons I want to study law is I thought I could give something back to my community. You know, open up a little law practice in my old neighborhood. I could do a lot more with a law degree than I can right now. But I can do more now than I can if I lose this job and don't replace it with something meaningful."

It became clear both to us and to Sharon that she had placed enormous stakes on this decision. At risk was her ability to give rather than receive orders. At risk was the chance to excel at a profession and to advance in the eyes of society. At risk was her sense of who she was as well as how she is perceived by others and her opportunity in life to contribute to her world and the next generation. And given the stakes, her iceberg belief that all risk is bad had led her to back away from her decision. As she came to see, though, her caution was not reality based. Her thinking styles and iceberg beliefs were holding her back unnecessarily.

Sharon made the decision to reach out. She completed her law degree two years ago and is currently working with a major firm in her hometown. Last time we spoke with her, she told us that, in a few years, with enough experience and the blessing of her current partners, she hopes to set up her own small practice.

Creating Meaning by Taking Risks

Of course, there are other ways to reach out. You can do simple things each day to have a richer, more meaningful life. At the very beginning of the book, we introduced you to Joan—a woman in her mid-sixties who values being open to new experiences and works hard to push back the horizon of her life. Some of you are probably like her. You like to try new things, and you look forward to the exhilaration that comes from taking risks—not dangerous risks but ones that help you to grow and expand the scope of your world. But our experience tells us that most people find themselves comfortably ensconced in a routine—eating the same foods, driving the same route, returning to the same vacation spots, reading the same kinds of books—and they feel nervous about breaking free.

Ask yourself this: When is the last time you tried a new food? Or talked with someone who was not your "type"? When was the last time you volunteered to work in your community? Or took a class in something unrelated to your profession? How long has it been since you went out to dinner alone (and didn't bury yourself in a book—hiding your aloneness from the other patrons)? In our conversations with people, it became clear that their beliefs were what held them back from breaking free of their routines, trying new things, and broadening their lives. Let's face it, the hard part is not figuring out what new thing to do (spend ten minutes and

315 * Resilience for Life

make a list of simple activities you could try—you'll see that making the list is the easy part); it's overcoming your beliefs that keep telling you to stick with what you know.

"Narrowing" beliefs—beliefs that keep you stuck in the same old routine and prevent you from taking risks—usually generate anxiety ("She's not going to want to talk with me," "I'm never going to be able to learn to paint—not unless 'painting by numbers' is allowed") or embarrassment ("I'll look like an idiot if I try do that" or "I'll miss all of the symbolism in the book and everyone else in the book club will have really deep things to say"). And anxiety then deters us from trying new things. Sheila is a woman we met in one of our seminars. She used the skills of resilience to challenge the beliefs that got in her way of reaching out.

"I've always wanted to take a cooking class in preparing Mexican food, but I'm frankly not a great cook. My family has learned to work around my attempts at seasoning by keeping a tray of spices as the centerpiece on our dining room table. Despite my many failed attempts at creating lively, vibrant flavors, I still believed that deep down inside there was a spicy cook waiting to be released."

Sheila saw a Mexican cooking class being offered in town and wanted to sign up. After much procrastination, she finally filled out the form, but as she drove to the first class, she was having second thoughts. Sheila used Real-time Resilience to keep herself from losing heart and turning the car around.

SHEILA'S BELIEF: *This is ridiculous. I should just face facts—I'm not a good cook. I bet everyone else is going to be these junior Emerils and I'm going to make a fool of myself.*

SHEILA'S REAL-TIME RESPONSE: *It's a cooking class, not a cooking show. I'm allowed to not know much—that's the whole point. We're all going to be in the same boat. No great cook is going to sign up for a class called "Hot Tamales: A Beginner's Journey through the Land of the Hot and Spicy."*

SHEILA'S BELIEF: *Not knowing much is one thing, but I'm the anticook. I swear my kids are losing weight, and I sometimes see a flash of fear in my husband's eyes when I put the food down on the table.*

SHEILA'S REAL-TIME RESPONSE: *Oh, relax! This is going to be fun. I'll learn a few things and meet a few people—it's not as if I'm about to launch a new restaurant. Anyway, it's good for my kids to see that I'm willing to try new things and that I'm not afraid to fail. That's much more important that having a mom who is a gourmet cook.*

SHEILA'S BELIEF: *But this is just dumb. I'm setting myself up for failure. I should be taking a course in something that I have some talent in. This must be some deep-rooted desire to humiliate myself.*

SHEILA'S REAL-TIME RESPONSE: *This isn't a deep-rooted desire to fail, it's a deep-rooted desire to cook. Instead of worrying so much, I should focus on my willingness to take risks. A lot of people don't do things because they're scared of failing, but I'm proving to myself that I'm not that kind of person. I'm proud of myself for doing this.*

If you find yourself shying away from new experiences, afraid to release your own inner cook, see if you can identify the beliefs that are holding you back. Then use the skills you've learned to challenge them.

Using the Resilience Skills to Heal after Loss

An inevitable part of life is mourning the loss of someone we love. We've often been asked whether resilience can help a person through such a difficult transition. What does it mean to mourn resiliently? First, we want to be clear that we do not believe that it makes much sense to test out the accuracy of your beliefs in the immediate aftermath of the loss. As we pointed out earlier, sometimes the events of our lives are so large and unambiguous that it is the event itself, not our interpretation of that event, that drives our reaction. But this is not to say that there is no role for resilience in coping with death of a loved one. Resilience can keep you connected to those around you, and by reaching out for support, the process of grieving will be easier.

Julie and Sophie talked on the phone a couple of times a day. They weren't long conversations—they called to say a quick hello between shuttling the kids to their various activities or to share a funny thing one of their kids said or even to get an idea for dinner—but the daily contact between the sisters had been a part of their relationship for as long as they could remember.

When the phone rang, Julie assumed it was Sophie. One o'clock was a standard how's-it-going call while the kids ate lunch. Instead, it was her mother; she called to say that there had been an accident and that Sophie had been killed. The weeks following her sister's death were horrible, but at least those first several weeks were filled with things to do: Funeral arrangements had to be made, relatives and friends contacted, meals prepared for her brother-in-law and the kids—on and on it went. Although Julie was devastated, she mainly felt numb and was focused on helping her sister's husband and kids as best she could and making sure her own family was getting through the trauma.

About two months after Sophie's death, it really hit Julie. She can recall the moment: "It was a Thursday afternoon. Beautiful day. My kids
were playing in a little wading pool, and the mail had just come. I was
looking through the catalogs and saw this pitcher that my sister would
love. Out of habit, I reached for the phone. Then suddenly I felt like I
had been punched in the stomach. I couldn't breathe and I started sob-
bing. I kept looking at that stupid blue pitcher and I just could not stop
crying"

The death of Julie's sister challenged her in a way that she had never
been challenged before. On the surface, she was holding it together—she
had to for her kids. But beneath the surface, the pain seemed unbearable.
Julie started withdrawing from her husband and friends. When the conversation turned to memories of Sophie, she would quietly leave the
room. When her mother brought over pictures that she had just had developed from the last time they were all together, Julie couldn't bring herself to look at them.

All of what Julie is experiencing is part of the normal grieving process.
There is not a correct way to grieve, just as there is not a correct way to
love. And while resilience can help you to heal following the death of a
loved one, it is not going to prevent you from feeling pain, anger, or sadness. Nor should it. These are healthy, normal human responses, and they
are important to experience. The resilience skills can help you to understand what you are feeling and stay connected to those you love as you
work your way through the complex emotions that are part of grief. And
resilience can help you when your grief interferes with your ability to
keep living your life, despite what you have lost.

One Sunday, about two months after Sophie died, Julie and her family were invited to a friend's house for a barbecue. David, Julie's husband,
was looking forward to some quiet time with friends and thought it would
be good for Julie to be in the company of people who knew her well and
cared so much about her. Julie was in a relatively good mood that morning, but it began to sour as they got ready to leave. By the time they arrived at George and Wendy's house, she had to work to keep from crying,
and almost everything out of Wendy's mouth irritated her. Julie wanted
to relax and accept the comfort her friends were desperate to offer, but
she felt like a pinball bouncing from emotion to emotion. We'll show
you how Julie used Real-time Resilience to stop her grief from driving a
wedge between herself and those who wanted to support her through the
crisis.

JULIE'S BELIEF: *How can they expect me to relax and have fun when they treat me like I'm so fragile—like if they say the wrong thing I might break into a thousand pieces? If they want me to have fun, they're gonna have tò stop treating me like I'm such a basket case.*

JULIE'S REAL-TIME RESPONSE: *I might be worried that I'll break into a thousand pieces, but that's not how they're treating me. They're probably feeling a little awkward because it's hard to know what to say to a person who's lost someone. But the awkwardness will go away if I relax a bit and let them know it's okay to talk about my sister.*

JULIE'S BELIEF: *Whom am I kidding? I'm a basket case! I miss her so much that even my hair aches. I can't keep feeling like this. I've got to pull myself together and move on—that's what Sophie would want.*

JULIE'S REAL-TIME RESPONSE: *What Sophie would want is for me to stop being so hard on myself. Grieving isn't a race. It's not a timed event. She was my sister. We shared a connection that I've never felt with anyone else. The world is a different place without her, and moving on isn't a concept that applies. I'm allowed to be sad and moody. But it's true that Sophie would want me to let other people help me through this. I don't get extra points for shouldering the burden alone.*

JULIE'S BELIEF: *Still, what was Wendy thinking when she told that story about her sister? Could she be any more insensitive? I mean, you don't have to have a degree in psychology to figure out that you shouldn't talk about your great relationship with your loving, beautiful sister with someone who just lost her loving, beautiful sister. What an ass.*

JULIE'S REAL-TIME RESPONSE: *Okay, perhaps it wasn't the best story to share at this particular moment, but she's doing the best she can. She clearly looked embarrassed after she started the story, but she probably didn't want to suddenly stop the story either because she knows that would make me feel even more uncomfortable. As hard as this is, I need to help my friends know what I want from them. If I can muster the strength to be more open about how I'm feeling, they'll be better able to help me through this.*

Julie used Real-time Resilience daily for the first few months after her sister died. For Julie, the resilience skills helped her to allow herself be comforted by others. For you, resilience might help you to understand the guilt you feel or to challenge the beliefs that are bringing intense anger or to identify deep beliefs that might be interfering with your ability to express your emotions with those you love. You can use the calming techniques to help you feel more calm and in control. It's important to remember that the goal is not to get yourself "back to normal." The goal is to help yourself heal and rely on your friends and family as you muddle your way through.

A Resilient Nation

At the beginning of this chapter we acknowledged that almost all of us lost something precious in the wake of September 11. We lost our sense of justice, and we lost our sense of safety. Justice is an essential component of how we see the world. We want to believe that the world is just: that good things happen to good people and bad things happen to bad people. This just-world belief is so strong that when we know someone is headed for misfortune, we assume they deserve it. It forms the basis of the common tendency to blame the victims of rape and other crimes.

Most of us have these just-world beliefs. But on September 11 they were shattered. We knew that the thousands of people who headed off to work that day had done nothing to bring the tragedy on themselves. We recognized that they had only done what we ourselves do every day—they had gone out to make a living to support the ones they love. We lost our sense of justice that day, our sense of fair play.

Not only do we believe the world is just, but most of us also develop deep beliefs that the world is basically safe—at least we work to convince ourselves of that as we go about our lives. It's a useful belief because it enables us to function in the world without constant worry. Psychologists understand the dreadful emotional consequences if that belief is shaken. In the very first chapter of this book we discussed posttraumatic stress disorder (PTSD)—a cluster of high-level anxiety symptoms that hit some people after significant trauma. Combat soldiers in Vietnam developed PTSD at significantly higher rates than their World War II counterparts. In World War II the fighting was more conventional. There was a front line; when you were at the front you were in danger, when you were not you were safe. The enemy wore uniforms. There were clear signals for safety and clear cues for danger. Not so in Vietnam. There was no front line. The enemy did not wear uniforms. In the minds of many allied soldiers, an elderly woman in a village could be just as deadly as a Vietcong foot soldier. Their beliefs about safety were assailed. Women who are raped in their homes or by someone they know are much more likely to develop PTSD than if the crime occurred in a strange place or was perpetrated by a stranger. Home is supposed to be safe. We are supposed to be safe with people we know.

The world should be just and fair. We should be able to come and go to work safely. September 11 decimated these beliefs—beliefs that are integral to our day-to-day functioning. But just as our basic beliefs about justice and safety have been eroded, they can be rebuilt.

Brenda is a researcher and part of her job requires flying to conferences. She was scheduled to attend a conference late September, but no one—not even her boss—minded when she canceled in the days after the terrorism of September 11. It became a problem, however, when in December she was still unwilling to fly and her boss was considering firing her. We met with Brenda and learned that for her, as for many Americans, the world suddenly seemed unsafe and unpredictable. The illusions that Brenda had constructed for herself, such as "Bad things only happen to bad people" or "That would never happen to someone like me," were clearly just illusions, and she struggled to find a way to feel safe again. The devastation of September 11 caused her to lose sight of the basic facts: Flying is still safe, probably safer; most of the people she passes on the street are basically good; opening the mail is not an anthrax risk.

Brenda, like many of us, began to catastrophize, and the more she catastrophized, the harder it was for her to go on with her life. Brenda used the skill of Putting It In Perspective to bring her anxiety back down to a manageable level, and she set herself the task of finding at least one piece of evidence every day that there was still justice and goodness in the world. She read the stories of how people around the world did whatever they could to help in the months following the attacks. She noticed the everyday acts of kindness that she used to overlook—the bus driver who waited as she ran down the street, the colleague who offered to help with a project so Brenda could leave early for a family function, the person who put a quarter in her parking meter so she wouldn't get a ticket. And Brenda made a point of seeing justice and fairness—the woman in the store who handed ten dollars back because she had been given too much change, the man who told the clerk that the other woman was in line before him, the news story about the human rights group that successfully got a Chinese woman released from jail. By forcing herself to see this evidence, gradually Brenda was able to reconstruct her basic faith in others and her fear subsided.

Our Hope for You

Our nation has come a long way since September 11. In little ways, every day, we are reconstructing our worlds. As we reach out a little more each day—travel to work and make it back home, see our children as we walk through the door, board the plane and return safely—we are piecing our beliefs back together. To paraphrase D. H. Lawrence: It may be hard work. There may no longer be a smooth road into the future. But we are a resilient nation. We are overcoming, steering through, bouncing back—and reaching out once again. We will live and we will thrive—no matter how many skies have fallen.

Together we've worked our way through the seven skills of resilience. We've shared with you stories of people who've used the skills to excel at work, to deepen their relationships with their partners and their children, and to embrace new experiences. The lives of those with whom we've worked didn't magically change overnight. Their lives changed because they took what we describe in this book and they made a commitment to become more resilient. Just like we as a nation have done, in little ways, every day, they reconstructed their worlds by changing the way they think.

They did it and so can you.

We hope that as you finish this book, you feel more confident in your ability to rise to life's challenges and strive for a life rich in meaning and purpose. As you use these skills each day, you'll find yourself more in control of your life—instead of being at the mercy of the day's events, *you'll* be in charge. The key is to use the skills every day. If you do, within weeks you'll find that the skills have become second nature—and that your basic approach to life has changed. You'll be happier and more optimistic. And when you're living a more resilient life, you'll be better able to connect deeply with those you love. All of our lives have twists and turns but with resilience you can thrive no matter what obstacles you face.

By changing the way you think, you can change your life for good.

ACKNOWLEDGMENTS

This book would not have been possible without the help of numerous people. We want to thank our colleagues and collaborators whom we worked with to develop and validate the Penn Resiliency Program (PRP) and the APEX program. These programs would not have existed without the hard work of Drs. Rob DeRubeis, Arthur Freeman, Jane Gillham, Steve Hollon, Lisa Jaycox, Martin Seligman, and Peter Schulman.

A special thanks goes to Jane Gillham, who has taken the lead in making sure the never-ending work on PRP actually gets done. Thank you, Jane.

We also want to thank Esteban Cardemil, who adapted the PRP manual for Latino inner-city children; David Yu, who adapted PRP for students in China; and Barbara Samuels, Andrea Levy, Marisa Lascher, and Samantha Litzinger, who have run the daily operations of PRP over the years. We especially want to acknowledge Derek Freres, who has been the key person in managing the administrative aspects of PRP. Thanks, Derek, we'd be lost without you.

The Penn Resiliency Program and the APEX program were developed at the University of Pennsylvania and first implemented in our own backyard. Over the years, however, a great many people worked hard to bring these programs to their neighborhoods, and we want to acknowledge them for their pioneering spirit. Simon Andrews in Adelaide, Australia; Darlene Hall in Toronto, Canada; Sam Moreno in Rock Island, Illinois; Diedre Quinlan in Duluth, Minnesota; Clare Roberts in Western Australia; Russell Roberts in Queensland, Australia; Ellen Lerner in Oakland, California; Joan Burnham in Austin, Texas; Terrill Hellander of Pasadena, California. Hal Bloss made sure that every fifth grader in the Hazelton Area School District learned the skills of PRP; and Skip McCann was the driving force behind bringing PRP to several school districts in Pennsylvania.

We also want to recognize the educators and administrators in and around Philadelphia who have been the mainstay of our PRP research over the last fifteen years. Three districts in particular have opened their doors to us and we are deeply grateful. Joe Galli, Barbara Shafer, Carolyn Felker, Ed Speer, and Jane Archibald of the Upper Darby School District gave us their unflagging support and devoted a great deal of their time to making sure the middle school students in their district were able to participate in our programs. In addition, thanks to Steve Bell, Wendy

Brown, Jean Cooney, Denise McDermott, Adair Ruff, Faith Mattison, Barbara Mendell, Annette Brandolini, Holly Farnese, Cheryl Macklin, Arlene Sarley, who implemented the programs with their students and deserve the credit for making PRP a great success.

The Wissahickon School District and the families that attend those schools have worked with us for several years and we appreciate their willingness to embark on this mission with us. Special thanks are due to Mary Hornyak, Neil Evans, and Bob Andersen as well as the schoolteachers who implemented the programs: Ginny Atlee, Cheryl Dillon, Mike Schneider, Kathy Briggs, Tom Finnegan, Victoria Rodney, and Sue Wyatt.

We are grateful to the administrators, teachers, and families in the Cherry Hill School District who worked with us on the development of the parent program. In particular, a big thank you is owed to Toni Rath, Nick Lorenzetti, Brian Betze, Tammy McDonald, and Ed Collins, who were instrumental in bringing the program to their district.

We want to thank Andrew's collaborators on the race research mentioned in Chapter 12: Lani Guinier, Veronica Rice, Susan Sturm, Esteban Cardemil, and an army of undergraduate researchers who made the work possible.

Our resilience programs are based on the pioneering work of Drs. Aaron Beck and Albert Ellis. We wish to thank them for providing us such a strong foundation on which to build our work.

We also want to thank the therapists and staff at the Center for Cognitive Therapy in Philadelphia, where we were therapists in training, and special thanks to our supervisors, Drs. Cory Newman and Robert DeRubeis, who helped us hone our skills and deepen our understanding of the cognitive model.

Thank you to all who contributed to Adaptiv Learning Systems, especially Dean Becker, Lou Berneman, Tony Jannetta, and Frank Slattery. We wish to particularly acknowledge Dean Becker—he has been our friend and business partner for the last five years, and this book simply would not have happened without him.

To all those who assisted in the creation of Adaptiv Training for Corporations. Patty Newbold was our instructional design consultant, and she helped us turn our materials into a program that would work in the corporate training room. Steve Hollon, Rob DeRubeis, Marty Seligman, Dan Oran, and Peter Schulman developed the predecessor program in the late eighties and we're grateful for having such a strong model on which to base our work.

Thanks also to the human resources and training department representatives in all the corporations in which we're worked, who have shown faith in our work and the efficacy of the skills, and to the thousands of people who have received Adaptiv Training. We also want to express our gratitude to all those who completed our Resilience Quotient Test, and thanks to the researchers who assisted us in its development and validation, especially to Jen Warren.

Several undergraduates at the University of Pennsylvania helped us with the research for this book: Alyssa Friede, Rachel King, Ella Masson, Jen Dibiase, and Susie Flood. We also want to thank the students in our resilience seminar who read drafts of the chapters and gave many insightful comments: Marilyn Arenas, Nicholas Balisciano, Elizabeth Beothy, J. Harley Chivers, Maria Dominguez, Rebecca Hashim, Sueihn Lee, Yuliya Lelchuk, Heather Lochridge, Sarah Master, and Talia Master.

And we want to thank our agent, Richard Pine, who encouraged us throughout this project and our editor, Stephanie Land, at Doubleday/Broadway, who has been passionate about this book from the very beginning.

Andrew would like to acknowledge:

Veronica. Without you, without your love, without your patience, without your resilience, I wouldn't have written a word.

Heartfelt thanks to my parents, Betty and Lloyd—you have always believed in me, even during those times when all the evidence indicated that your faith was sorely misplaced.

A special thank you to three wonderful friends, Gareth, Sarah, and Dara. You have buoyed me at every step with your humor, your company, and your genuine interest in this book. To Lou and Flo, who always seemed ready with a glass of wine and great conversation when I needed it most. To all the gang at McCrossen's, with special thanks to Bill Moriarty, Amanda Benner, Becca Raley, Ed Doty, Brian Lesher, Bill Roller, Togo Travalia—and g'day to Dale, Chris, and Matt.

And to Karen Reivich. It's been ten years since we first began our collaboration, and they've been the best years of my professional life—because of her. She's my friend, my confidante, and it was worth crossing the Pacific just to work with her.

Karen would like to acknowledge:

I would not have been able to write this book without my husband, Guy Diamond. Thank you, Guy, for all the weekends you took the boys on long hikes (*very* long hikes) so that I could have a quiet house in which to write, and for inspiring me with the passion you bring to all of your projects. My three sons, Jacob, Aaron, and Jonathan, spent many afternoons working on their "books" while I worked on mine. Thank you, boys, for interrupting me from my writing and reminding me what matters most in my life. You can finally stop asking, "Is the book done yet?" My mother, Joan Reivich, read drafts of every chapter and gave us detailed comments, but more important, she cheered me when my enthusiasm faltered, listened to me when I needed to think aloud, and did shtick with me when I needed to laugh. And thanks to my sister, Jennifer Jones, who called daily just to "check in" and give her love and support.

I also want to thank my friends Kate Kimbel and Peter Badgio, who always asked how the book was coming along and really cared about the answer.

And finally, of course, Andrew Shatté. Andrew has been my colleague since our days as graduate students at Penn. We worked on our dissertations together, started Adaptiv Learning Systems together, and, of course, wrote this book together. The best moments of my career have always been shared with Andrew. But more important, Andrew is a cherished friend. His compassion and great humor keep me going.

CHAPTER 1: *Resilience Matters*

1. We share many anecdotes and case studies in this book to illustrate resilience and the use of the resilience skills. Whenever possible, we present them exactly as they occurred. In some cases we have changed certain facts, or blended the facts of two or more cases, in order to protect the person's anonymity. In all cases, names have been changed.

2. The Harris Poll revealed that about 60 percent of people worry "a little" or "a lot" about aspects of their future. Of the more than one thousand respondents nationwide, 69 percent worry that they "will not have enough money to live comfortably," 60 percent worry that they "will not have enough health insurance to pay for large medical bills," 59 percent were concerned that their "spouse or someone very close to [them] will not live long," 60 percent worried that their "health will get much worse," and 61 percent worried that they would be "a victim of violent crime." These statistics are surprisingly high considering that the poll was conducted in October and November of 1999, well before the events of September 11, 2001, and the economic downturn that began in 2000. Source: www.gallup.com

3. John Gray (1992), *Men Are from Mars, Women Are from Venus* (New York: Harper-Collins).

4. Source: www.selfhelpmagazine.com

5. The skills presented in the four basic programs we've developed are based on the cognitive model developed by Aaron Beck, Albert Ellis, and Martin Seligman. We are also indebted to numerous colleagues who contributed substantially to the development of these programs.

6. The adverse effect on resilience of low birthweight, childhood poverty, and physical abuse has been studied extensively—and perhaps most thoroughly—by Suniya Luthar and Norman Garmezy. Each has provided an excellent review: N. Garmezy (1993), "Children in poverty: Resilience despite risk," *Psychiatry* 56, 127–36; S. Luthar (1991), "Vulnerability and resilience: A study of high-risk adolescents," *Child Development* 62, 600–16.

7. Perhaps the clearest summary statement of the three traditional uses of resilience is found in an article authored by Ann Masten, Karin Best, and Norman Garmezy in the journal *Development and Psychopathology*, entitled "Resilience and development: Contributions from the study of children who overcome adversity." They use the terms *overcoming, stress-resistance,* and *recovery* in place of the terms we use in this book—*overcoming, steering through,* and *bouncing back.* Our contribution to the work on the applications of resilience is to recognize that people use resilience not

just to fix what's broken, but to reach out to connect with others and to take on challenges and opportunities.

8. Dante Cicchetti and his colleagues have examined the dynamic relationship between aspects of the family, the internal life of the child, and the effect on future resilience in well-conducted longitudinal studies. An example is found in D. Cicchetti and F. A. Rogosch (1997). For the role of self-organization in the promotion of resilience in maltreated children, see *Development and Psychopathology* 9, 797–815.

9. The detrimental effects of poor family functioning on resilience is well documented, particularly by the eminent British researcher Michael Rutter.

10. The effects of different parenting styles as risk factors or protective factors for children are documented in A. Masten and D. Coatsworth (1998), "The development of competence in favorable and unfavorable environments: Lessons from research on successful children," *American Psychologist* 53, 205–20.

11. One study that demonstrates the positive effect of IQ on resilience is A. Masten, N. Garmezy, A. Tellegen, D. Pellegrini, K. Larkin, and A. Larsen (1988), "Competence and stress in school children: The moderating effects of individual and family qualities," *Journal of Child Psychiatry* 29, 754–64. Howard Gardner's excellent work on the nature of intelligence is very highly regarded. A sample of his theory on multiple intelligences can be found in: Howard H. Gardner, "Beyond a Modular View of Mind," in W. Damon (ed). (1989), *Child Development Today and Tomorrow*. The Jossey-Bass Social and Behavioral Science Series (222–39) (San Francisco: Jossey-Bass Inc., Publishers). You can read Peter Salovey's and John Mayer's early collaborative work in: P. Salovey and J. D. Mayer (1989), "Emotional Intelligence," *Imagination, Cognition & Personality* 9, 185–211.

12. Source: www.madd.org

13. J. Herman (1997), *Trauma and Recovery* (New York: Basic Books).

CHAPTER 2: *How Resilient Are You?*

1. E. Werner and R. Smith (2001), *Journeys from Childhood to Midlife: Risk, Resilience, and Recovery* (Ithaca, NY: Cornell University Press).

2. E. Werner (1989), "High-risk children in young adulthood: A longitudinal study from birth to 32 years," *American Journal of Orthopsychiatry* 59, 78.

3. Our work on the RQ Test began in 1997 with a series of statistical analyses called factor analyses. We came up with a few hundred questions that asked about a very wide range of aspects of resilience, ensuring that we covered overcoming, steering through, bouncing back, as well as items about reaching out, which we suspected was also an integral part of resilience. Factor analyses helped us determine what categories of items, or factors, made up the construct of resilience. After thousands of people had taken the RQ Test, we concluded that seven factors best accounted for the variance between people in their responses. For proprietary reasons the RQ Test in this book contains fifty-six questions rather than the standard seventy-item form we currently adminster.

4. Daniel Goleman (1995), *Emotional Intelligence* (New York: Bantam Books).

5. Eleanor H. Porter (1996), *Pollyanna* (New York: Puffin Books).

6. The concept of explanatory style was first raised in the article by L. Y. Abramson, M. E. P. Seligman, and J. D. Teasdale (1978), "Learned helplessness in humans: A critique and reformulation," *Journal of Abnormal Psychology* 97(1), 49–74.

CHAPTER 3: *Laying the Groundwork*

1. We are indebted to the entire resilience field for their contributions to our collective knowledge of resilience. We have been particularly influenced and inspired by the work of Dante Cicchetti, Norman Garmezy, Suniya Luthar, Ann Masten, Michael Rutter, Ruth Smith, and Emmy Werner.

2. Morton Hunt in his landmark book, *The Story of Psychology*, outlines exquisitely the development of what is modern psychology from its genesis in Roman and Greek philosophy. Hunt references this quote of B. F. Skinner, from Skinner's first TV appearance, to D. Hothersall (1984), *History of Psychology* (Philadelphia: Temple University Press).

3. Morton Hunt provides this quote in *The Story of Psychology* (New York: Doubleday), 257.

4. S. T. Fiske and S. E. Taylor (1984), *Social Cognition* (Reading, MA: Addison-Wesley), 88.

5. To read more about positive illusions see S. E. Taylor (1983), "Adjustment to threatening events: A theory of cognitive adaptation," *American Psychologist* 38, 1161–73 and S. E. Taylor and J. D. Brown (1988), "Illusion and well-being: A social psychological perspective on mental health," *Psychological Bulletin* 103, 193–210.

6. See J. Shedler, M. Mayman, and M. Manis (1993), "The illusion of mental health," *American Psychologist* 48, 1117–31. For a good overview of the issues related to the field of realistic optimism and positive illusions, see S. Schneider (2001), "In search of realistic optimism," *American Psychologist* 56(3), 250–63.

7. We wrote of this stage in psychology's history in: A. J. Shatté, M. E. P. Seligman, J. E. Gillham, and K. Reivich (in press), "The Role of Positive Psychology in Child, Adolescent, and Family Development." In R. E. Lerner, F. Jacobs, and D. Wertlieb, eds.), *Promoting Positive Child, Adolescent, and Family Development: A Handbook of Program and Policy Innovations* (Thousand Oaks, CA: Sage Publications).

8. Marty Seligman laid out his agenda for the construction of a new movement of positive psychology in the 1998 editions of the American Psychological Association (APA) Monitor.

9. The lifetime prevalence of clinical depression in the United States has increased dramatically in the last two generations, as reported in L. N. Robins, J. E. Helzer, M. M. Weissman, H. Orvaschel, E. Greunberg, J. D. Burke, and D. A. Reiger (1984), "Lifetime prevalence of specific psychiatric disorders in three sites," *Archives of General Psychiatry* 41, 949–58.

   Current estimates indicate that almost 10 percent of children experience clinical depression before the age of fourteen, and up to 20 percent of adolescents experience a clinical depression before they graduate from high school. P. M. Lewinsohn, H. Hops, R. Roberts, and J. Seeley (1993), "Adolescent psychopathology: I. Prevalence and incidence of depression and other DSM-III-R disorders in high school students," *Journal of Abnormal Psychology* 102, 110–20.

10. We are indebted to our colleagues Jane Gillham, Lisa Jaycox, Karen Reivich, and Marty Seligman who designed the original PRP program for children.

11. The research we conducted to prevent depression and promote resilience with adolescents and college students was funded by the National Institute of Mental Health (1 R01 MH52270-013 and 1 R01 MH63430-01). We are grateful for their continued support of this research.

12. The college program, called APEX, was developed by Robert DeRubeis, Art Freeman, Jane Gillham, Steven Hollon, Lisa Jayox, Karen Reivich, Peter Schulman, and Marty Seligman.

13. The results of the APEX study are reported in: M. E. P. Seligman, P. Schulman, R. J. DeRubeis, and S. D. Hollon (1999), "The prevention of depression and anxiety," *Prevention and Treatment.*

14. Jane Gillham was the first in our group to develop and test a parent companion to the children's PRP, and she continues to be a leading developer of the program today. The data cited is currently unpublished data collected during 2002 from research conducted by Jane, Karen, and Andrew.

15. We serve as the vice presidents of research and development with Adaptiv Learning Systems. For more information about Adaptiv, please access our website: www. adaptivlearning.com.

CHAPTER 4: *Learning Your ABCs*

1. There is a long history regarding what is an emotion, what causes emotion, and what functions emotions serve. In general, there are four basic traditions in the study of emotion: the evolutionary tradition, the psychophysiological tradition, the neurological tradition, and the dynamic tradition. Psychologists have also hotly debated the relationship between emotions and thoughts. Some psychologists, most notably Robert Zajonc, argue that emotions can precede thought—that thought is not a necessary condition of emotion. Others, for example, Richard Lazarus, have argued that emotions follow specific cognitive appraisals—such as anger follows the appraisal of harm. Robert Plutchik has written extensively about the evolutionary functions that emotions serve. For a review of the evolutionary account of emotions, see R. Plutchik (1984), "Emotions, a General Psychoevolutionary Theory," in K. Scherer and P. Ekman (eds.), *Approaches to Emotion* (Hillsdale, NJ: Lawrence Erlbaum Associates), 197–219.

2. P. Wong and B. Weiner (1981), "When people ask 'why' questions, and the heuristics of attributional search," *Journal of Personality and Social Psychology* 40, 650–62.

3. Psychologist Dolf Zillmann has studied the cognitive appraisals that elicit anger as well as the effects of anger on later cognitive processing. See D. Zillman (1994), "Cognition-excitation Interdependencies in the Escalation of Anger and Angry Aggression," in M. Potegal and J. F. Knutson (eds.), *The Dynamics of Aggression: Biological and Social Processes in Dyads and Groups* (Hillsdale, NJ: Lawrence Erlbaum Associates).

4. *The Nicomachean Ethics*: Aristotle's challenge.

5. For more information regarding the everyday experiences of guilt, see R. Baumeister, H. Reis, and P. Delespaul (1995), "Subjective and experiential correlates of guilt in daily life," *Personality and Social Psychology Bulletin* 21, 1256–68.

6. For a more detailed explanation of shame-proneness versus guilt proneness, see P. Niedenthal, J. Tangney, and I. Gavanski (1994), "'If only I were' versus 'If only I hadn't': Distinguishing shame and guilt in counterfactual thinking," *Journal of Personality and Social Psychology* 67, 585–95, or J. Tangney (1990), "Assessing individual differences in proneness to shame and guilt: Development of the self-conscious affect and attribution inventory," *Journal of Personality and Social Psychology* 59, 102–11.

7. For a thorough discussion of the cognitive perspective on anxiety, see A. Beck, G. Emery, and R. Greenberg (1985), *Anxiety Disorders and Phobias* (New York: Basic Books).

8. A. Modigliani (1968), "Embarrassment and embarrassability," *Sociometry* 32, 313–26.

9. For a broader discussion of the theories of embarrassment and how embarrassment and shame differ, see M. Babcock and J. Sabini (1990), "On differentiating embarrassment from shame," *European Journal of Social Psychology* 20, 151–69.

10. The phrase "amygdala hijack" was popularized by Daniel Goleman in *Emotional Intelligence*. For a detailed account of the role of the amygdala in the processing of emotional content and a thorough description of the latest research on how the brain processes sensory information, see J. LeDoux (1996), *The Emotional Brain* (New York: Simon & Schuster).

CHAPTER 5: *Avoiding Thinking Traps*

1. You may wish to read Aaron Beck's groundbreaking work yourself: A. T. Beck (1967), *Depression: Causes and Treatment* (Philadelphia: University of Pennsylvania Press). A. T. Beck (1976), *Cognitive Therapy and the Emotional Disorders* (New York: International Universities Press); A. T. Beck, A. J. Rush, B. F. Shaw, and G. Emery (1979), *Cognitive Therapy of Depression* (New York: Guilford Press).

2. P. Wason and J. Evans (1975). "Dual processes in reasoning?" *Cognition* 3, 141–54.

3. We owe much of the structure and information contained in this section to our teacher and colleague Jon Baron. We were privileged, as graduate students, to participate in Jon's class on thinking and decision making. We recommend his book to any reader interested in exploring further the vagaries of human reasoning: J. Baron (1988), *Thinking and Deciding* (Cambridge: Cambridge University Press).

4. A. Tversky and D. Kahneman (1983), "Extensional versus intuitive reasoning: The conjunction fallacy in probability judgment," *Psychological Review* 90, 297.

CHAPTER 6: *Detecting Icebergs*

1. A. Beck, G. Emery, and R. Greenberg (1985), *Anxiety Disorders and Phobias* (New York: Basic Books).

CHAPTER 7: *Challenging Beliefs*

1. You can read more about trephined skulls in T. Stewart (1957), *Stone Age Surgery: A general review, with emphasis on the New World. Annual Review of the Smithsonian Institution* (Washington, DC: Smithsonian Institution).

2. We follow here the scoring system devised by Seligman and his colleagues when they first developed the Attributional Style (Explanatory Style) Questionnaire.

3. For an excellent summary of the research evidence of the causal role of pessimistic explanatory style in depression: C. Robins and A. Hayes (1995), "The Role of Causal Attributions in the Prediction of Depression," in G. Buchanan and M. Seligman (eds.), *Explanatory Style* (Hillsdale, NJ: Lawrence Erlbaum).

4. Buchanan and Seligman's book, *Explanatory Style*, cited above, is an excellent summary of the research on pessimism and optimism in the areas of school, work, sports, and physical health.

5. One of our graduate-student colleagues, Dr. Jason Satterfield, conducted one of the first studies to indicate that in some domains, optimism was a hindrance. Jason and his colleagues measured the explanatory styles of almost 400 law students prior to their entering law school, and followed their progress longitudinally across their law

school experience. They found that in this milieu, students who made "me," "always," and "everything" explanations for negative events outperformed more optimistic students on both grade point average and law journal success: J. Satterfield, J. Monahan, and M. Seligman (1997), "Law school performance predicted by explanatory style," *Behavioral Sciences & the Law* 15(1), 95–105. In addition, our research with undergraduates demonstrates that extreme optimism is not predictive of course grade.

CHAPTER 8: *Putting It in Perspective*

1. We develop this connection between explanatory style, thinking style for past events, and future or "what next" beliefs in: A Shatté, K. Reivich, and J. Gillham (1999), "Learned Optimism in Children," in C. Snyder (ed.). *Coping Skills* (Oxford: Oxford University Press), 165–81.
2. Taylor and her colleagues found that men who had tested positive for HIV were actually more optimistic about not developing AIDS than their HIV-negative peers: S. Taylor, M. Kemeny, L. Aspinwall, S. Schneider, S. Rodriguez, and M. Herbert (1992), "Optimism, coping, psychological distress, and high-risk sexual behavior among men at risk for AIDS," *Journal of Personality and Social Psychology* 63, 460–73.
3. W. Middleton, P. Harris, and M. Surman. (1996), "Give 'em enough rope: Perception of health and safety risks in bungee jumpers," *Journal of Social and Clinical Psychology* 15(1), 68–79.

CHAPTER 9: *The Fast Skills: Calming and Focusing and Real-time Resilience*

1. S. Cohen, D. Tyrrell, and A. Smith (1991), "Psychological stress and susceptibility to the common cold," *New England Journal of Medicine* 329 (9), 606–11.
2. D. Krantz, D. Sheps, R. Carney, and B. Natelson (2000), "Effects of mental stress in patients wth coronary artery disease: Evidence and clinical implications," *Journal of the American Medical Association* 283(14), 1800–02.
3. W. Jiang, M. Babyak, D. Krantz, R. Waugh, E. Coleman, M. Hanson, D. Frid, S. McNulty, J. Morris, C. O'Connor, J. Blumenthal (1996), "Mental-stress induced myocardial ischemia and cardiac events," *Journal of the American Medical Association* 275(21), 1651–56.
4. For example, the natural killer cell activity (cells which provide defense against virus-infected cells and cancer cells) was lower in medical students when they were feeling stressed by their exams than compared with their functioning during less stressful times of the semester. This and other studies underscore the toxicity of stress: Stress compromises your immune system, and a compromised immune system means that you will get sick more often. For more information regarding the effects of stress on natural killer cell activity, see R. Glaser, J. Rice, C. E. Spiecher, J. C. Stout, and J. K. Kiecolt-Glaser (1986), "Stress depresses interferon production by leukocytes concomitant with a decrease in natural killer cell activity," *Brain, Behavior, and Immunity* 1, 7–20. For a review of the importance of social support on coping with stress and immunological functioning, see W. Stroebe and M. Stroebe (1996), "The Social Psychology of Social Support," in E. T. Higgins and A. W. Kruglanski (eds.), *Social psychology: Handbook of Basic Principles* (New York: Guilford Press). And for a review of the positive effects of marriage on mortality

and coronary artery disease, see A. Reifman (1995), "Social relationships, recovery from illness, and survival," *Annals of Behavioral Medicine* 17, 124–31.

5. Research shows that some positive events, such as the birth of a baby and marriage, are rated as more stressful than negative events, such as the death of a friend. T. H. Holmes and R. H. Rahe (1967), "The social readjustment rating scale," *Journal of Psychosomatic Research* 11, 213–18.

6. Dr. Suzanne Kobasa has studied the affects of commitment, control, and challenge in minimizing the effects of stress on health. In general, she finds that people who are high on these personality variables stay healthier than people low on these variables despite similar levels of stress. See S. Kobasa (1990), "Stress-resistant Personality," in R. Ornstein and C. Swencionis, (eds), *The Healing Brain: A scientific reader* (New York: Guilford Press), or S. Kobasa and M. Puccetti (1983), "Personality and social resources in stress resistance," *Journal of Personality & Social Psychology* 45(4), 839–50.

7. For a detailed description of techniques for dealing with stress and how to avoid common problems implementing the techniques, see D. Barlow and R. Rapee (1991), *Mastering Stress: A Lifestyle Approach* (Dallas, TX: American Health Publishing Company).

8. For a description of the response-style theory and the effects of rumination and distraction on depressed mood, see S. Nolen-Hoeksema (1991), "Responses to depression and their effects on the duration of the depressive episode," *Journal of Abnormal Psychology* 109, 569–82.

9. It's important to point out that while women are twice as likely to get depressed as men, this is not to say that all distraction techniques are healthy. For example, drinking as a means to cope with or distract oneself from a depressed mood is a dangerous practice. Indeed, alcohol abuse and dependence are much more common in males than females, with a male to female ratio as high as 5:1.

10. S. Lyubomirsky, K. Tucker, N. Caldwell, and K. Berg (1999), "Why ruminators are poor problem solvers: Clues from the phenomenology of dysphoric rumination," *Journal of Personality and Social Psychology* 77(5), 1041–60.

CHAPTER 10: *Resilience in Marriage and Long-term Relationships*

1. Two books on how to improve your relationships which we found most useful and grounded in science are: H. J. Markman, S. M. Stanley, and S. L. Blumberg (2001), *Fighting for Your Marriage* (San Francisco: Jossey-Bass) and J. M. Gottman and N. Silver (1999), *The Seven Principles for Making Marriage Work* (New York: Three Rivers Press).

2. Markman and colleagues in *Fighting for Your Marriage* describe five communication filters: distractions (such as external stimuli like the television or internal stimuli like your thoughts), emotional states, beliefs and expectations, differences in style (such as one person is open and expressive, and the other is quiet and reluctant to share his or her beliefs or feelings), and self-protection or the fear of being rejected. These filters operate outside of our awareness and influence how we communicate with our partner or how we interpret what our partner communicates to us.

3. For an excellent review of the importance of beliefs in fighting and the effects on marriage, see F. D. Fincham and T. N. Bradbury (1990), *The Psychology of Marriage* (New York: Guilford Press).

For research on the effects of fighting on children, see R. E. Emery (1982), "Interparental conflict and the children of discord and divorce," *Psychological Bulletin*

92, 310–33; E. M. Cummings and P. Davies (1994), *Children and Marital Conflict* (New York: Guilford Press); M. A. Easterbrooks, E. M. Cummings, and R. N. Emde (1994), "Young children's responses to constructive marital disputes," *Merrill-Palmer Quarterly*, 42, 1–21. For more information on the emotional security hypothesis, see P. T. Davies and E. M. Cummings (1998), "Exploring children's emotional security as a mediator of the link between marital relations and child adjustment," *Child Development* 69(1), 124–39.

4. Gottman describes six attributes that he has found to predict divorce, some of which are not specific to a couple's style of fighting. Gottman describes each of these attributes in *The Seven Principles for Making Marriage Work*.

5. Gottman in *The Seven Principles for Making Marriage Work* describes solveable versus perpetual problems and includes exercises for helping the reader to differentiate between the two.

6. Gottman describes other creative activities for overcoming relationship gridlock in *The Seven Principles for Making Marriage Work*.

CHAPTER 11: *Resilience in Parenting*

1. These figures are a subset of the findings published by the Centers for Disease Control. To see the full report, go to www.cdc.gov/mmwr/preview.

2. P. Lewinsohn, P. Rohde, J. Seeley, and S. Fischer (1993), "Age-cohort changes in the lifetime occurrence of depression and other mental disorders," *Journal of Abnormal Psychology* 102, 110–20; C. Garrison, C. Addy, K. Jackson, et al. (1992), "Major depressive disorder and dysthymia in young adolescents," *American Journal of Epidemiology* 135, 792–802.

3. There are numerous studies that show a variety of problems that co-occur with children and adolescents who are experiencing symptoms of depression, such as symptoms of anxiety, conduct disorder, smoking, drug use, poor academic performance, increased rates of pregnancy, physical health problems, and suicide. For empirical research supporting these relationships see G. Downey and J. C. Coyne (1990), "Children of depressed parents: An integrative review," *Psychological Bulletin* 108, 50–76; J. Garber, M. R. Kriss, M. Koch, and L. Lindholm (1988), "Recurrent depression in adolescents: A follow-up study," *Journal of the American Academy of Child and Adolescent Psychiatry* 27, 49–54; R. Harrington, H. Fudge, M. Rutter, A. Pickles, and J. Hill (1990), "Adult outcomes of childhood and adolescent depression," *Archives of General Psychiatry* 47, 465–73; and P. Rohde, P. Lewinsohn, and J. R. Seeley (1991), "Comorbidity of unipolar depression: II. Comorbidity with other mental disorders in adolescents and adults," *Journal of Abnormal Psychology* 100, 214–22.

4. The direction of causality between self-esteem and a whole host of outcomes such as academic performance, substance use, and violence is one of ongoing debate. For examples of arguments that suggest low self-esteem causes these negative outcomes, see E. Gondolf (1985), *Men Who Batter* (Holmes Beach, FL: Learning Publications), or J. Levin and J. McDevitt (1993), *Hate Crimes* (New York: Plenum Press). For evidence that violence is not caused by low self-esteem see R. F. Baumeister, B. J. Bushman, and W. K. Campbell (2000), "Self-esteem, narcissism, and aggression: Does violence result from low self-esteem or from threatened egotism?" *Psychological Science* 9(1), 26–29.

5. For further reading on the relationship between self-esteem and violence, see R. Baumeister (1997), *Evil: Inside human violence and cruelty* (New York:

W. H. Freeman), or B. Bushman and R. Baumeister (1998), "Threatened egotism, narcissism, self-esteem, and direct and displaced aggression: Does self-love or self-hate lead to violence?" *Journal of Personality and Social Psychology* 75, 219–29.

6. The concept of attachment was first popularized by the psychiatrist John Bowlby. Bowlby and colleague Mary Ainsworth have written extensively about the importance of what they call the "attachment bond"—the attachment a child has to a stronger and wiser adult—and how this bond is instrumental in the social and emotional development of the child. For a more detailed description of the attachment theory and guidelines for child rearing based on attachment theory, see J. Bowlby (1988), *A Secure Base* (New York: Basic Books). For the importance of attachment across the lifespan, see M. D. S. Ainsworth (1989), "Attachments beyond infancy," *American Psychologist* 44, 709–16.

7. There have been numerous studies that have shown that behavioral problems in adolescence are linked to poor attachment with parents. See M. Dadds and T. A. McCugh (1992), "Social support and treatment outcome in behavioral family therapy for child outcome problems," *Journal of Consulting and Clinical Psychology* 60, 252–59; G. R. Patterson and R. J. Dishion (1985), "Contribution of families and peers to delinquency," *Criminology* 23, 63–79; R. Loeber (1990), "Development and risk factors of juvenile antisocial behavior and delinquency," *Clinical Psychology Review* 10, 1–14.

8. For a more detailed description of the parenting styles, see D. Baumrind (1967), "Child care practices anteceding three patterns of preschool behavior," *Genetic Psychology Monographs* 75, 327–33, and E. E. Maccoby (1992), "The role of parents in the socialization of children: An historical overview," *Developmental Psychology* 28(6), 1006–17.

9. D. Baumrind (1967), "Child care practices anteceding three patterns of preschool behavior," *Genetic Psychology Monographs* 75, 327–33.

10. J. Shedler and J. Block (1990), "Adolescent drug use and psychological health," *American Psychologist* 45(5), 612–30.

11. The effects of permissive parenting on children vary depending on whether the parents are permissive but warm or permissive and indifferent. See L. D. Steinberg, N. Darling, A. Fletcher, B. Brown, and S. Dornbusch (1995), "Authoritative Parenting and Adolescent Adjustment: An Ecological Journey," in P. Moen, G. H. Elder, and K. Luscher (eds.), *Linking Lives and Contexts: Perspectives on the Ecology of Human Development* (Washington, DC: American Psychological Association).

12. There are many studies that show that children who have authoritative parents do better across a variety of domains than children raised with either of the other styles of parenting. For a summary of this research, see E. E. Maccoby (1992), "The role of parents in the socialization of children: An historical overview," *Developmental Psychology* 28(6), 1006–17.

13. The skills in Chapter 11 come from the work we have done with our colleagues Drs. Jane Gillham, Lisa Jaycox, and Martin Seligman over the last 13 years. We know that these skills work because we have evaluated their effectiveness with thousands of schoolchildren in the U.S., Australia, and China. In our first large-scale study, the goal was to prevent depression in fifth and sixth graders at heightened risk. Before the program began, 24 percent of the children in both the control group and the prevention group reported moderate to severe depression; but immediately after the resiliency group ended, only 13 percent of the students who learned the skills had

moderate to severe depression, whereas the control group remained at 23 percent. More important, two years later, 44 percent of the control group was experiencing moderate to severe depression, but only 22 percent of the children who learned the resilience skills were in that range. We also tested whether the resilience skills increased the children's optimism and we found that it did. In fact, the children who showed the greatest increases in optimism were also the children who showed the greatest decreases in depression. When we looked at the data at two and a half years and three years, we found that the program's effect on depression had faded—the differences between the groups was no longer significant. The program's effect on optimism, however, remained strong. After two and a half years, children may have forgotten some of the skills they learned in the program, and would benefit from "booster sessions" that reinforced the skills as they transitioned through adolescence. This is exactly what we are now doing in our current large-scale implementation of the resilience program. And, we should point out, even if the program *only* staved off the natural rise in depression for two years, think of the enormous difference that translates to: two years of less depression means two years without the many problems that depression brings—suicidality, drug use, academic failure, pregnancy. Preventing depression for two years could very well change the trajectory of a child's life. Since that first study, we have conducted several others, each of which show that children who learn the skills of PRP show fewer symptoms of depression across a two-year period than children in a no-intervention control condition. Additionally, we did a study in which middle school children participated in the standard PRP and their parents attended a six-week parent version of the program. We found that the "family" intervention reduced symptoms of depression and anxiety in the children and, as in previous studies of PRP, the effect has grown stronger with time. By the six-month follow-up, one third of controls reported moderate to severe levels of depression symptoms. In contrast, only 10 percent of intervention participants reported symptoms in this range. To learn more about the full resilience program for children read M. Seligman, K. Reivich, L. Jaycox, and J. Gillham (1995), *The Optimistic Child* (New York: Houghton Mifflin). For more detail regarding the actual studies and results, see L. H. Jaycox, K. Reivich, J. Gillham, and M. Seligman (1994), "Preventing depressive symptoms in schoolchildren," *Behavior Research and Therapy*, 32, 8, 801–16; J. E. Gillham, K. Reivich, L. H. Jaycox, and M. Seligman (1995), "Preventing depressive symptoms in schoolchildren: Two-year follow-up," *Psychological Science*, 6, 343–51; J. E. Gillham and K. Reivich (1999), "Prevention of depressive symptoms in schoolchildren: A research update," *Psychological Science*, 10, 461–62.

CHAPTER 12: *Resilience at Work*

1. Gallup poll statistics. Source: www.gallup.com
2. These data were released by the World Health Organization, the United Nations International Labor Organization, and the National Council on Compensation Insurance.
3. The story of this study is well known among consultants and psychologists. It appears to be apochryphal—we could locate no such study in the research literature.
4. These figures were published on-line by the U.S. Department of Labor.
5. Carol Gilligan (1977), "In a different voice: Women's conception of the self and of morality," *Harvard Educational Review* 47(4), 481–517, 577.

6. These figures reflect Gallup polls conducted over nearly 30 years. Source: www.gallup.com.

CHAPTER 13: *Resilience for Life*

1. Viktor E. Frankl (1959), *Man's Search for Meaning* (New York: Simon and Schuster), 94–95.

INDEX

© DEBORAH BOARDMAN

KAREN REIVICH, Ph.D., is a co-director of the Penn Resiliency Project at the Positive Psychology Center and a research associate in the Department of Psychology at the University of Pennsylvania, where she also teaches. She is a leader in the field of depression prevention, resilience, positive psychology interventions, and school-based intervention research. In addition, Dr. Reivich has a coaching practice and provides consultation to organizations around the themes of resilience, optimism, and strength development. Dr. Reivich and her work have been featured in a variety of news and media outlets including *Oprah*, *The Early Show*, *ABC News*, *Parenting* magazine, and the *New York Times*.

Dr. ANDREW SHATTÉ, Ph.D., is a research assistant professor in the Department of Family and Community Medicine at the University of Arizona. He is executive director of the Phoenix Life Academy—an organization focused on researching and boosting resilience and connection to life and work. Dr. Shatté is faculty with the Institute for Management Studies and the Brookings Institution for his work on resilience.